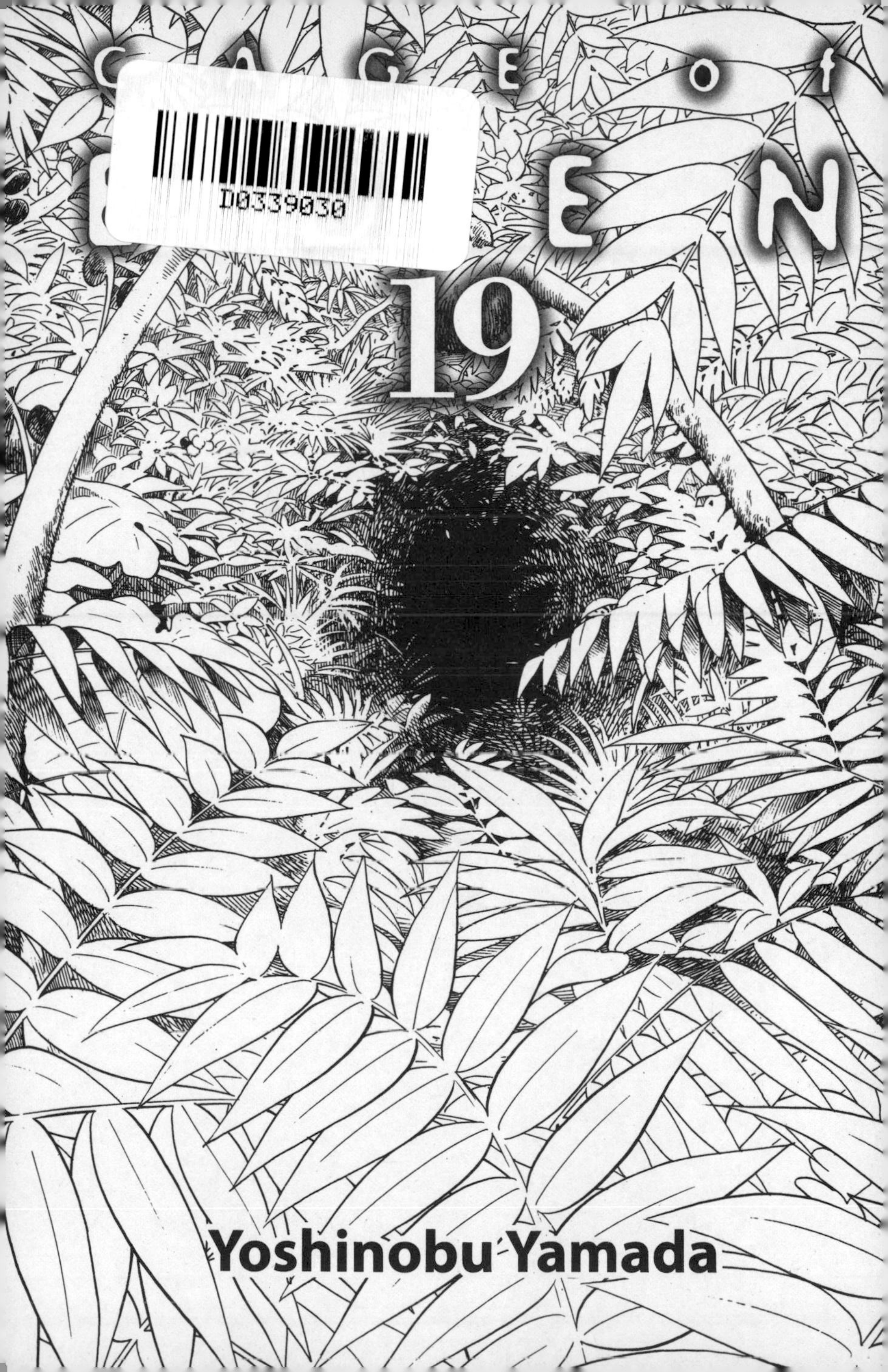
CAGE of
EN
19
Yoshinobu Yamada

CAGE of EDEN

CONTENTS

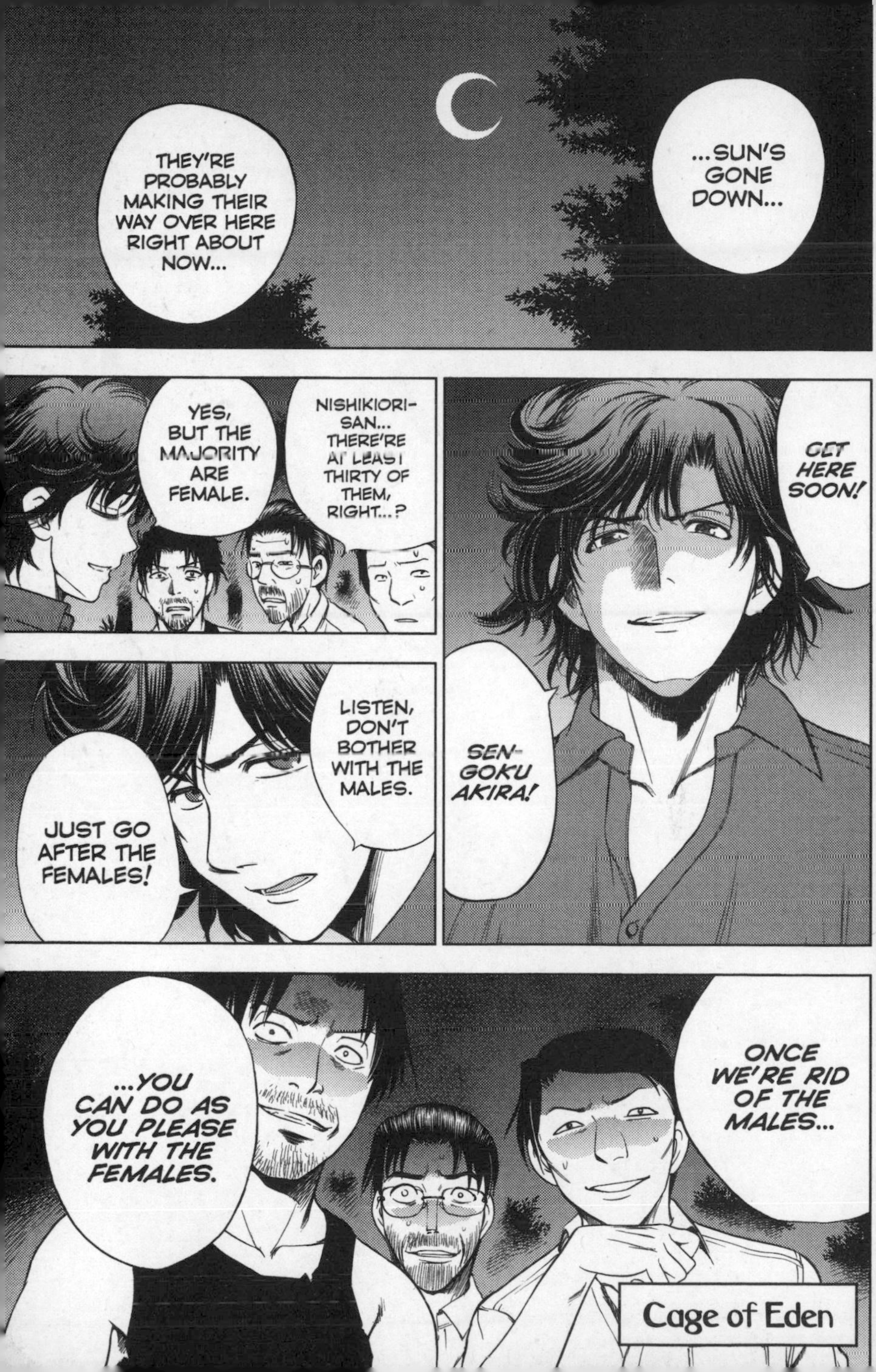
...SUN'S GONE DOWN...
THEY'RE PROBABLY MAKING THEIR WAY OVER HERE RIGHT ABOUT NOW...
GET HERE SOON!
SEN-GOKU AKIRA!
NISHIKIORI-SAN... THERE'RE AT LEAST THIRTY OF THEM, RIGHT...?
YES, BUT THE MAJORITY ARE FEMALE.
LISTEN, DON'T BOTHER WITH THE MALES.
JUST GO AFTER THE FEMALES!
ONCE WE'RE RID OF THE MALES...
...YOU CAN DO AS YOU PLEASE WITH THE FEMALES.
Cage of Eden

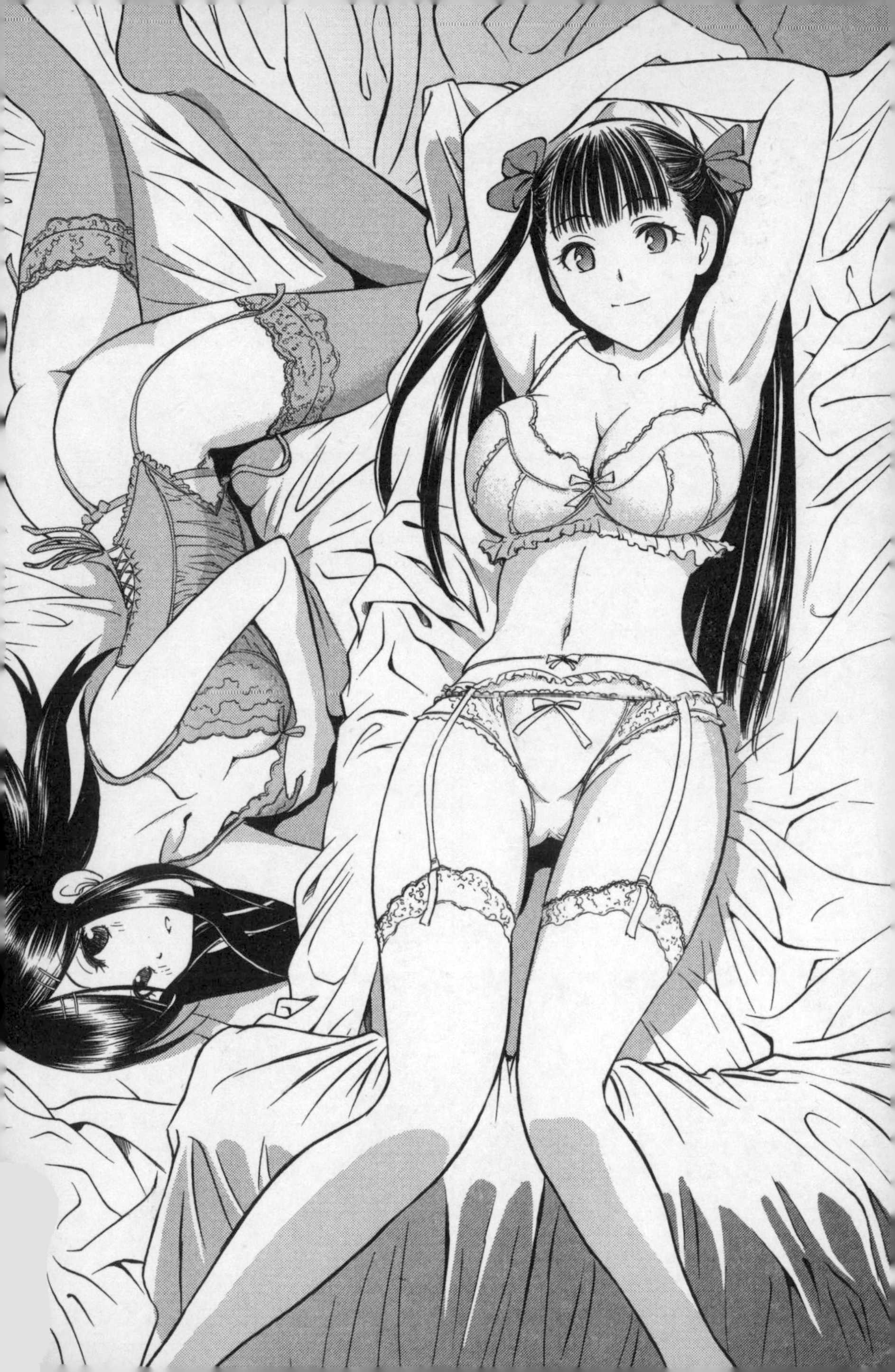

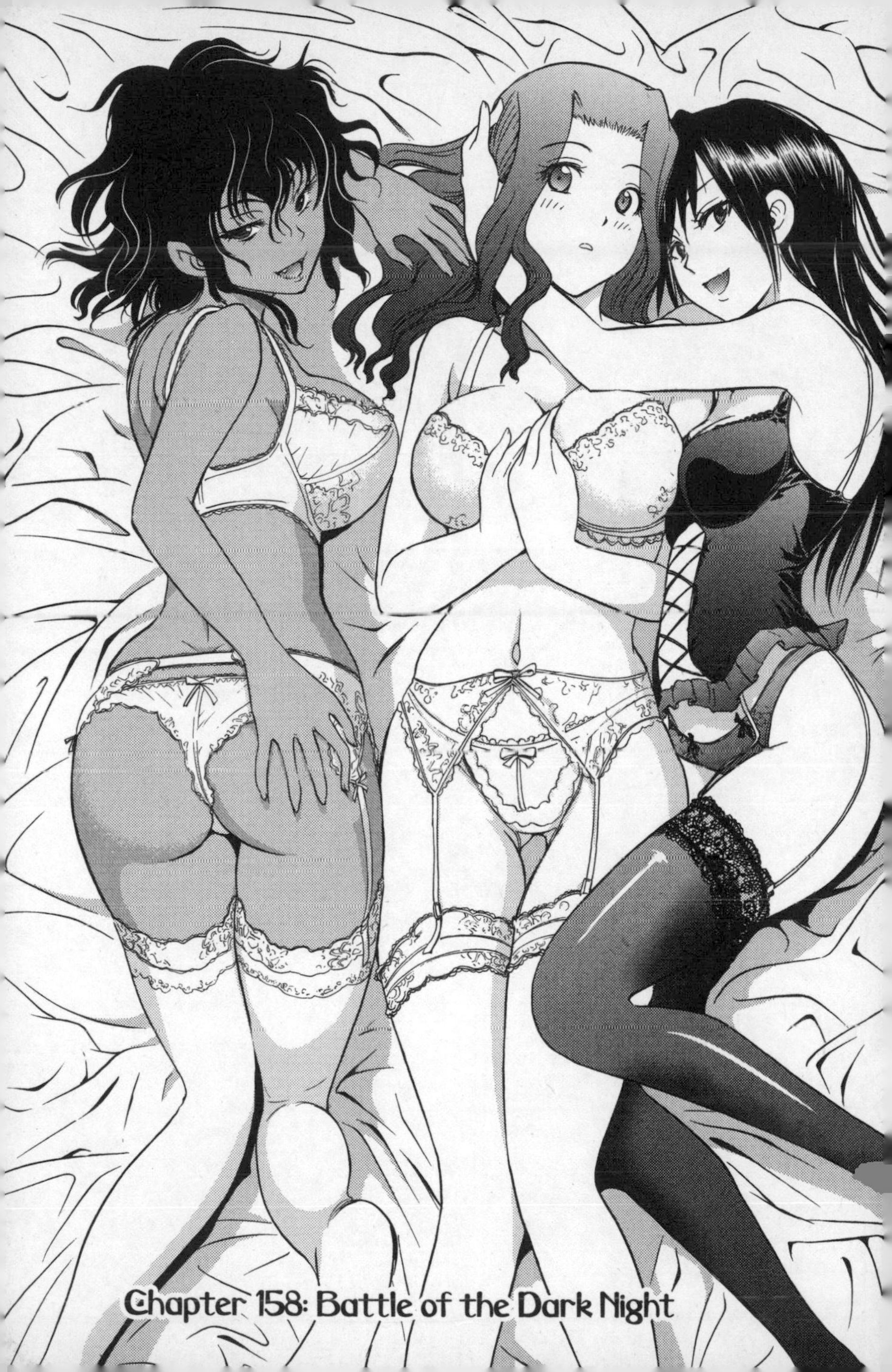
Chapter 158: Battle of the Dark Night

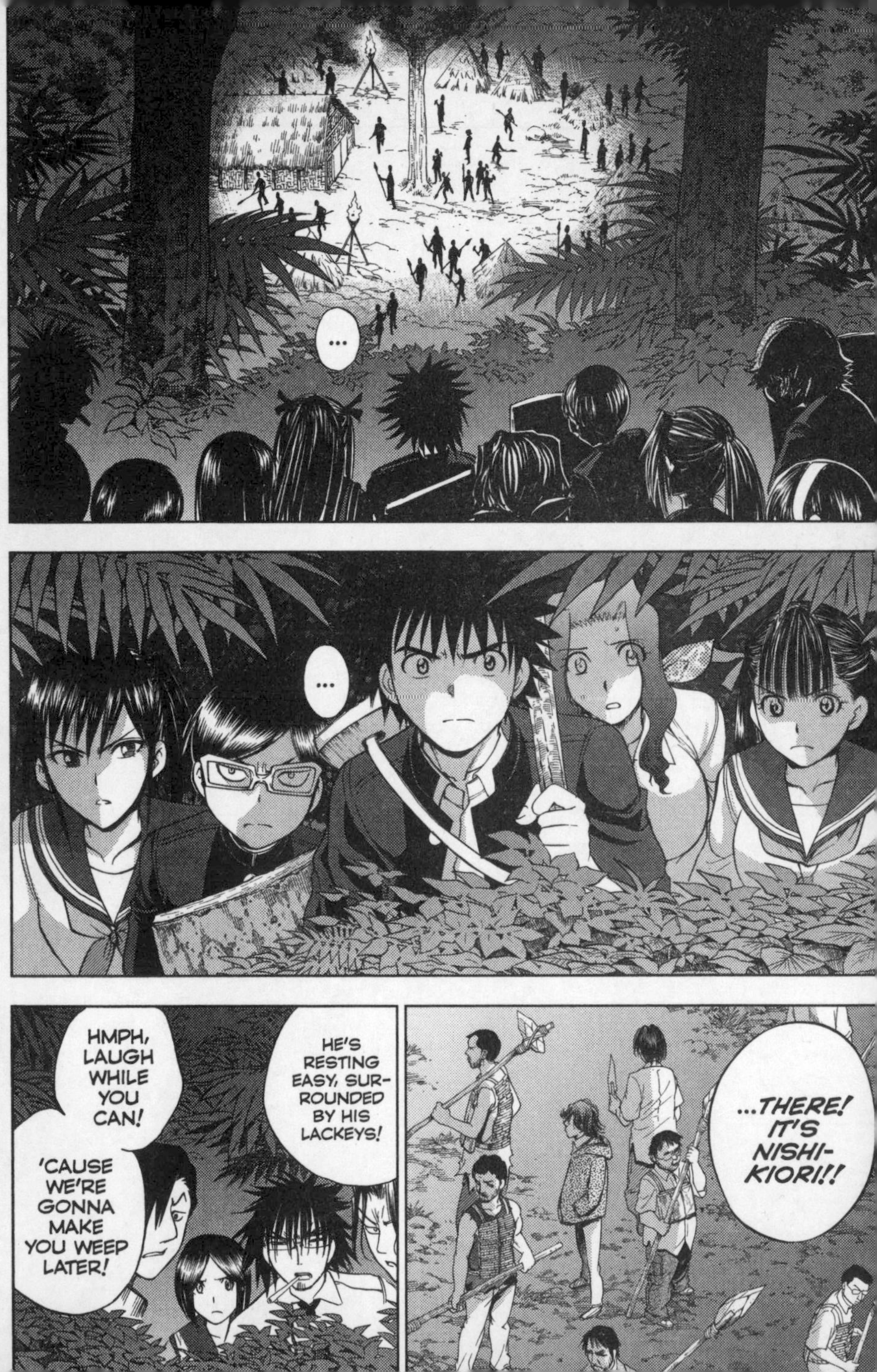
...
...
...THERE! IT'S NISHI-KIORI!!
HE'S RESTING EASY, SUR-ROUNDED BY HIS LACKEYS!
HMPH, LAUGH WHILE YOU CAN!
'CAUSE WE'RE GONNA MAKE YOU WEEP LATER!

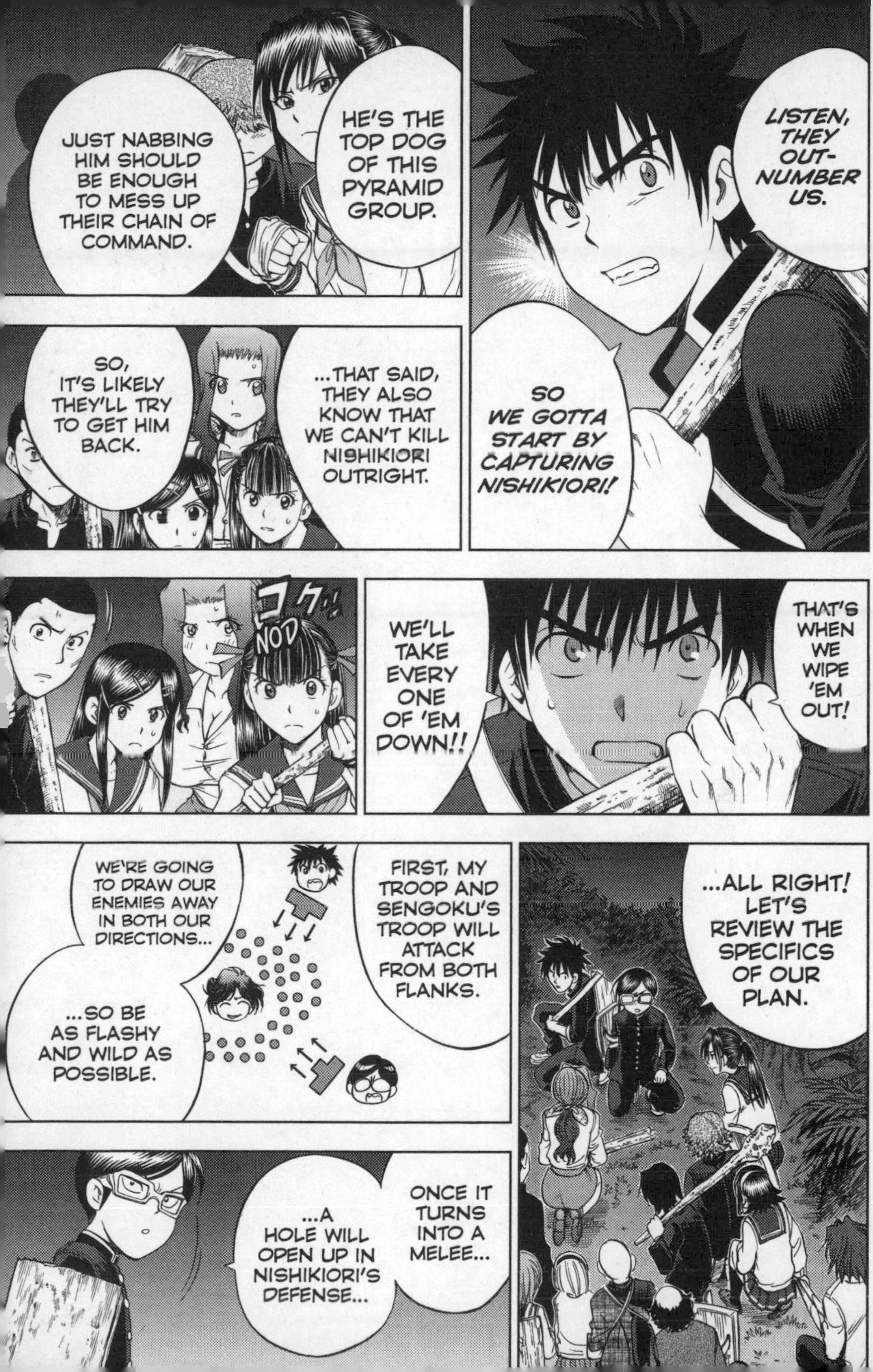
LISTEN, THEY OUT-NUMBER US.
SO WE GOTTA START BY CAPTURING NISHIKIORI!
HE'S THE TOP DOG OF THIS PYRAMID GROUP.
JUST NABBING HIM SHOULD BE ENOUGH TO MESS UP THEIR CHAIN OF COMMAND.
...THAT SAID, THEY ALSO KNOW THAT WE CAN'T KILL NISHIKIORI OUTRIGHT.
SO, IT'S LIKELY THEY'LL TRY TO GET HIM BACK.
THAT'S WHEN WE WIPE 'EM OUT!
WE'LL TAKE EVERY ONE OF 'EM DOWN!!
コクッ
NOD
...ALL RIGHT! LET'S REVIEW THE SPECIFICS OF OUR PLAN.
FIRST, MY TROOP AND SENGOKU'S TROOP WILL ATTACK FROM BOTH FLANKS.
WE'RE GOING TO DRAW OUR ENEMIES AWAY IN BOTH OUR DIRECTIONS...
...SO BE AS FLASHY AND WILD AS POSSIBLE.
ONCE IT TURNS INTO A MELEE...
...A HOLE WILL OPEN UP IN NISHIKIORI'S DEFENSE...

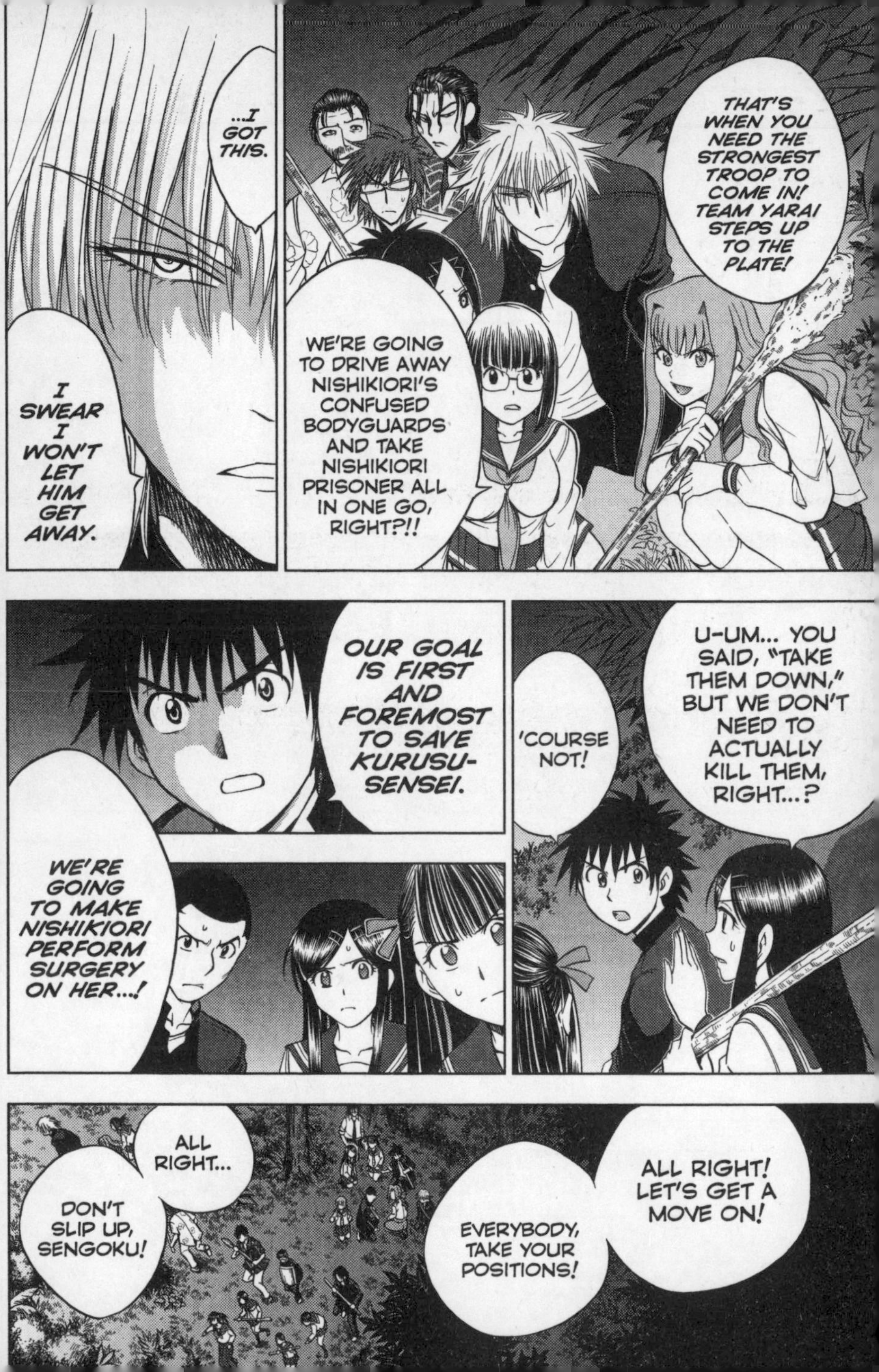

THAT'S WHEN YOU NEED THE STRONGEST TROOP TO COME IN! TEAM YARAI STEPS UP TO THE PLATE!
WE'RE GOING TO DRIVE AWAY NISHIKIORI'S CONFUSED BODYGUARDS AND TAKE NISHIKIORI PRISONER ALL IN ONE GO, RIGHT?!!
...I GOT THIS.
I SWEAR I WON'T LET HIM GET AWAY.
U-UM... YOU SAID, "TAKE THEM DOWN," BUT WE DON'T NEED TO ACTUALLY KILL THEM, RIGHT...?
'COURSE NOT!
OUR GOAL IS FIRST AND FOREMOST TO SAVE KURUSU-SENSEI.
WE'RE GOING TO MAKE NISHIKIORI PERFORM SURGERY ON HER...!
ALL RIGHT! LET'S GET A MOVE ON!
EVERYBODY, TAKE YOUR POSITIONS!
ALL RIGHT...
DON'T SLIP UP, SENGOKU!

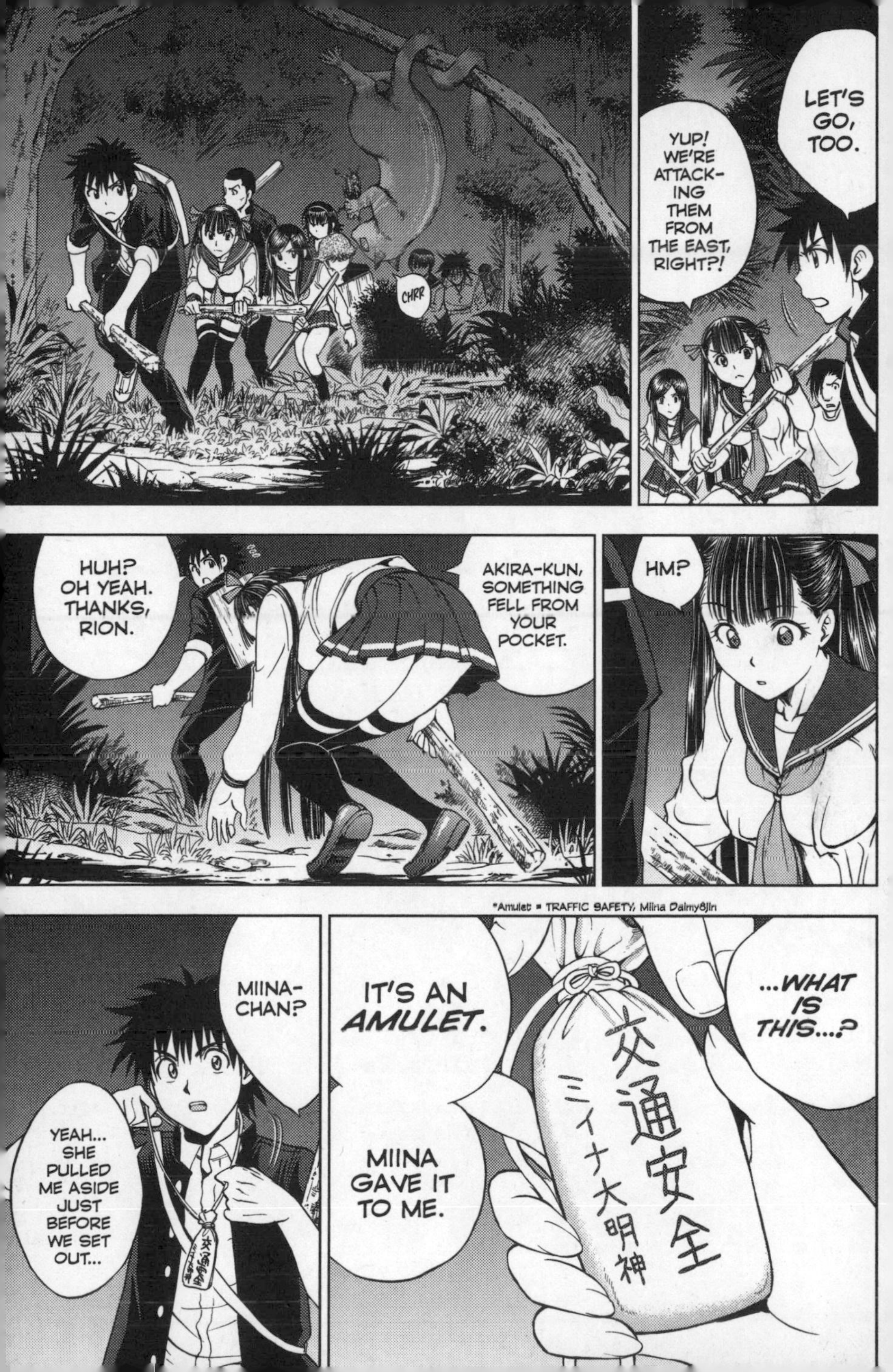
LET'S GO, TOO.
YUP! WE'RE ATTACKING THEM FROM THE EAST, RIGHT?!
CHRR
HM?
AKIRA-KUN, SOMETHING FELL FROM YOUR POCKET.
HUH? OH YEAH. THANKS, RION.
...WHAT IS THIS...?
IT'S AN *AMULET*.
交通安全
ミイナ大明神
MIINA GAVE IT TO ME.
MIINA-CHAN?
YEAH... SHE PULLED ME ASIDE JUST BEFORE WE SET OUT...

*Amulet = TRAFFIC SAFETY, Miina Daimyōjin

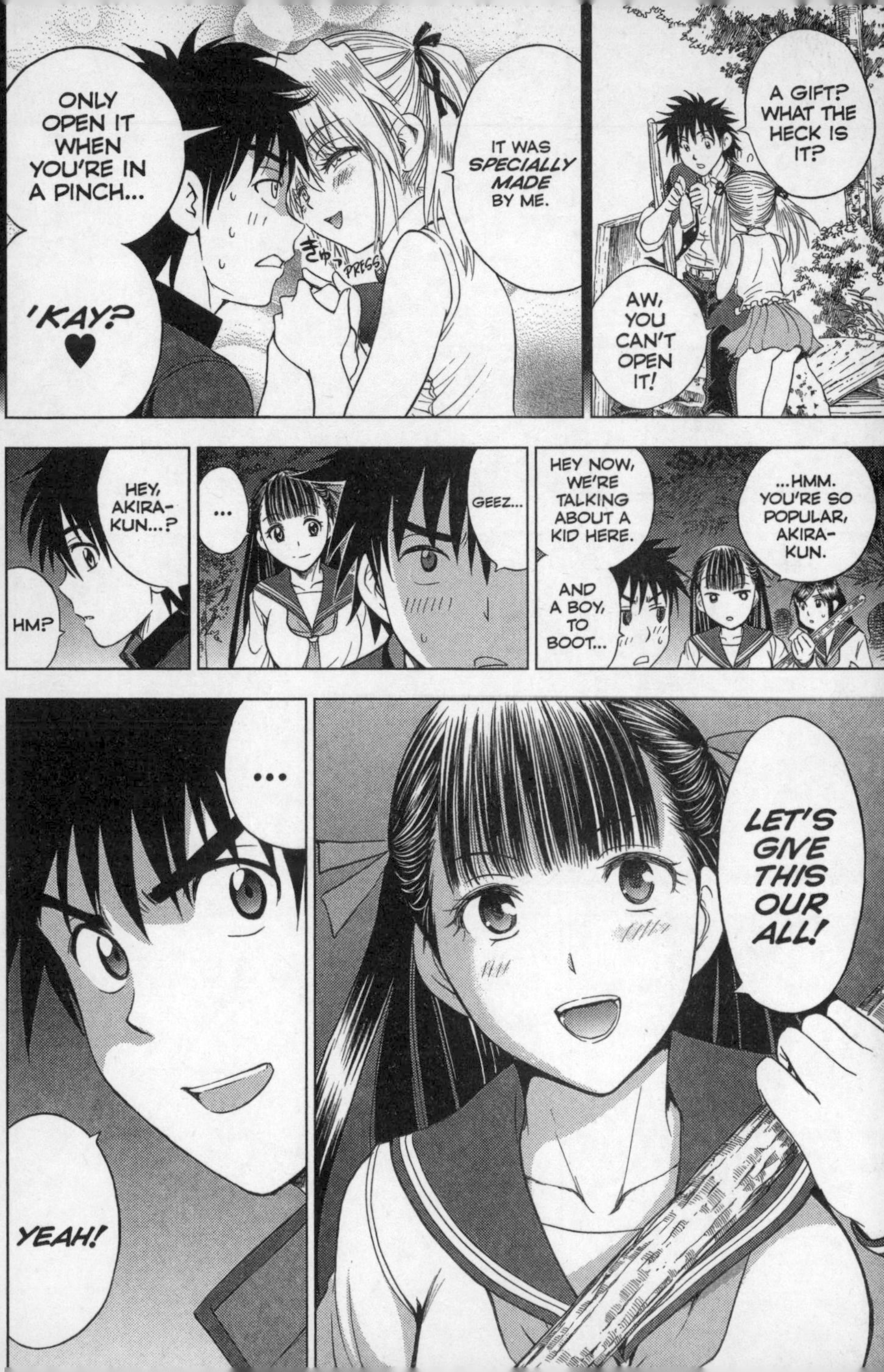
A GIFT? WHAT THE HECK IS IT?
AW, YOU CAN'T OPEN IT!
IT WAS SPECIALLY MADE BY ME.
きゅっ PRESS
ONLY OPEN IT WHEN YOU'RE IN A PINCH...
'KAY? ♥
...HMM. YOU'RE SO POPULAR, AKIRA-KUN.
HEY NOW, WE'RE TALKING ABOUT A KID HERE.
AND A BOY, TO BOOT...
GEEZ...
...
HEY, AKIRA-KUN...?
HM?
LET'S GIVE THIS OUR ALL!
...
YEAH!

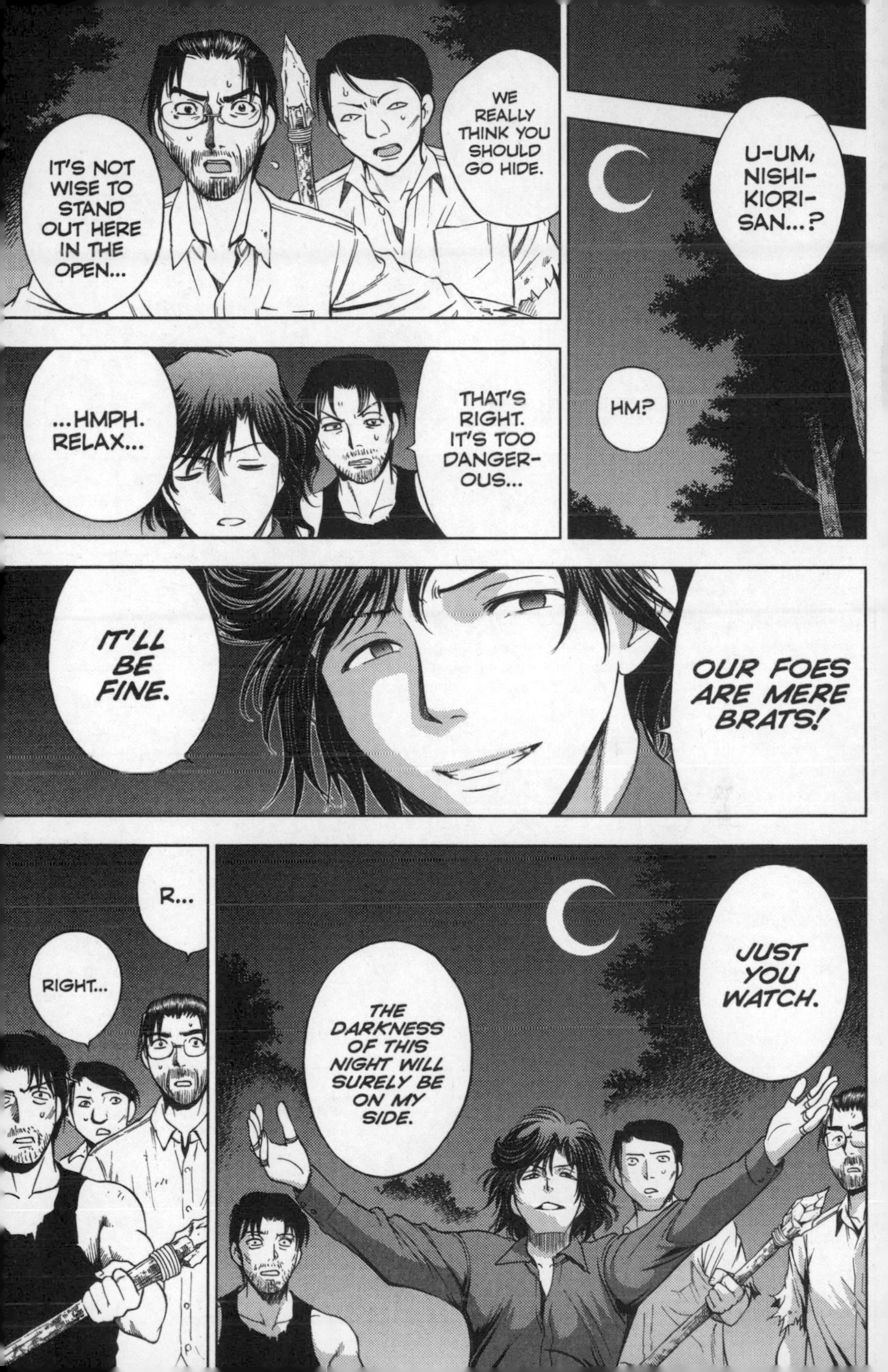
U-UM, NISHIKIORI-SAN...?
HM?
WE REALLY THINK YOU SHOULD GO HIDE.
IT'S NOT WISE TO STAND OUT HERE IN THE OPEN...
THAT'S RIGHT. IT'S TOO DANGEROUS...
...HMPH. RELAX...
OUR FOES ARE MERE BRATS!
IT'LL BE FINE.
JUST YOU WATCH.
THE DARKNESS OF THIS NIGHT WILL SURELY BE ON MY SIDE.
R...
RIGHT...

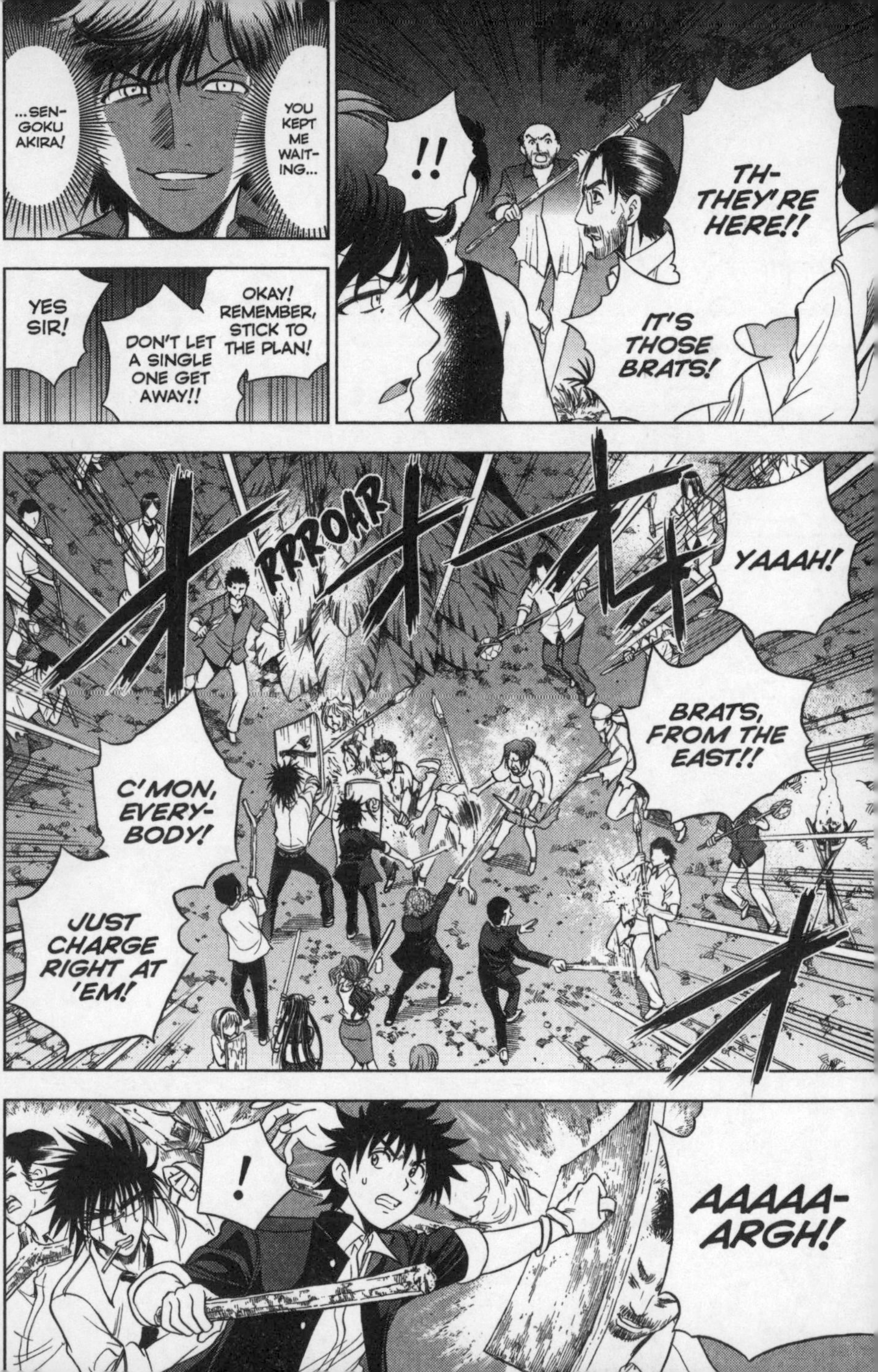
TH-THEY'RE HERE!!
!!
IT'S THOSE BRATS!
YOU KEPT ME WAITING...
...SENGOKU AKIRA!
OKAY! REMEMBER, STICK TO THE PLAN!
DON'T LET A SINGLE ONE GET AWAY!!
YES SIR!
YAAAH!
RRROAR
BRATS, FROM THE EAST!!
C'MON, EVERYBODY!
JUST CHARGE RIGHT AT 'EM!
AAAAA-ARGH!
!

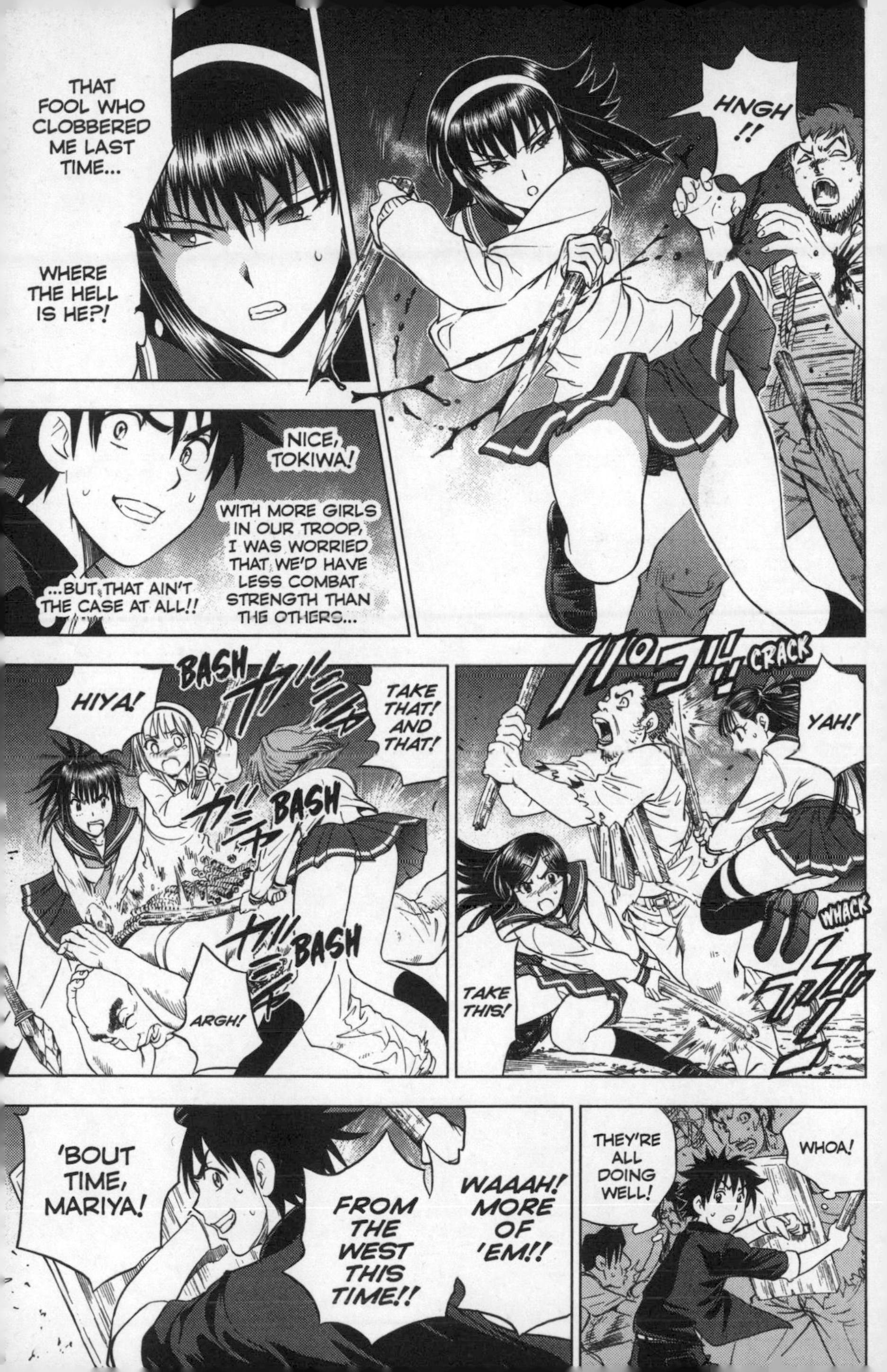
HNGH !!
THAT FOOL WHO CLOBBERED ME LAST TIME...
WHERE THE HELL IS HE?!
NICE, TOKIWA!
WITH MORE GIRLS IN OUR TROOP, I WAS WORRIED THAT WE'D HAVE LESS COMBAT STRENGTH THAN THE OTHERS...
...BUT THAT AIN'T THE CASE AT ALL!!
CRACK
YAH!
WHACK
TAKE THIS!
TAKE THAT! AND THAT!
BASH
HIYA!
BASH
BASH
ARGH!
WHOA!
THEY'RE ALL DOING WELL!
WAAAH! MORE OF 'EM!!
FROM THE WEST THIS TIME!!
'BOUT TIME, MARIYA!

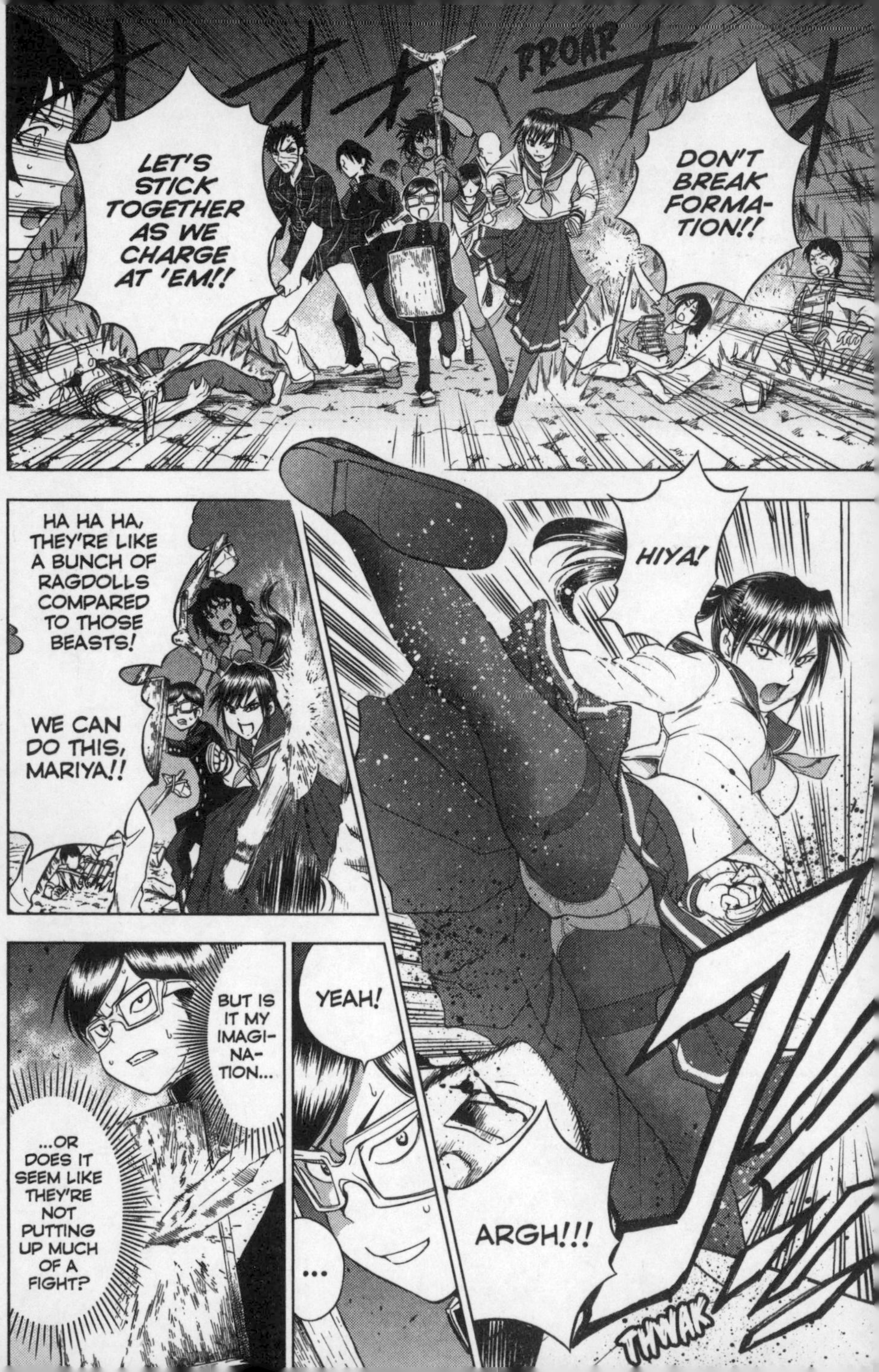
DON'T BREAK FORMA-TION!!
KROAR
LET'S STICK TOGETHER AS WE CHARGE AT 'EM!!
HIYA!
HA HA HA, THEY'RE LIKE A BUNCH OF RAGDOLLS COMPARED TO THOSE BEASTS!
WE CAN DO THIS, MARIYA!!
YEAH!
BUT IS IT MY IMAGI-NA-TION...
...OR DOES IT SEEM LIKE THEY'RE NOT PUTTING UP MUCH OF A FIGHT?
...
ARGH!!!
THWAK

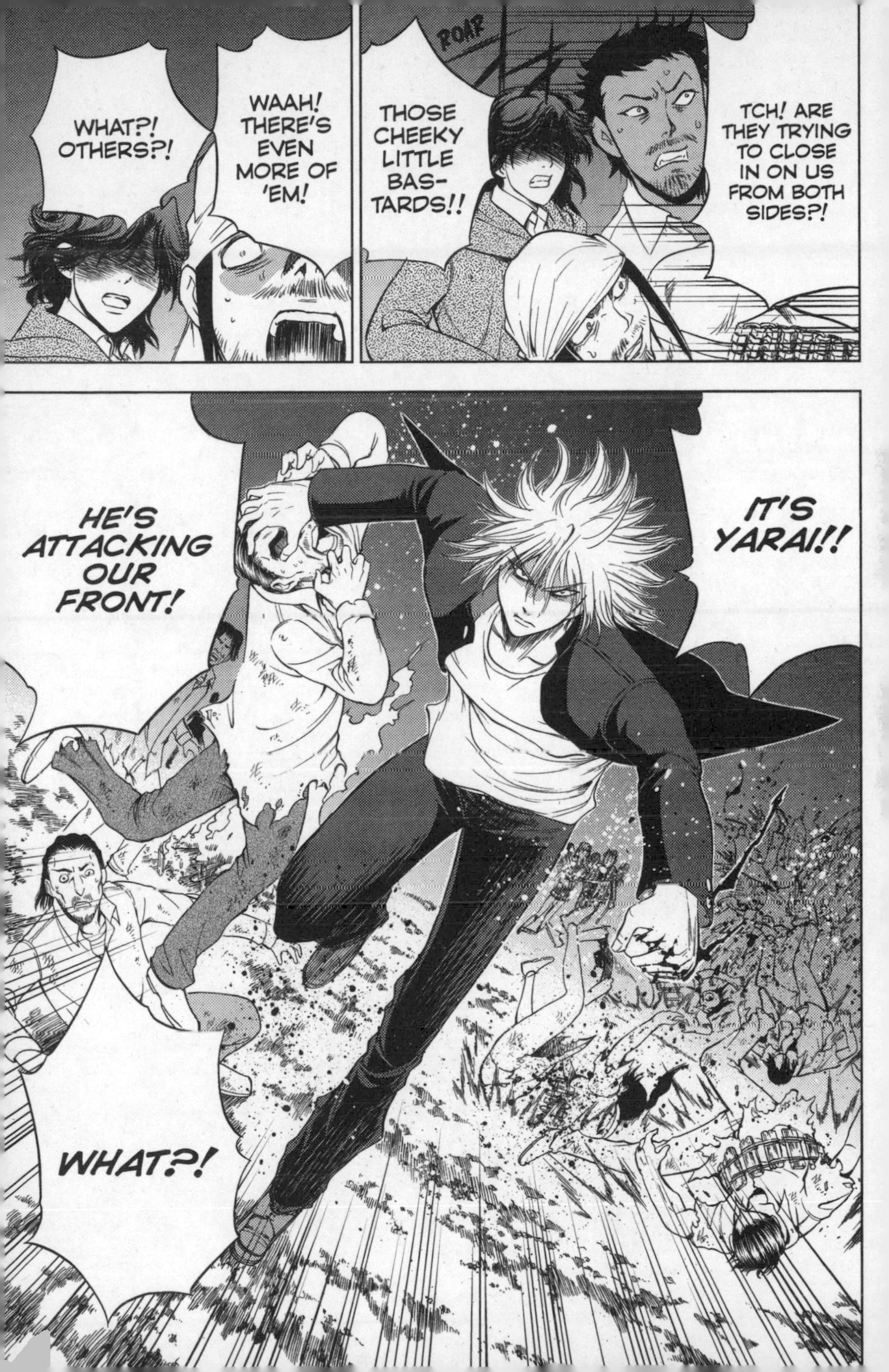

TCH! ARE THEY TRYING TO CLOSE IN ON US FROM BOTH SIDES?!
ROAR
THOSE CHEEKY LITTLE BAS-TARDS!!
WAAH! THERE'S EVEN MORE OF 'EM!
WHAT?! OTHERS?!
IT'S YARAI!!
HE'S ATTACKING OUR FRONT!
WHAT?!

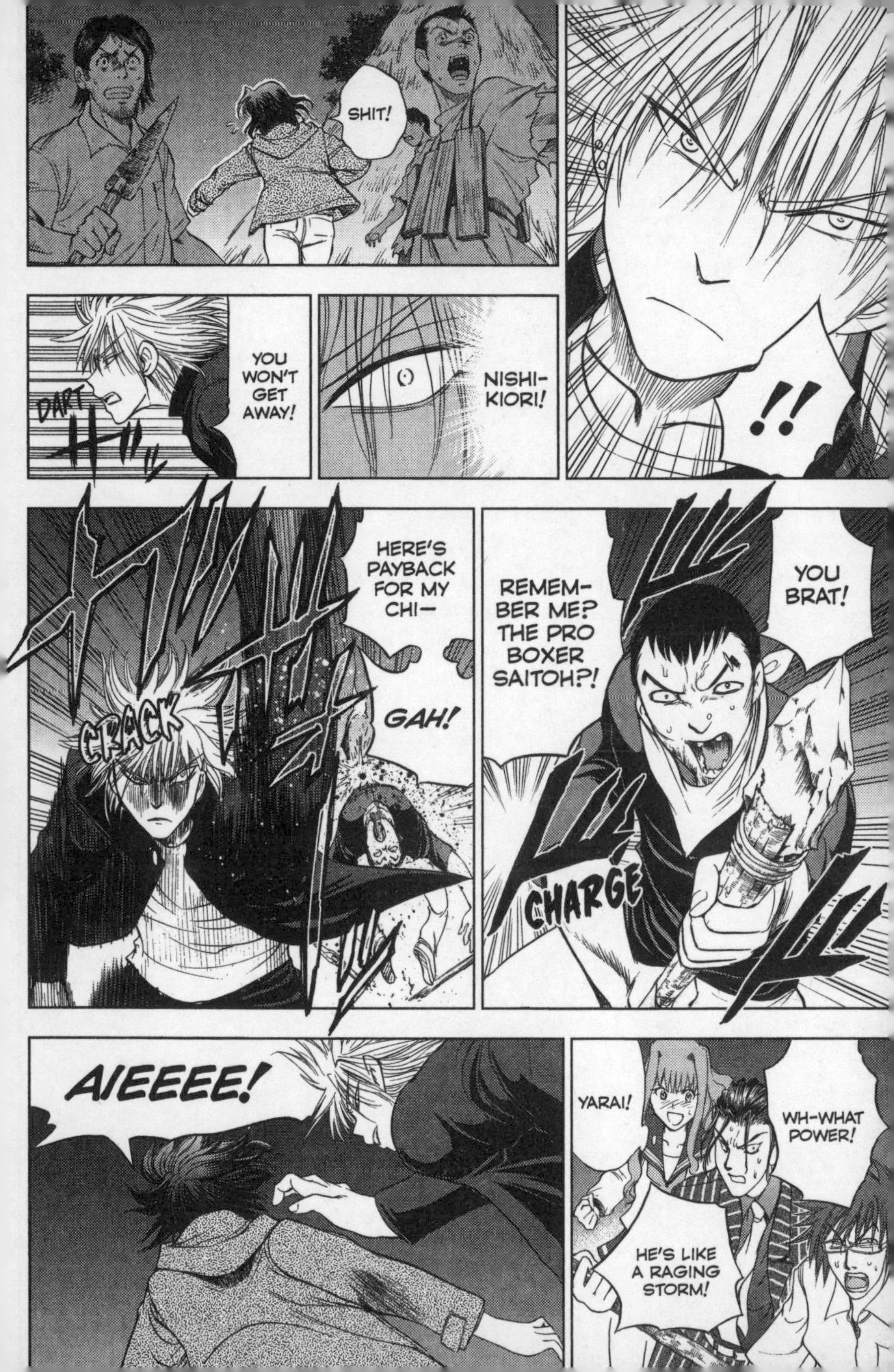
!!
SHIT!
NISHI-KIORI!
YOU WON'T GET AWAY!
DART
YOU BRAT!
REMEMBER ME? THE PRO BOXER SAITOH?!
CHARGE
HERE'S PAYBACK FOR MY CHI—
GAH!
CRACK
WH-WHAT POWER!
YARAI!
HE'S LIKE A RAGING STORM!
AIEEEE!

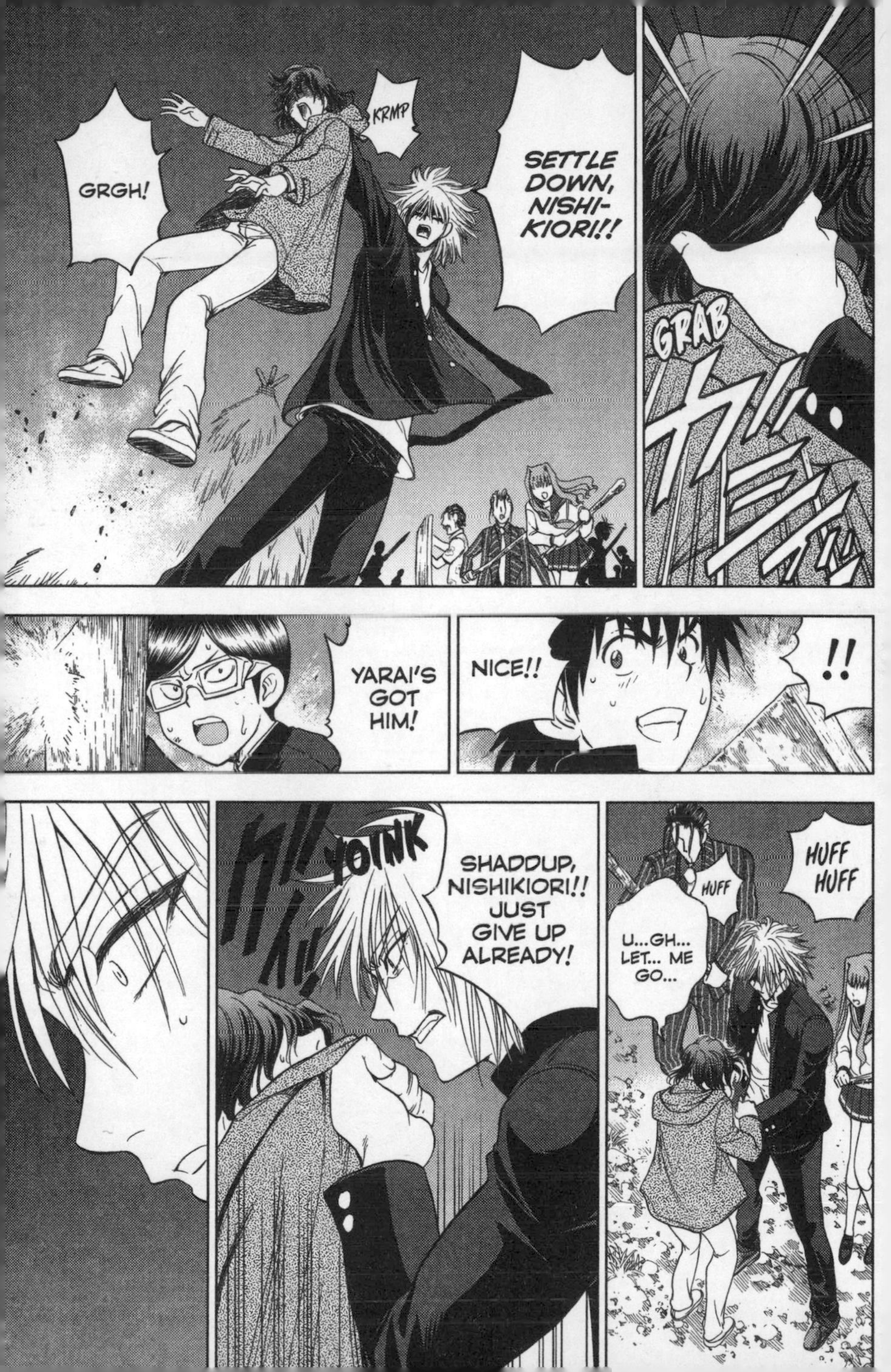
GRAB
SETTLE DOWN, NISHIKIORI!!
KRMP
GRGH!
!!
NICE!!
YARAI'S GOT HIM!
HUFF HUFF
HUFF
U...GH... LET... ME GO...
SHADDUP, NISHIKIORI!! JUST GIVE UP ALREADY!
YOINK

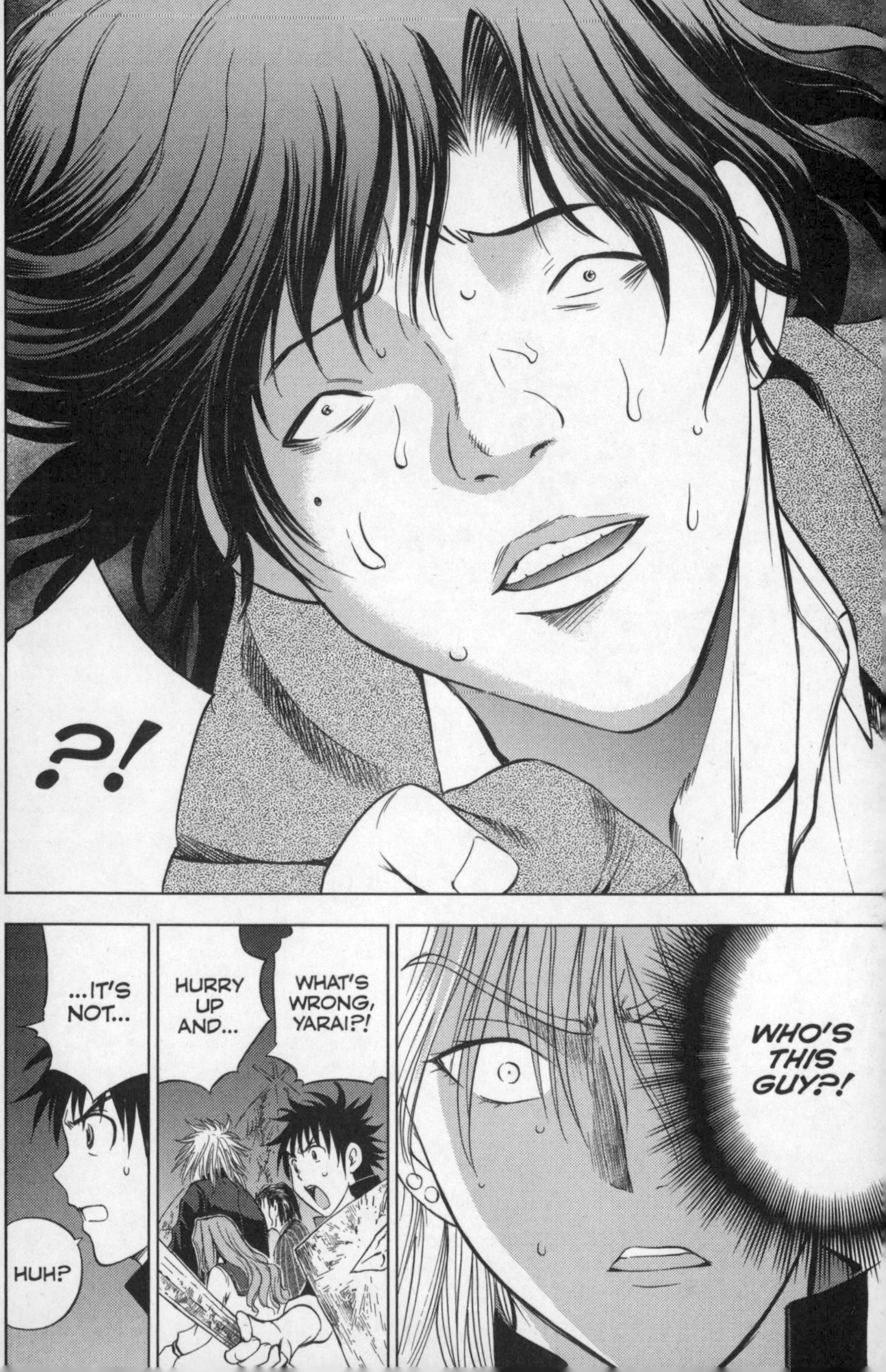
?!
WHO'S THIS GUY?!
WHAT'S WRONG, YARAI?!
HURRY UP AND...
...IT'S NOT...
HUH?

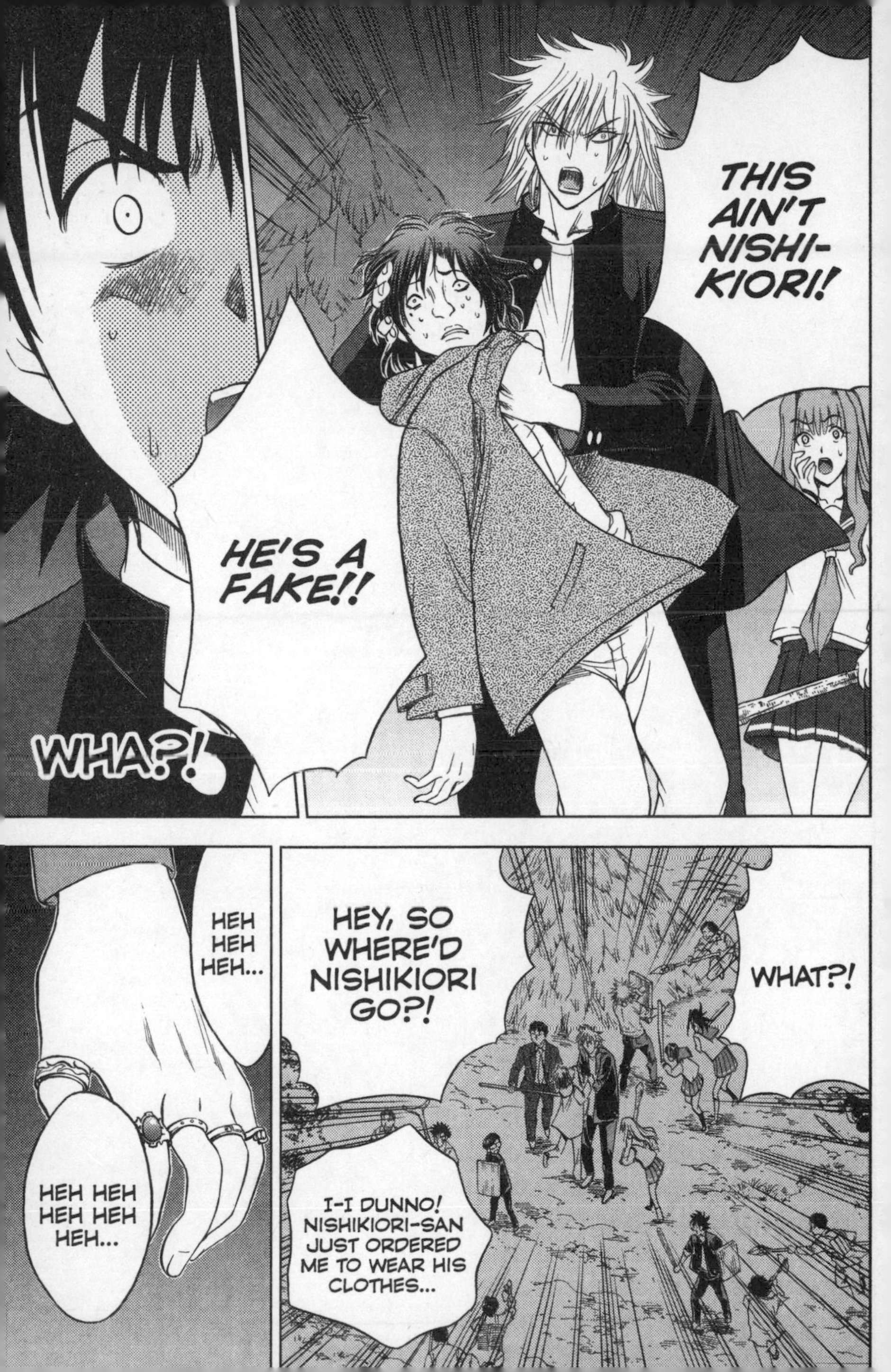
THIS AIN'T NISHI-KIORI!
HE'S A FAKE!!
WHA?!
WHAT?!
HEY, SO WHERE'D NISHIKIORI GO?!
I-I DUNNO! NISHIKIORI-SAN JUST ORDERED ME TO WEAR HIS CLOTHES...
HEH HEH HEH...
HEH HEH HEH HEH HEH...

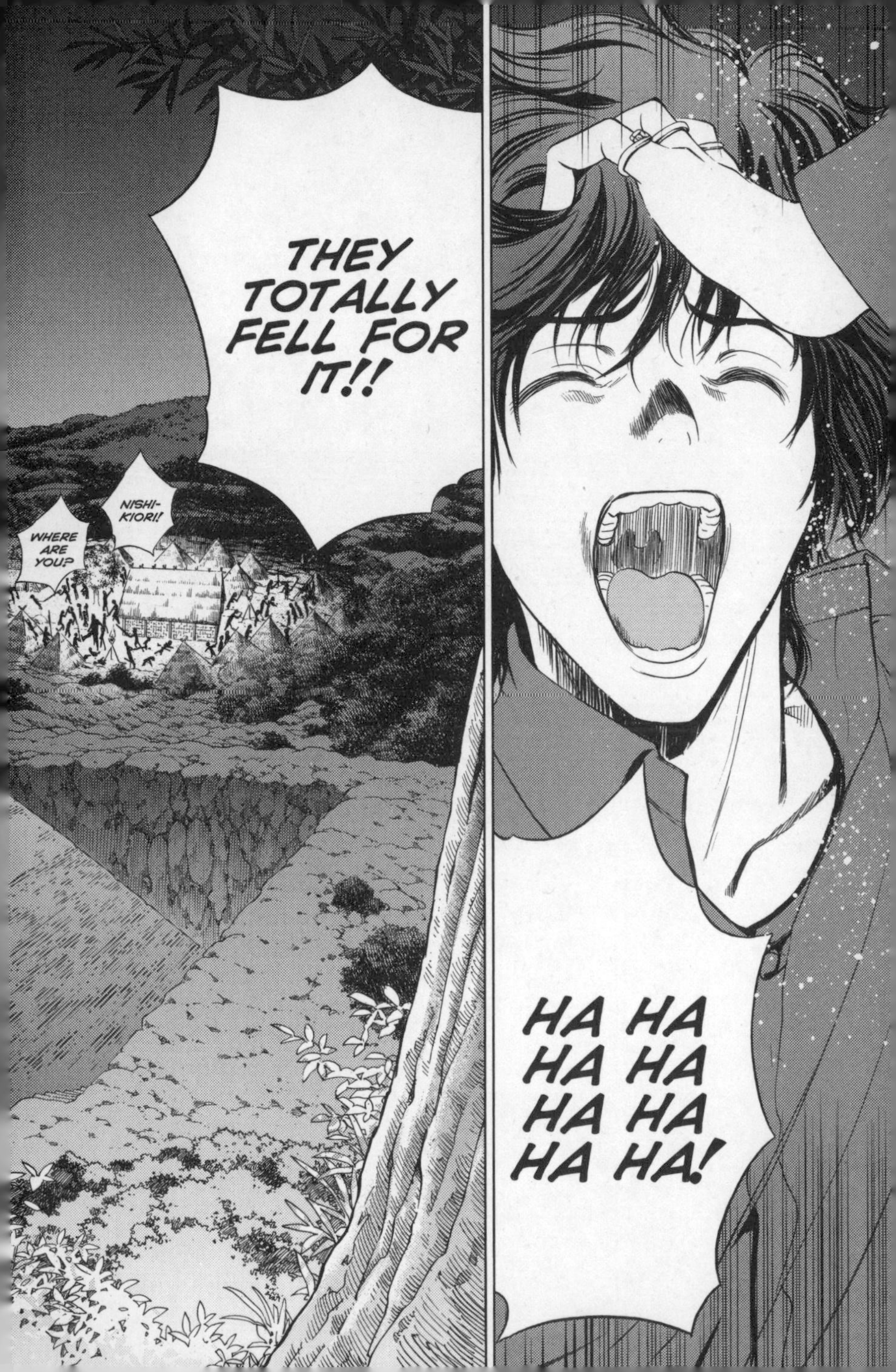
HA HA HA HA HA HA HA HA!
THEY TOTALLY FELL FOR IT!!
NISHI-KIORI!
WHERE ARE YOU?

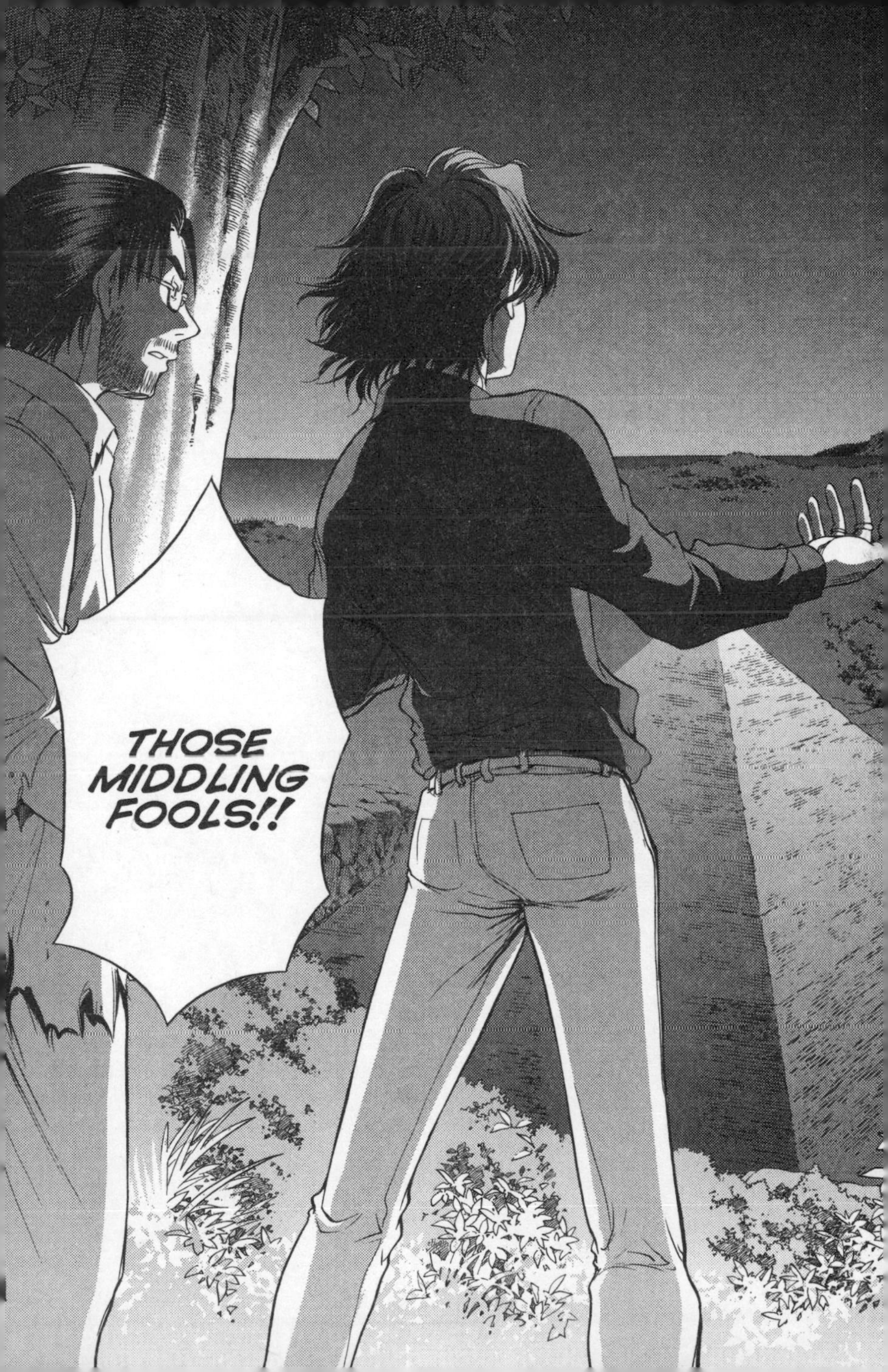
THOSE MIDDLING FOOLS!!

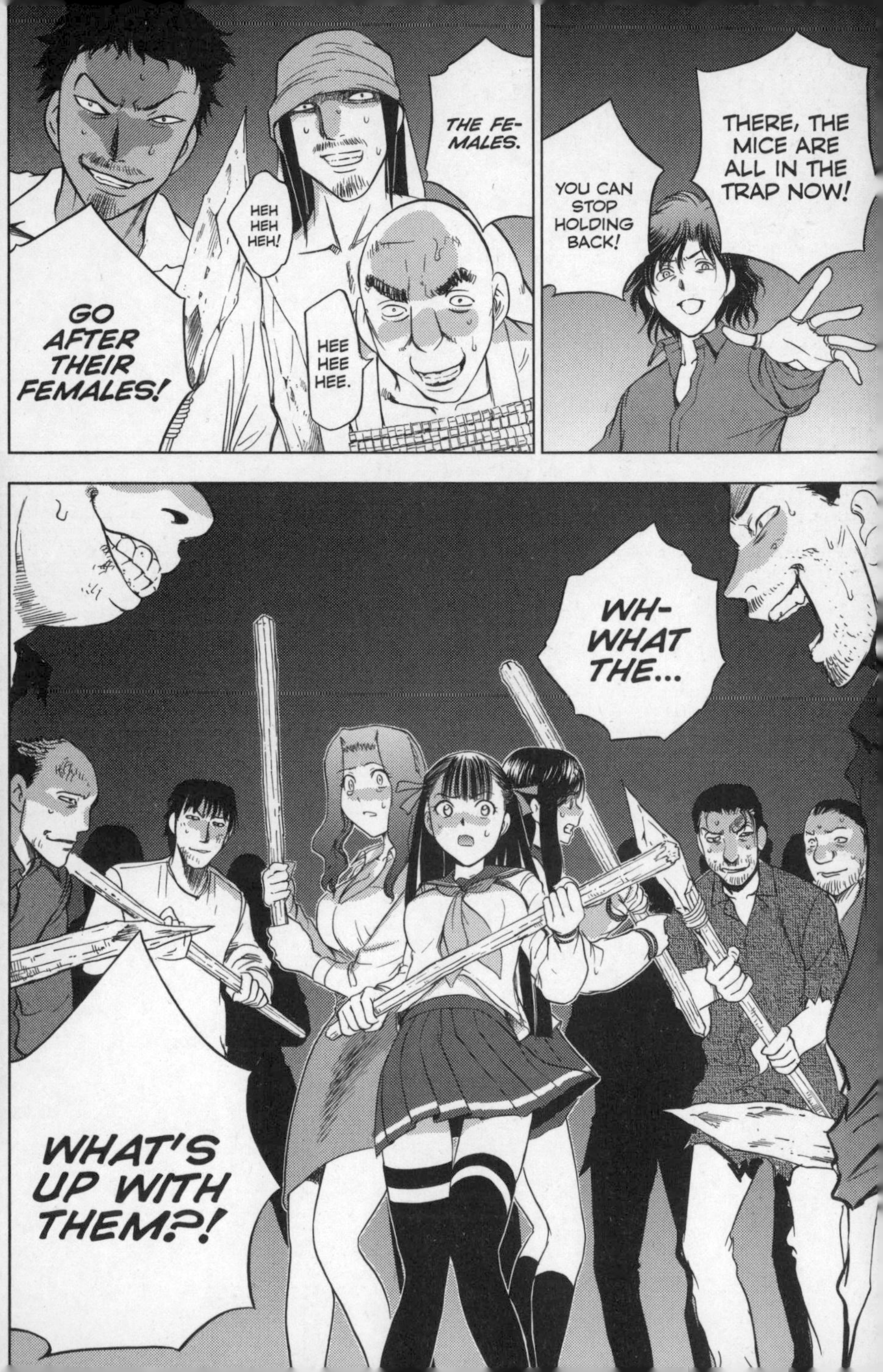

THERE, THE MICE ARE ALL IN THE TRAP NOW!
YOU CAN STOP HOLDING BACK!
THE FE-MALES.
HEH HEH HEH!
HEE HEE HEE.
GO AFTER THEIR FEMALES!
WH-WHAT THE...
WHAT'S UP WITH THEM?!

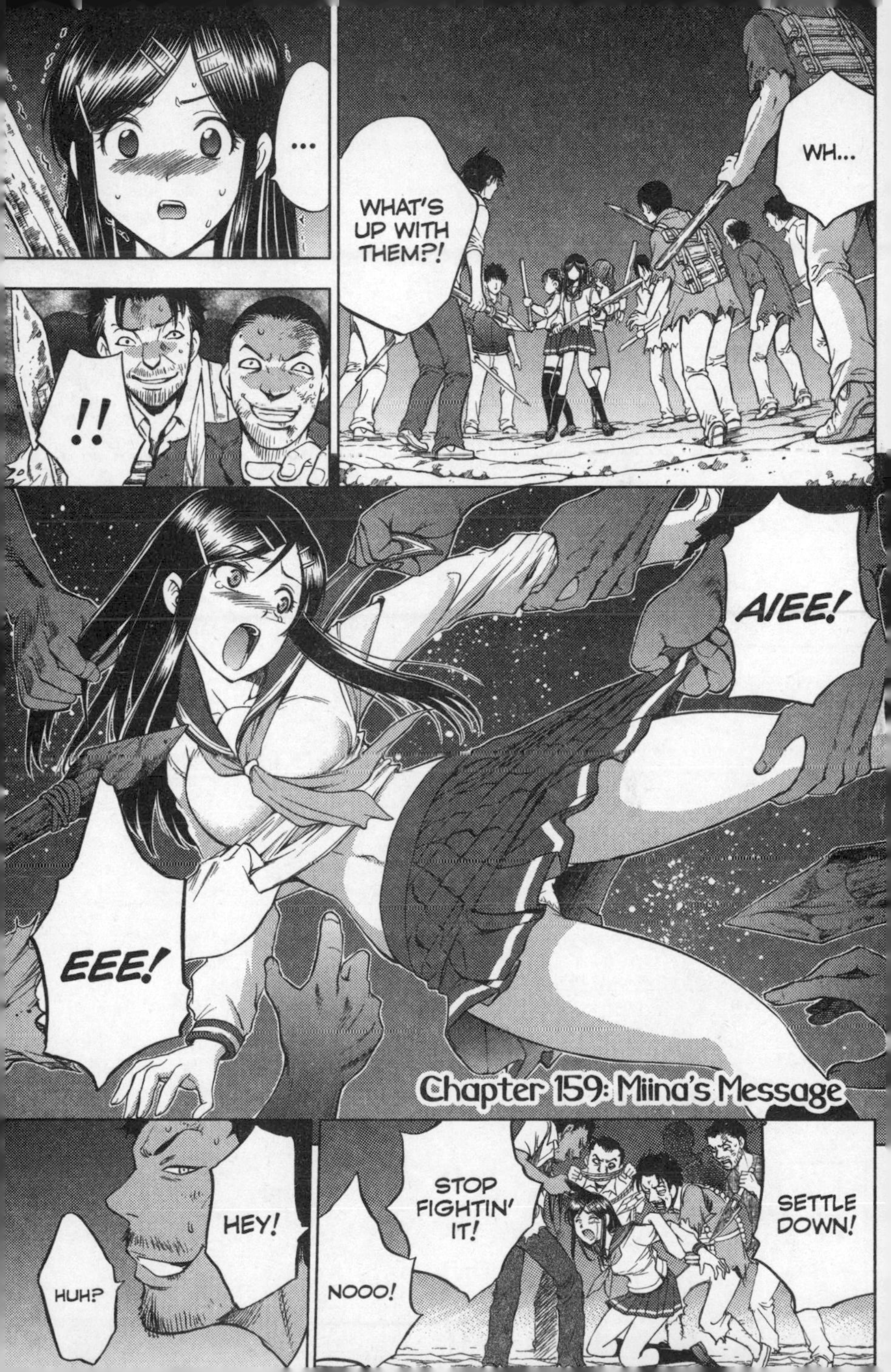
WH...
WHAT'S UP WITH THEM?!
...
!!
AIEE!
EEE!
Chapter 159: Miina's Message
SETTLE DOWN!
STOP FIGHTIN' IT!
NOOO!
HEY!
HUH?

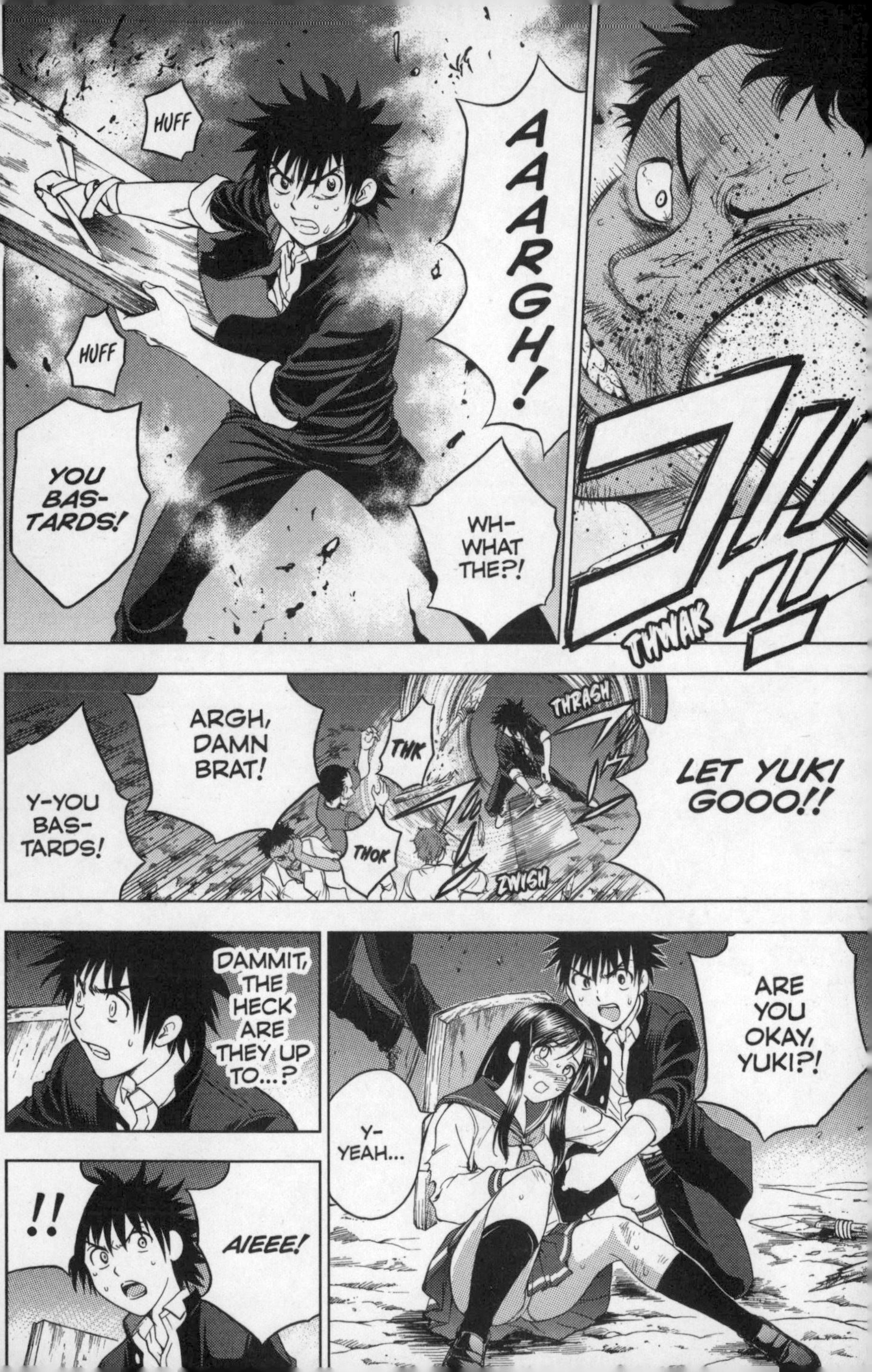
THWAK
AAARGH!
HUFF
HUFF
WH-WHAT THE?!
YOU BASTARDS!
LET YUKI GOOOO!!
THRASH
THK
ARGH, DAMN BRAT!
Y-YOU BASTARDS!
THOK
ZWISH
ARE YOU OKAY, YUKI?!
Y-YEAH...
DAMMIT, THE HECK ARE THEY UP TO...?
!!
AIEEE!

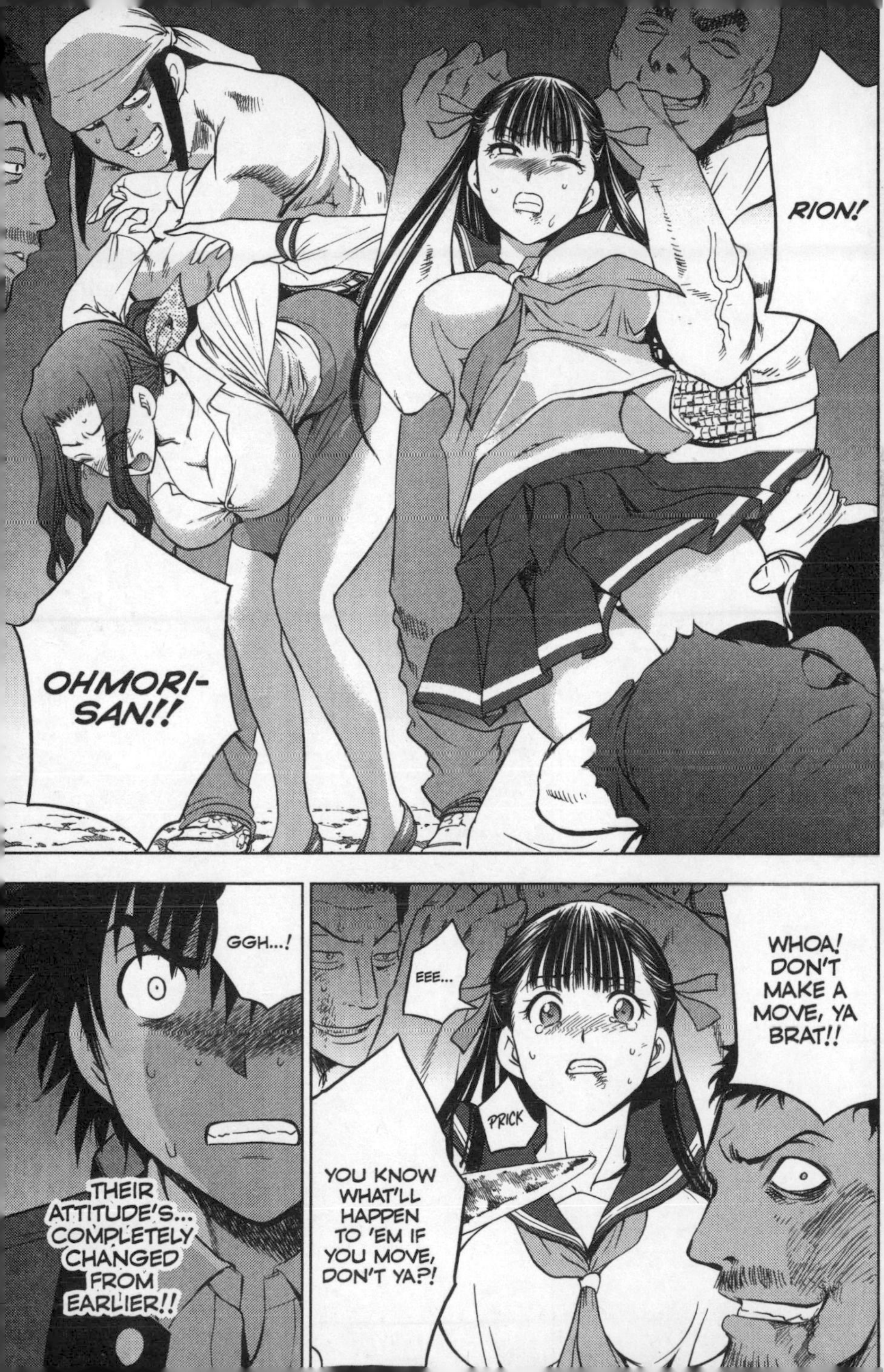
RION!
OHMORI-SAN!!
WHOA! DON'T MAKE A MOVE, YA BRAT!!
EEE...
PRICK
YOU KNOW WHAT'LL HAPPEN TO 'EM IF YOU MOVE, DON'T YA?!
GGH...!
THEIR ATTITUDE'S... COMPLETELY CHANGED FROM EARLIER!!

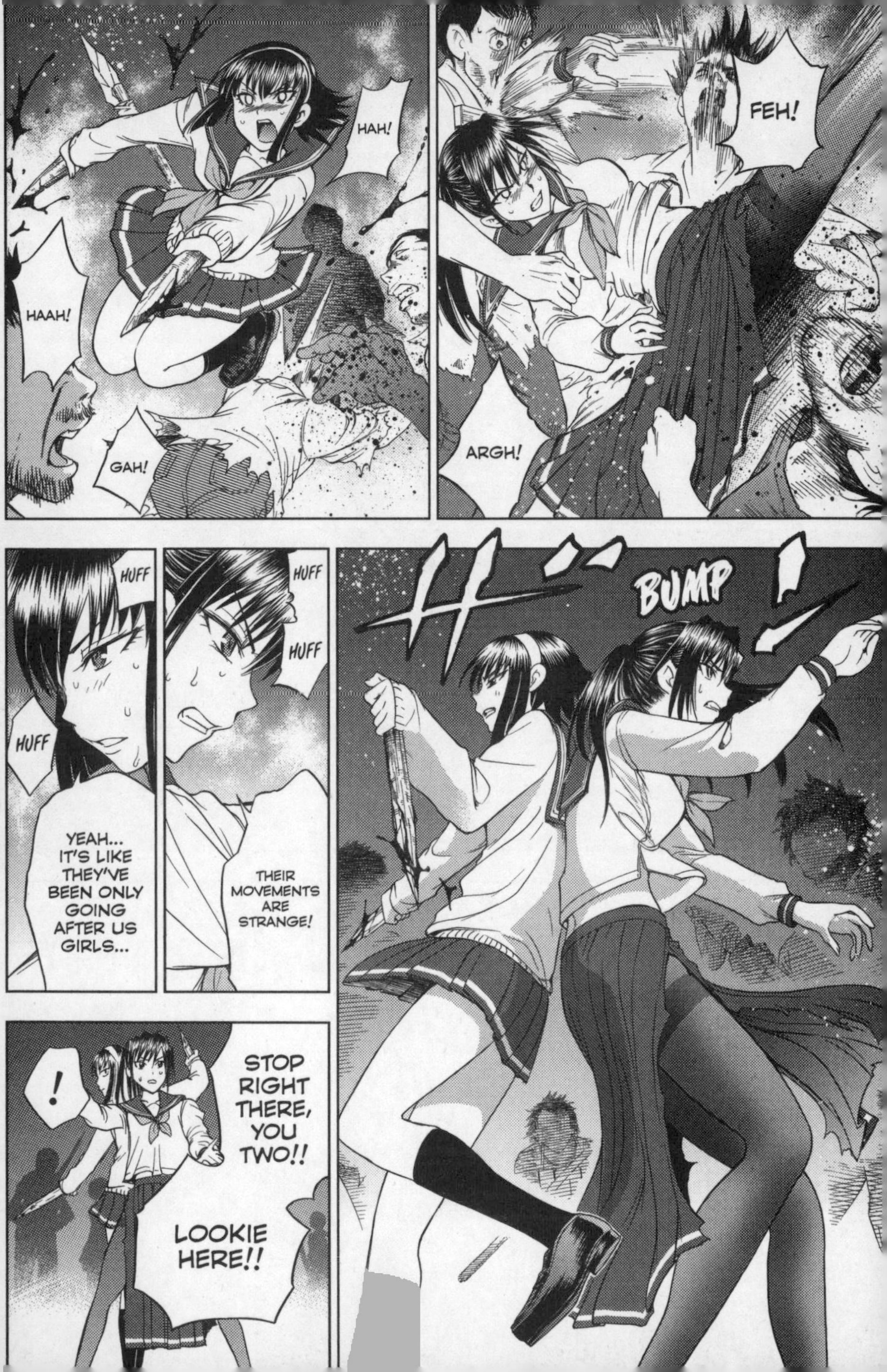
FEH!
ARGH!
HAH!
HAAH!
GAH!
BUMP
!
HUFF
HUFF
THEIR MOVEMENTS ARE STRANGE!
HUFF
HUFF
YEAH... IT'S LIKE THEY'VE BEEN ONLY GOING AFTER US GIRLS...
STOP RIGHT THERE, YOU TWO!!
!
LOOKIE HERE!!

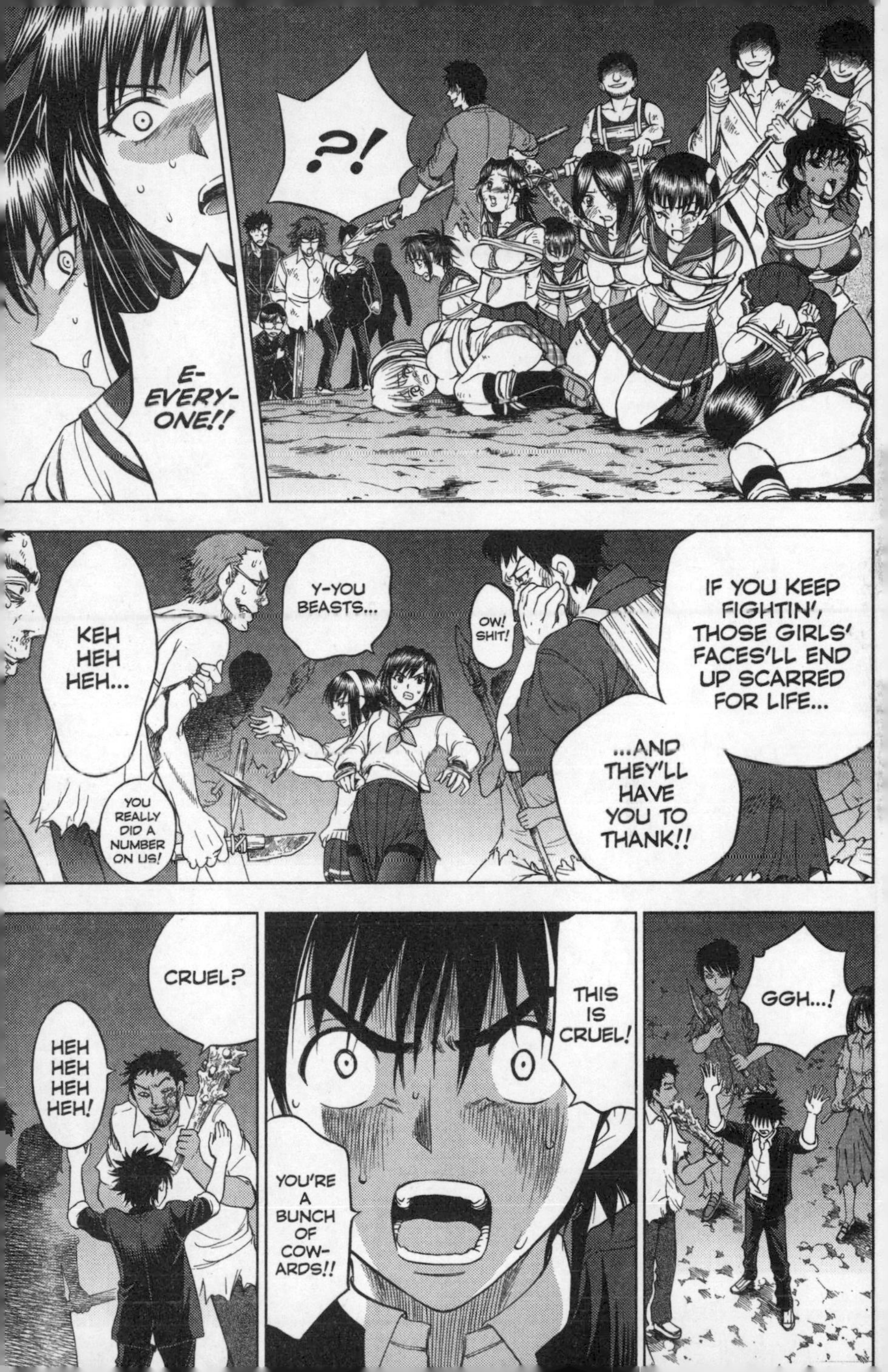
?!
E-EVERYONE!!
IF YOU KEEP FIGHTIN', THOSE GIRLS' FACES'LL END UP SCARRED FOR LIFE...
...AND THEY'LL HAVE YOU TO THANK!!
OW! SHIT!
Y-YOU BEASTS...
KEH HEH HEH...
YOU REALLY DID A NUMBER ON US!
GGH...!
THIS IS CRUEL!
YOU'RE A BUNCH OF COWARDS!!
CRUEL?
HEH HEH HEH HEH!

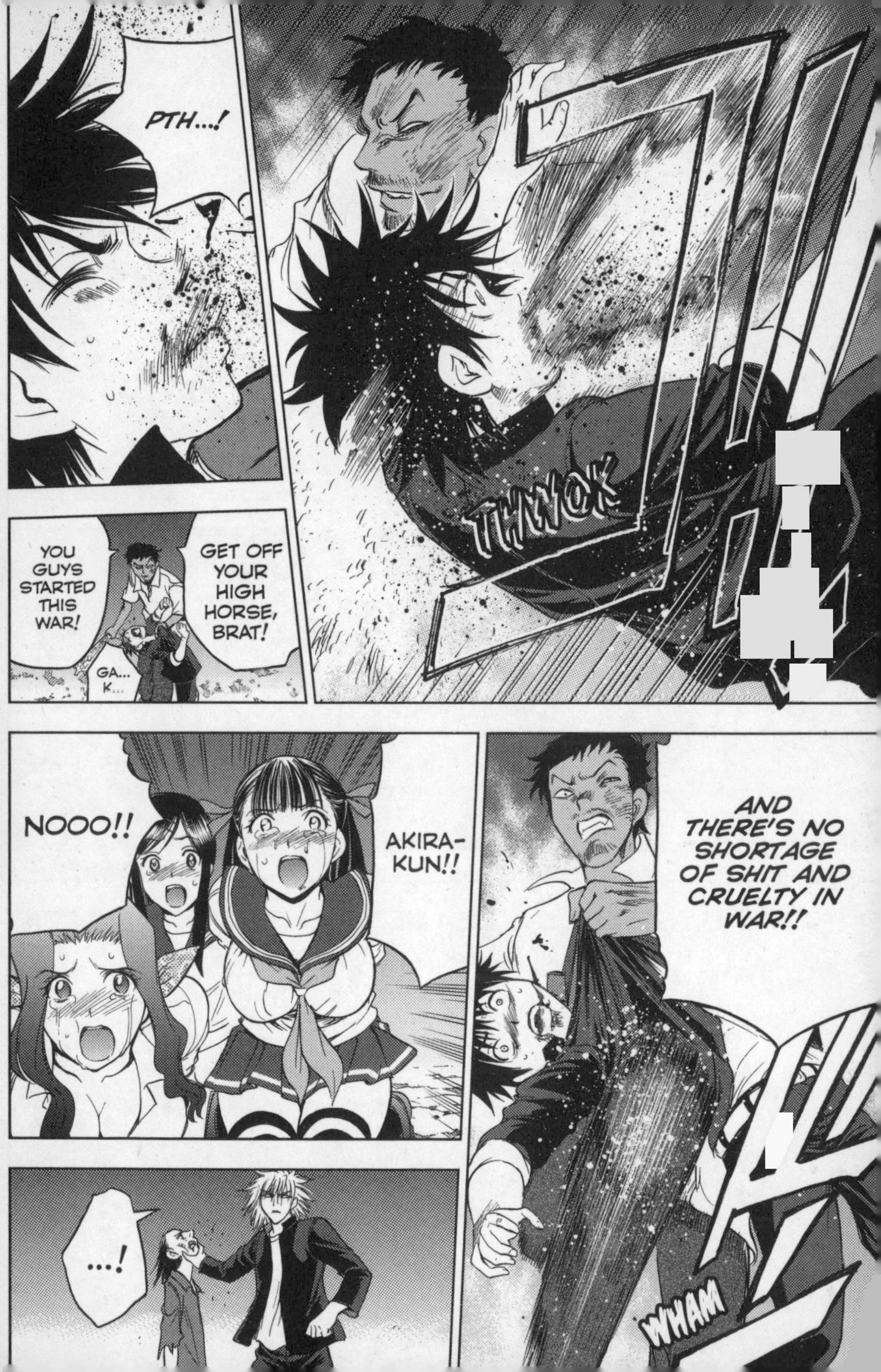
THWOCK
PTH...!
GET OFF YOUR HIGH HORSE, BRAT!
YOU GUYS STARTED THIS WAR!
GA... K...
AND THERE'S NO SHORTAGE OF SHIT AND CRUELTY IN WAR!!
WHAM
AKIRA-KUN!!
NOOO!!
...!

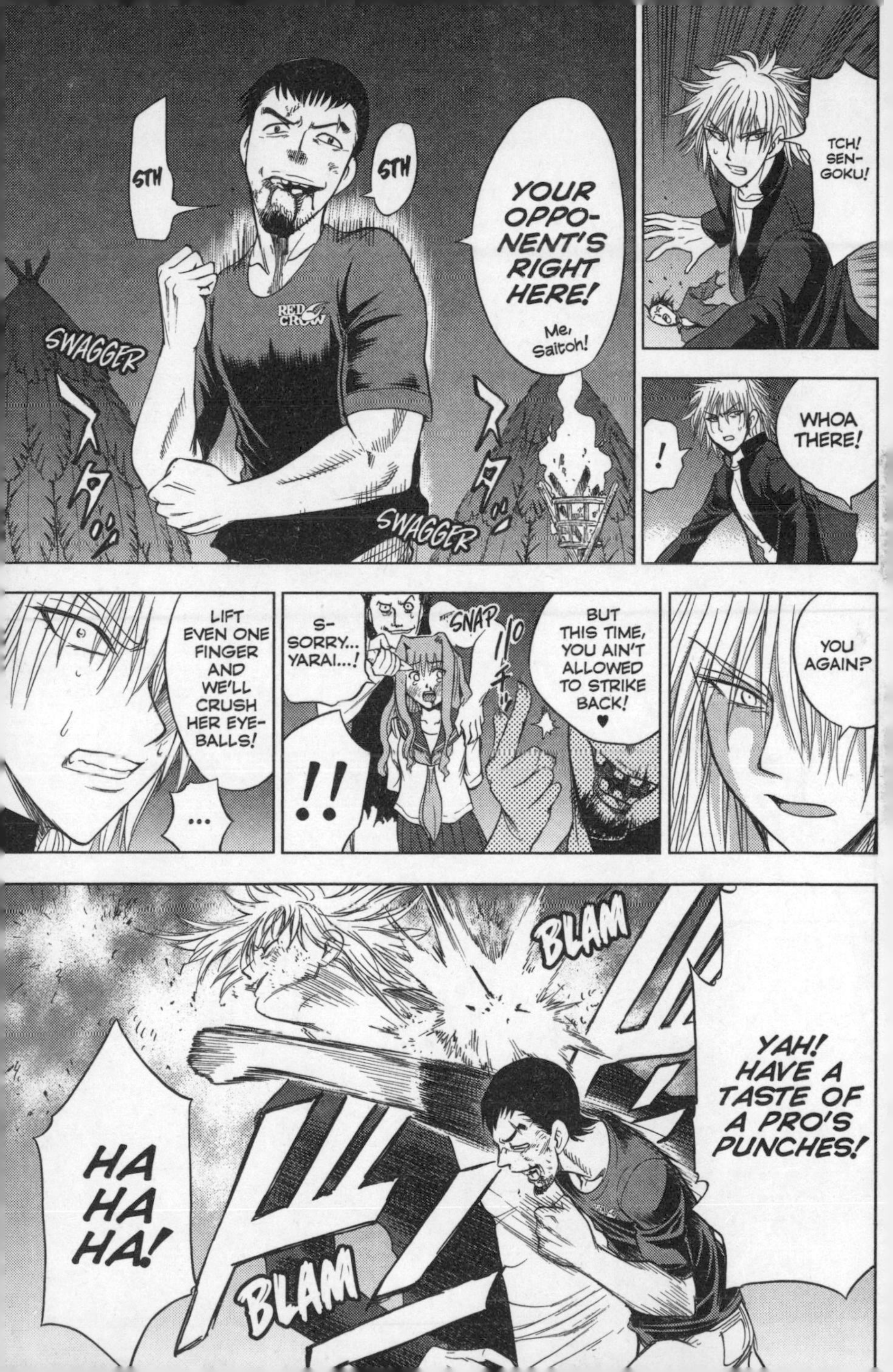
TCH! SEN-GOKU!
!
WHOA THERE!
YOUR OPPONENT'S RIGHT HERE!
Me, Saitoh!
STH
STH
RED CROW
SWAGGER
SWAGGER
YOU AGAIN?
BUT THIS TIME, YOU AIN'T ALLOWED TO STRIKE BACK! ♥
SNAP
S-SORRY... YARAI...!
!!
LIFT EVEN ONE FINGER AND WE'LL CRUSH HER EYE-BALLS!
...
BLAM
YAH! HAVE A TASTE OF A PRO'S PUNCHES!
HA HA HA HA!
BLAM

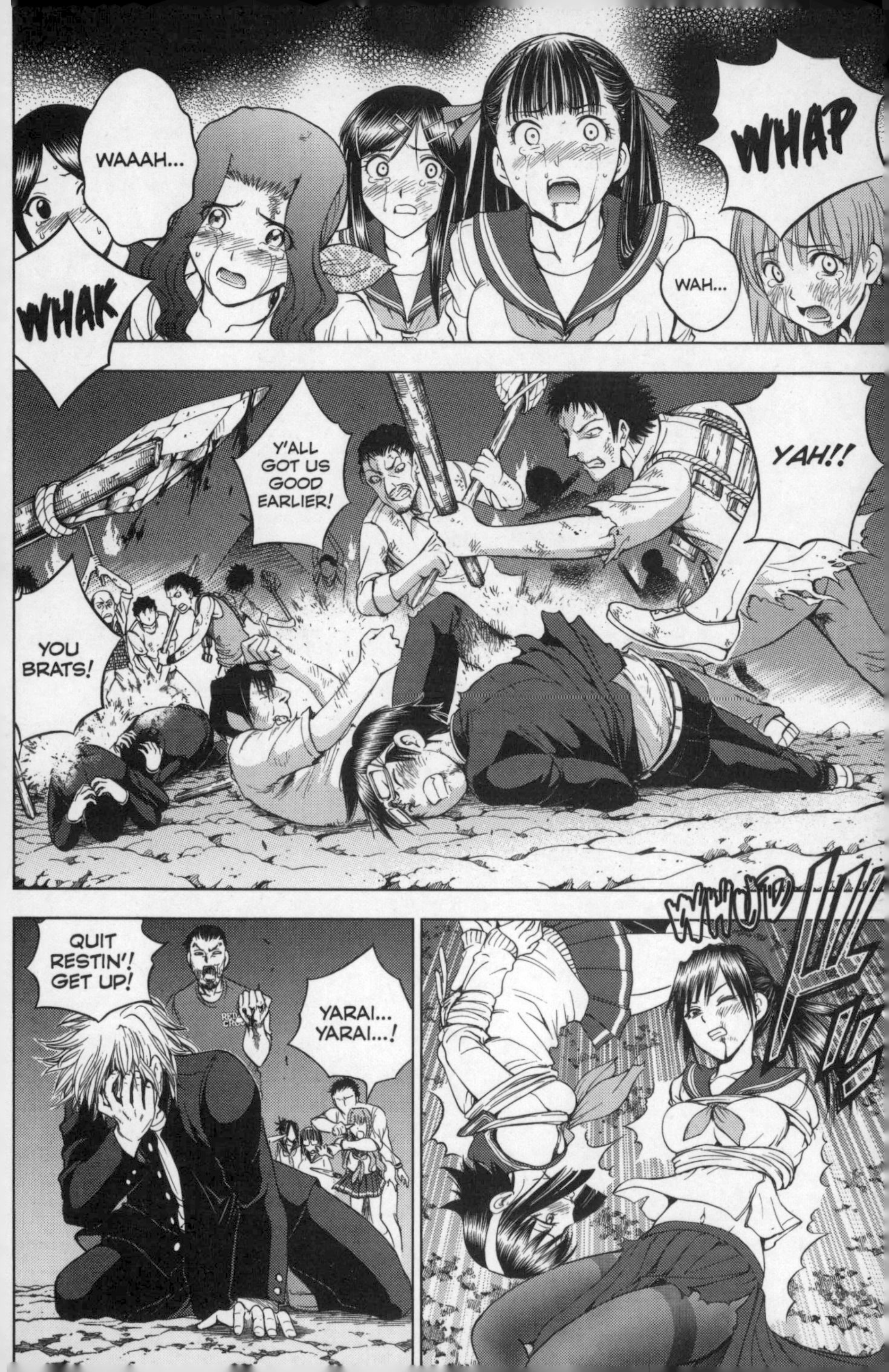
WHAP
WAH...
WAAAH...
WHAK
YAH!!
Y'ALL GOT US GOOD EARLIER!
YOU BRATS!
WHUD
QUIT RESTIN'! GET UP!
YARAI... YARAI...!

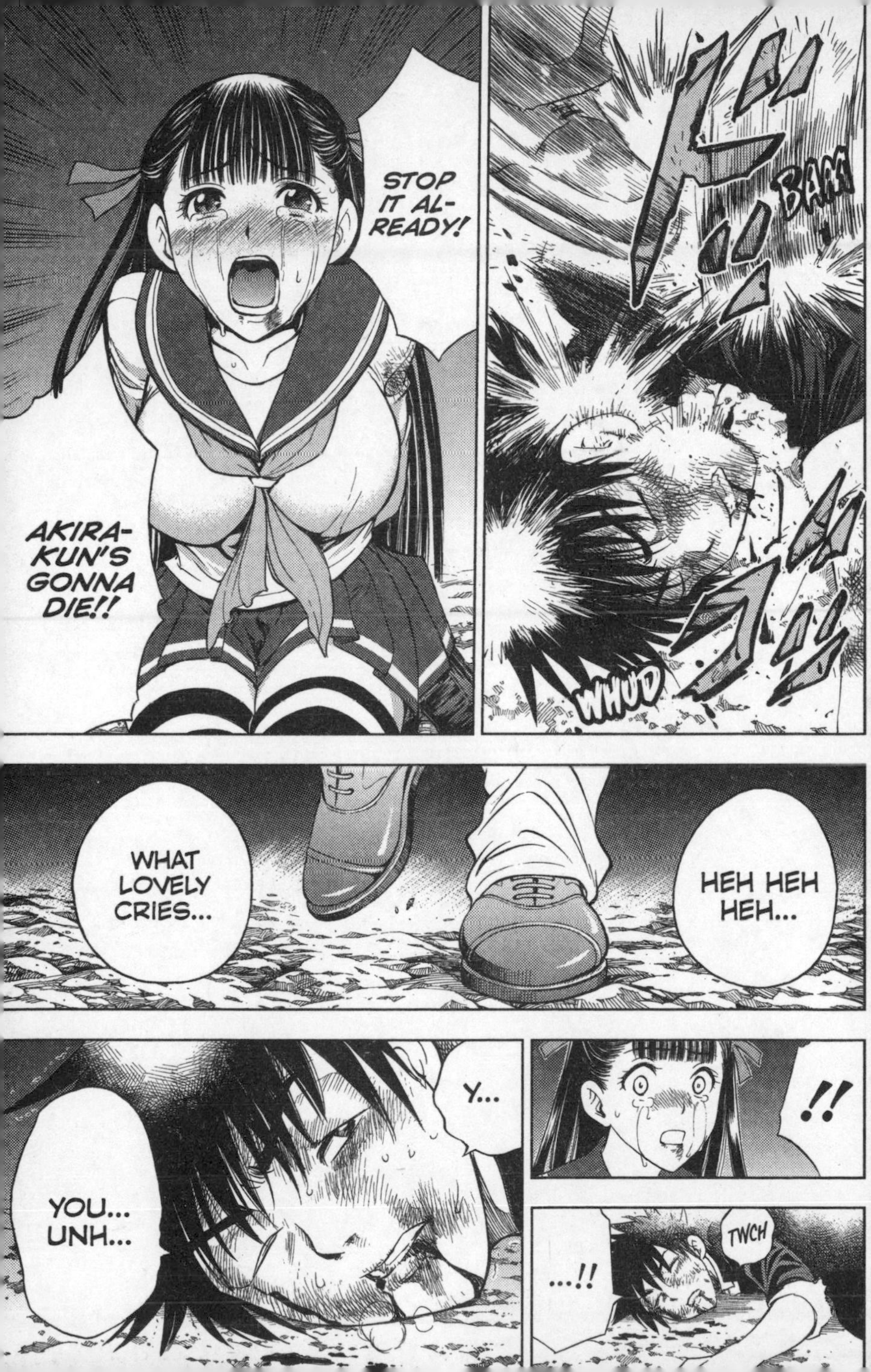
BAM
WHUD
STOP IT AL-READY!
AKIRA-KUN'S GONNA DIE!!
HEH HEH HEH...
WHAT LOVELY CRIES...
!!
TWCH
...!!
Y...
YOU... UNH...

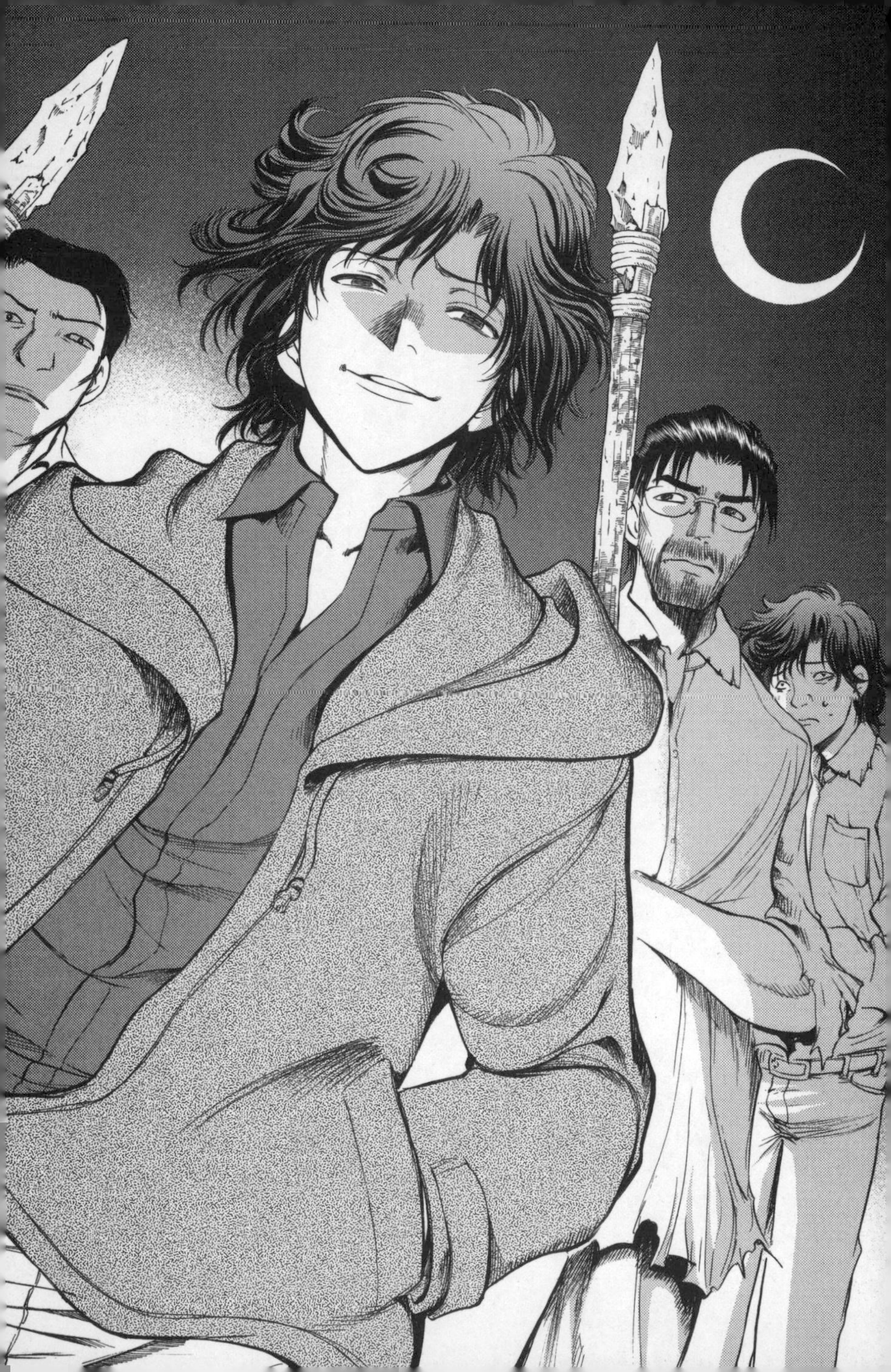

NISHI-KI...

...ORI...

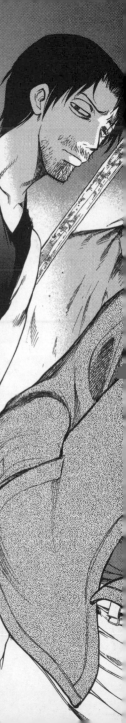

HMPH!

THAT'S QUITE A NICE LOOK ON YOU, SENGOKU AKIRA.

HMPH.

KICK

WELL...? DO YOU GET IT NOW? YOU CAN'T DEFY ME.

...

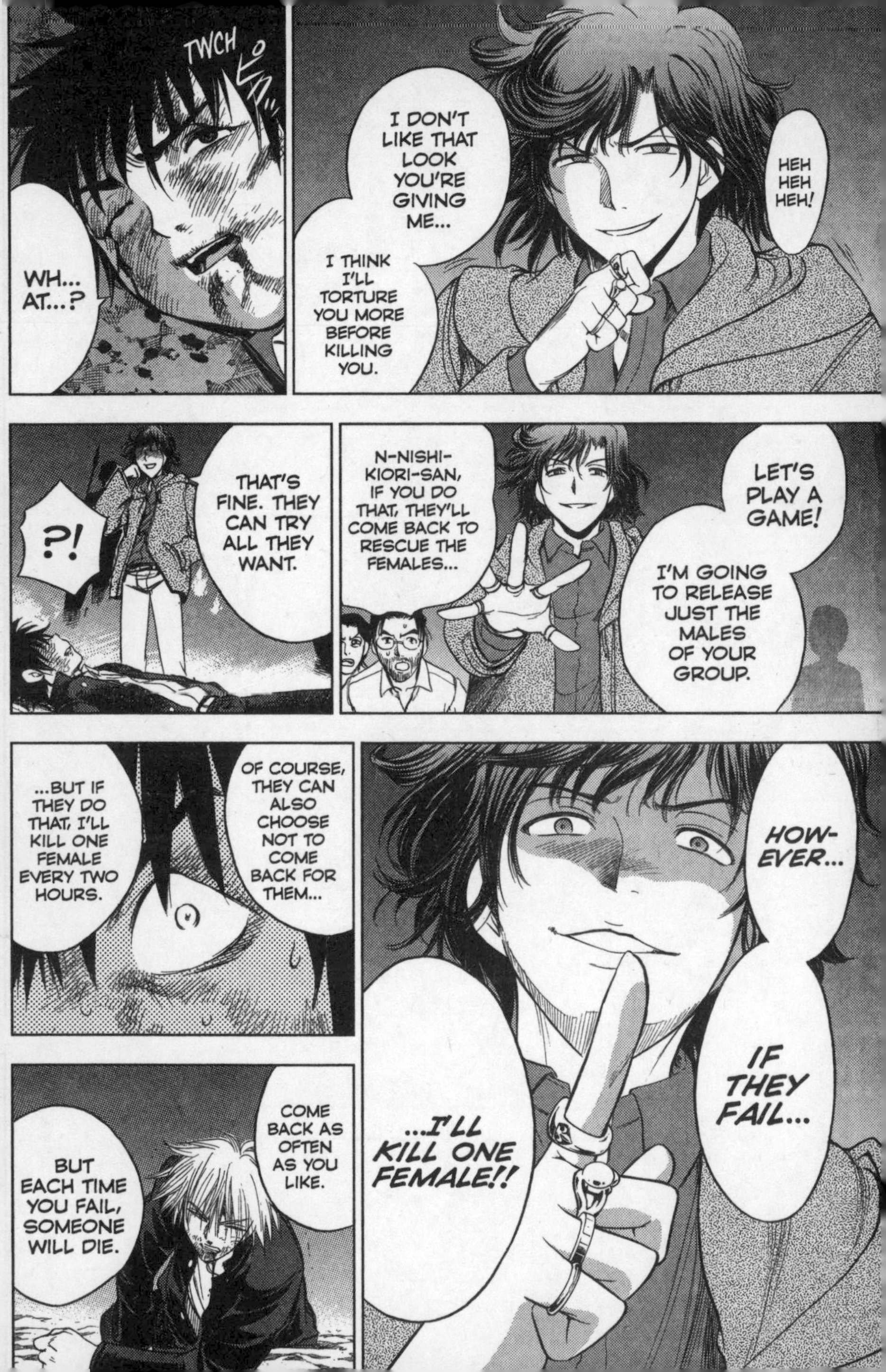
HEH HEH HEH!
I DON'T LIKE THAT LOOK YOU'RE GIVING ME...
I THINK I'LL TORTURE YOU MORE BEFORE KILLING YOU.
TWCH
WH... AT...?
LET'S PLAY A GAME!
I'M GOING TO RELEASE JUST THE MALES OF YOUR GROUP.
N-NISHIKIORI-SAN, IF YOU DO THAT, THEY'LL COME BACK TO RESCUE THE FEMALES...
THAT'S FINE. THEY CAN TRY ALL THEY WANT.
?!
HOW-EVER...
IF THEY FAIL...
...I'LL KILL ONE FEMALE!!
OF COURSE, THEY CAN ALSO CHOOSE NOT TO COME BACK FOR THEM...
...BUT IF THEY DO THAT, I'LL KILL ONE FEMALE EVERY TWO HOURS.
COME BACK AS OFTEN AS YOU LIKE.
BUT EACH TIME YOU FAIL, SOMEONE WILL DIE.

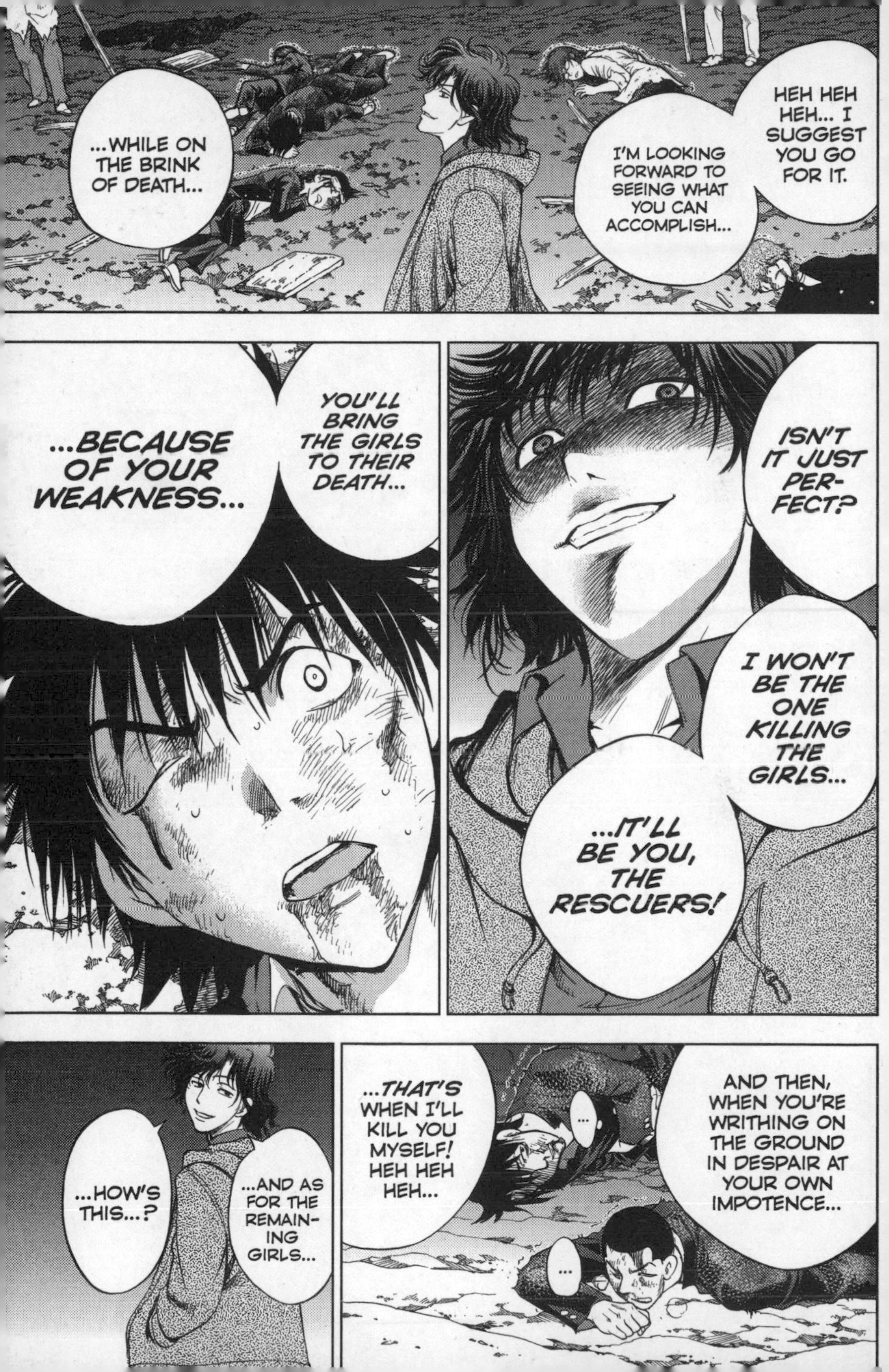
HEH HEH HEH... I SUGGEST YOU GO FOR IT.
I'M LOOKING FORWARD TO SEEING WHAT YOU CAN ACCOMPLISH...
...WHILE ON THE BRINK OF DEATH...
ISN'T IT JUST PER-FECT?
I WON'T BE THE ONE KILLING THE GIRLS...
...IT'LL BE YOU, THE RESCUERS!
YOU'LL BRING THE GIRLS TO THEIR DEATH...
...BECAUSE OF YOUR WEAKNESS...
AND THEN, WHEN YOU'RE WRITHING ON THE GROUND IN DESPAIR AT YOUR OWN IMPOTENCE...
...THAT'S WHEN I'LL KILL YOU MYSELF! HEH HEH HEH...
...
...
...AND AS FOR THE REMAINING GIRLS...
...HOW'S THIS...?

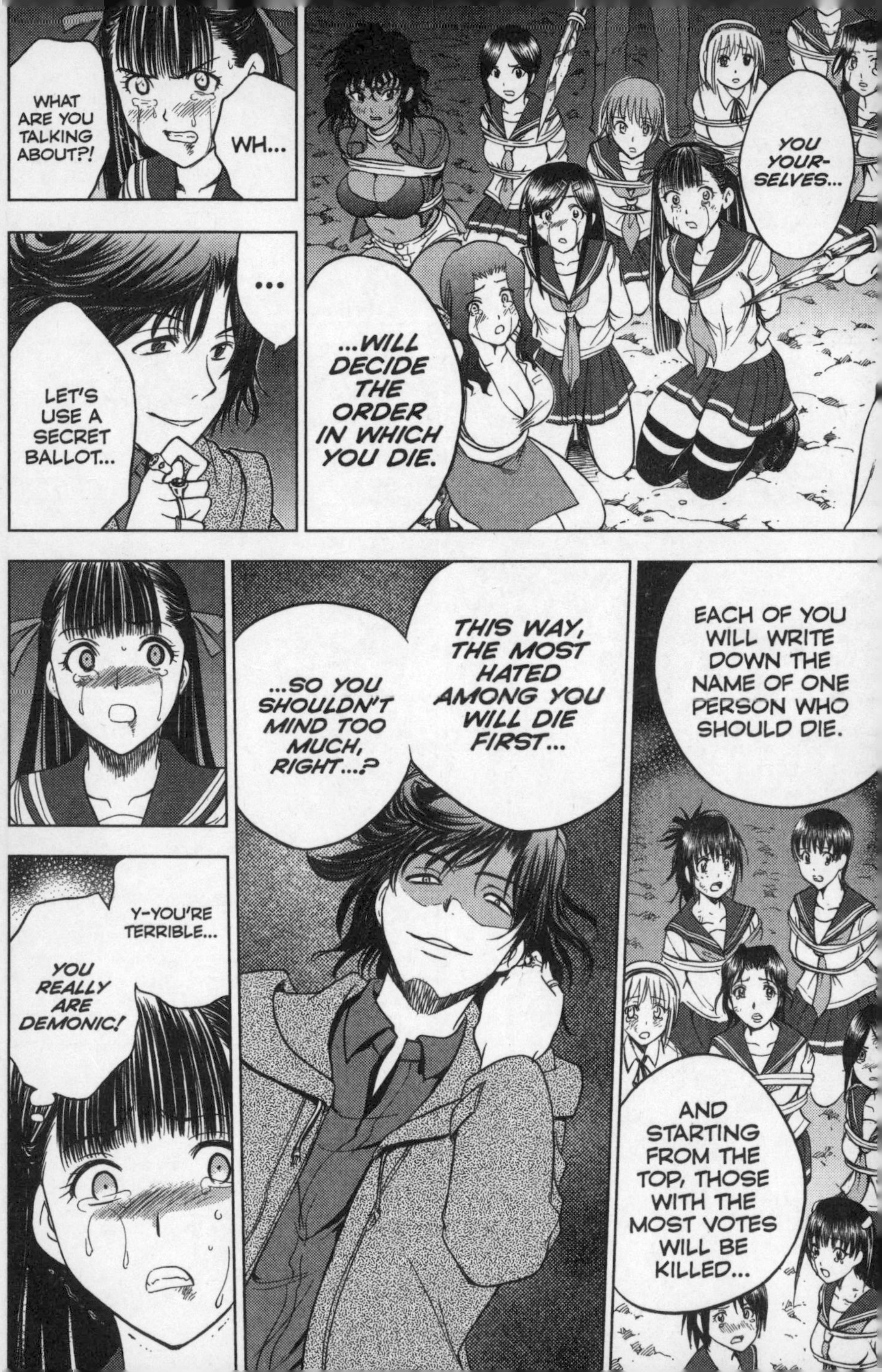
YOU YOURSELVES...
...WILL DECIDE THE ORDER IN WHICH YOU DIE.
WH...
WHAT ARE YOU TALKING ABOUT?!
...
LET'S USE A SECRET BALLOT...
EACH OF YOU WILL WRITE DOWN THE NAME OF ONE PERSON WHO SHOULD DIE.
AND STARTING FROM THE TOP, THOSE WITH THE MOST VOTES WILL BE KILLED...
THIS WAY, THE MOST HATED AMONG YOU WILL DIE FIRST...
...SO YOU SHOULDN'T MIND TOO MUCH, RIGHT...?
Y-YOU'RE TERRIBLE...
YOU REALLY ARE DEMONIC!

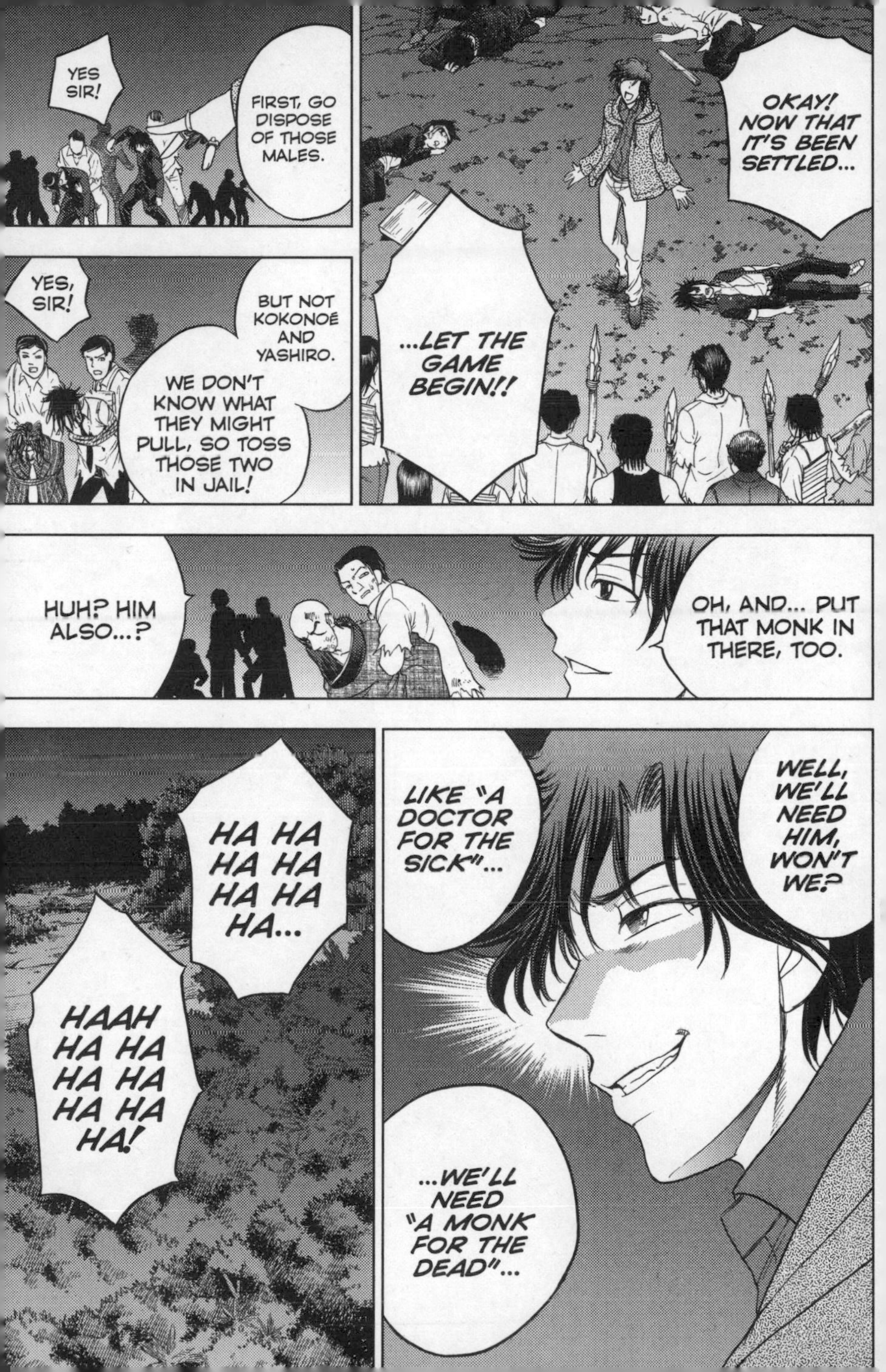
OKAY! NOW THAT IT'S BEEN SETTLED...
...LET THE GAME BEGIN!!
FIRST, GO DISPOSE OF THOSE MALES.
YES SIR!
BUT NOT KOKONOÉ AND YASHIRO.
WE DON'T KNOW WHAT THEY MIGHT PULL, SO TOSS THOSE TWO IN JAIL!
YES, SIR!
OH, AND... PUT THAT MONK IN THERE, TOO.
HUH? HIM ALSO...?
WELL, WE'LL NEED HIM, WON'T WE?
LIKE "A DOCTOR FOR THE SICK"...
...WE'LL NEED "A MONK FOR THE DEAD"...
HA HA HA HA HA HA HA...
HAAH HA HA HA HA HA HA HA!

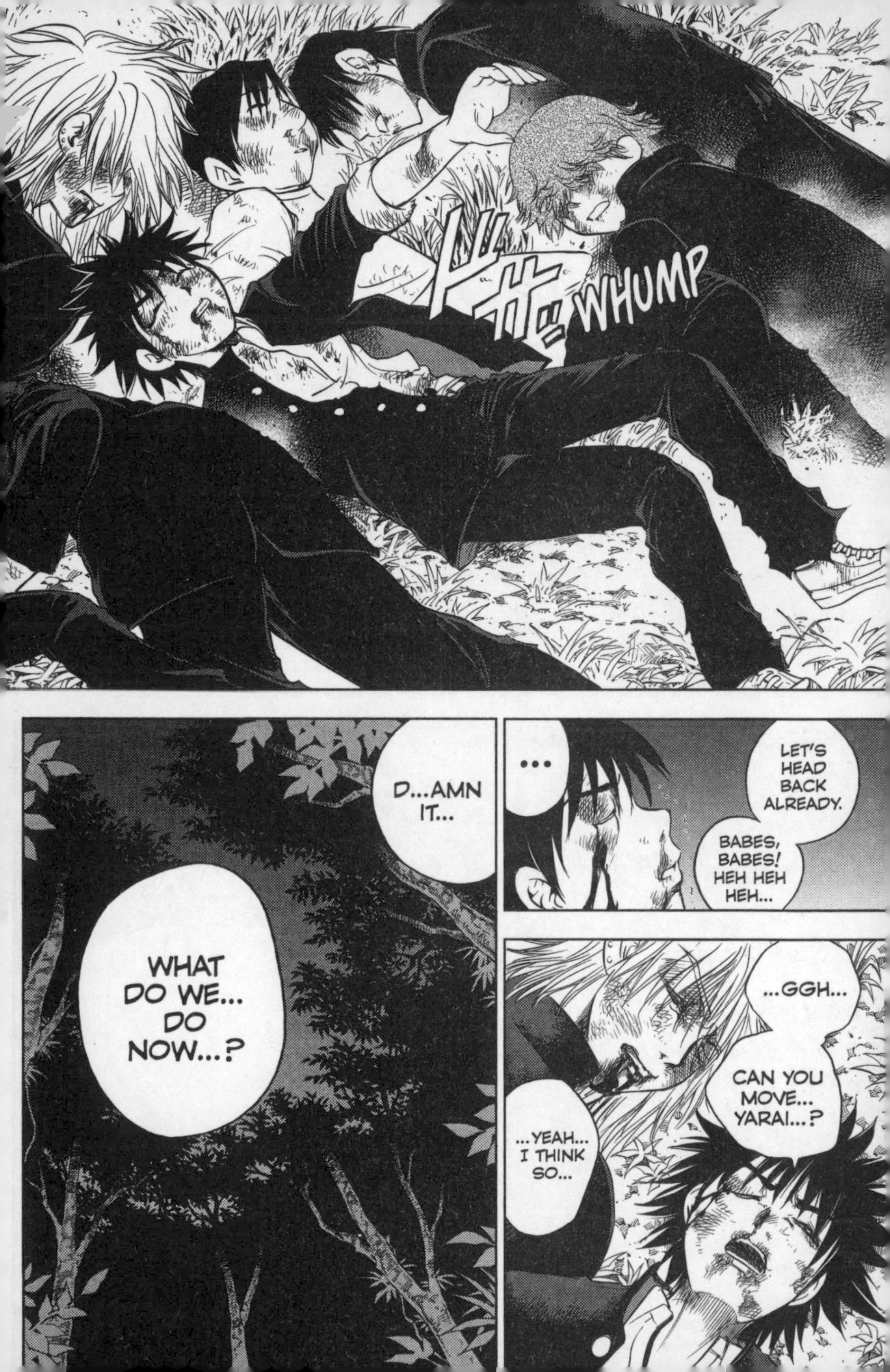
ドサッ
WHUMP
LET'S HEAD BACK ALREADY.
BABES, BABES! HEH HEH HEH...
...
...GGH...
CAN YOU MOVE... YARAI...?
...YEAH... I THINK SO...
D...AMN IT...
WHAT DO WE... DO NOW...?

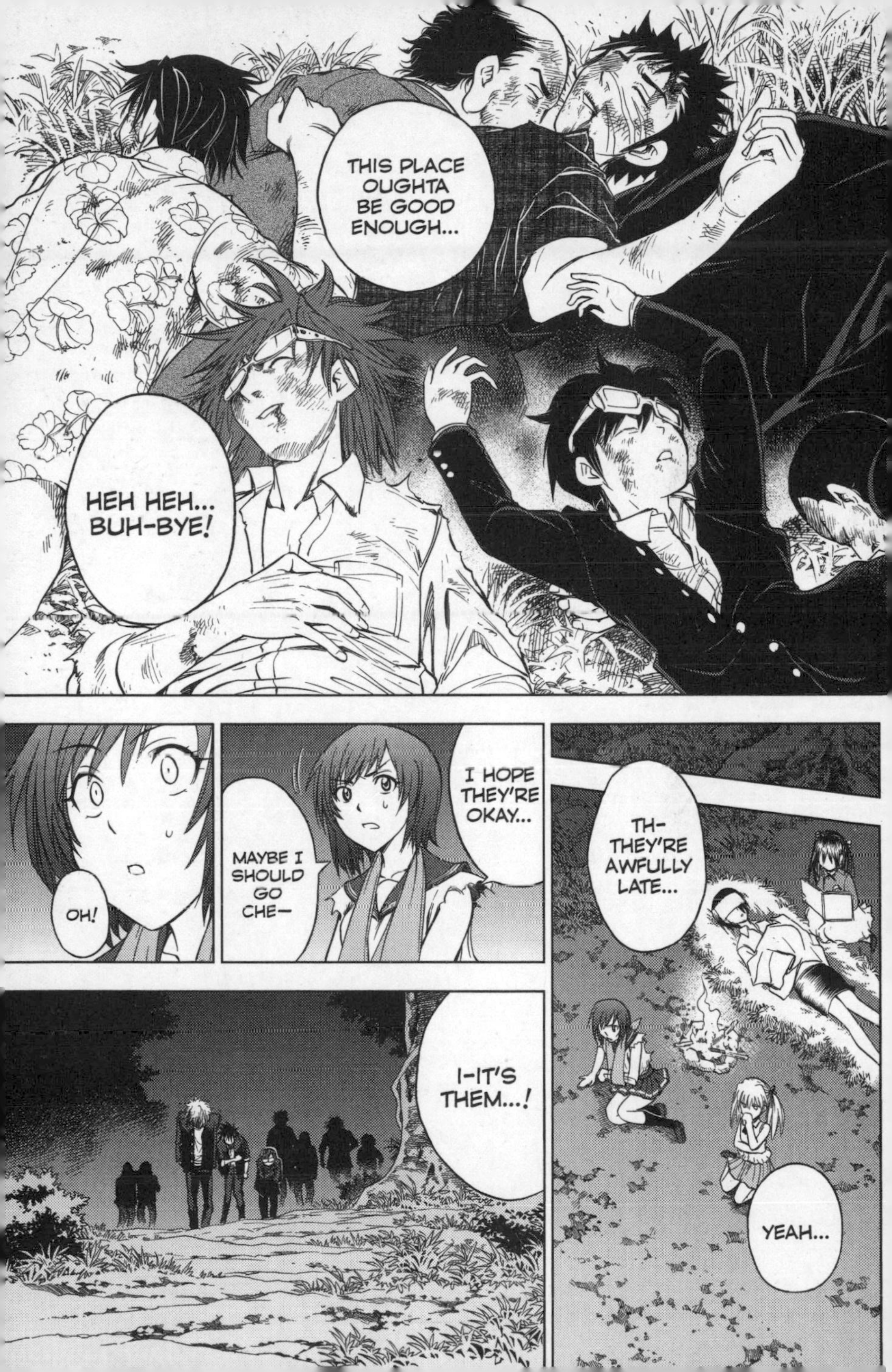

THIS PLACE OUGHTA BE GOOD ENOUGH...
HEH HEH... BUH-BYE!
TH- THEY'RE AWFULLY LATE...
YEAH...
I HOPE THEY'RE OKAY...
MAYBE I SHOULD GO CHE—
OH!
I-IT'S THEM...!

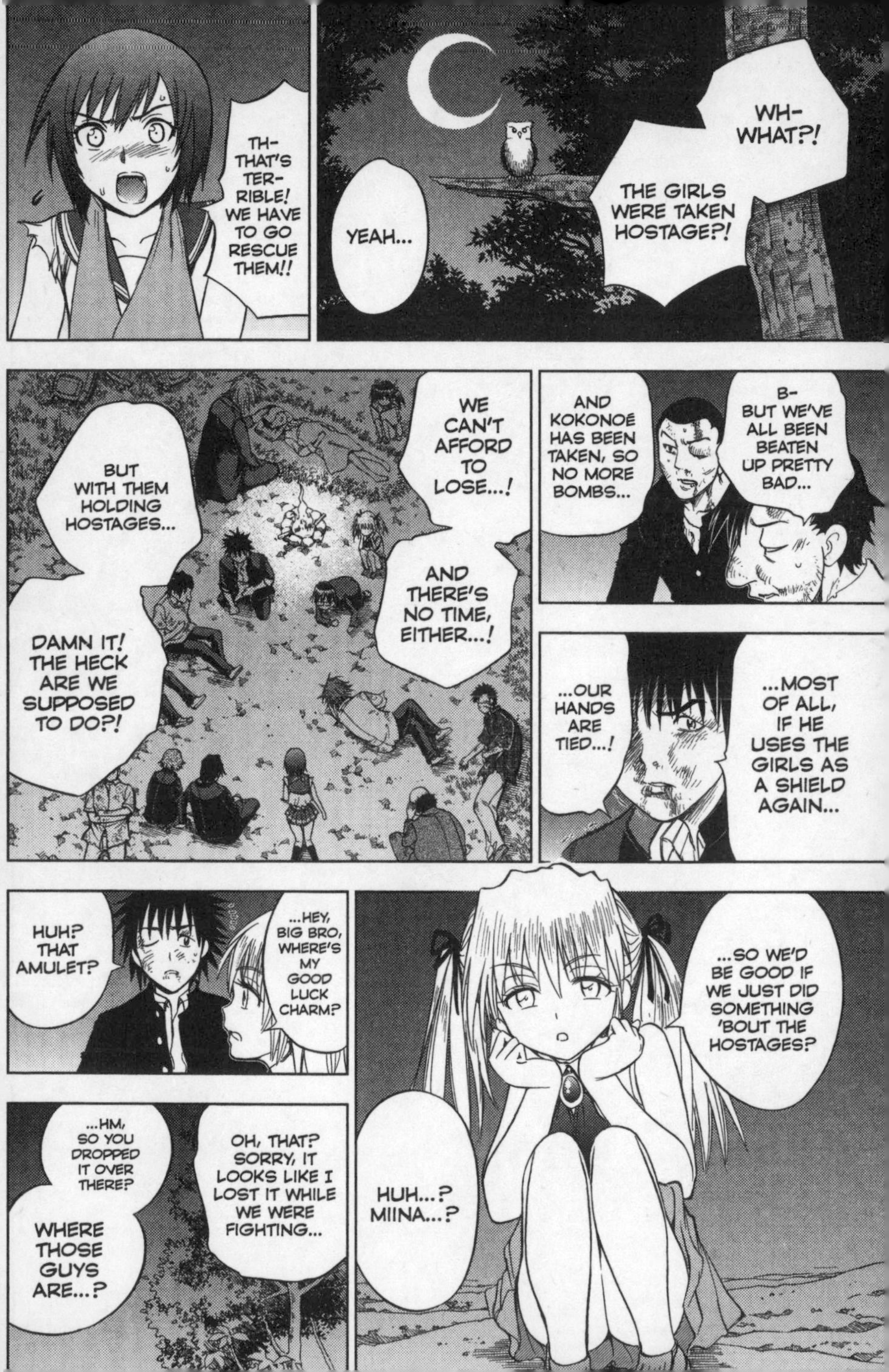
WH- WHAT?!
THE GIRLS WERE TAKEN HOSTAGE?!
YEAH...
TH- THAT'S TER- RIBLE! WE HAVE TO GO RESCUE THEM!!
B- BUT WE'VE ALL BEEN BEATEN UP PRETTY BAD...
AND KOKONOE HAS BEEN TAKEN, SO NO MORE BOMBS...
...MOST OF ALL, IF HE USES THE GIRLS AS A SHIELD AGAIN...
...OUR HANDS ARE TIED...!
WE CAN'T AFFORD TO LOSE...!
BUT WITH THEM HOLDING HOSTAGES...
AND THERE'S NO TIME, EITHER...!
DAMN IT! THE HECK ARE WE SUPPOSED TO DO?!
...SO WE'D BE GOOD IF WE JUST DID SOMETHING 'BOUT THE HOSTAGES?
HUH...? MIINA...?
...HEY, BIG BRO, WHERE'S MY GOOD LUCK CHARM?
HUH? THAT AMULET?
OH, THAT? SORRY, IT LOOKS LIKE I LOST IT WHILE WE WERE FIGHTING...
...HM, SO YOU DROPPED IT OVER THERE?
WHERE THOSE GUYS ARE...?

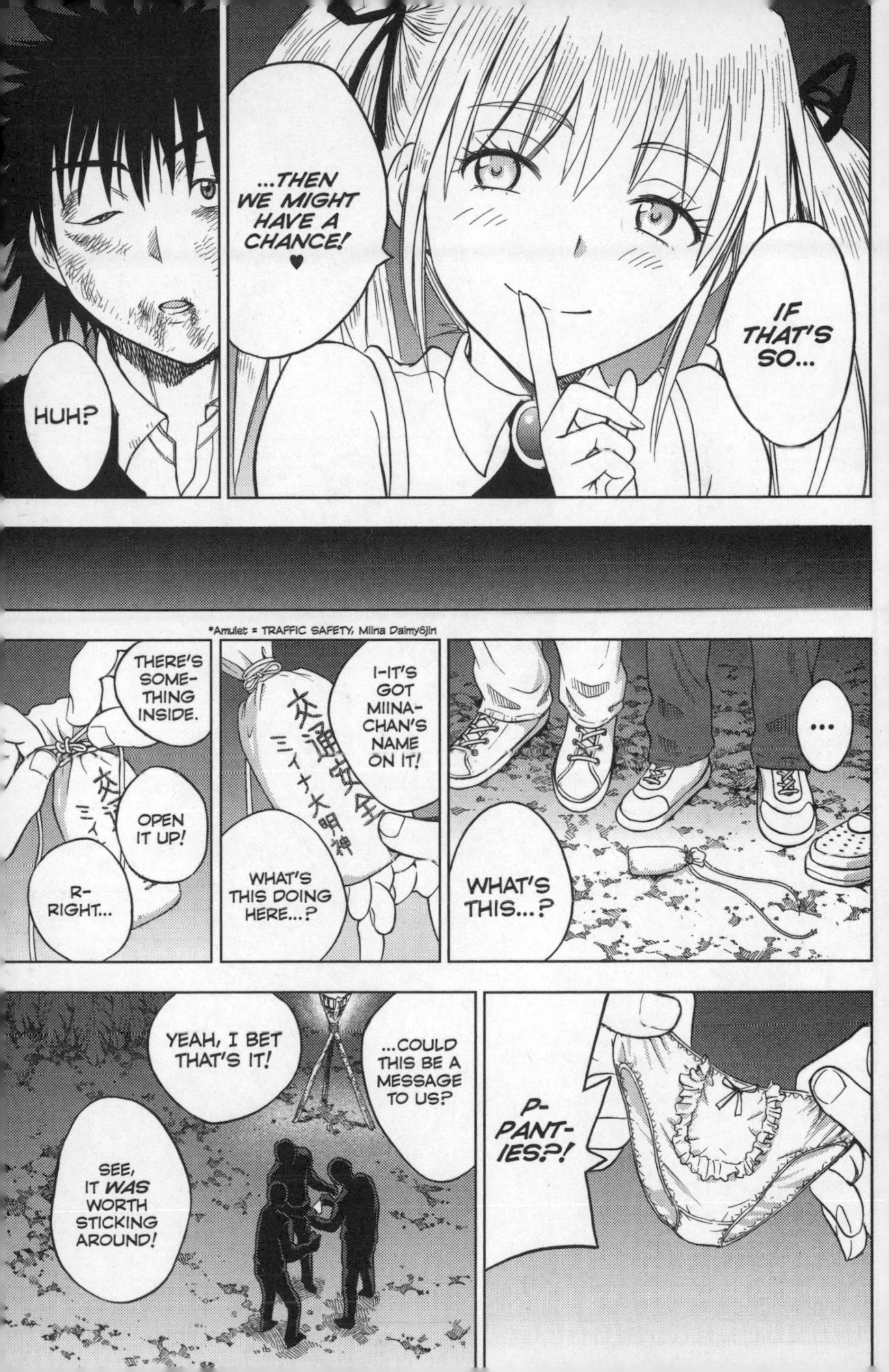
IF THAT'S SO...
...THEN WE MIGHT HAVE A CHANCE! ♥
HUH?
*Amulet = TRAFFIC SAFETY, Miina Daimyōjin
...
WHAT'S THIS...?
I-IT'S GOT MIINA-CHAN'S NAME ON IT!
交通安全 ミイナ大明神
WHAT'S THIS DOING HERE...?
THERE'S SOME-THING INSIDE.
OPEN IT UP!
R-RIGHT...
P-PANT-IES?!
...COULD THIS BE A MESSAGE TO US?
YEAH, I BET THAT'S IT!
SEE, IT *WAS* WORTH STICKING AROUND!

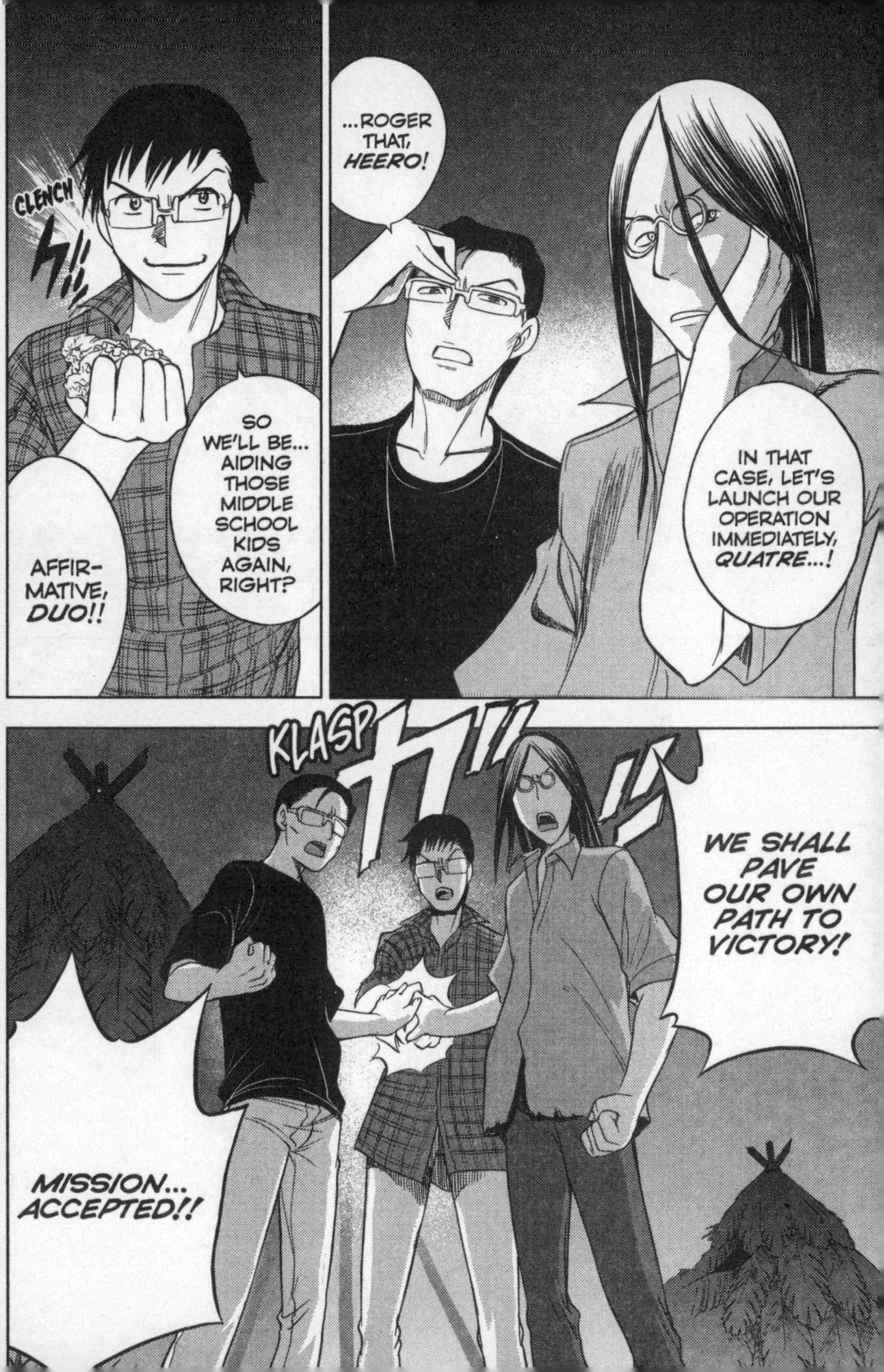
...ROGER THAT, HEERO!
IN THAT CASE, LET'S LAUNCH OUR OPERATION IMMEDIATELY, QUATRE...!
CLENCH
SO WE'LL BE... AIDING THOSE MIDDLE SCHOOL KIDS AGAIN, RIGHT?
AFFIRMATIVE, DUO!!
KLASP
WE SHALL PAVE OUR OWN PATH TO VICTORY!
MISSION... ACCEPTED!!

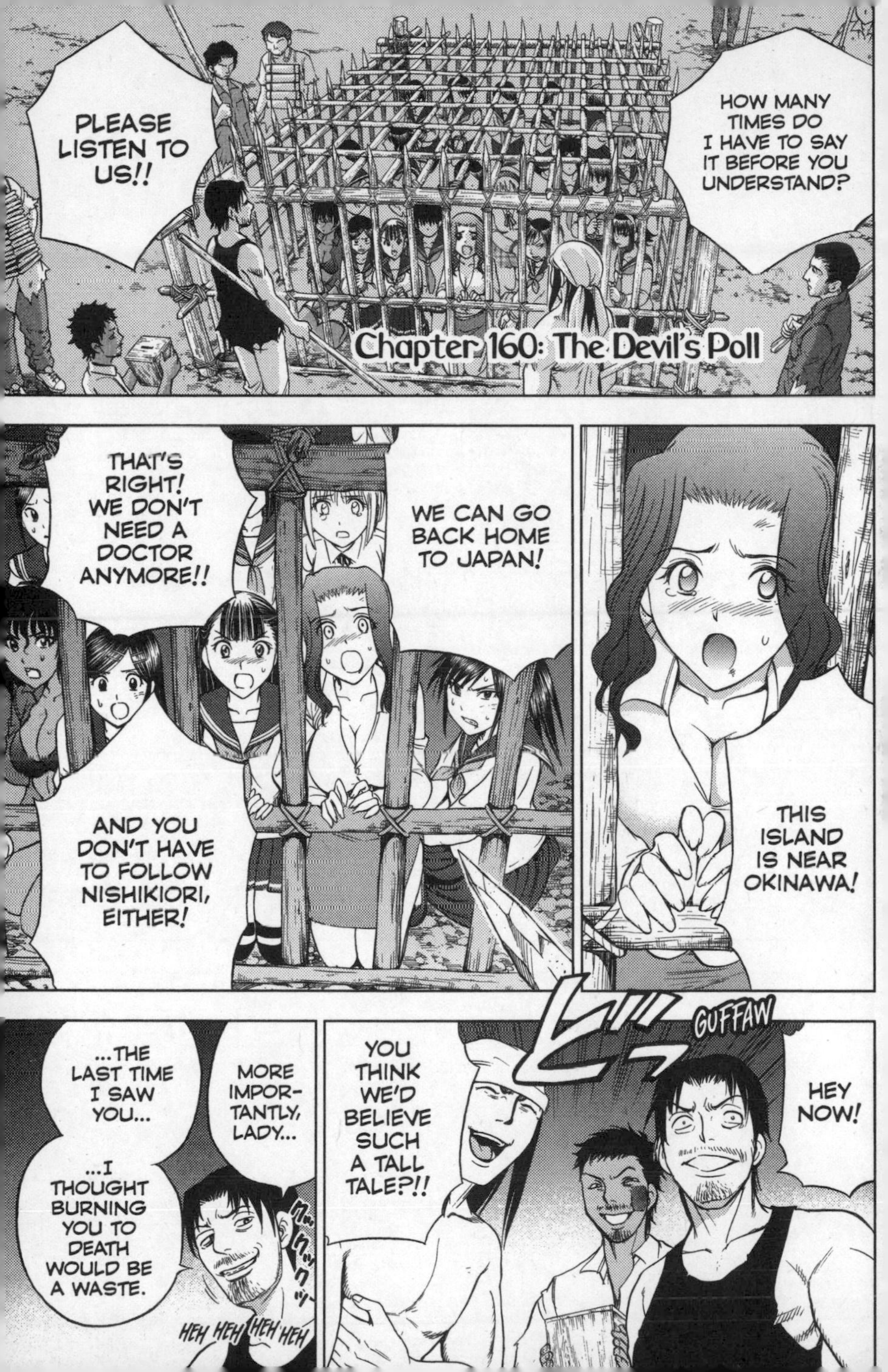
HOW MANY TIMES DO I HAVE TO SAY IT BEFORE YOU UNDERSTAND?
PLEASE LISTEN TO US!!
Chapter 160: The Devil's Poll
THIS ISLAND IS NEAR OKINAWA!
WE CAN GO BACK HOME TO JAPAN!
THAT'S RIGHT! WE DON'T NEED A DOCTOR ANYMORE!!
AND YOU DON'T HAVE TO FOLLOW NISHIKIORI, EITHER!
GUFFAW
HEY NOW!
YOU THINK WE'D BELIEVE SUCH A TALL TALE?!!
MORE IMPORTANTLY, LADY...
...THE LAST TIME I SAW YOU...
...I THOUGHT BURNING YOU TO DEATH WOULD BE A WASTE.
HEH HEH HEH HEH

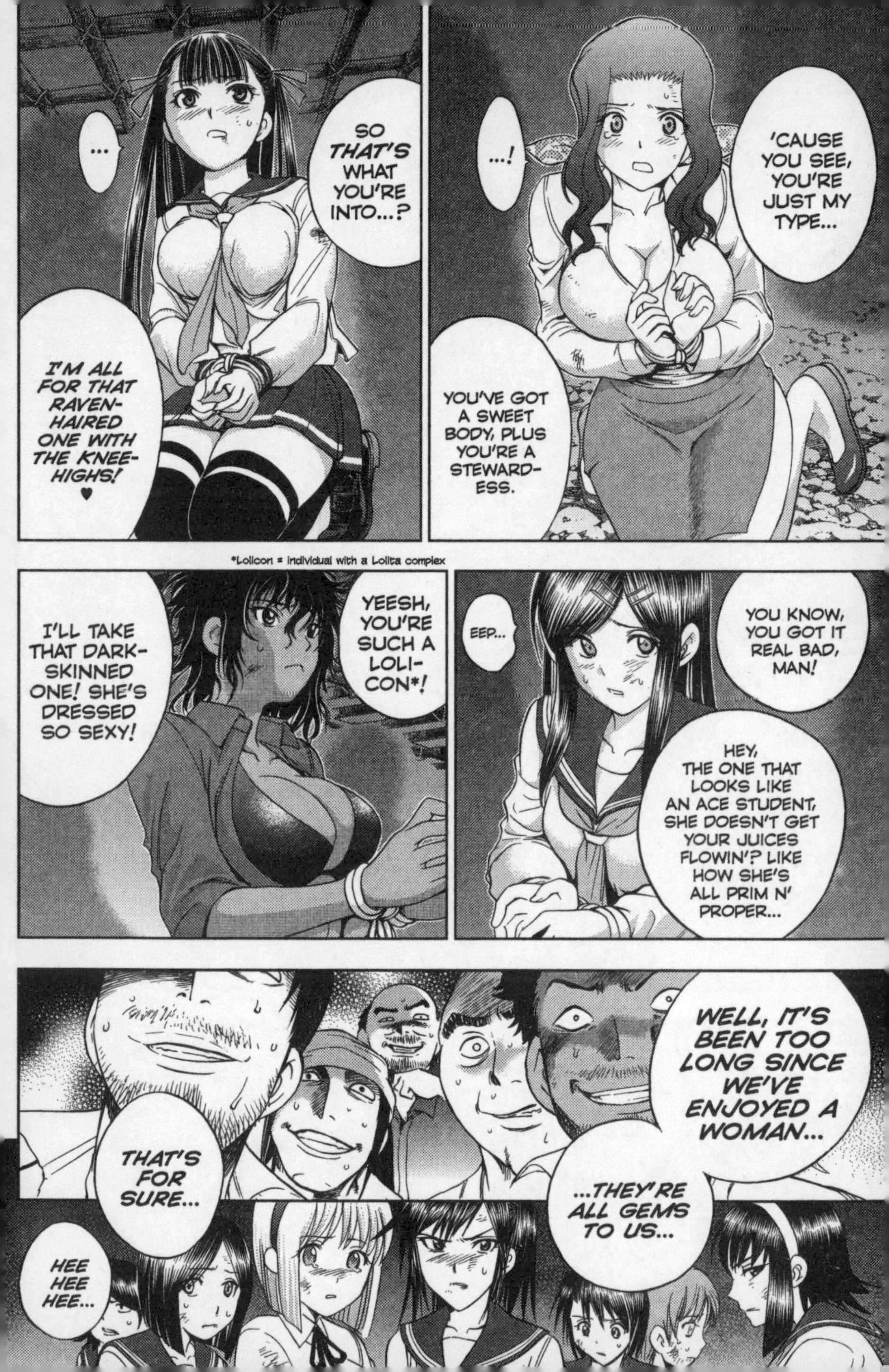
'CAUSE YOU SEE, YOU'RE JUST MY TYPE...
...!
YOU'VE GOT A SWEET BODY, PLUS YOU'RE A STEWARD-ESS.
SO *THAT'S* WHAT YOU'RE INTO...?
...
I'M ALL FOR THAT RAVEN-HAIRED ONE WITH THE KNEE-HIGHS! ♥
YOU KNOW, YOU GOT IT REAL BAD, MAN!
EEP...
HEY, THE ONE THAT LOOKS LIKE AN ACE STUDENT, SHE DOESN'T GET YOUR JUICES FLOWIN'? LIKE HOW SHE'S ALL PRIM N' PROPER...
YEESH, YOU'RE SUCH A LOLI-CON*!
I'LL TAKE THAT DARK-SKINNED ONE! SHE'S DRESSED SO SEXY!
WELL, IT'S BEEN TOO LONG SINCE WE'VE ENJOYED A WOMAN...
THAT'S FOR SURE...
...THEY'RE ALL GEMS TO US...
HEE HEE HEE...

*Lolicon = individual with a Lolita complex

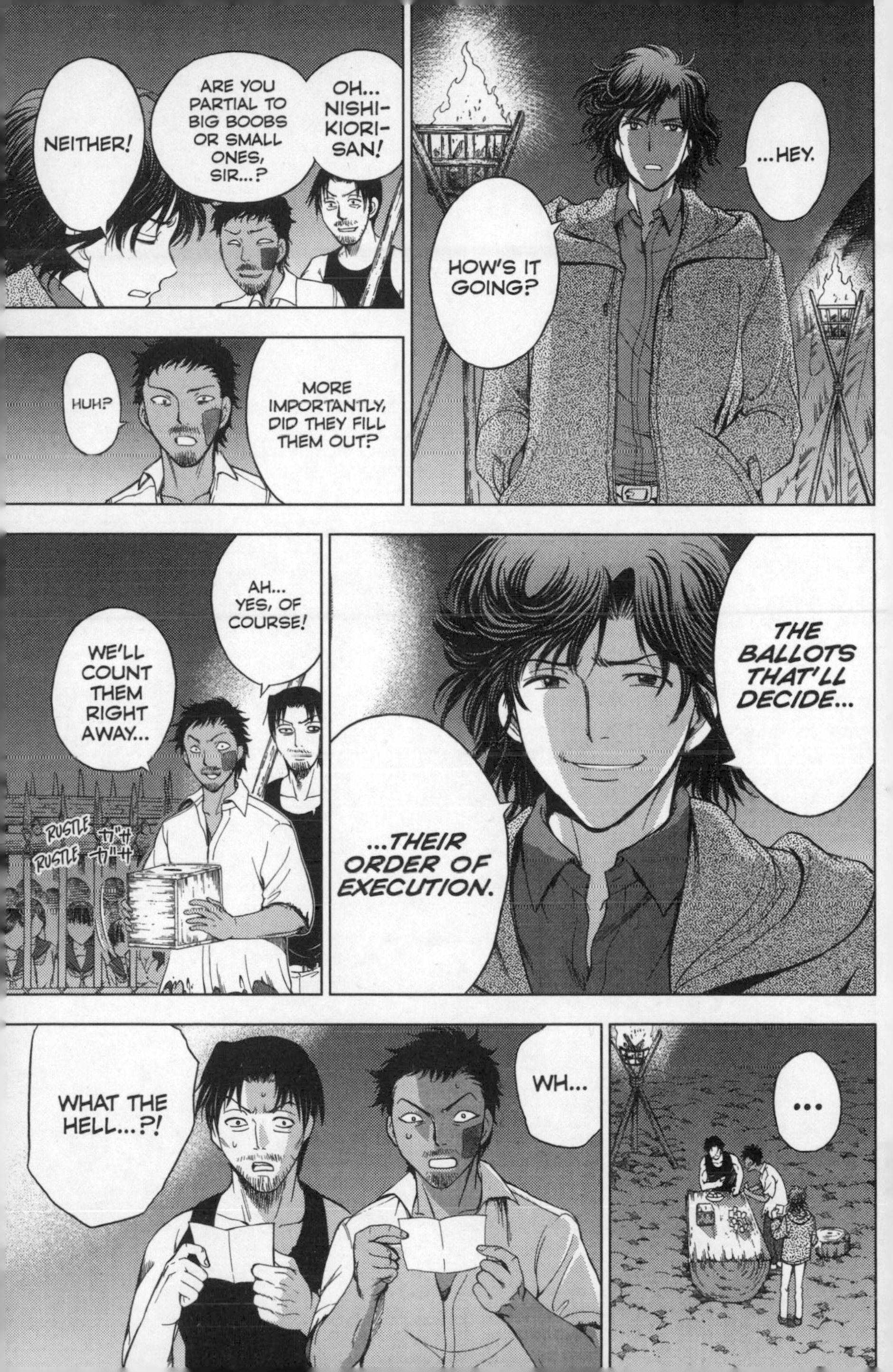
...HEY.
HOW'S IT GOING?
OH... NISHIKIORI-SAN!
ARE YOU PARTIAL TO BIG BOOBS OR SMALL ONES, SIR...?
NEITHER!
MORE IMPORTANTLY, DID THEY FILL THEM OUT?
HUH?
THE BALLOTS THAT'LL DECIDE...
...THEIR ORDER OF EXECUTION.
AH... YES, OF COURSE!
WE'LL COUNT THEM RIGHT AWAY...
RUSTLE ガサ
RUSTLE ガサ
...
WH...
WHAT THE HELL...?!

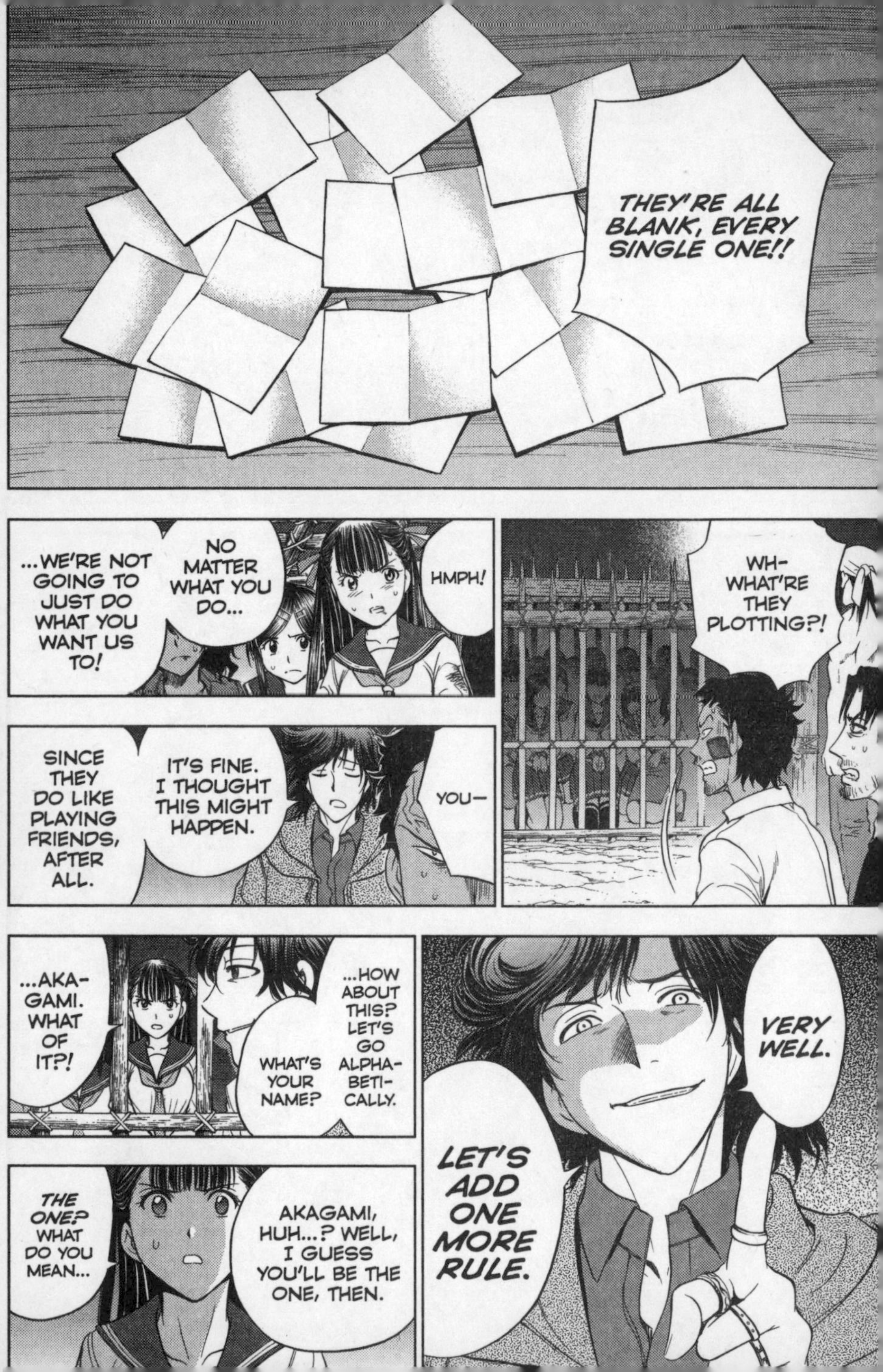
THEY'RE ALL BLANK, EVERY SINGLE ONE!!
WH-WHAT'RE THEY PLOTTING?!
HMPH!
NO MATTER WHAT YOU DO...
...WE'RE NOT GOING TO JUST DO WHAT YOU WANT US TO!
YOU—
IT'S FINE. I THOUGHT THIS MIGHT HAPPEN.
SINCE THEY DO LIKE PLAYING FRIENDS, AFTER ALL.
VERY WELL.
LET'S ADD ONE MORE RULE.
...HOW ABOUT THIS? LET'S GO ALPHABETICALLY.
WHAT'S YOUR NAME?
...AKAGAMI. WHAT OF IT?!
AKAGAMI, HUH...? WELL, I GUESS YOU'LL BE THE ONE, THEN.
THE ONE? WHAT DO YOU MEAN...

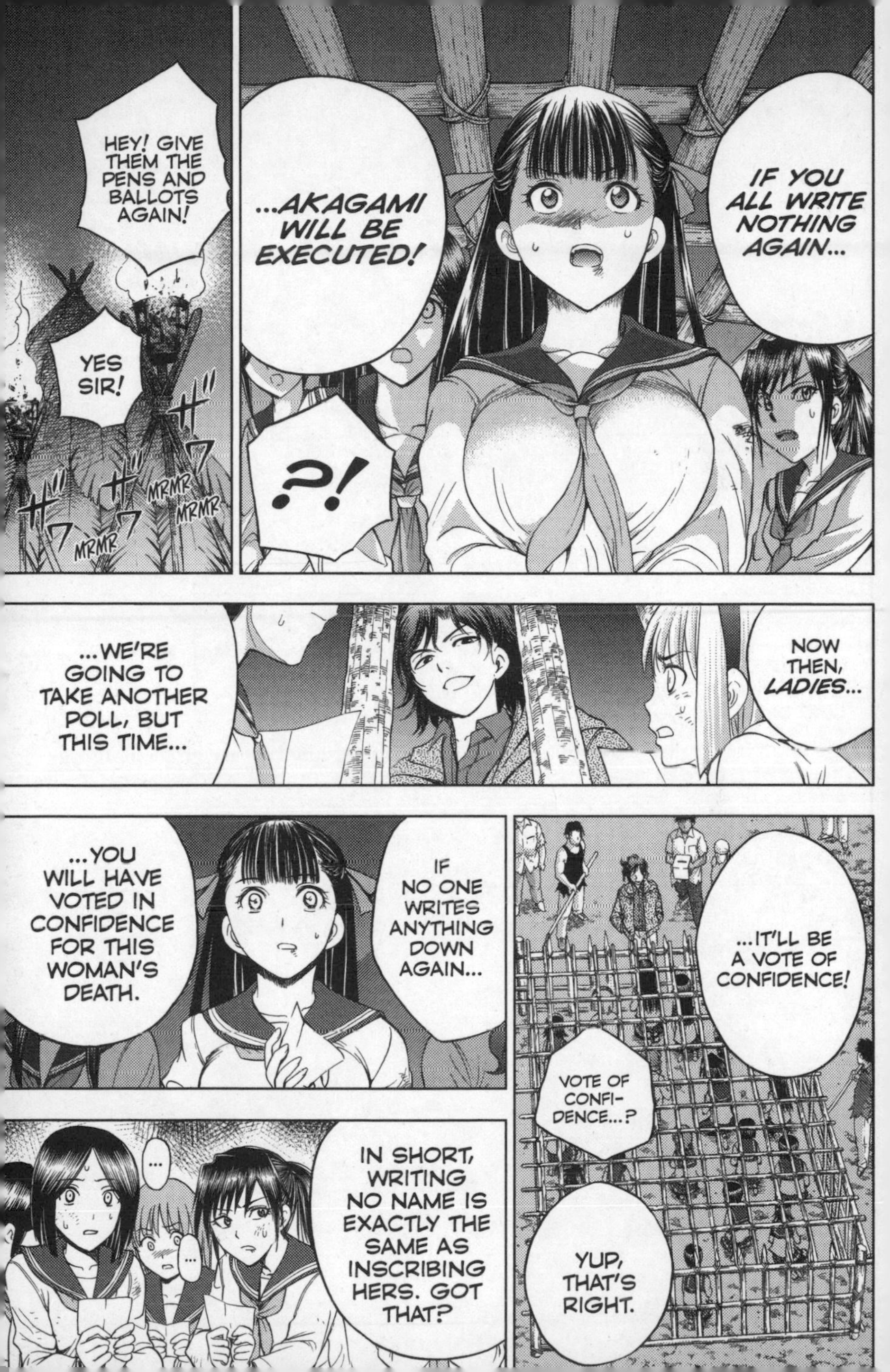
IF YOU ALL WRITE NOTHING AGAIN...
...AKAGAMI WILL BE EXECUTED!
?!
HEY! GIVE THEM THE PENS AND BALLOTS AGAIN!
YES SIR!
MRMR MRMR
MRMR
NOW THEN, LADIES...
...WE'RE GOING TO TAKE ANOTHER POLL, BUT THIS TIME...
...IT'LL BE A VOTE OF CONFIDENCE!
VOTE OF CONFI- DENCE...?
YUP, THAT'S RIGHT.
IF NO ONE WRITES ANYTHING DOWN AGAIN...
...YOU WILL HAVE VOTED IN CONFIDENCE FOR THIS WOMAN'S DEATH.
IN SHORT, WRITING NO NAME IS EXACTLY THE SAME AS INSCRIBING HERS. GOT THAT?
...
...

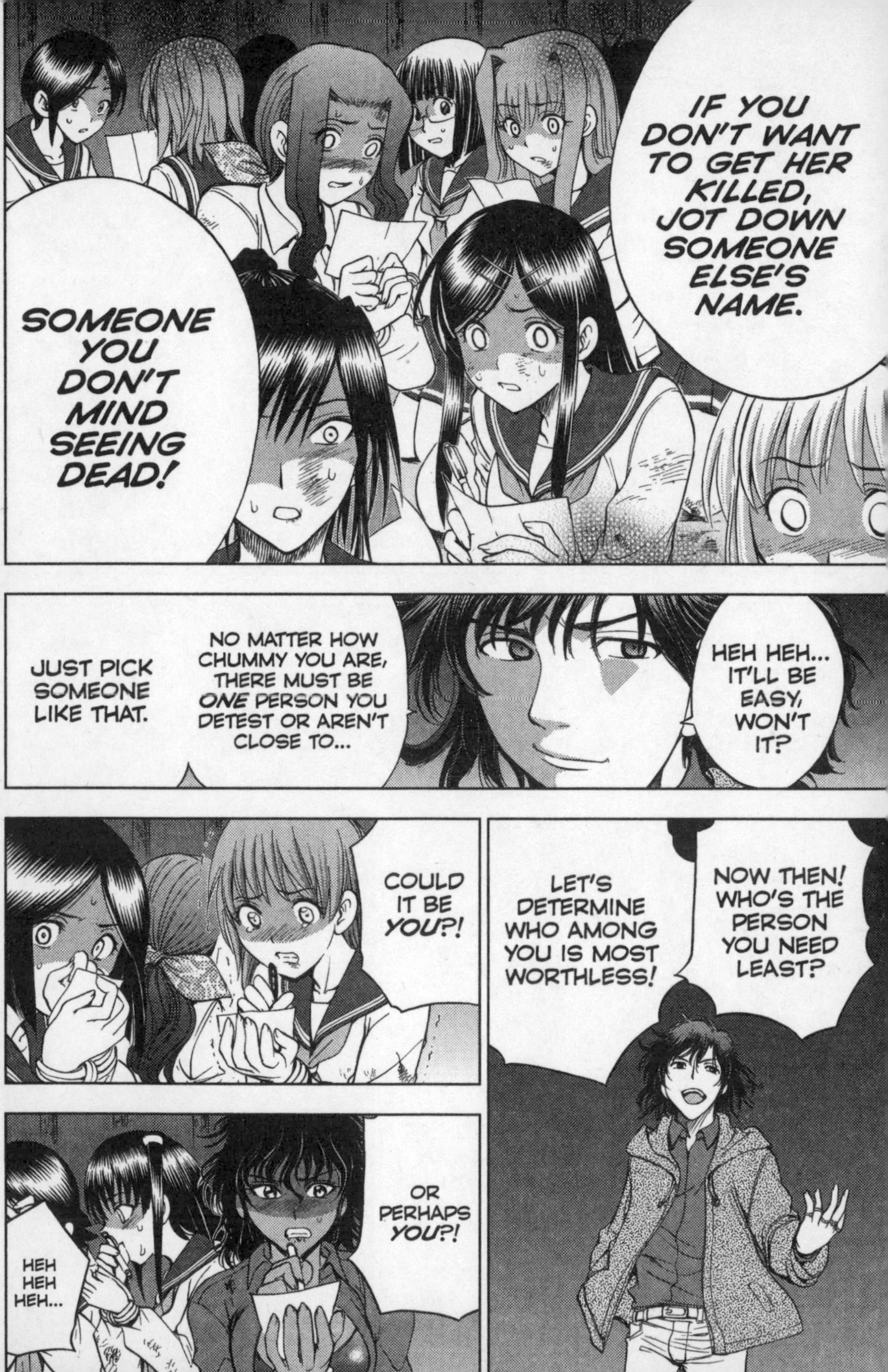
IF YOU DON'T WANT TO GET HER KILLED, JOT DOWN SOMEONE ELSE'S NAME.
SOMEONE YOU DON'T MIND SEEING DEAD!
HEH HEH... IT'LL BE EASY, WON'T IT?
NO MATTER HOW CHUMMY YOU ARE, THERE MUST BE *ONE* PERSON YOU DETEST OR AREN'T CLOSE TO...
JUST PICK SOMEONE LIKE THAT.
NOW THEN! WHO'S THE PERSON YOU NEED LEAST?
LET'S DETERMINE WHO AMONG YOU IS MOST WORTHLESS!
COULD IT BE *YOU*?!
OR PERHAPS *YOU*?!
HEH HEH HEH...

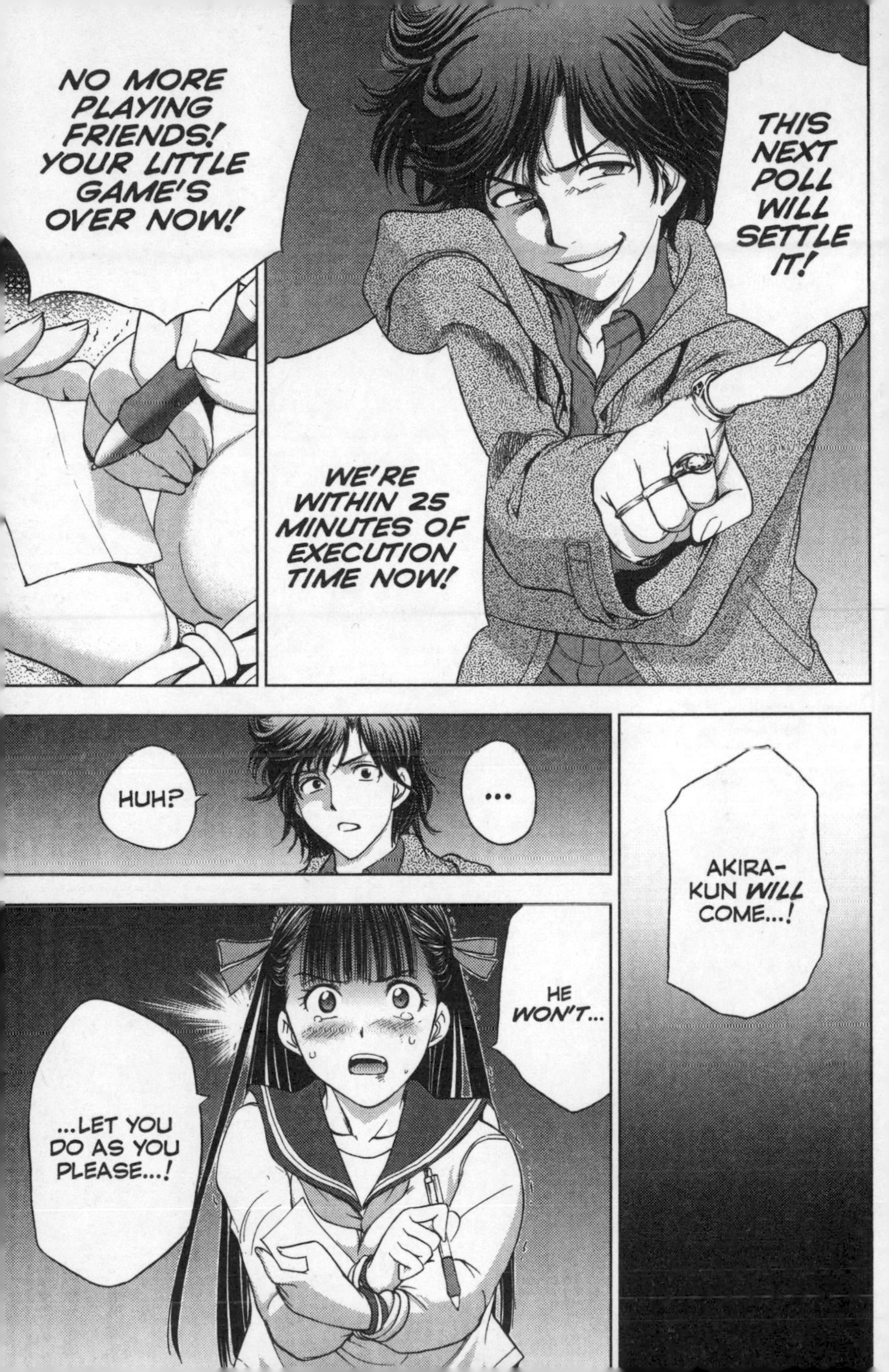
THIS NEXT POLL WILL SETTLE IT!
NO MORE PLAYING FRIENDS! YOUR LITTLE GAME'S OVER NOW!
WE'RE WITHIN 25 MINUTES OF EXECUTION TIME NOW!
AKIRA-KUN *WILL* COME...!
...
HUH?
HE *WON'T*...
...LET YOU DO AS YOU PLEASE...!

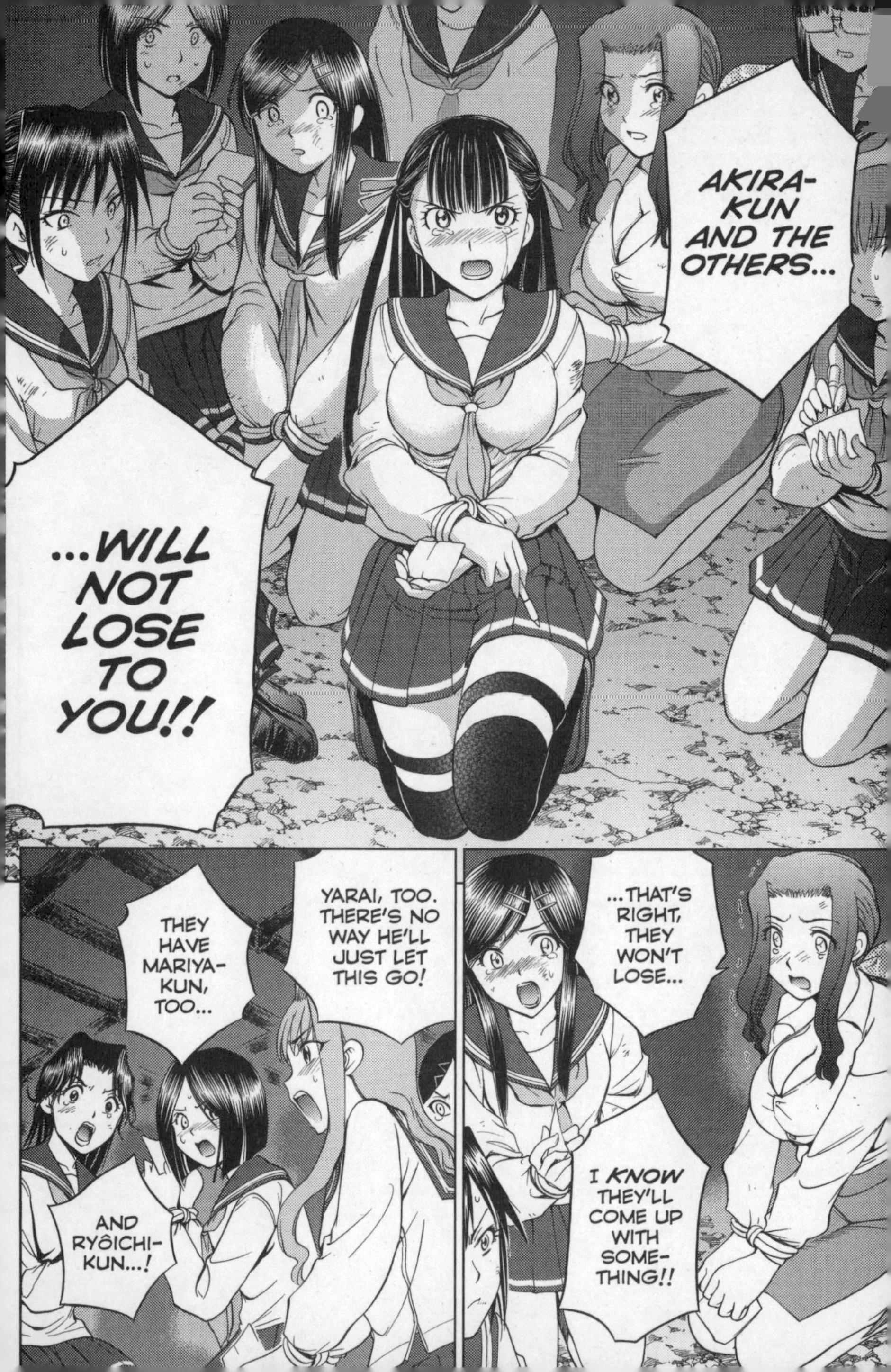
AKIRA-KUN AND THE OTHERS...
...WILL NOT LOSE TO YOU!!
...THAT'S RIGHT, THEY WON'T LOSE...
I *KNOW* THEY'LL COME UP WITH SOME-THING!!
YARAI, TOO. THERE'S NO WAY HE'LL JUST LET THIS GO!
THEY HAVE MARIYA-KUN, TOO...
AND RYÔICHI-KUN...!

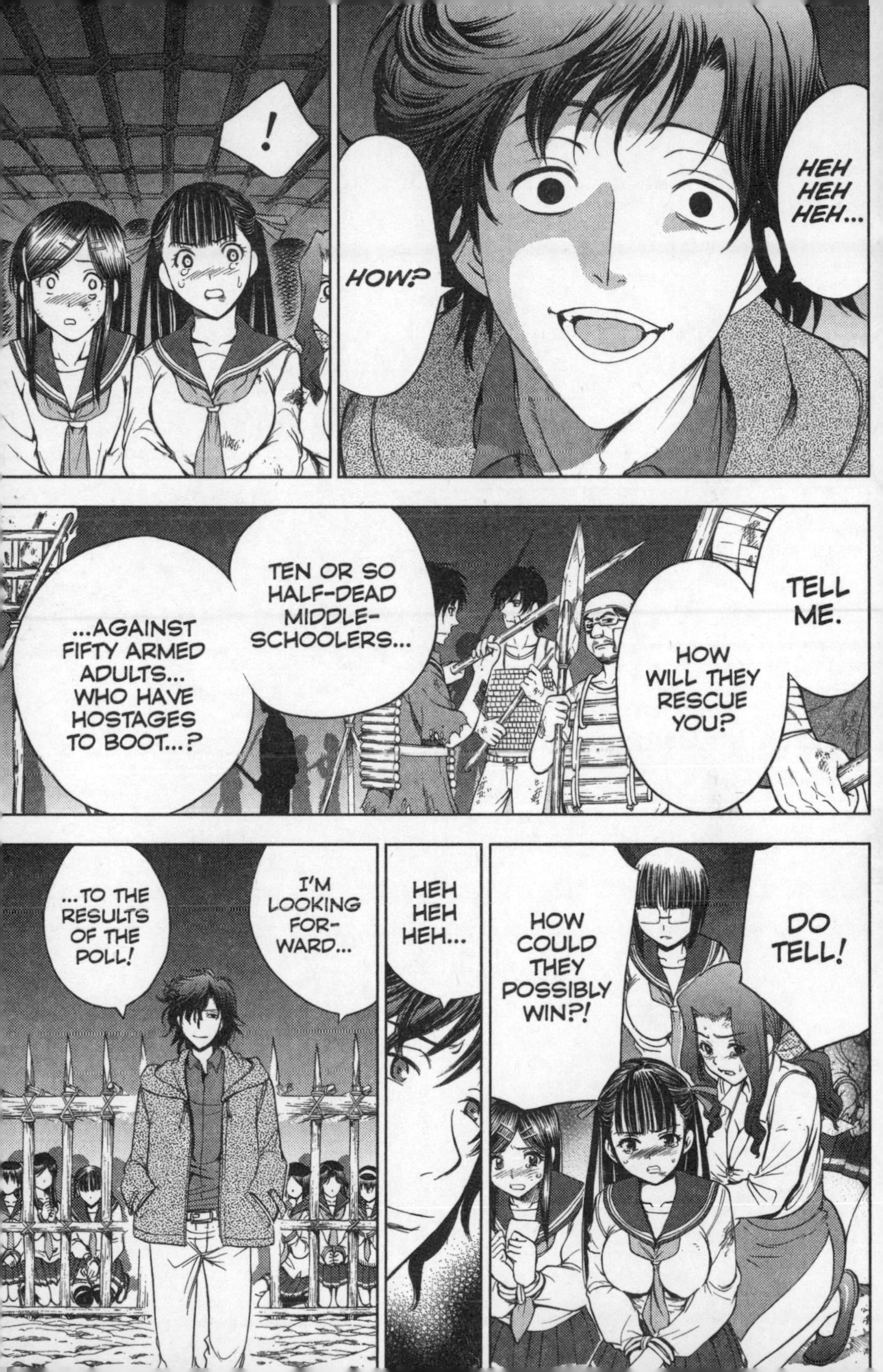
HEH HEH HEH...
HOW?
!
TELL ME.
HOW WILL THEY RESCUE YOU?
TEN OR SO HALF-DEAD MIDDLE-SCHOOLERS...
...AGAINST FIFTY ARMED ADULTS... WHO HAVE HOSTAGES TO BOOT...?
DO TELL!
HOW COULD THEY POSSIBLY WIN?!
HEH HEH HEH...
I'M LOOKING FOR-WARD...
...TO THE RESULTS OF THE POLL!

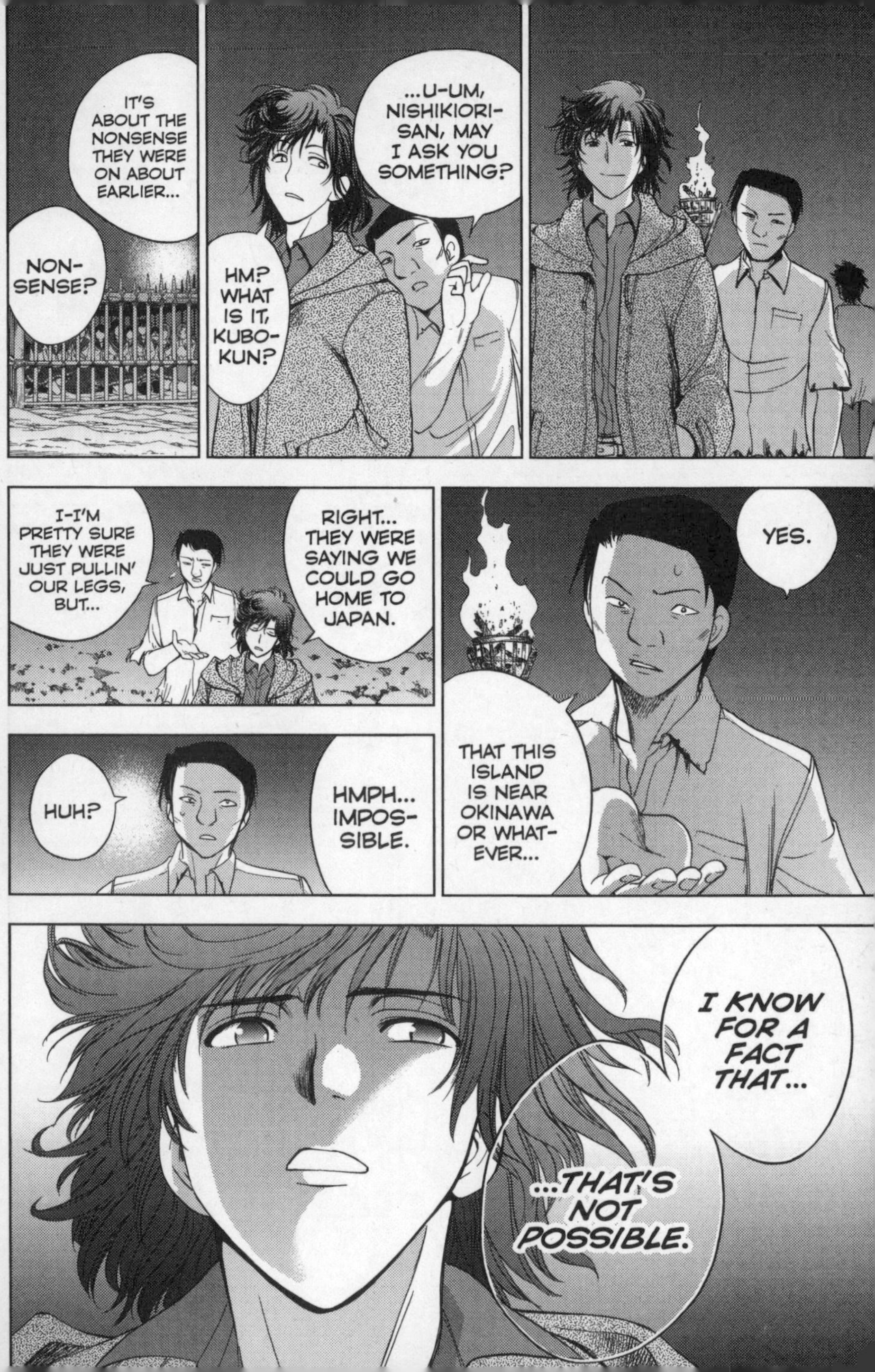
...U-UM, NISHIKIORI-SAN, MAY I ASK YOU SOMETHING?
HM? WHAT IS IT, KUBO-KUN?
IT'S ABOUT THE NONSENSE THEY WERE ON ABOUT EARLIER...
NON-SENSE?
YES.
THAT THIS ISLAND IS NEAR OKINAWA OR WHAT-EVER...
RIGHT... THEY WERE SAYING WE COULD GO HOME TO JAPAN.
I-I'M PRETTY SURE THEY WERE JUST PULLIN' OUR LEGS, BUT...
HMPH... IMPOS-SIBLE.
HUH?
I KNOW FOR A FACT THAT...
...THAT'S NOT POSSIBLE.

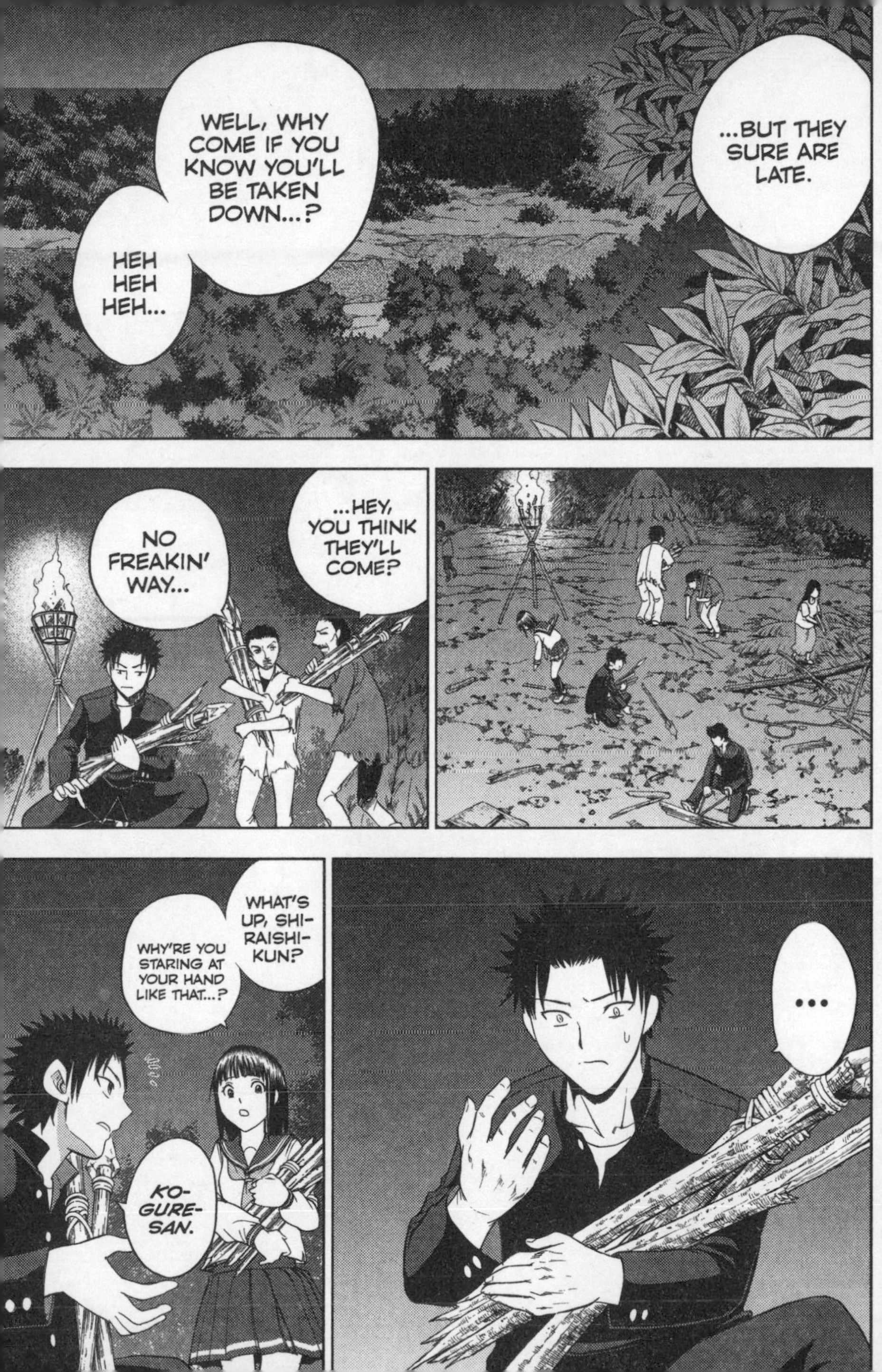
...BUT THEY SURE ARE LATE.
WELL, WHY COME IF YOU KNOW YOU'LL BE TAKEN DOWN...?
HEH HEH HEH...
...HEY, YOU THINK THEY'LL COME?
NO FREAKIN' WAY...
...
WHAT'S UP, SHI-RAISHI-KUN?
WHY'RE YOU STARING AT YOUR HAND LIKE THAT...?
KO-GURE-SAN.

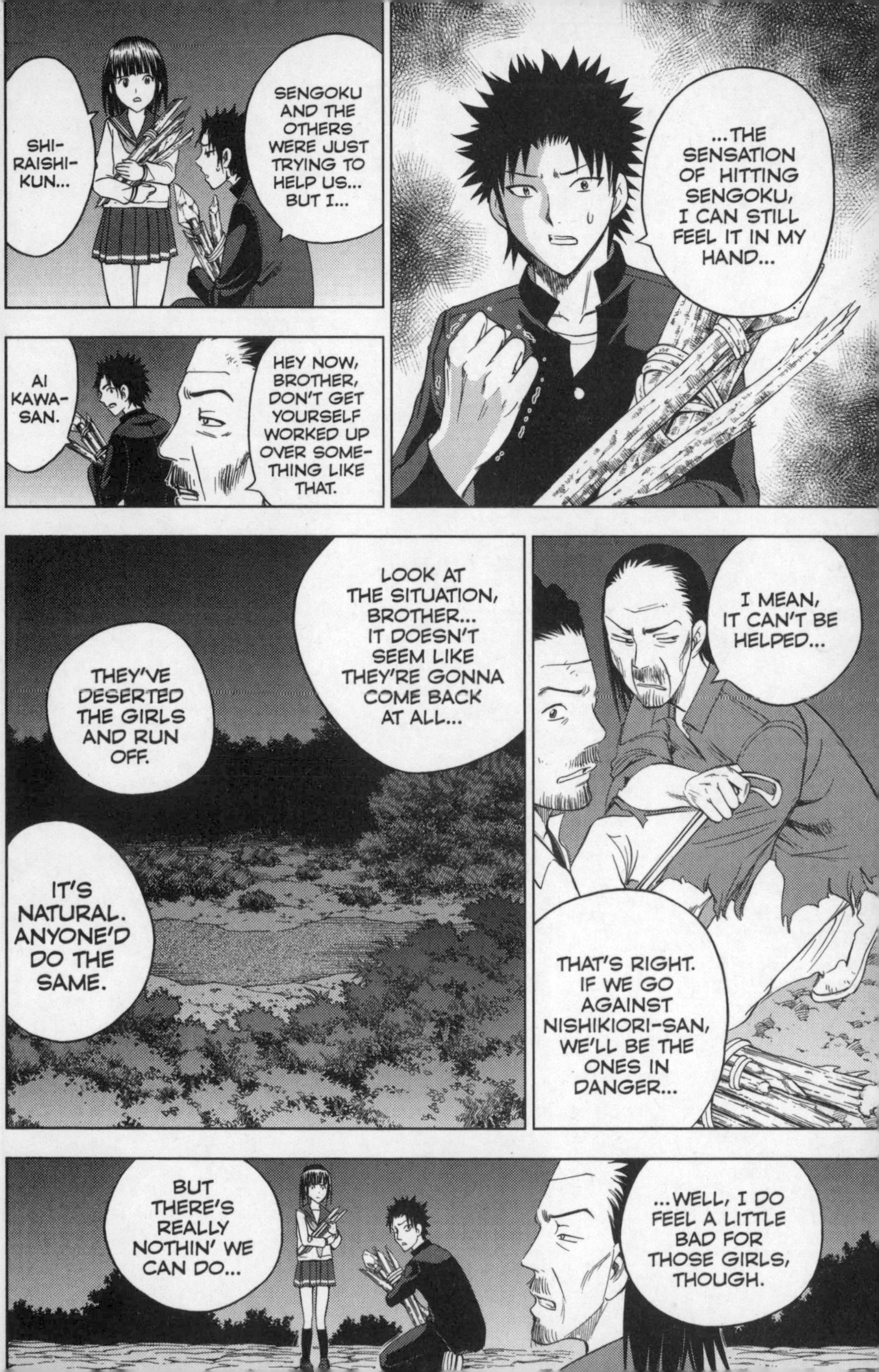
...THE SENSATION OF HITTING SENGOKU, I CAN STILL FEEL IT IN MY HAND...
SENGOKU AND THE OTHERS WERE JUST TRYING TO HELP US... BUT I...
SHI-RAISHI-KUN...
HEY NOW, BROTHER, DON'T GET YOURSELF WORKED UP OVER SOME-THING LIKE THAT.
AI KAWA-SAN.
I MEAN, IT CAN'T BE HELPED...
THAT'S RIGHT. IF WE GO AGAINST NISHIKIORI-SAN, WE'LL BE THE ONES IN DANGER...
LOOK AT THE SITUATION, BROTHER... IT DOESN'T SEEM LIKE THEY'RE GONNA COME BACK AT ALL...
THEY'VE DESERTED THE GIRLS AND RUN OFF.
IT'S NATURAL. ANYONE'D DO THE SAME.
...WELL, I DO FEEL A LITTLE BAD FOR THOSE GIRLS, THOUGH.
BUT THERE'S REALLY NOTHIN' WE CAN DO...

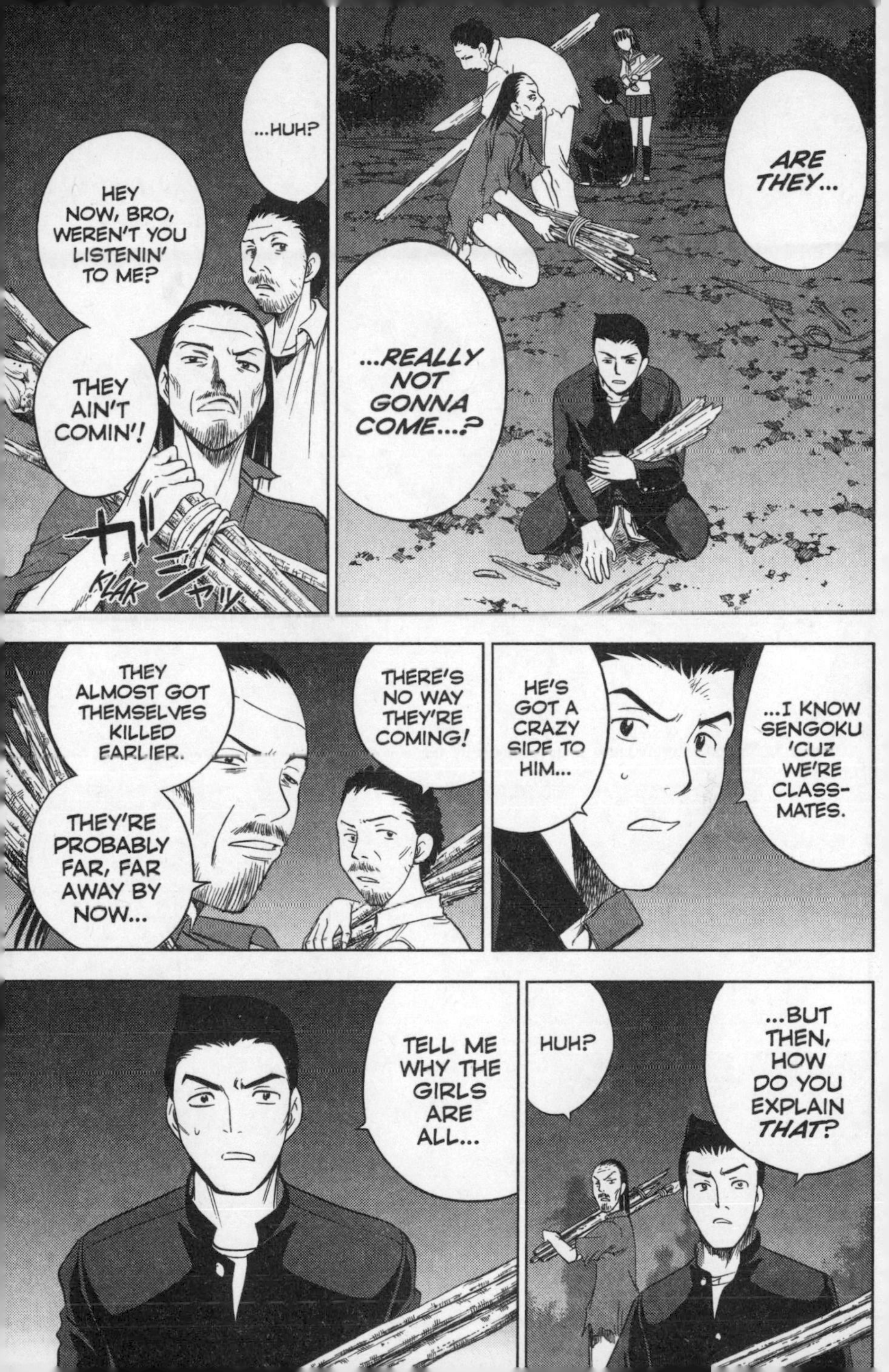
ARE THEY...
...REALLY NOT GONNA COME...?
...HUH?
HEY NOW, BRO, WEREN'T YOU LISTENIN' TO ME?
THEY AIN'T COMIN'!
KLAK
...I KNOW SENGOKU 'CUZ WE'RE CLASSMATES.
HE'S GOT A CRAZY SIDE TO HIM...
THERE'S NO WAY THEY'RE COMING!
THEY ALMOST GOT THEMSELVES KILLED EARLIER.
THEY'RE PROBABLY FAR, FAR AWAY BY NOW...
...BUT THEN, HOW DO YOU EXPLAIN *THAT*?
HUH?
TELL ME WHY THE GIRLS ARE ALL...

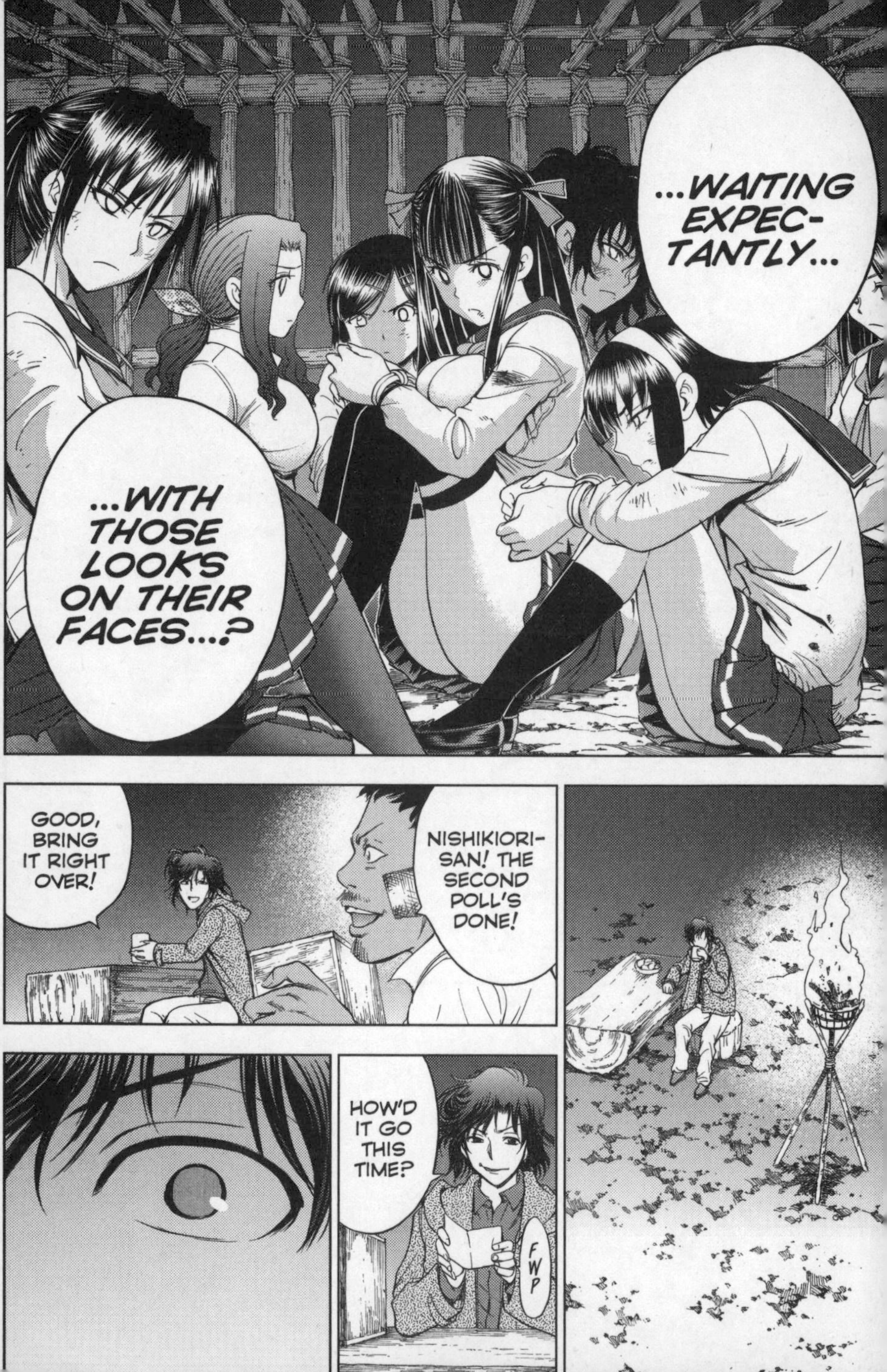
...WAITING EXPECTANTLY...
...WITH THOSE LOOKS ON THEIR FACES...?
NISHIKIORI-SAN! THE SECOND POLL'S DONE!
GOOD, BRING IT RIGHT OVER!
HOW'D IT GO THIS TIME?
FWP

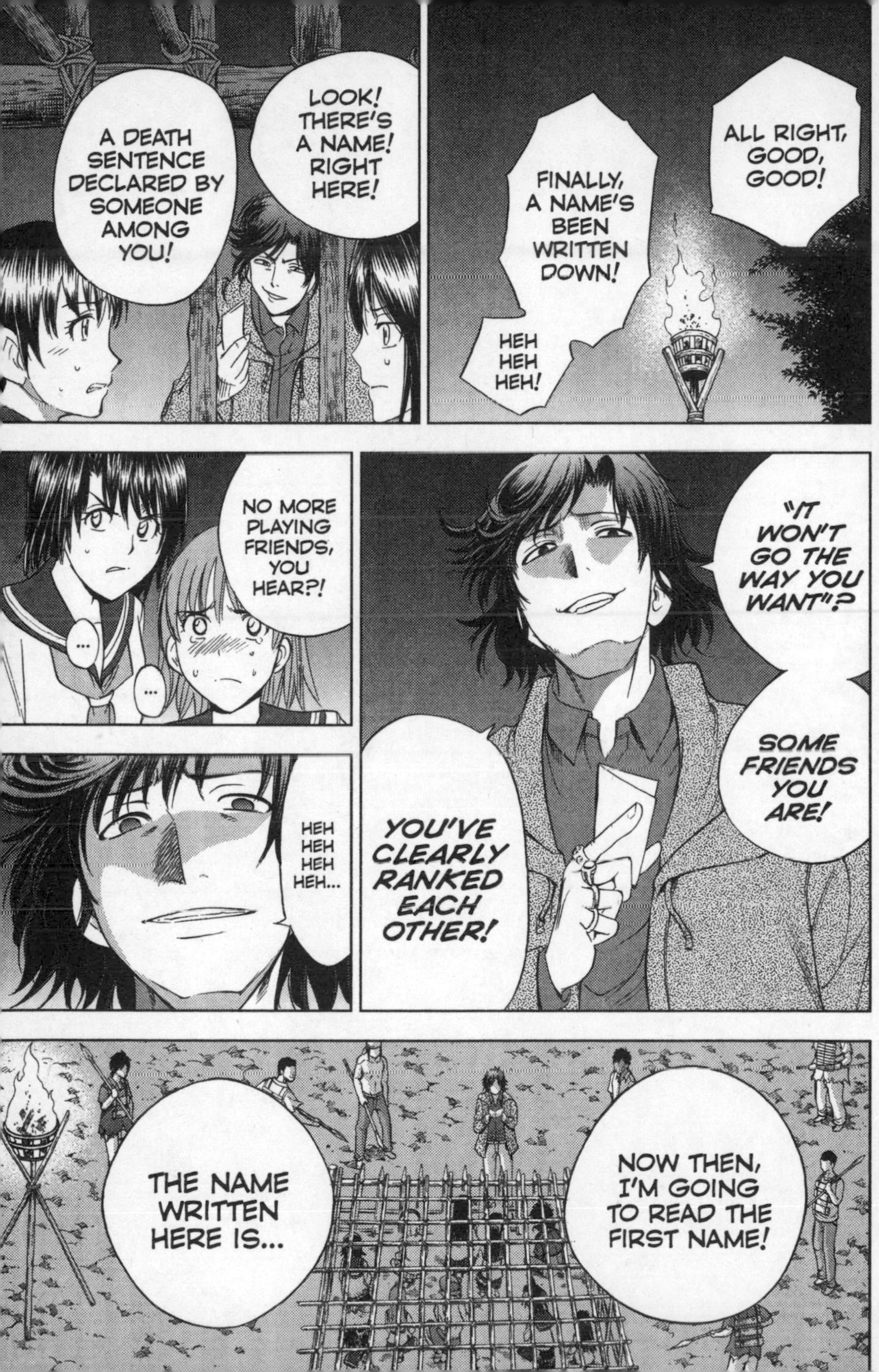
ALL RIGHT, GOOD, GOOD!
FINALLY, A NAME'S BEEN WRITTEN DOWN!
HEH HEH HEH!
LOOK! THERE'S A NAME! RIGHT HERE!
A DEATH SENTENCE DECLARED BY SOMEONE AMONG YOU!
"IT WON'T GO THE WAY YOU WANT"?
SOME FRIENDS YOU ARE!
YOU'VE CLEARLY RANKED EACH OTHER!
NO MORE PLAYING FRIENDS, YOU HEAR?!
...
...
HEH HEH HEH HEH...
NOW THEN, I'M GOING TO READ THE FIRST NAME!
THE NAME WRITTEN HERE IS...

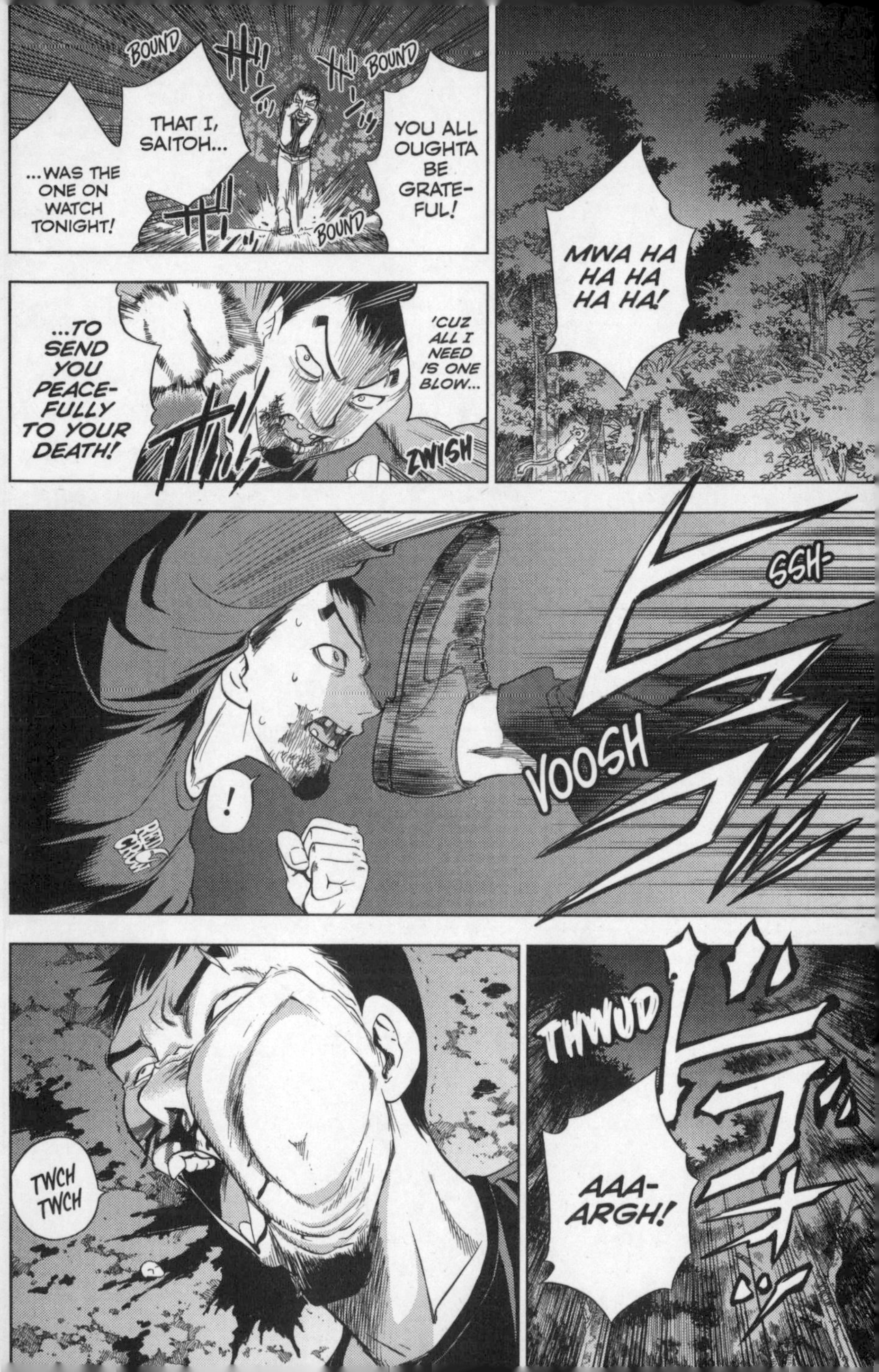
MWA HA HA HA HA HA!
BOUND
BOUND
YOU ALL OUGHTA BE GRATE-FUL!
THAT I, SAITOH...
...WAS THE ONE ON WATCH TONIGHT!
BOUND
'CUZ ALL I NEED IS ONE BLOW...
...TO SEND YOU PEACE-FULLY TO YOUR DEATH!
ZWISH
SSH-
VOOSH
!
THWUD
AAA-ARGH!
TWCH TWCH

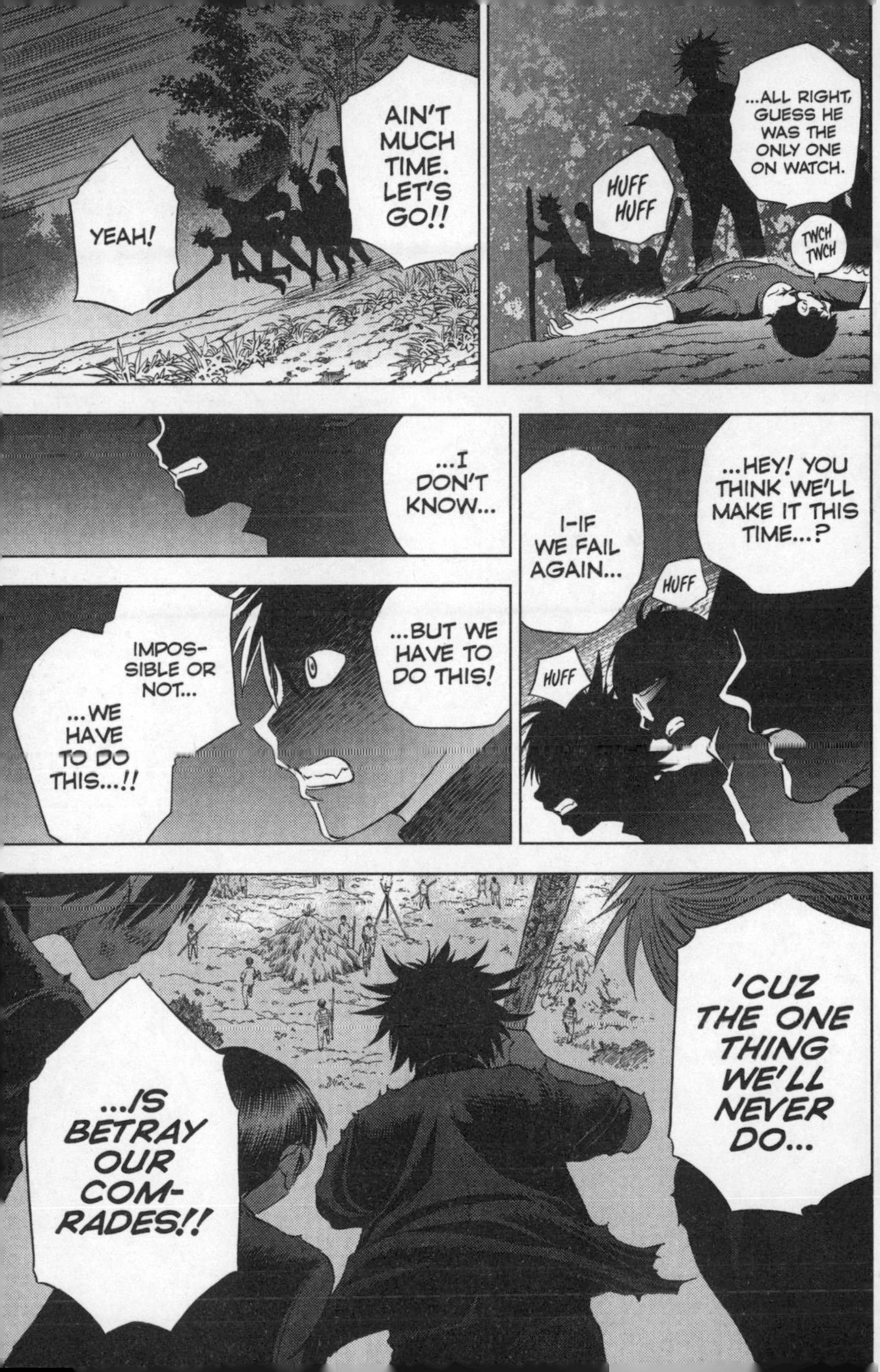
...ALL RIGHT, GUESS HE WAS THE ONLY ONE ON WATCH.
HUFF HUFF
TWCH TWCH
AIN'T MUCH TIME. LET'S GO!!
YEAH!
...HEY! YOU THINK WE'LL MAKE IT THIS TIME...?
I-IF WE FAIL AGAIN...
HUFF
HUFF
...I DON'T KNOW...
...BUT WE HAVE TO DO THIS!
IMPOS-SIBLE OR NOT...
...WE HAVE TO DO THIS...!!
'CUZ THE ONE THING WE'LL NEVER DO...
...IS BETRAY OUR COM-RADES!!

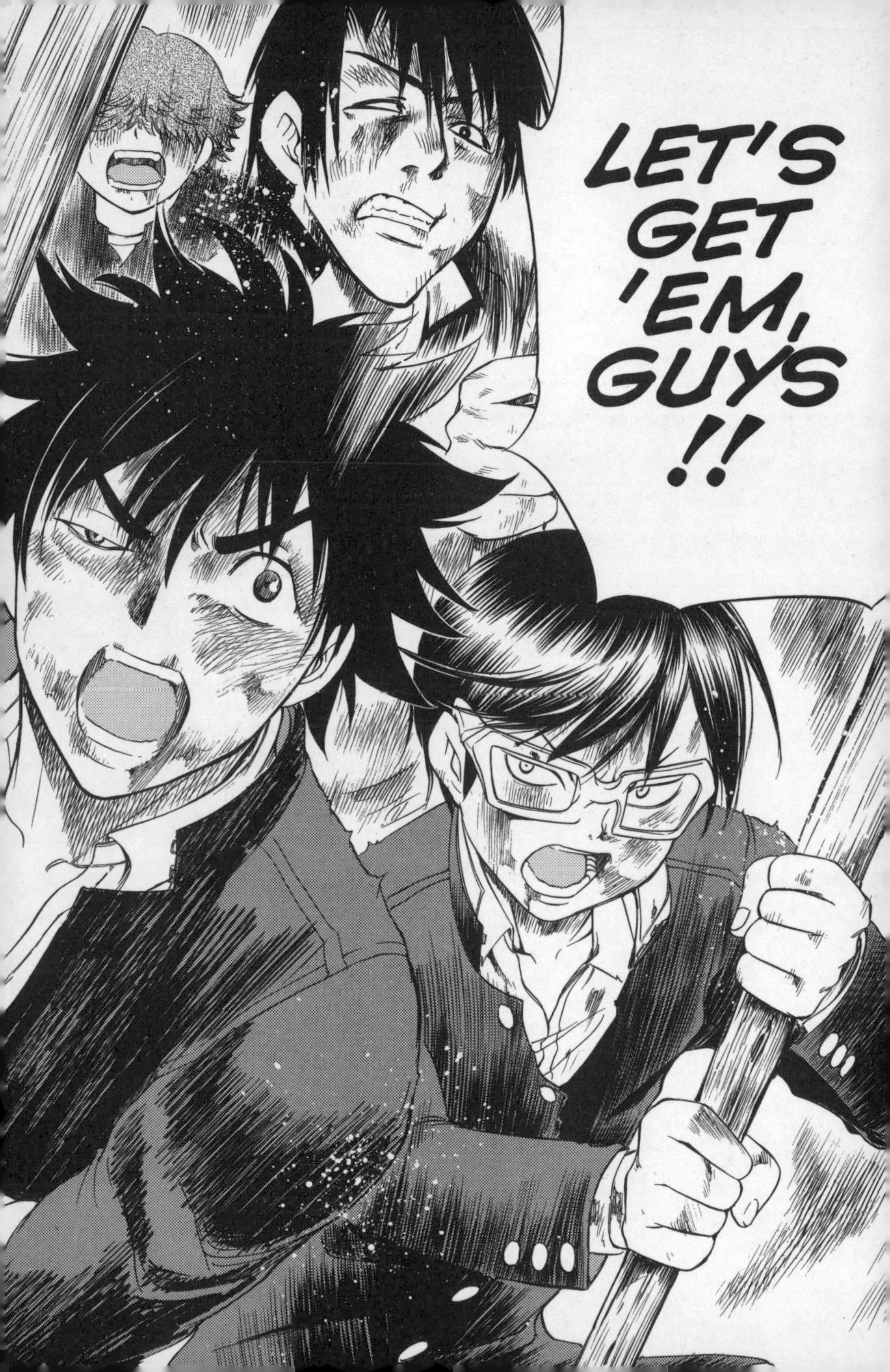
LET'S GET 'EM, GUYS!!

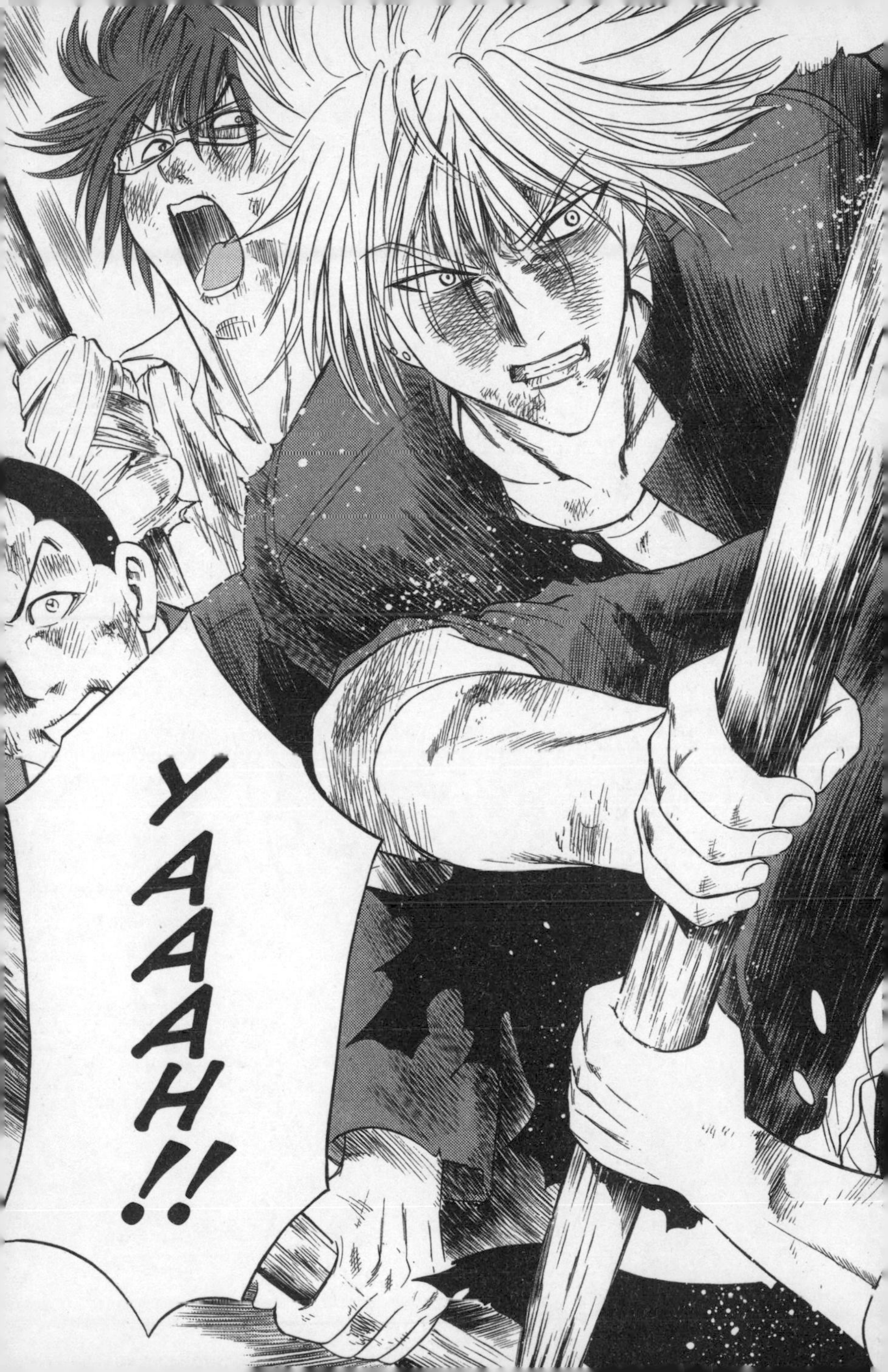
YAAAH!!

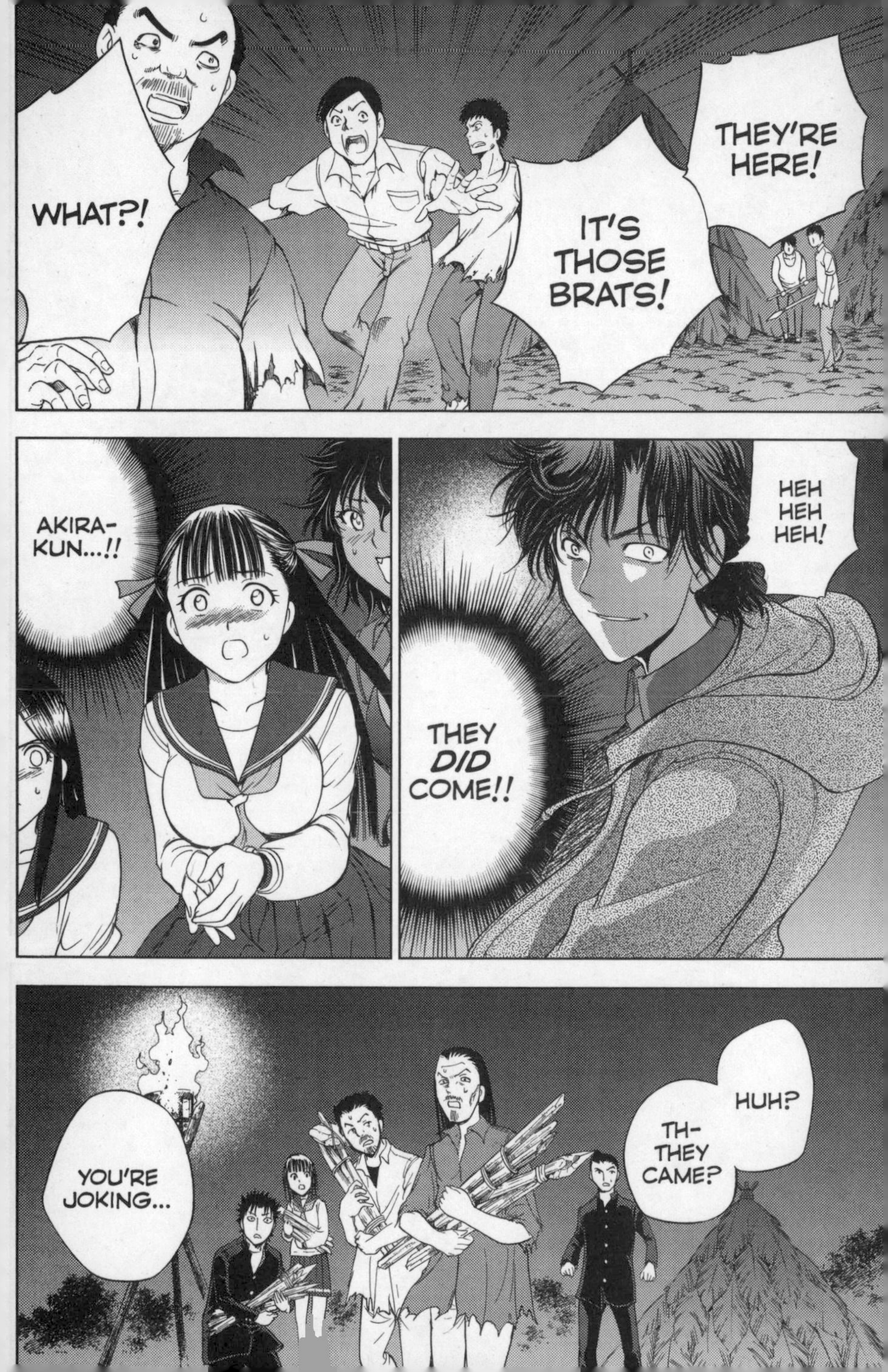

THEY'RE HERE!
IT'S THOSE BRATS!
WHAT?!
HEH HEH HEH!
THEY *DID* COME!!
AKIRA-KUN...!!
HUH?
TH-THEY CAME?
YOU'RE JOKING...

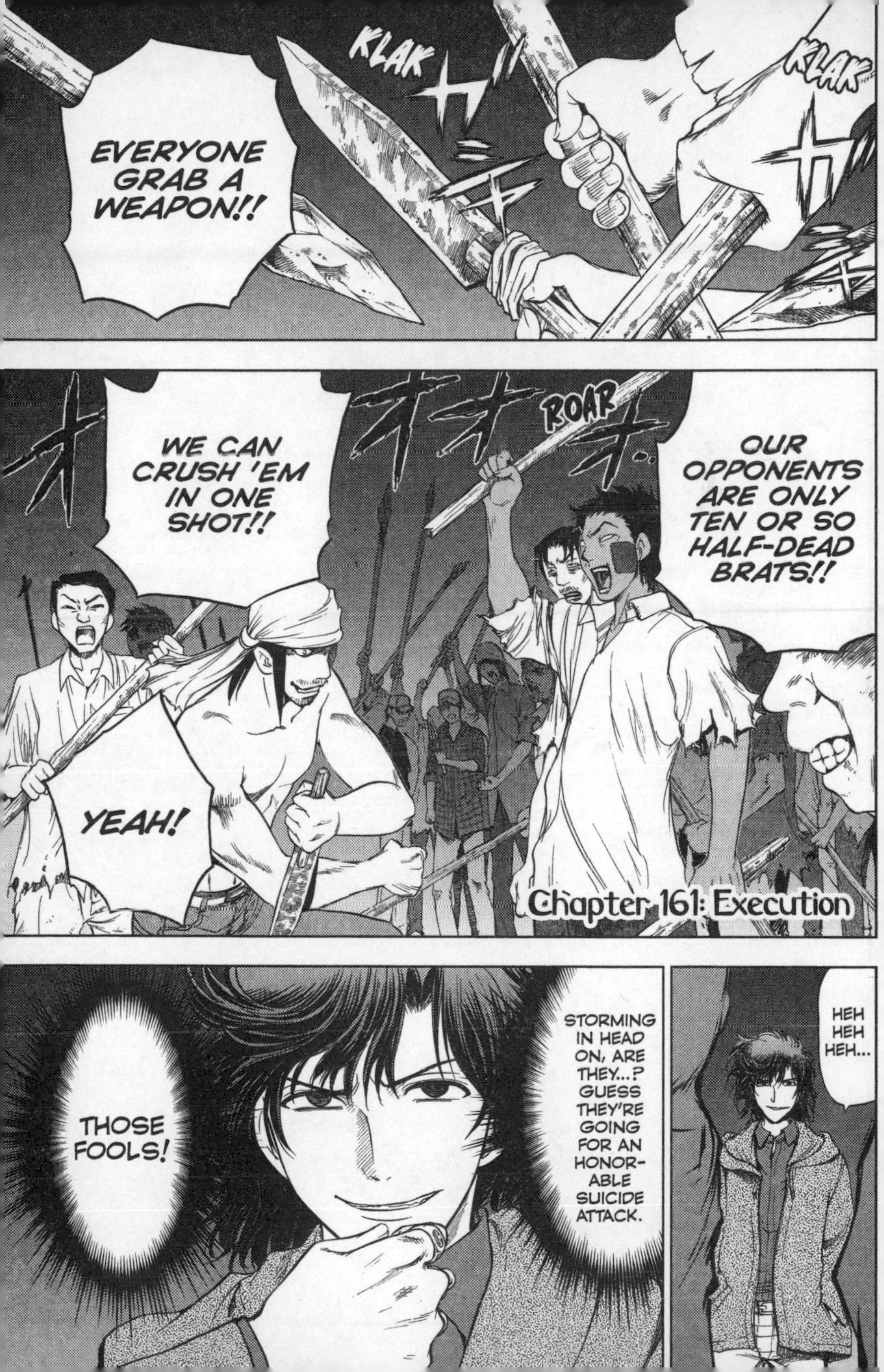
KLAK
KLAK
EVERYONE GRAB A WEAPON!!
OUR OPPONENTS ARE ONLY TEN OR SO HALF-DEAD BRATS!!
ROAR
WE CAN CRUSH 'EM IN ONE SHOT!!
YEAH!
Chapter 161: Execution
HEH HEH HEH...
STORMING IN HEAD ON, ARE THEY...? GUESS THEY'RE GOING FOR AN HONOR-ABLE SUICIDE ATTACK.
THOSE FOOLS!

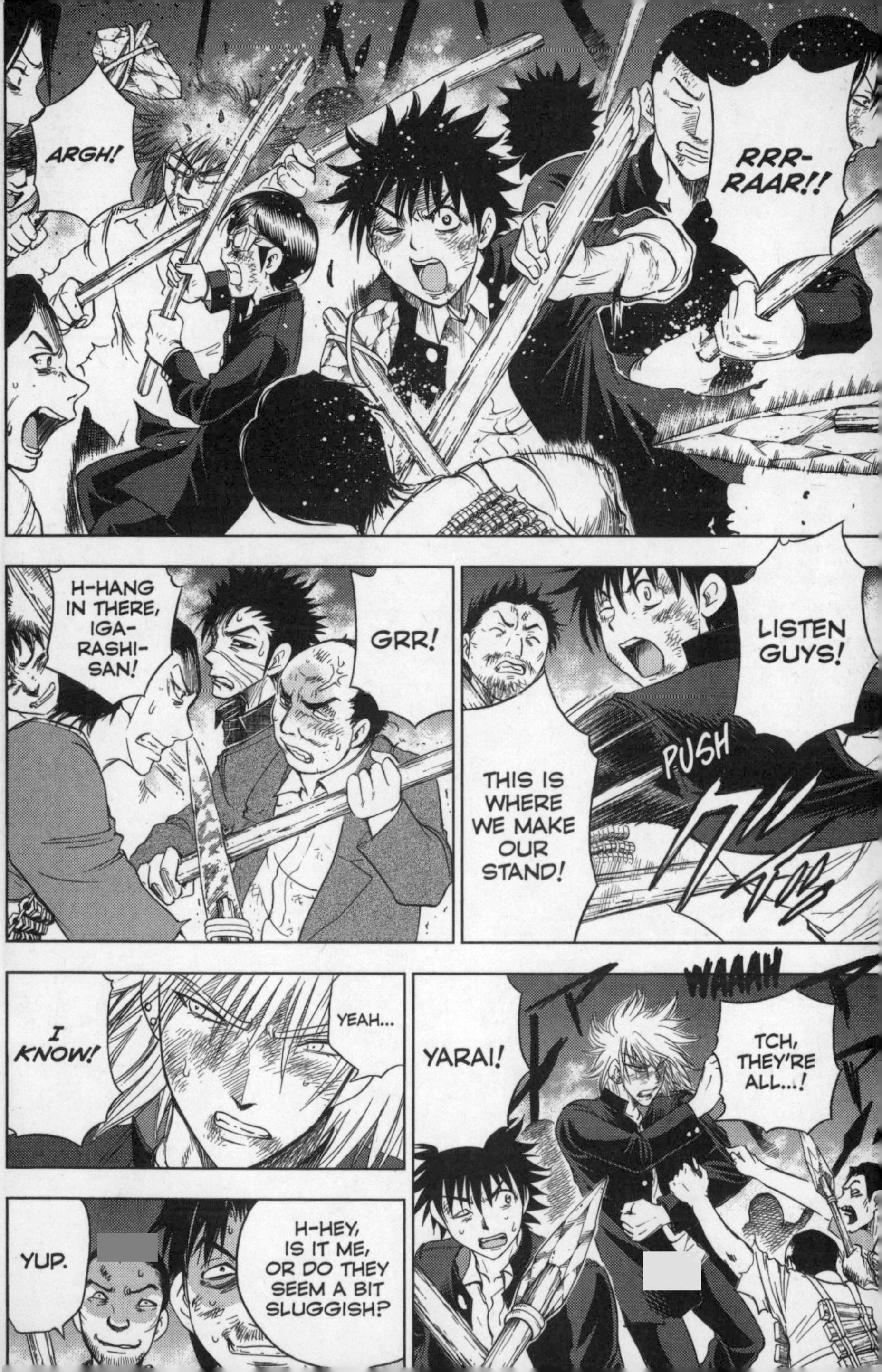
RRR-RAAR!!
ARGH!
LISTEN GUYS!
PUSH
THIS IS WHERE WE MAKE OUR STAND!
GRR!
H-HANG IN THERE, IGA-RASHI-SAN!
WAAAH
TCH, THEY'RE ALL...!
YARAI!
YEAH...
I KNOW!
H-HEY, IS IT ME, OR DO THEY SEEM A BIT SLUGGISH?
YUP.

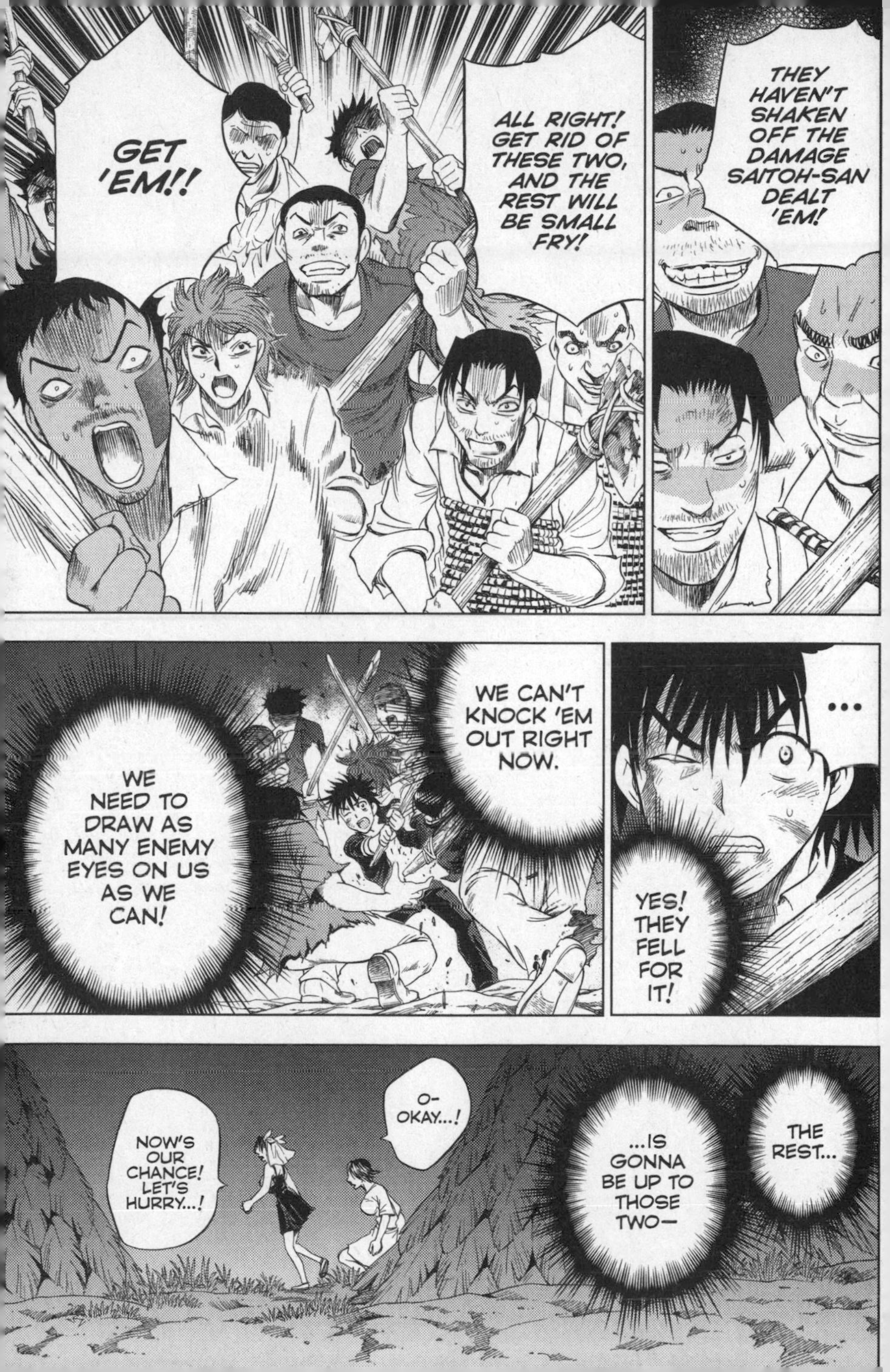
THEY HAVEN'T SHAKEN OFF THE DAMAGE SAITOH-SAN DEALT 'EM!
ALL RIGHT! GET RID OF THESE TWO, AND THE REST WILL BE SMALL FRY!
GET 'EM!!
...
YES! THEY FELL FOR IT!
WE CAN'T KNOCK 'EM OUT RIGHT NOW.
WE NEED TO DRAW AS MANY ENEMY EYES ON US AS WE CAN!
THE REST...
...IS GONNA BE UP TO THOSE TWO—
O-OKAY...!
NOW'S OUR CHANCE! LET'S HURRY...!

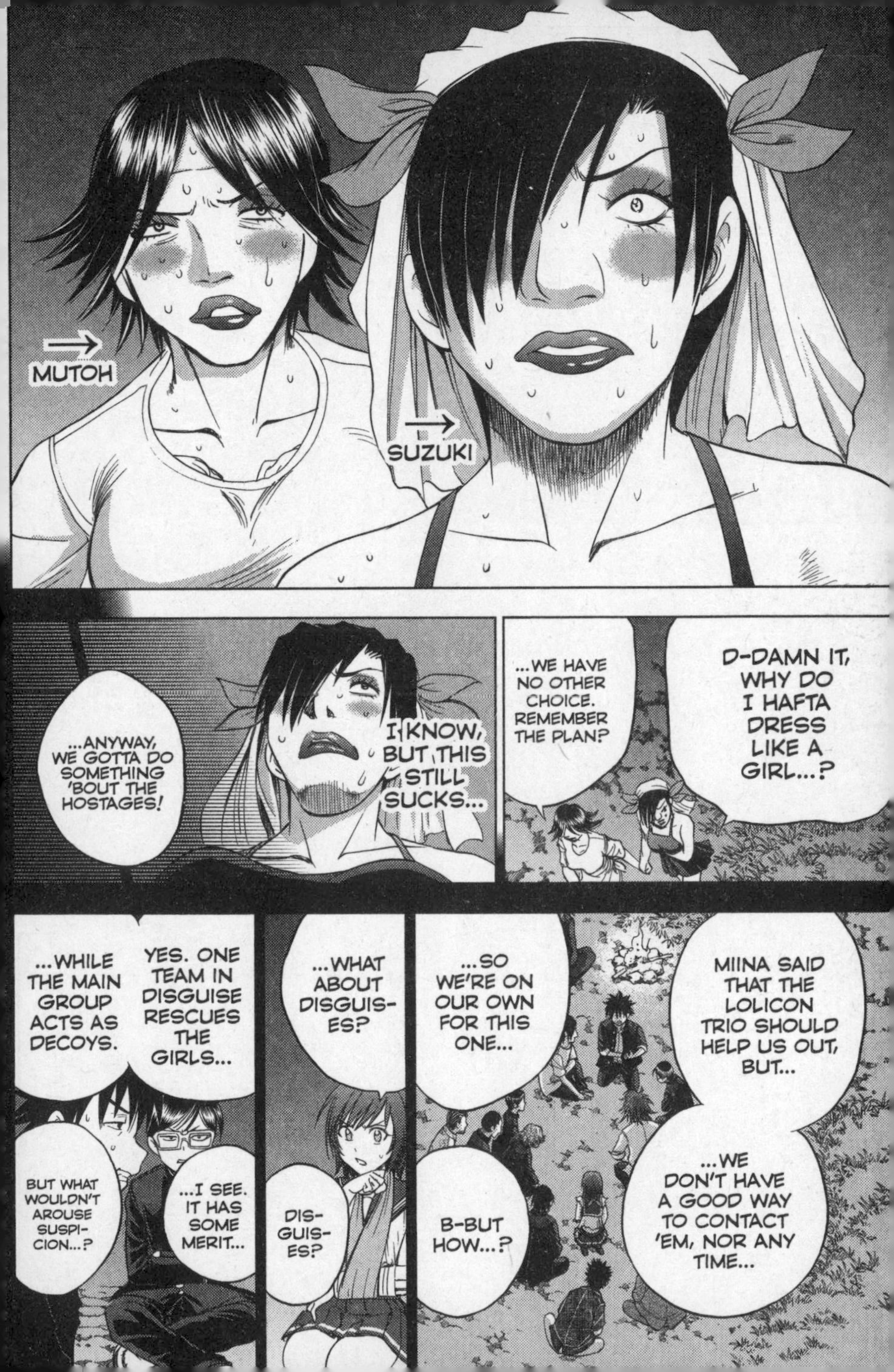
SUZUKI
MUTOH
D-DAMN IT, WHY DO I HAFTA DRESS LIKE A GIRL...?
...WE HAVE NO OTHER CHOICE. REMEMBER THE PLAN?
I KNOW, BUT THIS STILL SUCKS...
...ANYWAY, WE GOTTA DO SOMETHING 'BOUT THE HOSTAGES!
MIINA SAID THAT THE LOLICON TRIO SHOULD HELP US OUT, BUT...
...WE DON'T HAVE A GOOD WAY TO CONTACT 'EM, NOR ANY TIME...
...SO WE'RE ON OUR OWN FOR THIS ONE...
B-BUT HOW...?
...WHAT ABOUT DISGUIS-ES?
DIS-GUIS-ES?
YES. ONE TEAM IN DISGUISE RESCUES THE GIRLS...
...WHILE THE MAIN GROUP ACTS AS DECOYS.
...I SEE. IT HAS SOME MERIT...
BUT WHAT WOULDN'T AROUSE SUSPI-CION...?

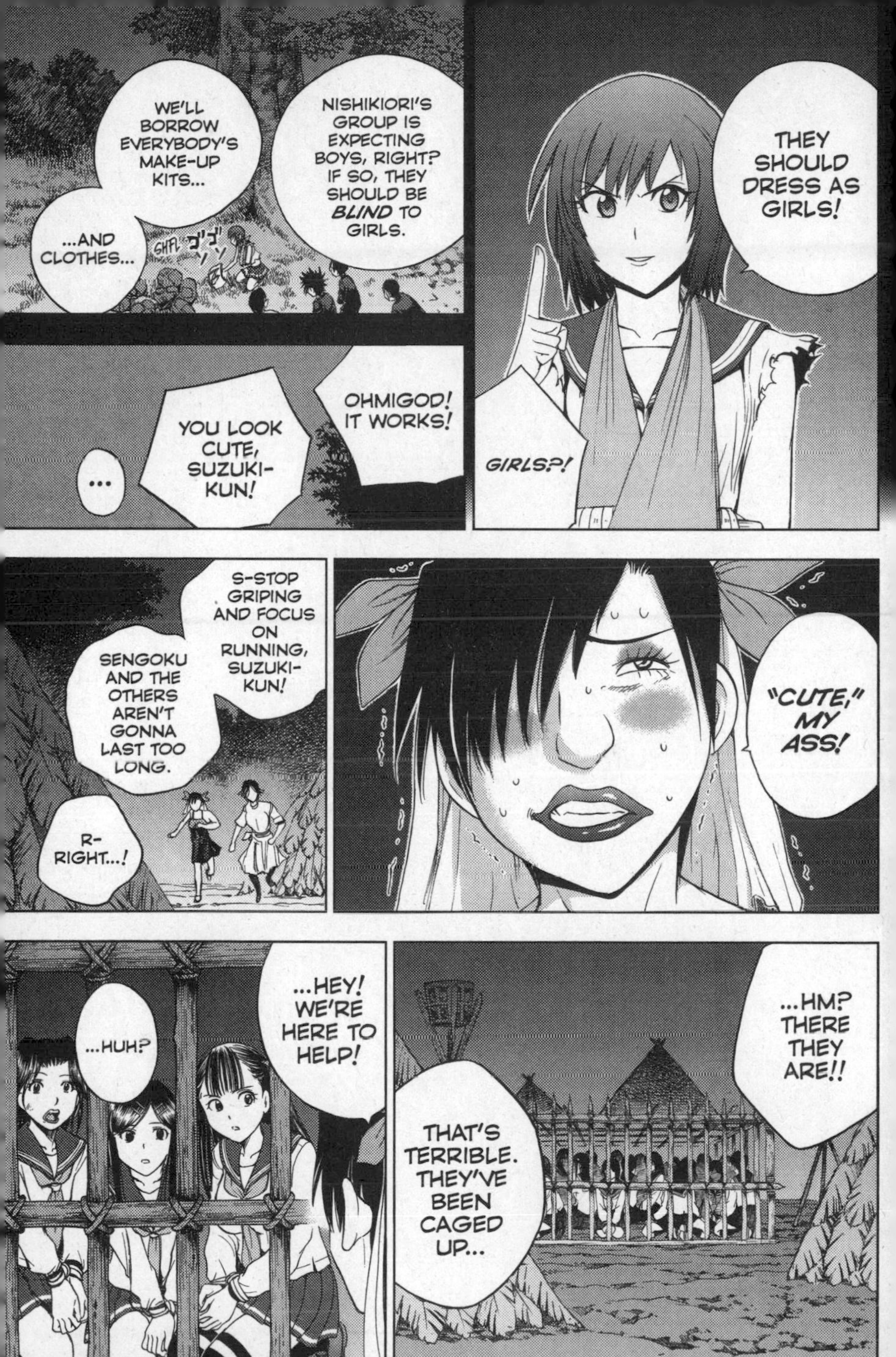
THEY SHOULD DRESS AS GIRLS!
GIRLS?!
NISHIKIORI'S GROUP IS EXPECTING BOYS, RIGHT? IF SO, THEY SHOULD BE *BLIND* TO GIRLS.
WE'LL BORROW EVERYBODY'S MAKE-UP KITS...
...AND CLOTHES...
SHFL
OHMIGOD! IT WORKS!
YOU LOOK CUTE, SUZUKI-KUN!
...
"CUTE," MY ASS!
S-STOP GRIPING AND FOCUS ON RUNNING, SUZUKI-KUN!
SENGOKU AND THE OTHERS AREN'T GONNA LAST TOO LONG.
R-RIGHT...!
...HM? THERE THEY ARE!!
THAT'S TERRIBLE. THEY'VE BEEN CAGED UP...
...HEY! WE'RE HERE TO HELP!
...HUH?

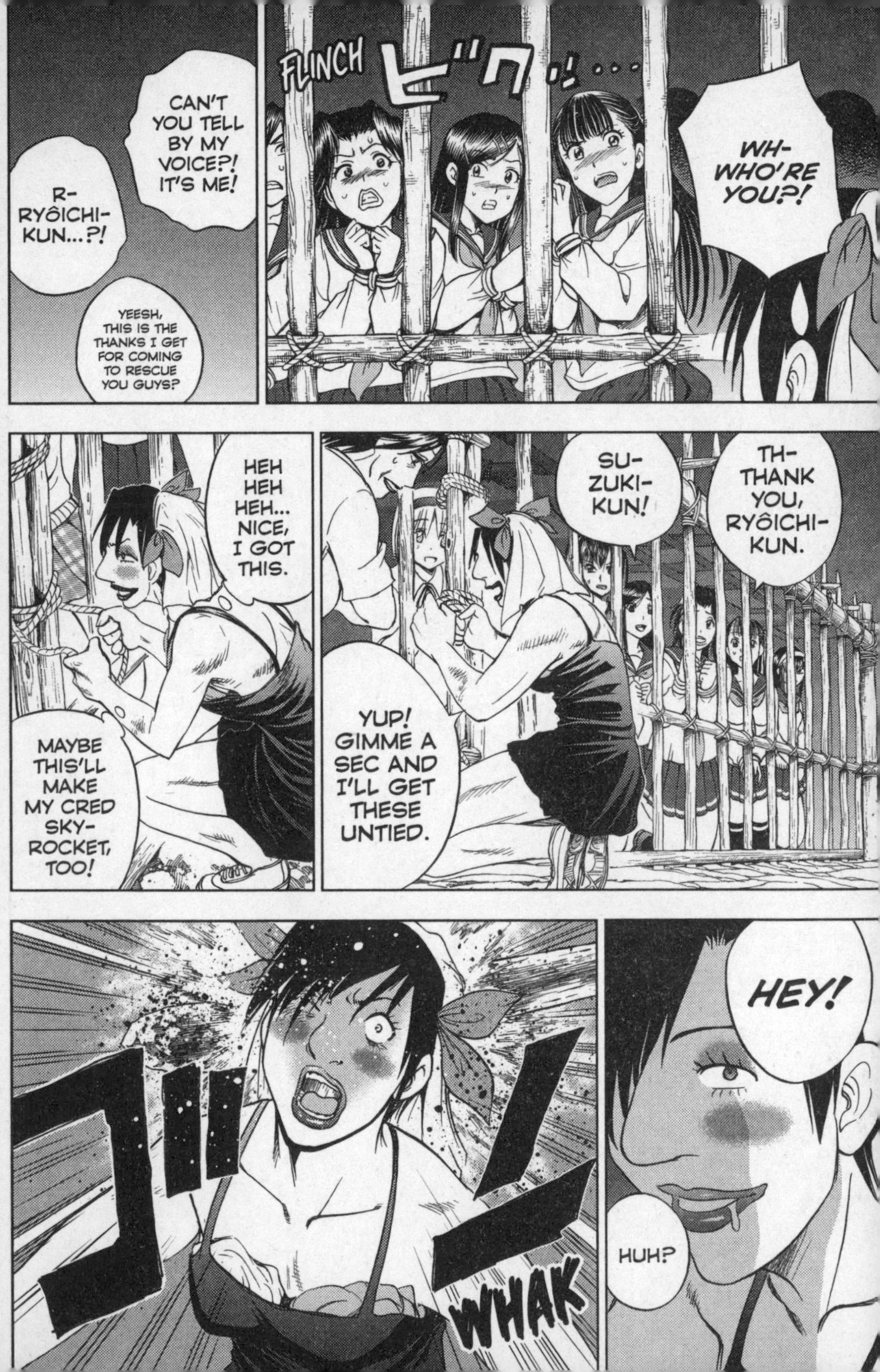
FLINCH
ビクッ!!...
WH- WHO'RE YOU?!
CAN'T YOU TELL BY MY VOICE?! IT'S ME!
R-RYÔICHI-KUN...?!
YEESH, THIS IS THE THANKS I GET FOR COMING TO RESCUE YOU GUYS?
TH-THANK YOU, RYÔICHI-KUN.
SU-ZUKI-KUN!
YUP! GIMME A SEC AND I'LL GET THESE UNTIED.
HEH HEH HEH... NICE, I GOT THIS.
MAYBE THIS'LL MAKE MY CRED SKY-ROCKET, TOO!
HEY!
HUH?
WHAK

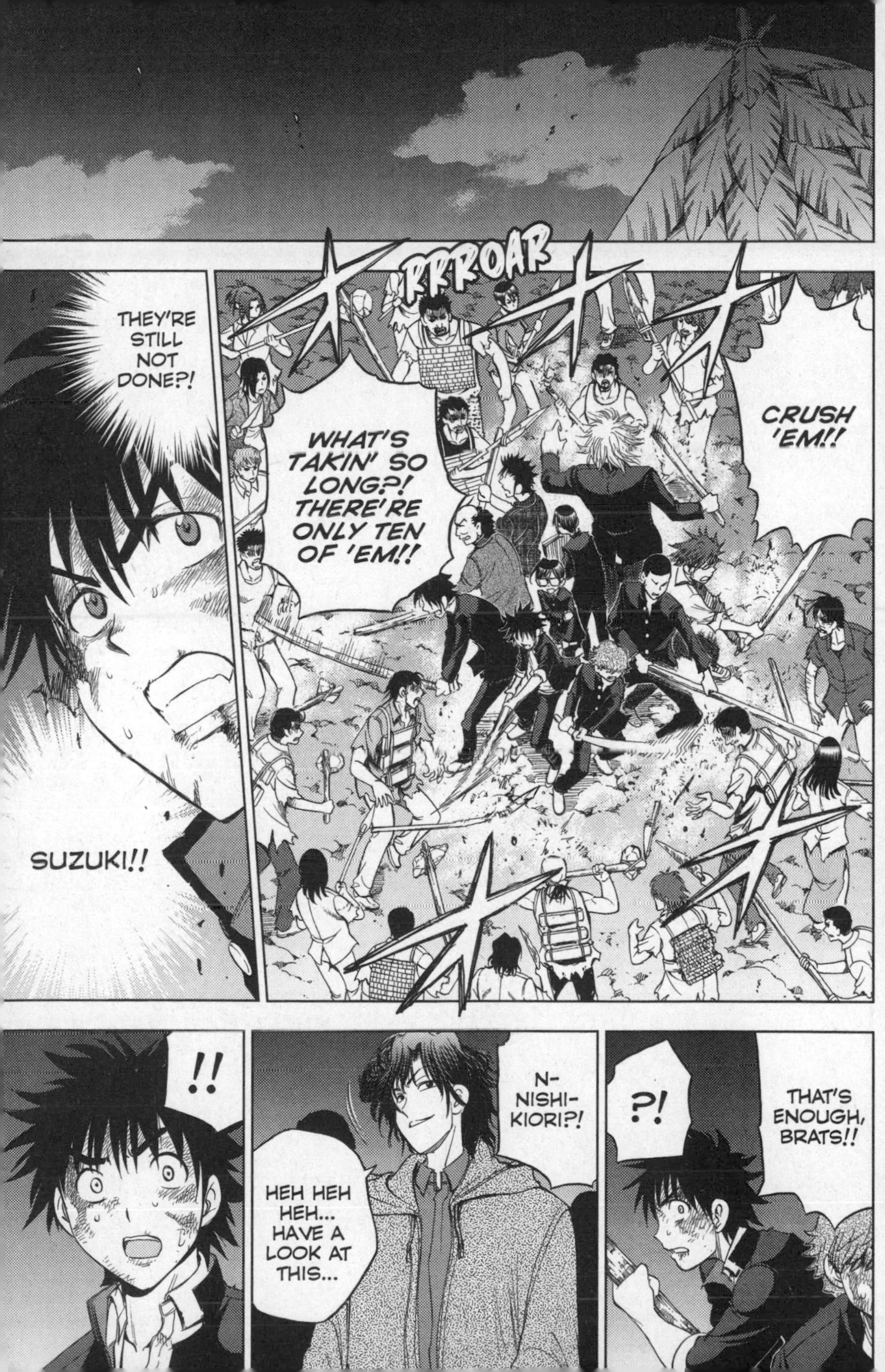
RRROAR
CRUSH 'EM!!
WHAT'S TAKIN' SO LONG?! THERE'RE ONLY TEN OF 'EM!!
THEY'RE STILL NOT DONE?!
SUZUKI!!
THAT'S ENOUGH, BRATS!!
?!
N-NISHIKIORI?!
HEH HEH HEH... HAVE A LOOK AT THIS...
!!

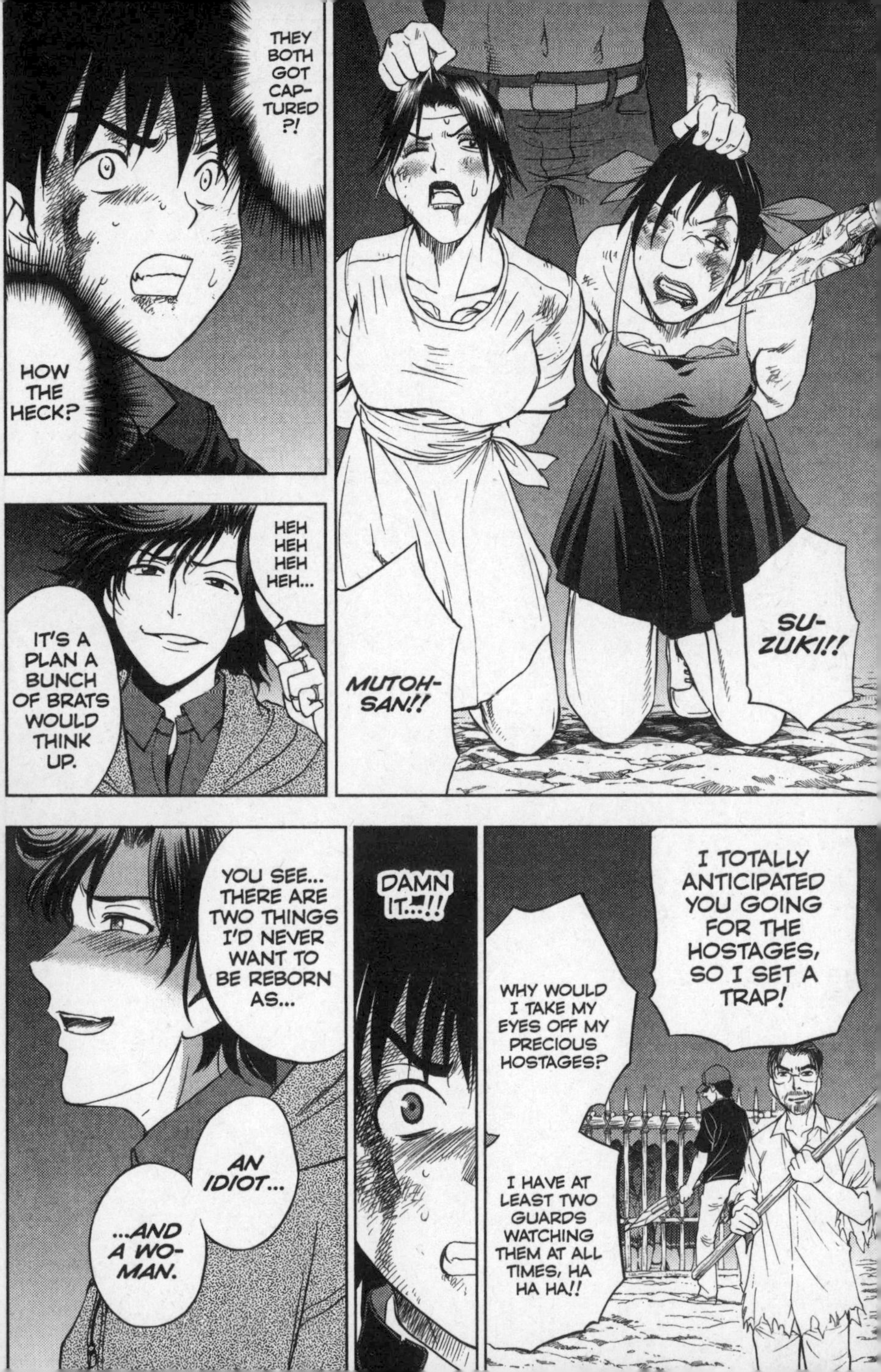
SU-ZUKI!!
MUTOH-SAN!!
THEY BOTH GOT CAP-TURED?!
HOW THE HECK?
HEH HEH HEH HEH...
IT'S A PLAN A BUNCH OF BRATS WOULD THINK UP.
I TOTALLY ANTICIPATED YOU GOING FOR THE HOSTAGES, SO I SET A TRAP!
WHY WOULD I TAKE MY EYES OFF MY PRECIOUS HOSTAGES?
I HAVE AT LEAST TWO GUARDS WATCHING THEM AT ALL TIMES, HA HA HA!!
DAMN IT...!!
YOU SEE... THERE ARE TWO THINGS I'D NEVER WANT TO BE REBORN AS...
AN IDIOT...
...AND A WO-MAN.

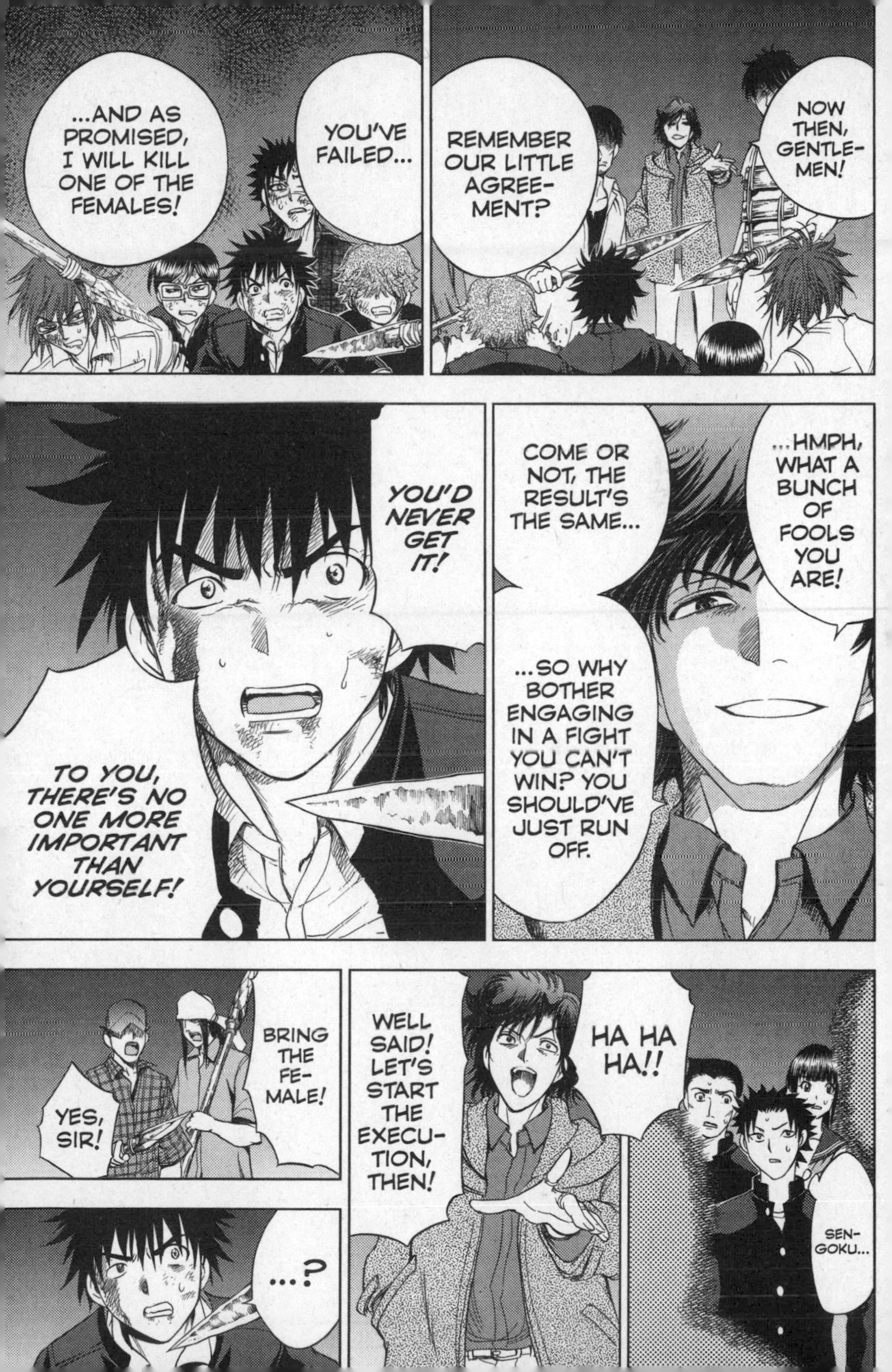
NOW THEN, GENTLEMEN!
REMEMBER OUR LITTLE AGREEMENT?
YOU'VE FAILED...
...AND AS PROMISED, I WILL KILL ONE OF THE FEMALES!
...HMPH, WHAT A BUNCH OF FOOLS YOU ARE!
COME OR NOT, THE RESULT'S THE SAME...
...SO WHY BOTHER ENGAGING IN A FIGHT YOU CAN'T WIN? YOU SHOULD'VE JUST RUN OFF.
YOU'D NEVER GET IT!
TO YOU, THERE'S NO ONE MORE IMPORTANT THAN YOURSELF!
HA HA HA!!
WELL SAID! LET'S START THE EXECUTION, THEN!
SEN-GOKU...
BRING THE FE-MALE!
YES, SIR!
...?

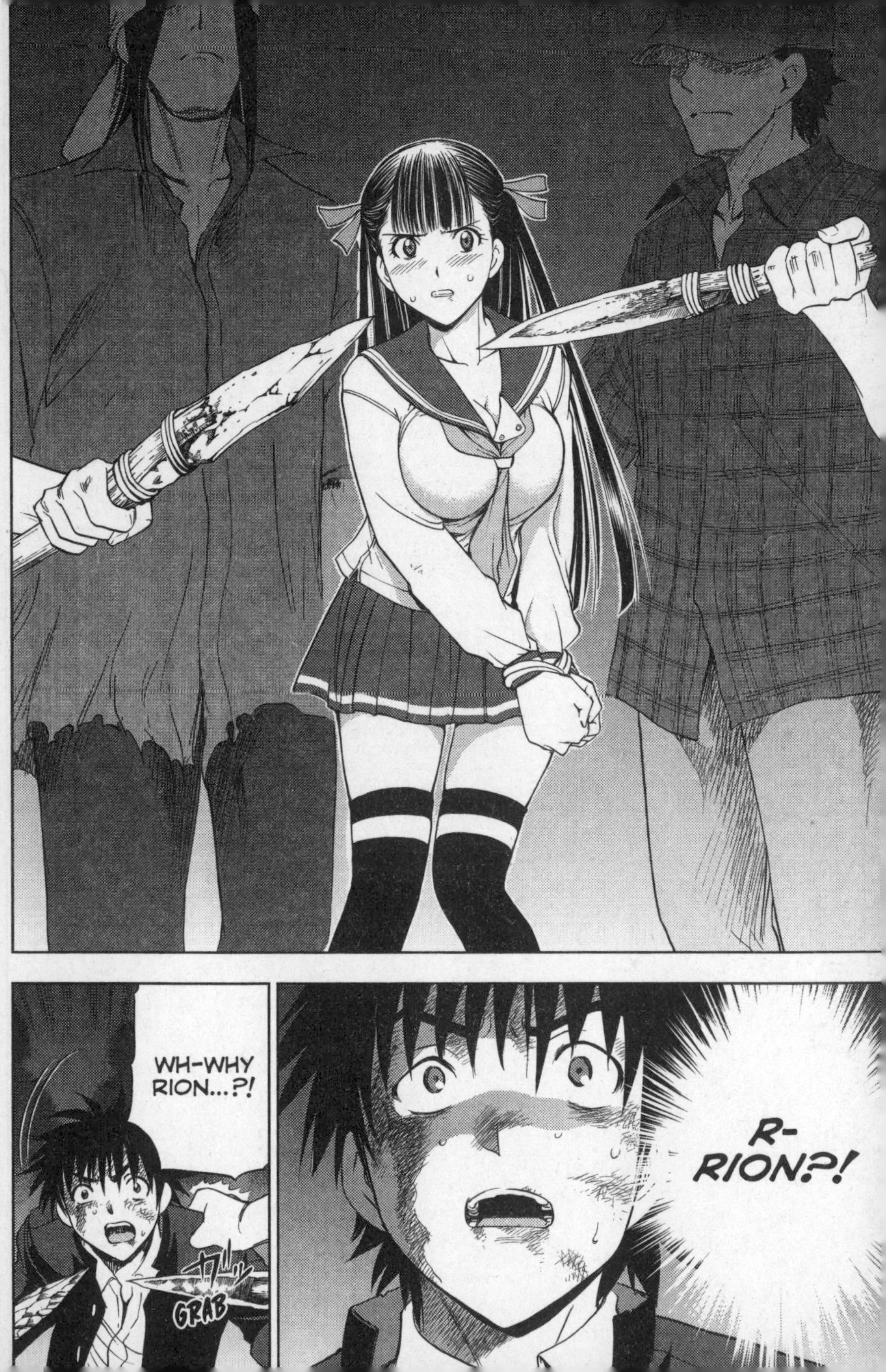
R-
RION?!
WH-WHY
RION...?!
GRAB

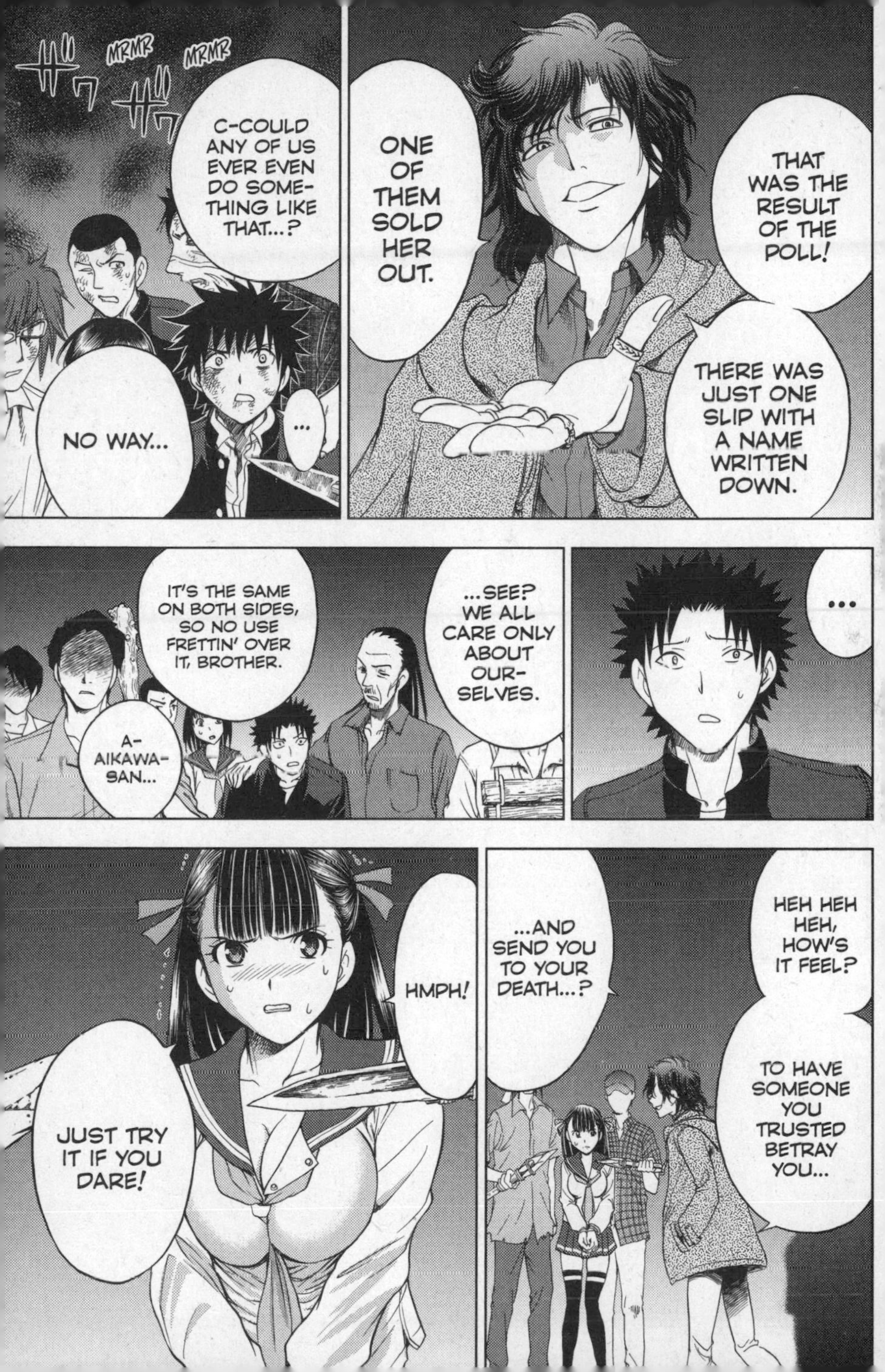
THAT WAS THE RESULT OF THE POLL!
THERE WAS JUST ONE SLIP WITH A NAME WRITTEN DOWN.
ONE OF THEM SOLD HER OUT.
ザワ ザワ
MRMR
MRMR
C-COULD ANY OF US EVER EVEN DO SOME-THING LIKE THAT...?
NO WAY...
...
...
...SEE? WE ALL CARE ONLY ABOUT OUR-SELVES.
IT'S THE SAME ON BOTH SIDES, SO NO USE FRETTIN' OVER IT, BROTHER.
A- AIKAWA-SAN...
HEH HEH HEH, HOW'S IT FEEL?
TO HAVE SOMEONE YOU TRUSTED BETRAY YOU...
...AND SEND YOU TO YOUR DEATH...?
HMPH!
JUST TRY IT IF YOU DARE!

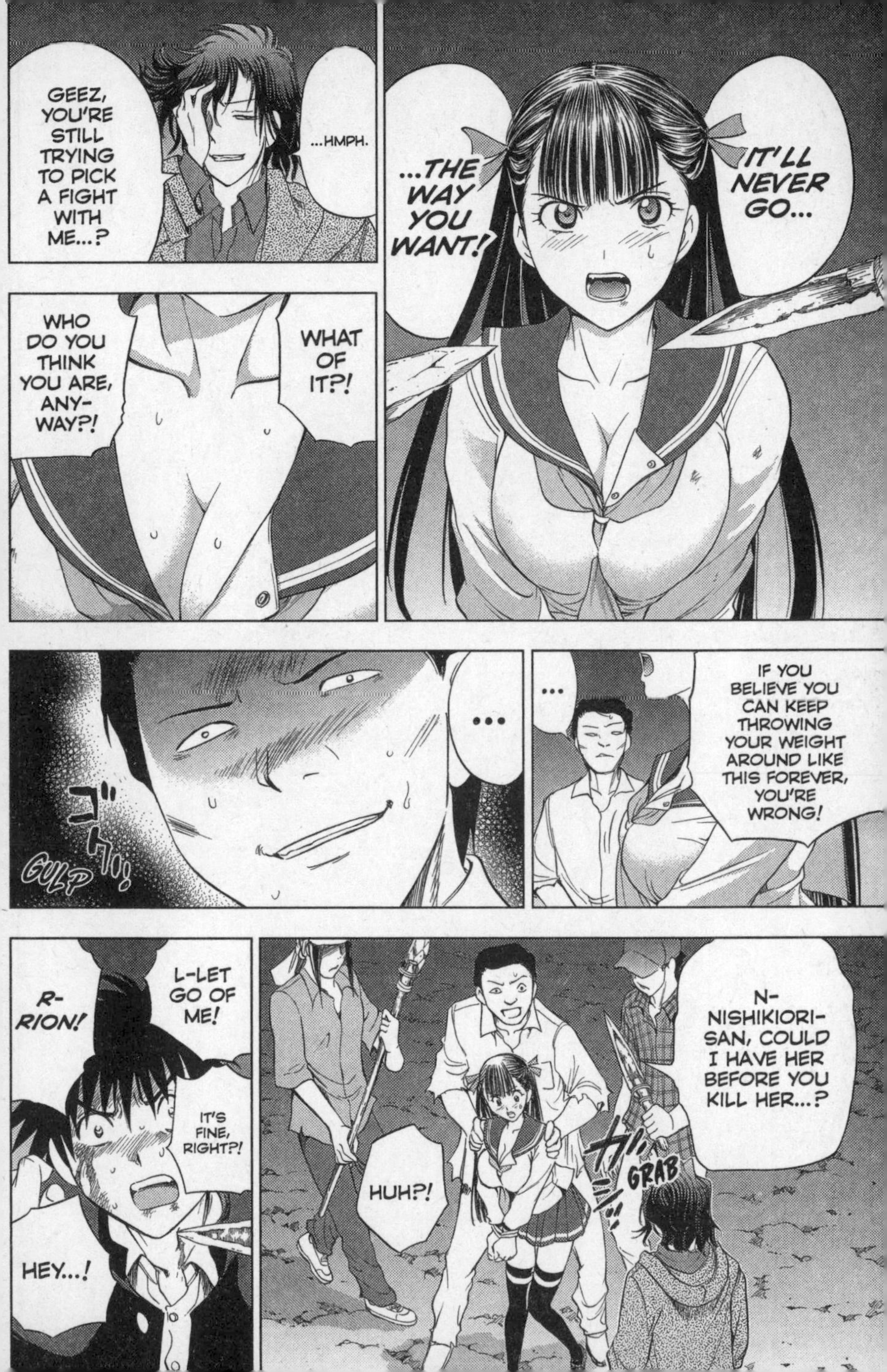
IT'LL NEVER GO...
...THE WAY YOU WANT!
...HMPH.
GEEZ, YOU'RE STILL TRYING TO PICK A FIGHT WITH ME...?
WHAT OF IT?!
WHO DO YOU THINK YOU ARE, ANY-WAY?!
IF YOU BELIEVE YOU CAN KEEP THROWING YOUR WEIGHT AROUND LIKE THIS FOREVER, YOU'RE WRONG!
...
...
GULP
N-NISHIKIORI-SAN, COULD I HAVE HER BEFORE YOU KILL HER...?
GRAB
HUH?!
L-LET GO OF ME!
R-RION!
IT'S FINE, RIGHT?!
HEY...!

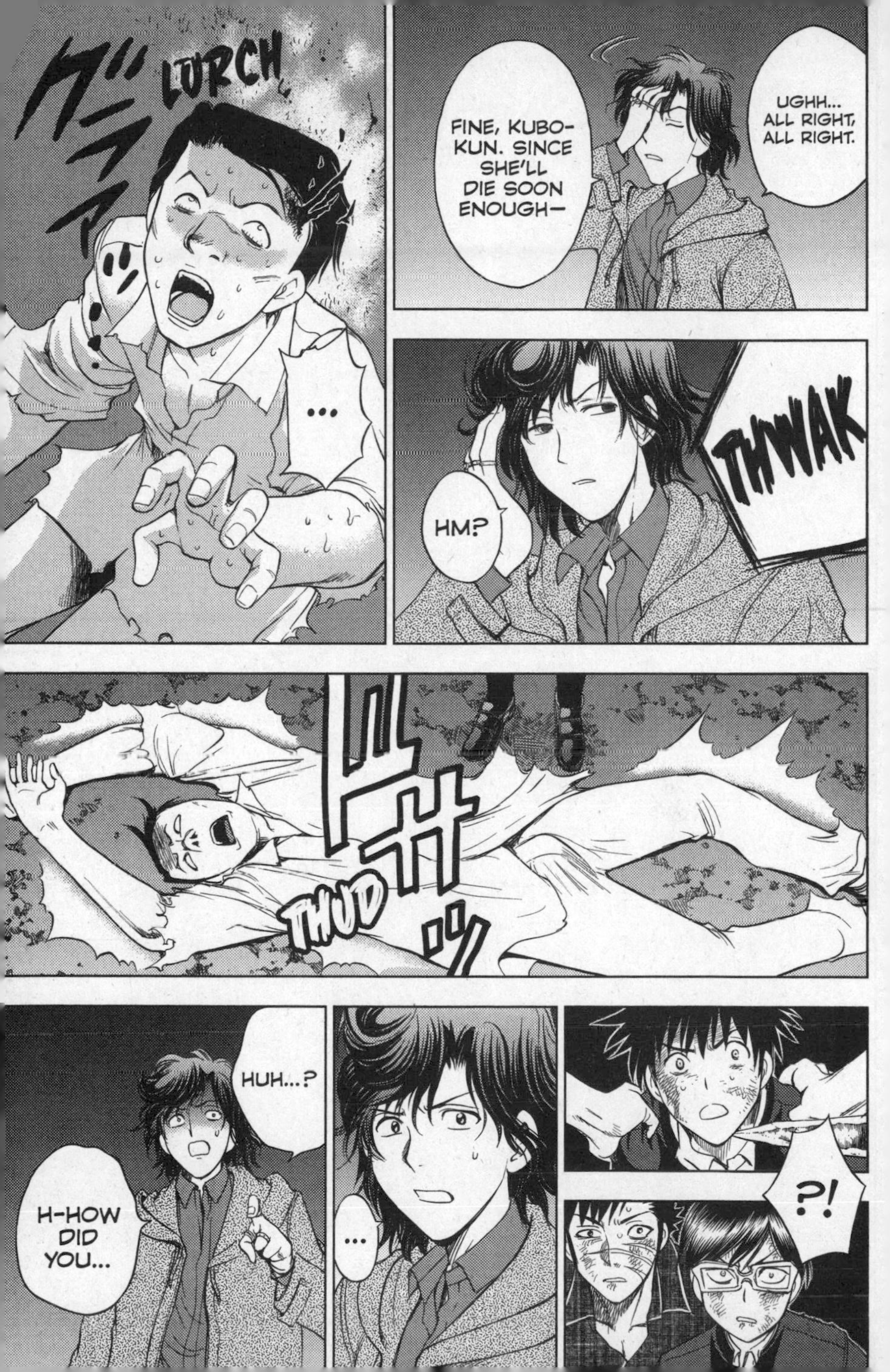
UGHH... ALL RIGHT, ALL RIGHT.
FINE, KUBO-KUN. SINCE SHE'LL DIE SOON ENOUGH—
THWAK
HM?
LURCH
...
THUD
?!
...
HUH...?
H-HOW DID YOU...

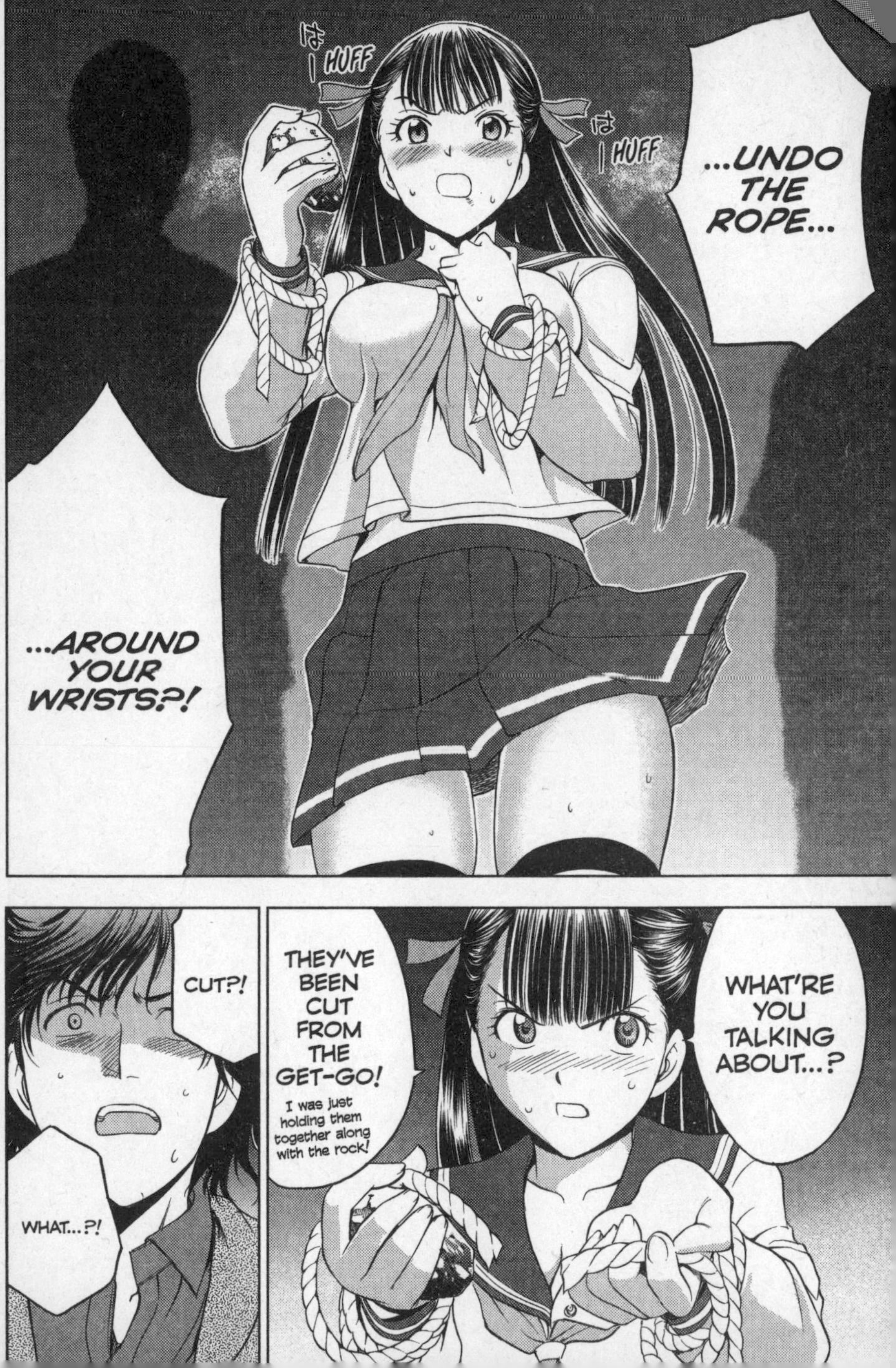

...UNDO THE ROPE...
は HUFF
は HUFF
...AROUND YOUR WRISTS?!
WHAT'RE YOU TALKING ABOUT...?
THEY'VE BEEN CUT FROM THE GET-GO!
I was just holding them together along with the rock!
CUT?!
WHAT...?!

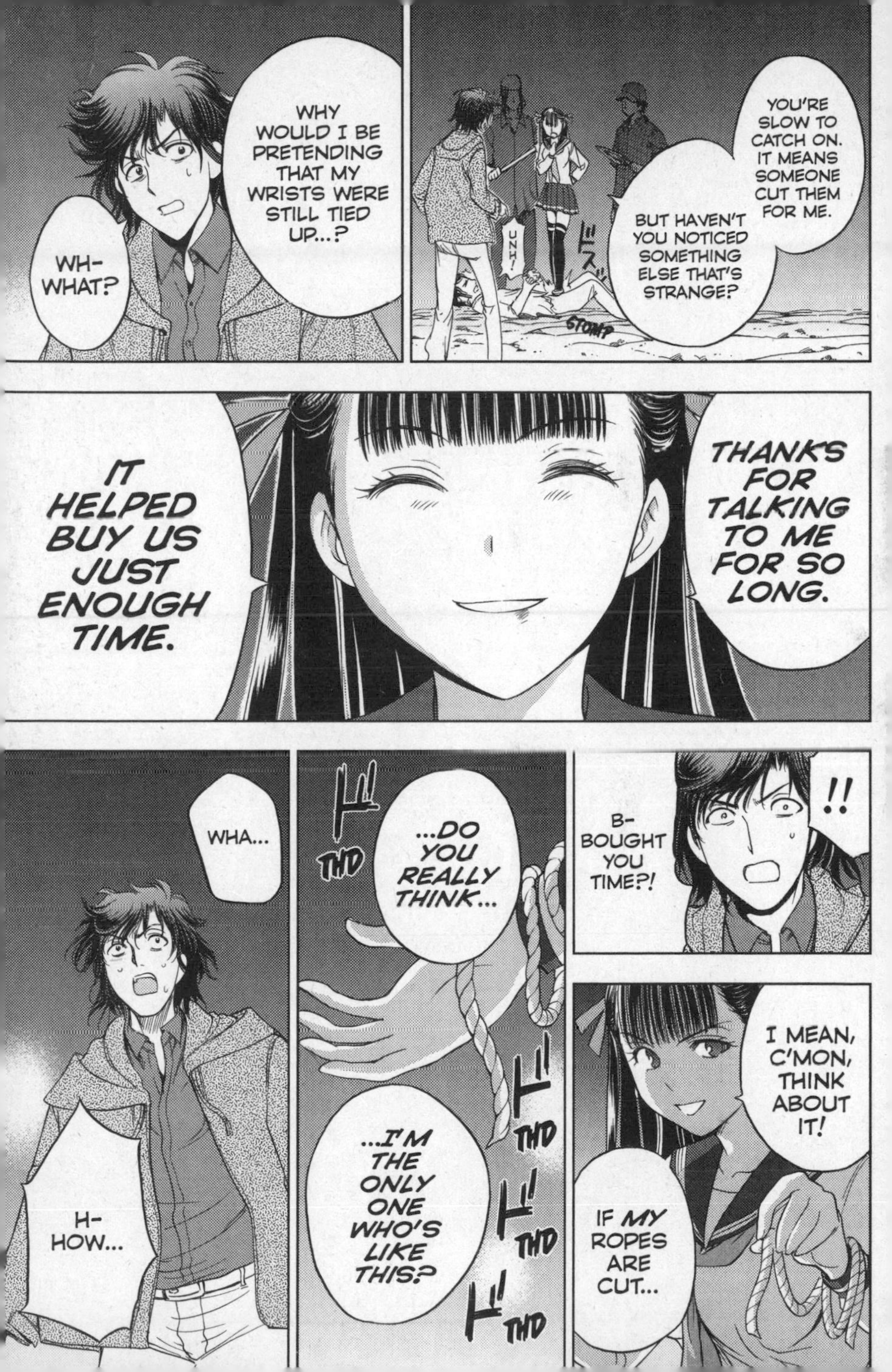
YOU'RE SLOW TO CATCH ON. IT MEANS SOMEONE CUT THEM FOR ME.
BUT HAVEN'T YOU NOTICED SOMETHING ELSE THAT'S STRANGE?
UNH!
STOMP
WHY WOULD I BE PRETENDING THAT MY WRISTS WERE STILL TIED UP...?
WH- WHAT?
THANKS FOR TALKING TO ME FOR SO LONG.
IT HELPED BUY US JUST ENOUGH TIME.
!!
B- BOUGHT YOU TIME?!
I MEAN, C'MON, THINK ABOUT IT!
IF MY ROPES ARE CUT...
...DO YOU REALLY THINK...
THD
...I'M THE ONLY ONE WHO'S LIKE THIS?
THD
THD
THD
WHA...
H- HOW...

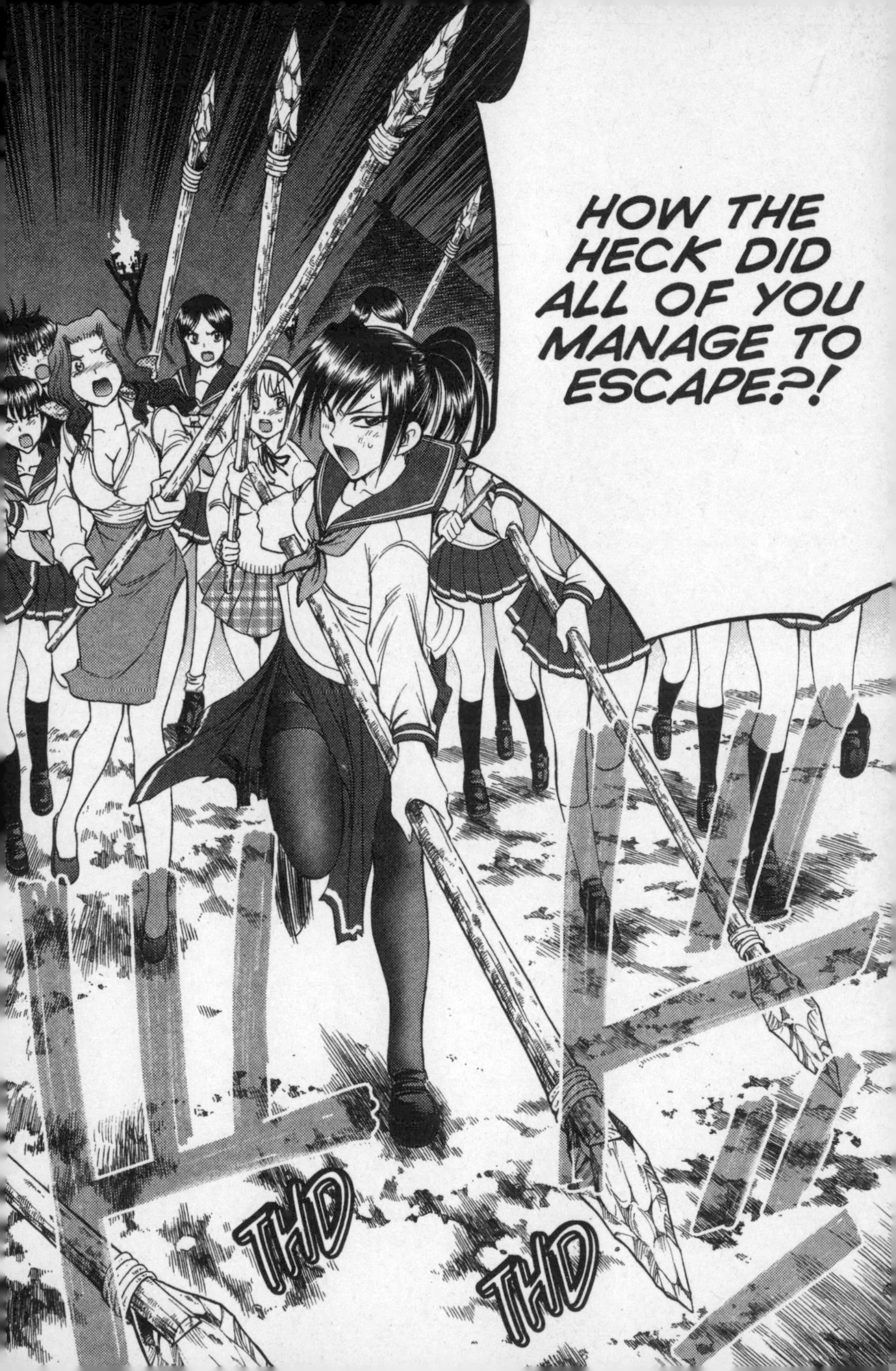
HOW THE HECK DID ALL OF YOU MANAGE TO ESCAPE?!
THD
THD

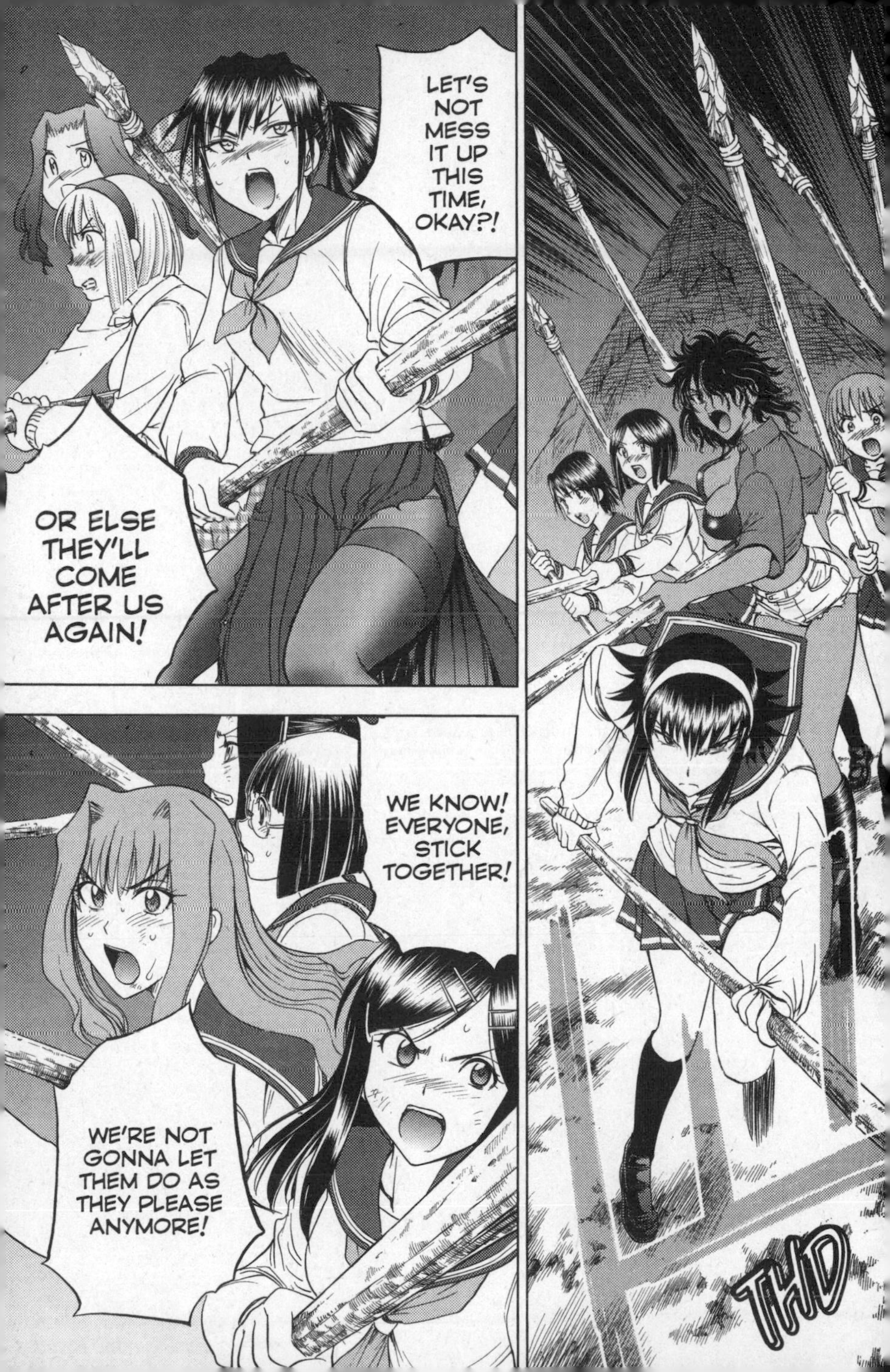
THD
LET'S NOT MESS IT UP THIS TIME, OKAY?!
OR ELSE THEY'LL COME AFTER US AGAIN!
WE KNOW! EVERYONE, STICK TOGETHER!
WE'RE NOT GONNA LET THEM DO AS THEY PLEASE ANYMORE!

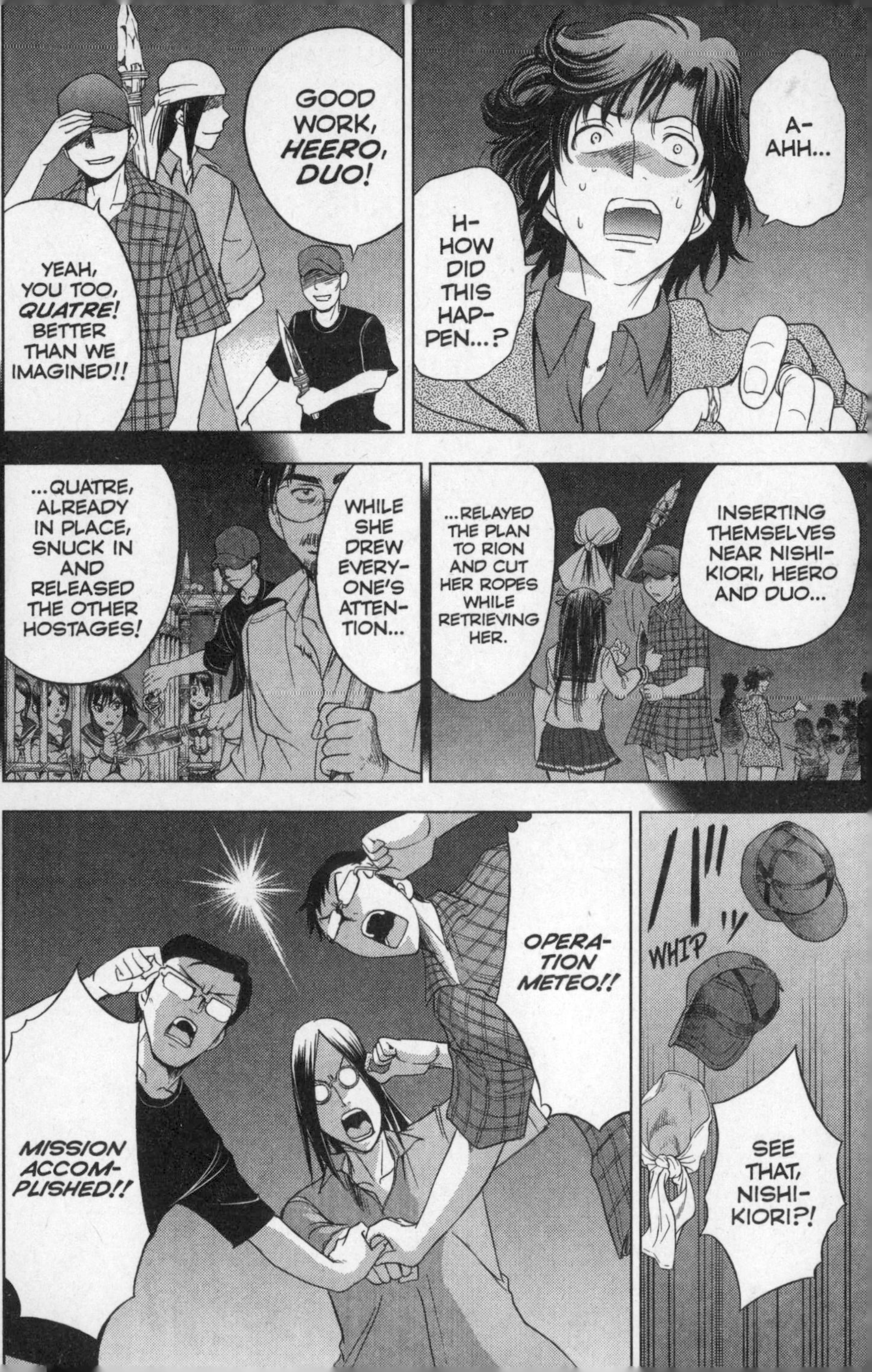
A- AHH...
H- HOW DID THIS HAP- PEN...?
GOOD WORK, HEERO, DUO!
YEAH, YOU TOO, QUATRE! BETTER THAN WE IMAGINED!!
INSERTING THEMSELVES NEAR NISHI- KIORI, HEERO AND DUO...
...RELAYED THE PLAN TO RION AND CUT HER ROPES WHILE RETRIEVING HER.
WHILE SHE DREW EVERY- ONE'S ATTEN- TION...
...QUATRE, ALREADY IN PLACE, SNUCK IN AND RELEASED THE OTHER HOSTAGES!
WHIP
SEE THAT, NISHI- KIORI?!
OPERA- TION METEO!!
MISSION ACCOM- PLISHED!!

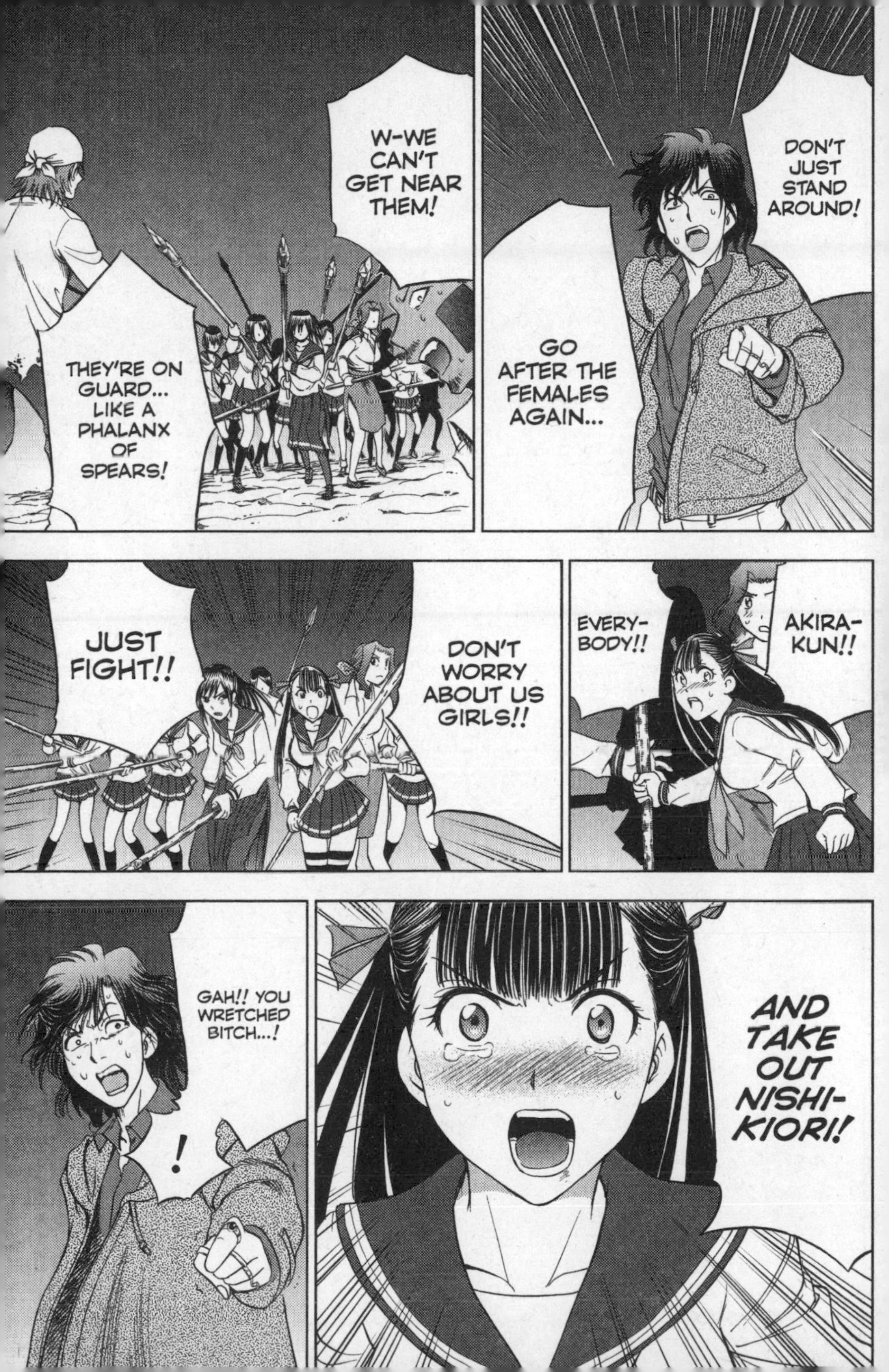
DON'T JUST STAND AROUND!
GO AFTER THE FEMALES AGAIN...
W-WE CAN'T GET NEAR THEM!
THEY'RE ON GUARD... LIKE A PHALANX OF SPEARS!
AKIRA-KUN!!
EVERY-BODY!!
DON'T WORRY ABOUT US GIRLS!!
JUST FIGHT!!
AND TAKE OUT NISHI-KIORI!
GAH!! YOU WRETCHED BITCH...!
!

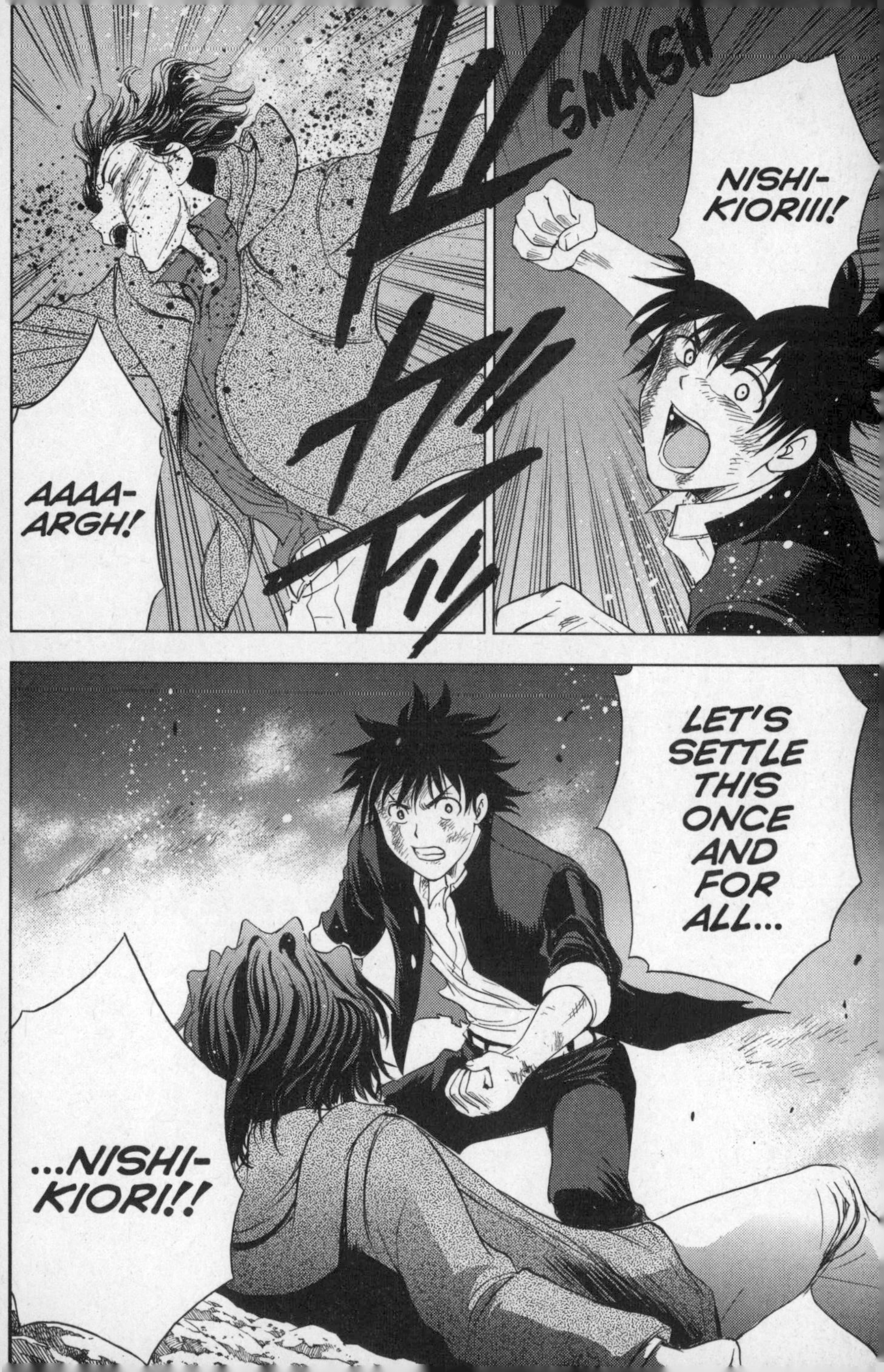
SMASH
NISHI-KIORIII!
AAAA-ARGH!
LET'S SETTLE THIS ONCE AND FOR ALL...
...NISHI-KIORI!!

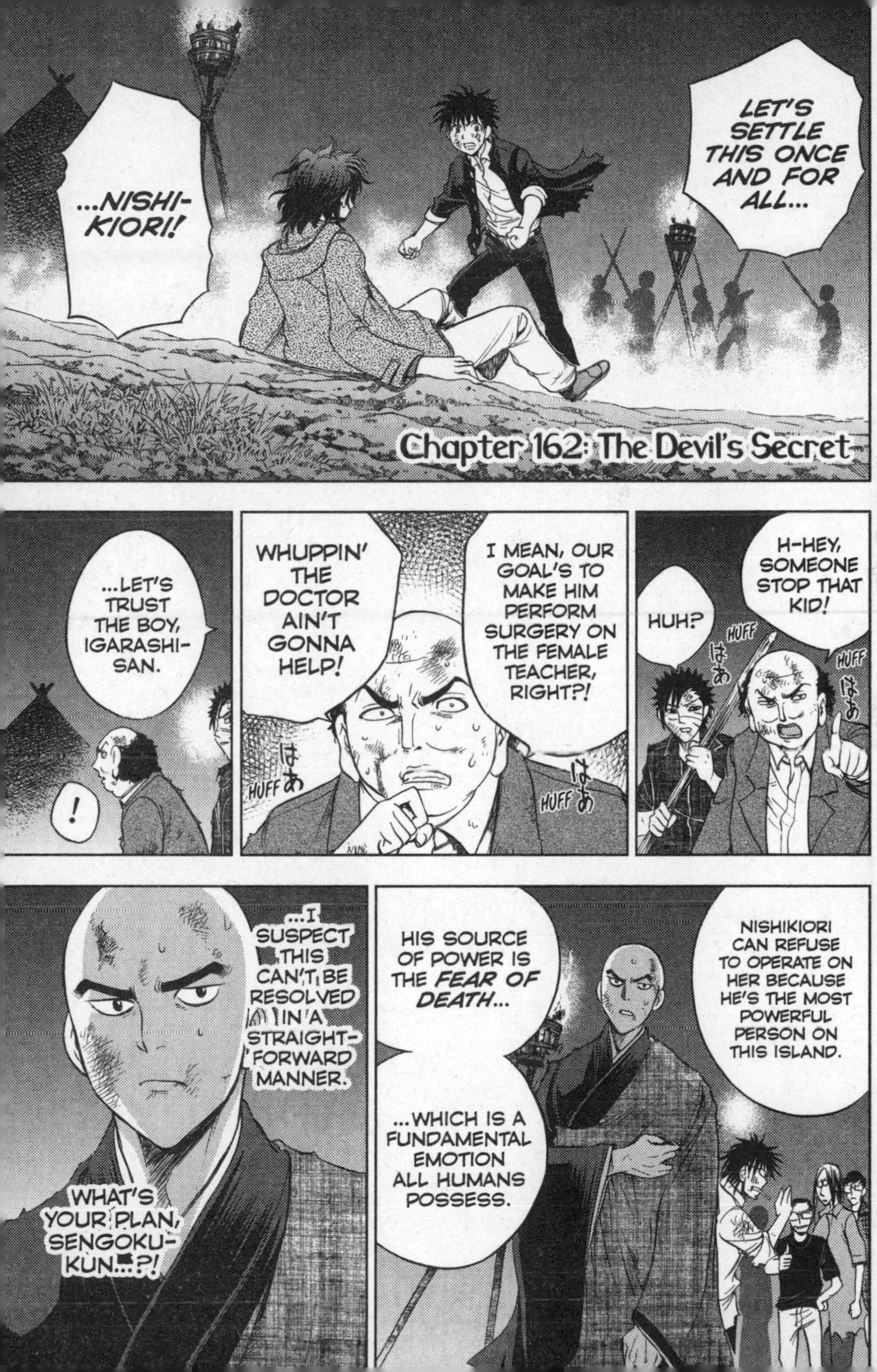
LET'S SETTLE THIS ONCE AND FOR ALL...
...NISHIKIORI!
Chapter 162: The Devil's Secret
H-HEY, SOMEONE STOP THAT KID!
HUFF はあ
HUH?
HUFF はあ
I MEAN, OUR GOAL'S TO MAKE HIM PERFORM SURGERY ON THE FEMALE TEACHER, RIGHT?!
WHUPPIN' THE DOCTOR AIN'T GONNA HELP!
HUFF はあ
HUFF はあ
...LET'S TRUST THE BOY, IGARASHI-SAN.
!
NISHIKIORI CAN REFUSE TO OPERATE ON HER BECAUSE HE'S THE MOST POWERFUL PERSON ON THIS ISLAND.
HIS SOURCE OF POWER IS THE FEAR OF DEATH...
...WHICH IS A FUNDAMENTAL EMOTION ALL HUMANS POSSESS.
...I SUSPECT THIS CAN'T BE RESOLVED IN A STRAIGHTFORWARD MANNER.
WHAT'S YOUR PLAN, SENGOKU-KUN...?!

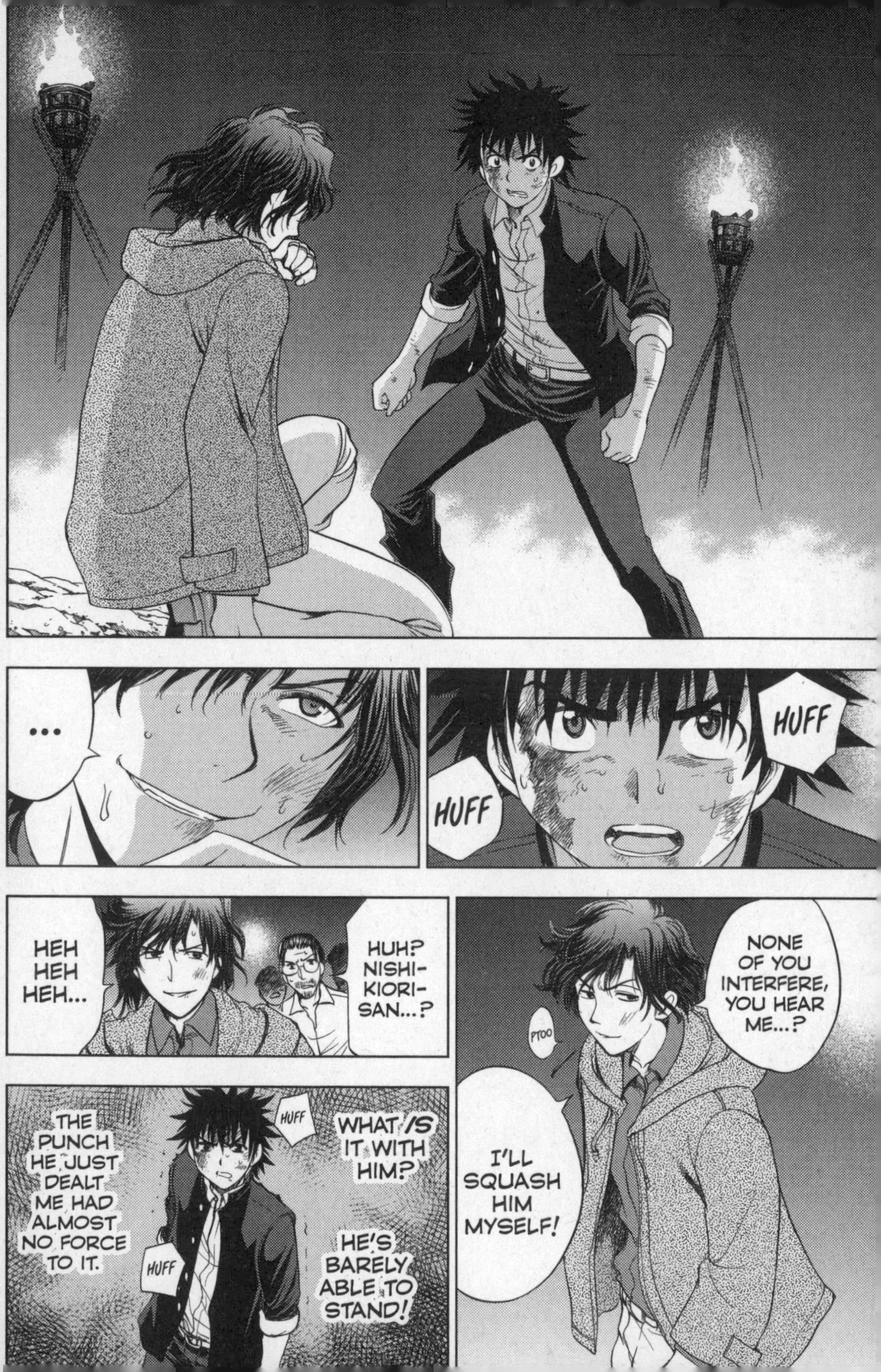
HUFF
HUFF
...
NONE OF YOU INTERFERE, YOU HEAR ME...?
PTOO
I'LL SQUASH HIM MYSELF!
HUH? NISHIKIORI-SAN...?
HEH HEH HEH...
HUFF
WHAT IS IT WITH HIM?
HE'S BARELY ABLE TO STAND!
THE PUNCH HE JUST DEALT ME HAD ALMOST NO FORCE TO IT.
HUFF

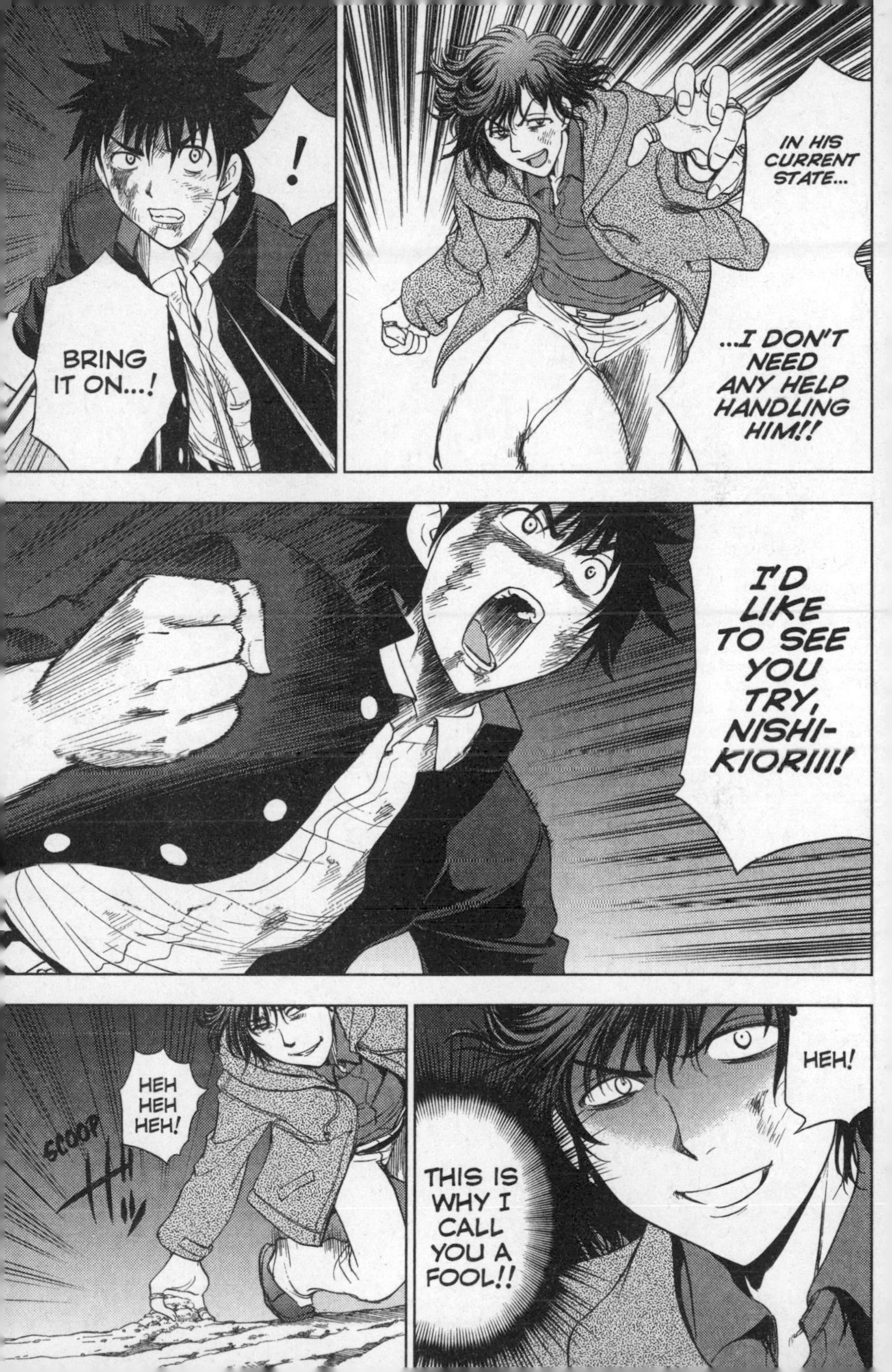
IN HIS CURRENT STATE...
...I DON'T NEED ANY HELP HANDLING HIM!!
!
BRING IT ON...!
I'D LIKE TO SEE YOU TRY, NISHI-KIORIII!
HEH!
THIS IS WHY I CALL YOU A FOOL!!
HEH HEH HEH!
SCOOP

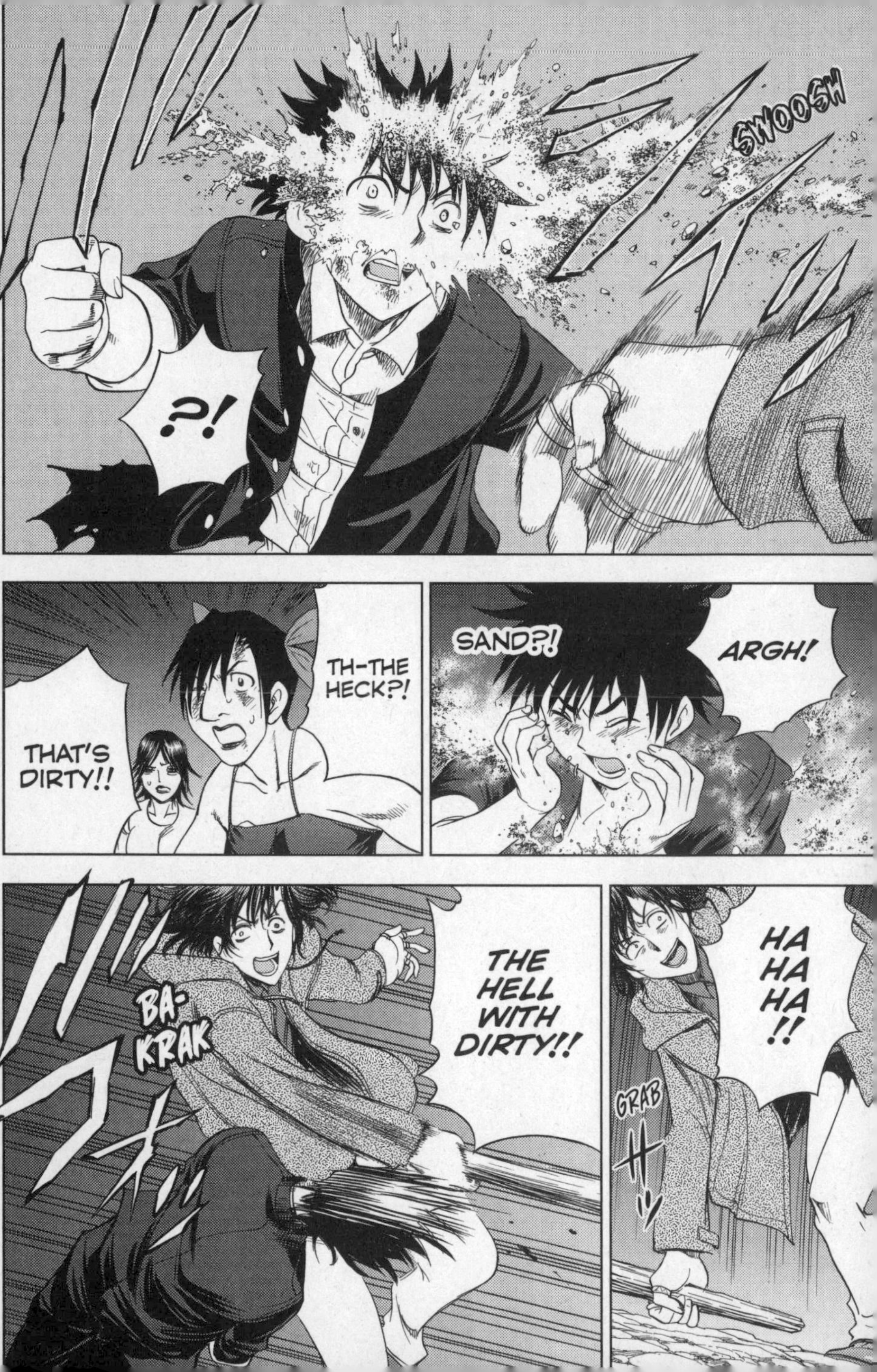
SWOOSH
?!
ARGH!
SAND?!
TH-THE HECK?!
THAT'S DIRTY!!
HA HA HA!!
GRAB
THE HELL WITH DIRTY!!
BA-KRAK

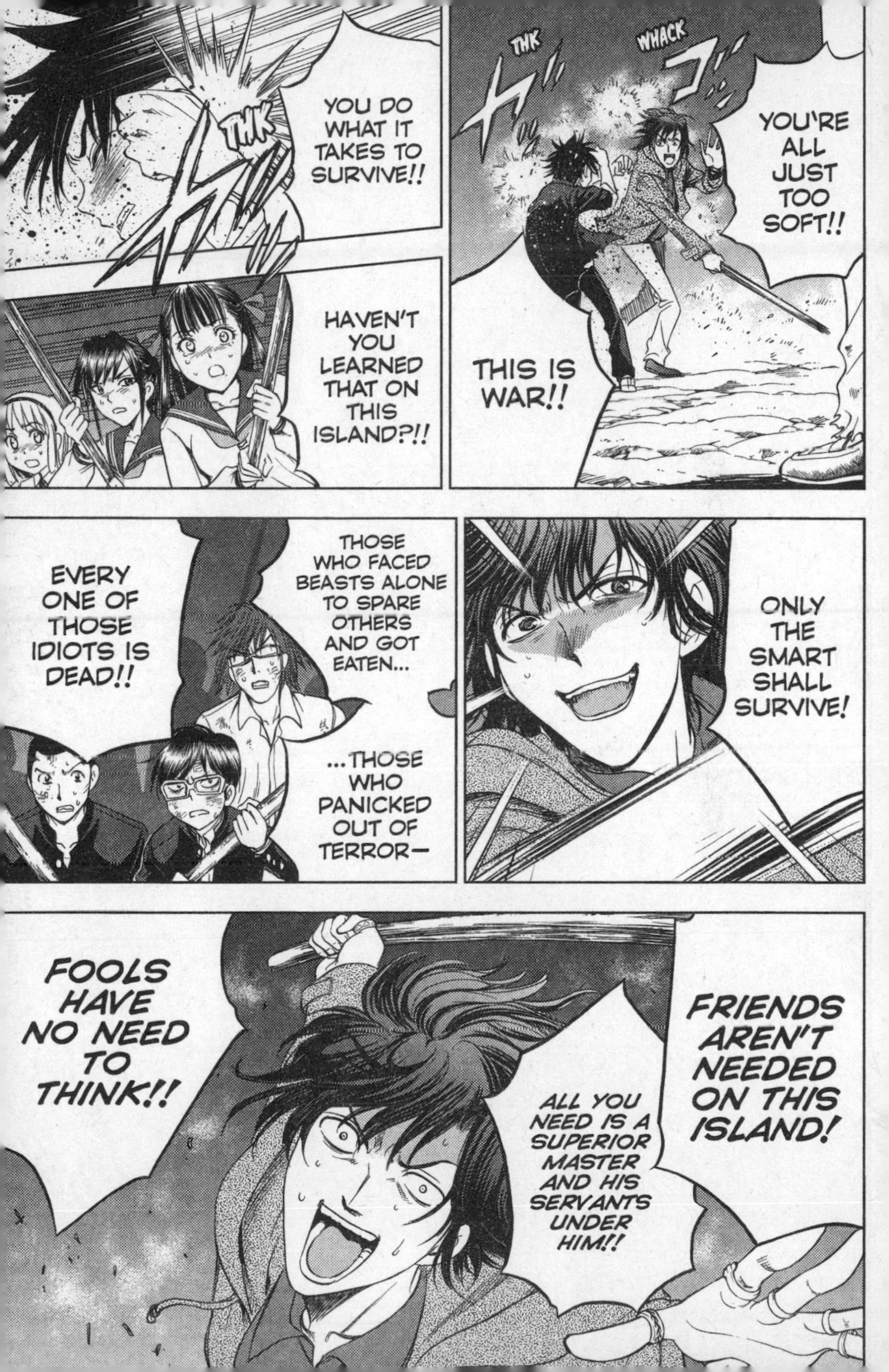
THK
WHACK
YOU'RE ALL JUST TOO SOFT!!
THIS IS WAR!!
YOU DO WHAT IT TAKES TO SURVIVE!!
THK
HAVEN'T YOU LEARNED THAT ON THIS ISLAND?!!
ONLY THE SMART SHALL SURVIVE!
THOSE WHO FACED BEASTS ALONE TO SPARE OTHERS AND GOT EATEN...
...THOSE WHO PANICKED OUT OF TERROR—
EVERY ONE OF THOSE IDIOTS IS DEAD!!
FRIENDS AREN'T NEEDED ON THIS ISLAND!
ALL YOU NEED IS A SUPERIOR MASTER AND HIS SERVANTS UNDER HIM!!
FOOLS HAVE NO NEED TO THINK!!

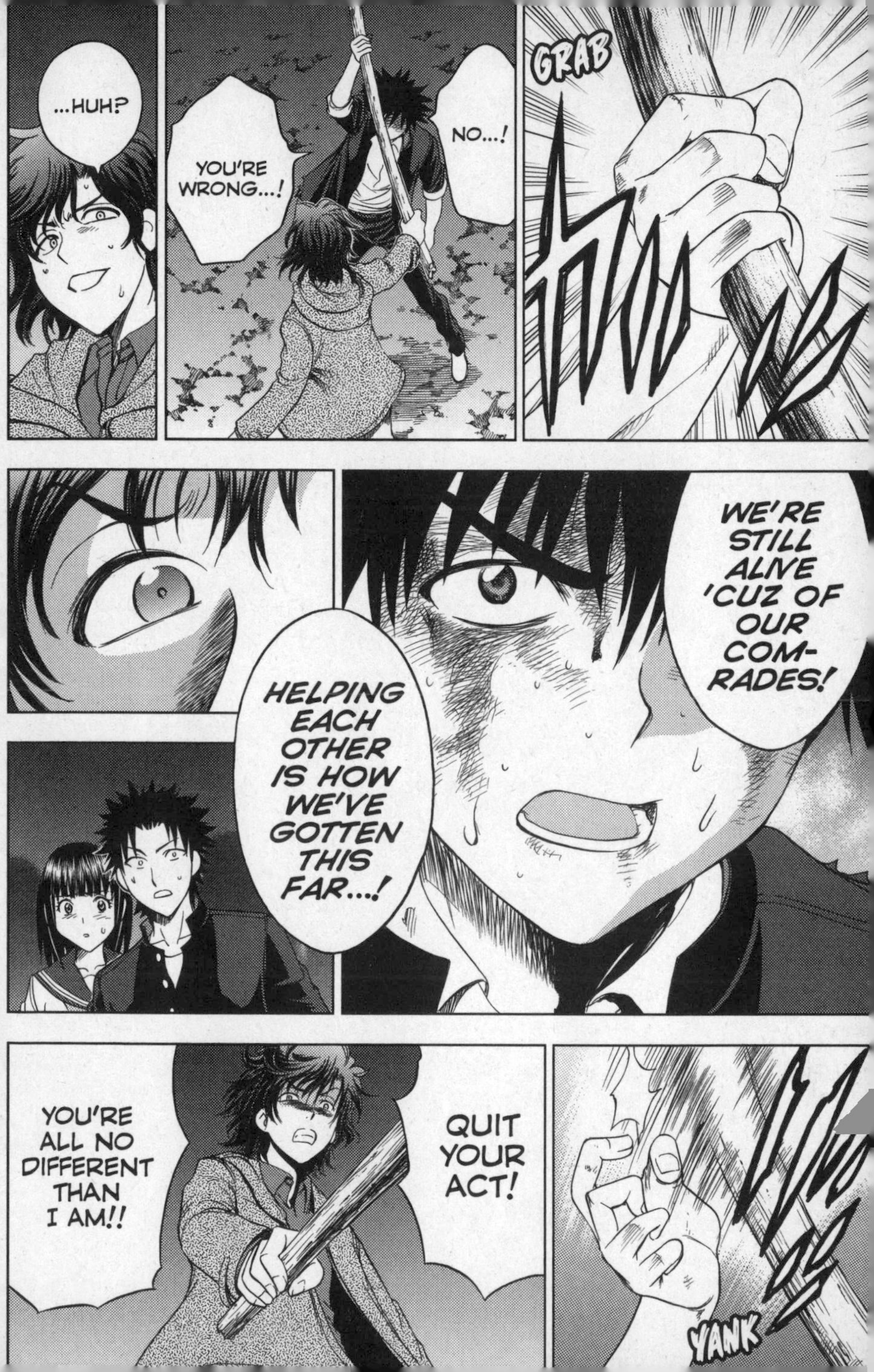
GRAB
NO...!
YOU'RE WRONG...!
...HUH?
WE'RE STILL ALIVE 'CUZ OF OUR COM-RADES!
HELPING EACH OTHER IS HOW WE'VE GOTTEN THIS FAR...!
YANK
QUIT YOUR ACT!
YOU'RE ALL NO DIFFERENT THAN I AM!!

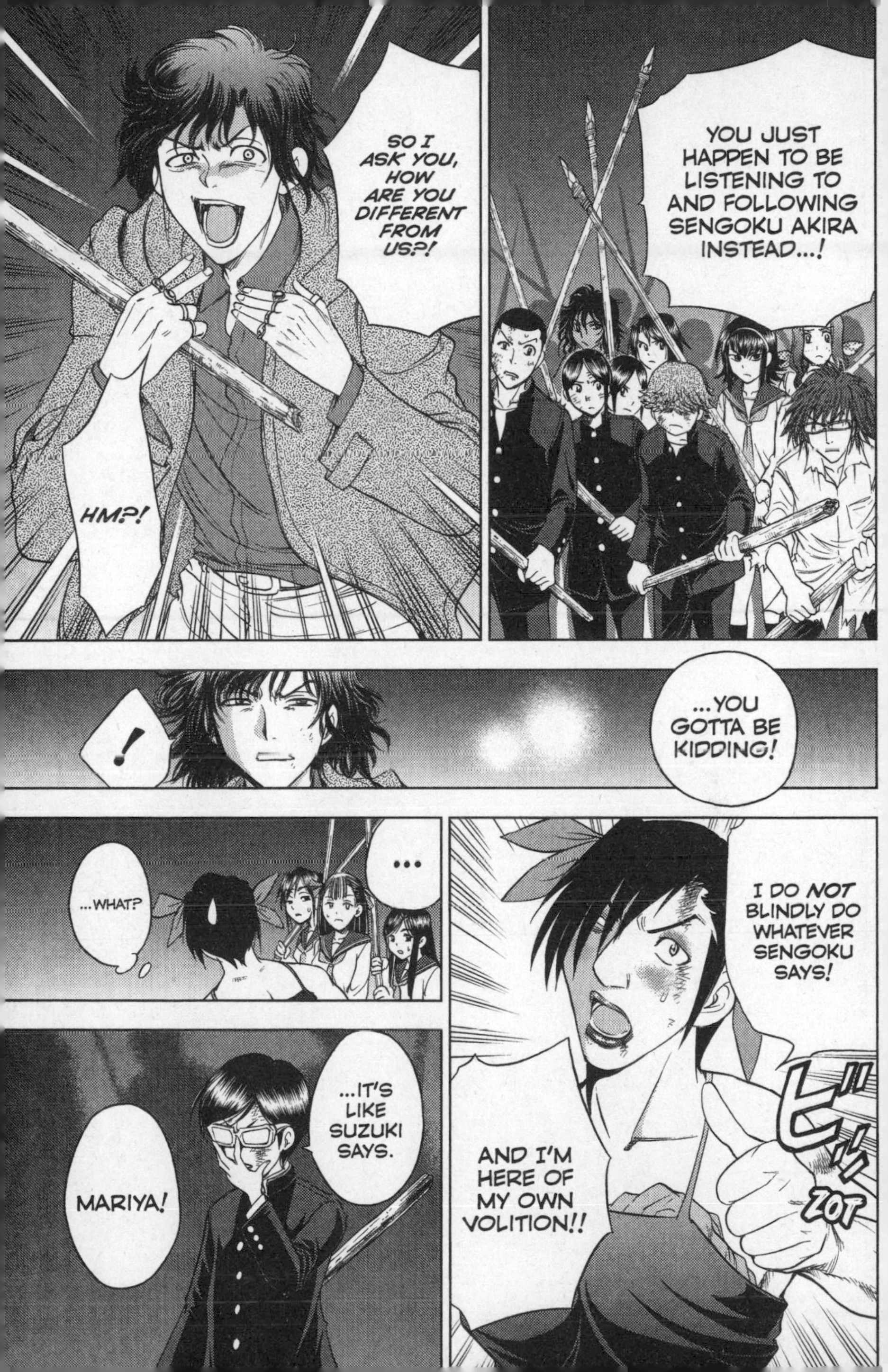
YOU JUST HAPPEN TO BE LISTENING TO AND FOLLOWING SENGOKU AKIRA INSTEAD...!
SO I ASK YOU, HOW ARE YOU DIFFERENT FROM US?!
HM?!
...YOU GOTTA BE KIDDING!
!
I DO *NOT* BLINDLY DO WHATEVER SENGOKU SAYS!
AND I'M HERE OF MY OWN VOLITION!!
ZOT
...
...WHAT?
...IT'S LIKE SUZUKI SAYS.
MARIYA!

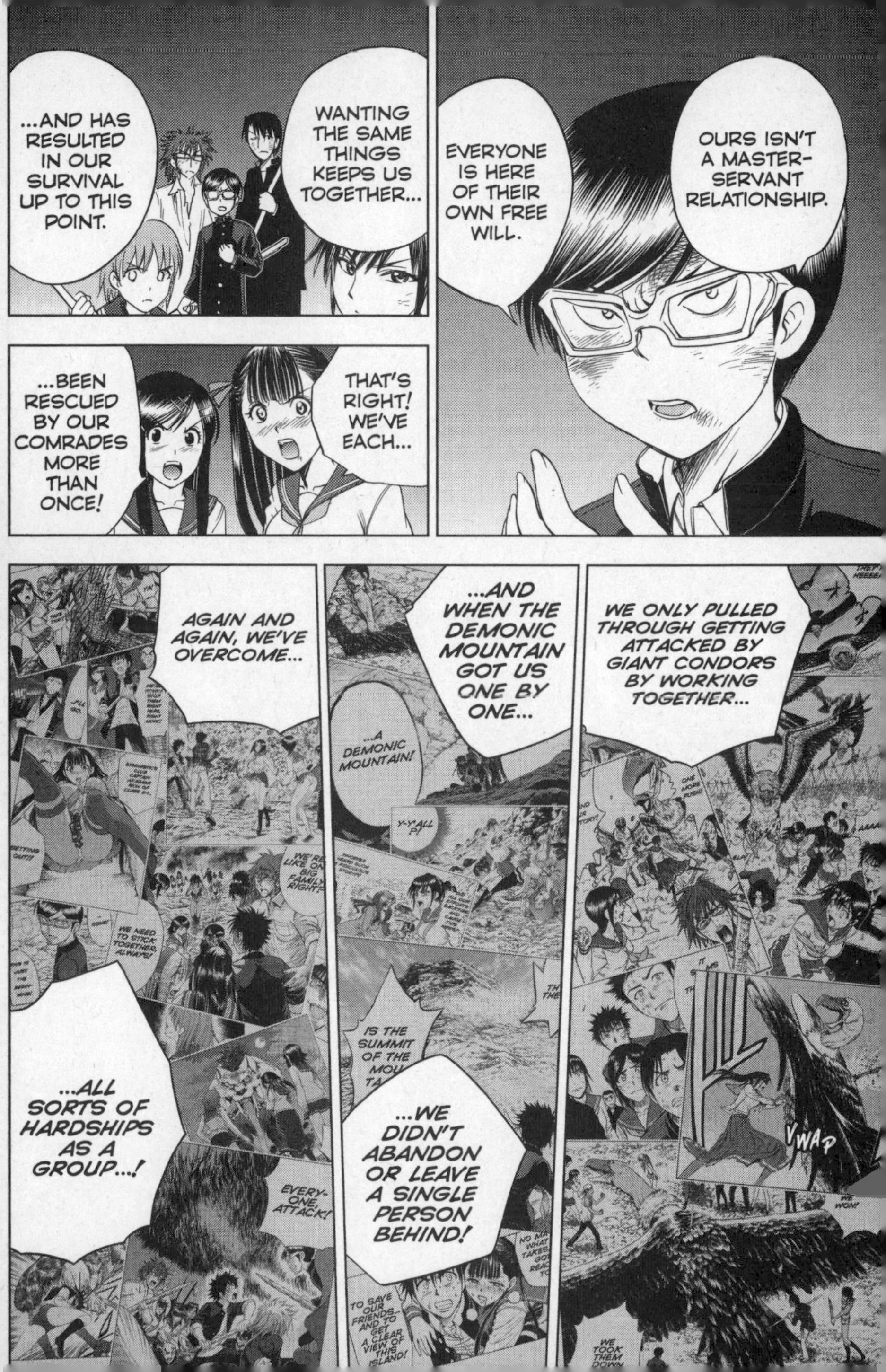
OURS ISN'T A MASTER-SERVANT RELATIONSHIP.
EVERYONE IS HERE OF THEIR OWN FREE WILL.
WANTING THE SAME THINGS KEEPS US TOGETHER...
...AND HAS RESULTED IN OUR SURVIVAL UP TO THIS POINT.
THAT'S RIGHT! WE'VE EACH...
...BEEN RESCUED BY OUR COMRADES MORE THAN ONCE!
WE ONLY PULLED THROUGH GETTING ATTACKED BY GIANT CONDORS BY WORKING TOGETHER...
VWAP
WE WON!
WE TOOK THEM DOWN
...AND WHEN THE DEMONIC MOUNTAIN GOT US ONE BY ONE...
...A DEMONIC MOUNTAIN!
...WE DIDN'T ABANDON OR LEAVE A SINGLE PERSON BEHIND!
TO SAVE OUR FRIENDS... AND TO GET A CLEAR VIEW OF THIS ISLAND!
AGAIN AND AGAIN, WE'VE OVERCOME...
WE NEED TO STICK TOGETHER, ALWAYS!
...ALL SORTS OF HARDSHIPS AS A GROUP...!
EVERY-ONE, ATTACK!

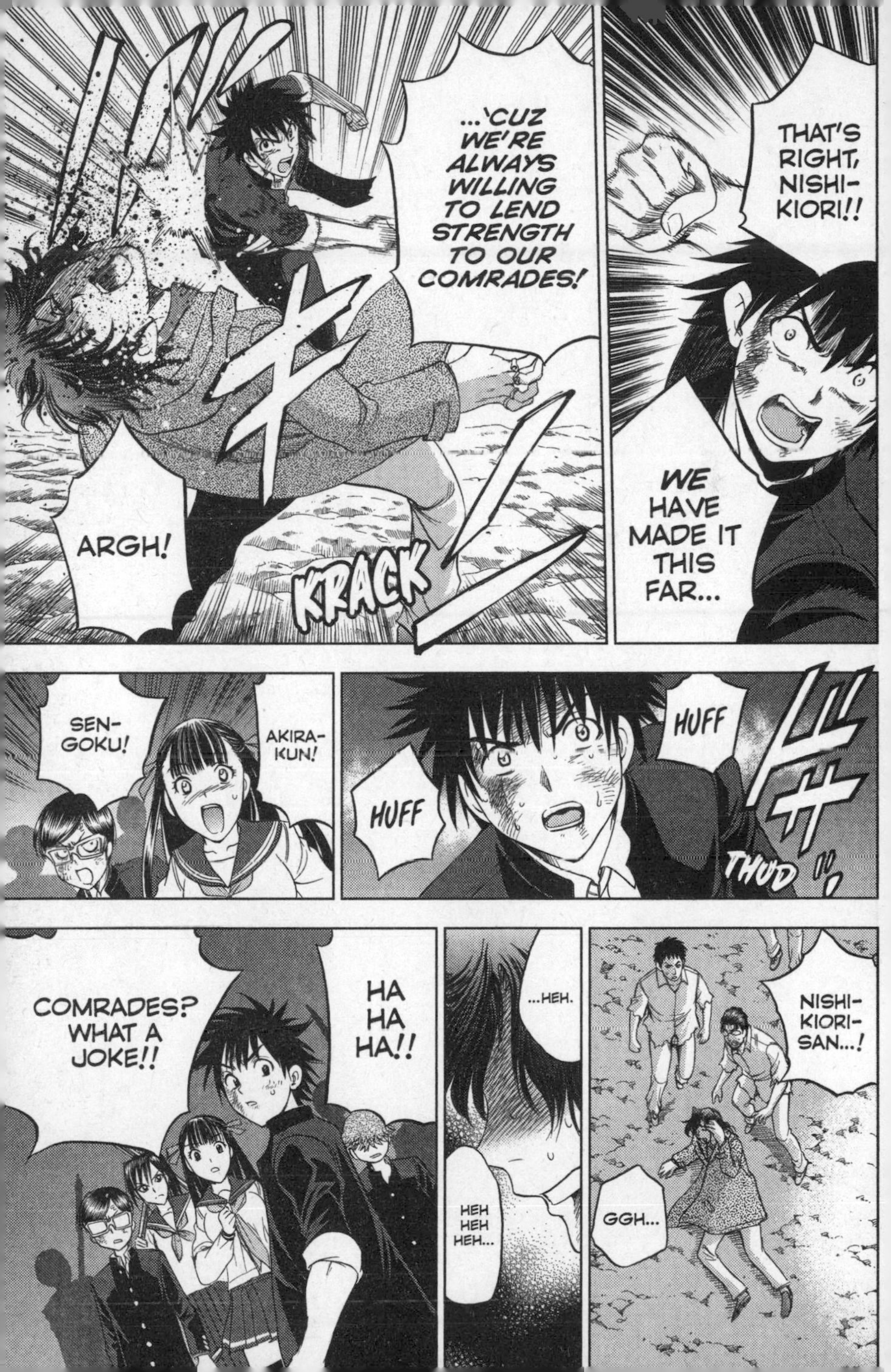
THAT'S RIGHT, NISHI-KIORI!!
WE HAVE MADE IT THIS FAR...
...'CUZ WE'RE ALWAYS WILLING TO LEND STRENGTH TO OUR COMRADES!
ARGH!
KRACK
HUFF
HUFF
THUD
AKIRA-KUN!
SEN-GOKU!
NISHI-KIORI-SAN...!
GGH...
...HEH.
HEH HEH HEH...
HA HA HA!!
COMRADES? WHAT A JOKE!!

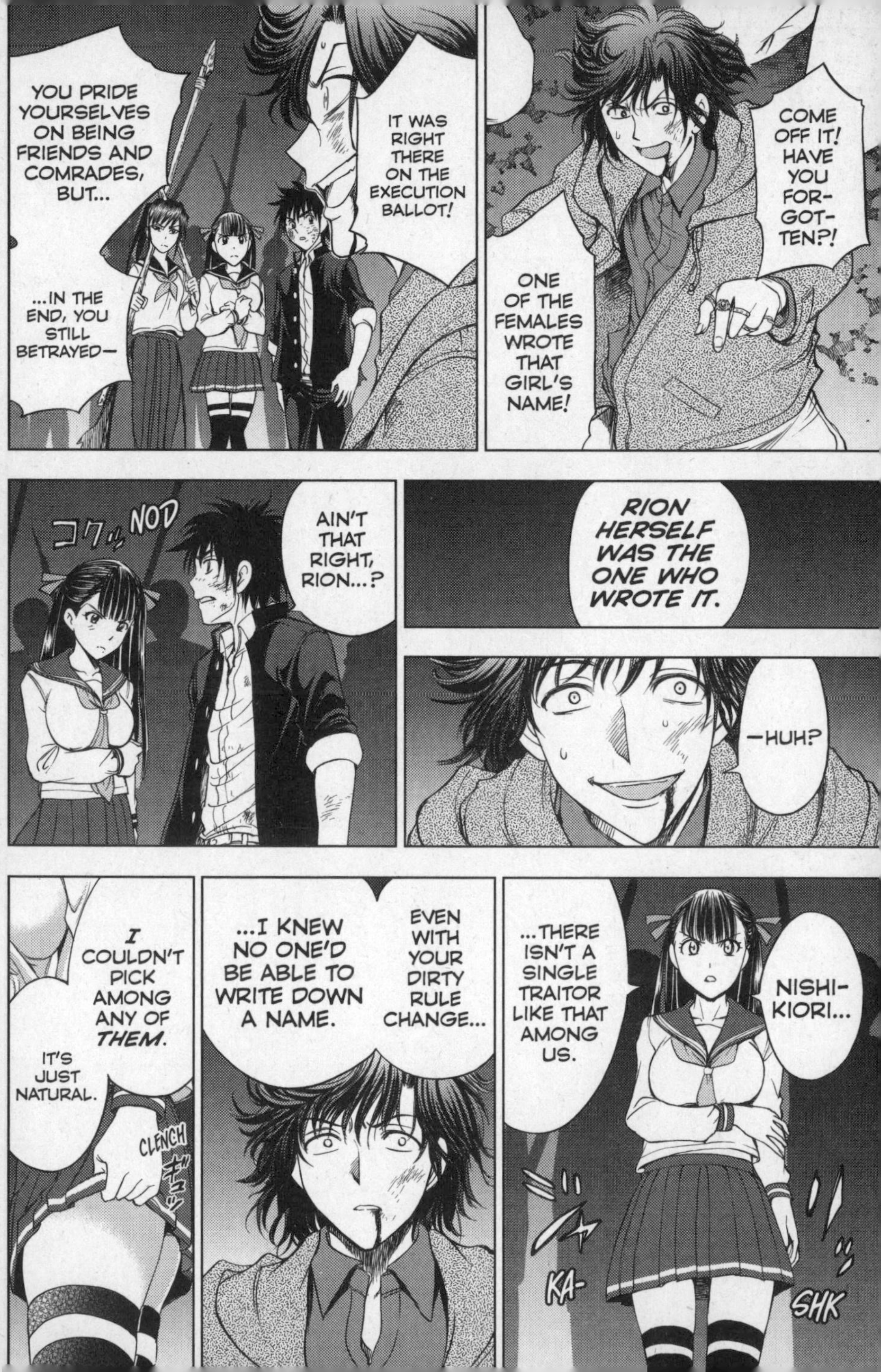
COME OFF IT! HAVE YOU FORGOTTEN?!
ONE OF THE FEMALES WROTE THAT GIRL'S NAME!
IT WAS RIGHT THERE ON THE EXECUTION BALLOT!
YOU PRIDE YOURSELVES ON BEING FRIENDS AND COMRADES, BUT...
...IN THE END, YOU STILL BETRAYED—
RION HERSELF WAS THE ONE WHO WROTE IT.
—HUH?
AIN'T THAT RIGHT, RION...?
コクッ NOD
NISHIKIORI...
...THERE ISN'T A SINGLE TRAITOR LIKE THAT AMONG US.
KA-SHK
EVEN WITH YOUR DIRTY RULE CHANGE...
...I KNEW NO ONE'D BE ABLE TO WRITE DOWN A NAME.
I COULDN'T PICK AMONG ANY OF *THEM*.
IT'S JUST NATURAL.
CLENCH ギュッ

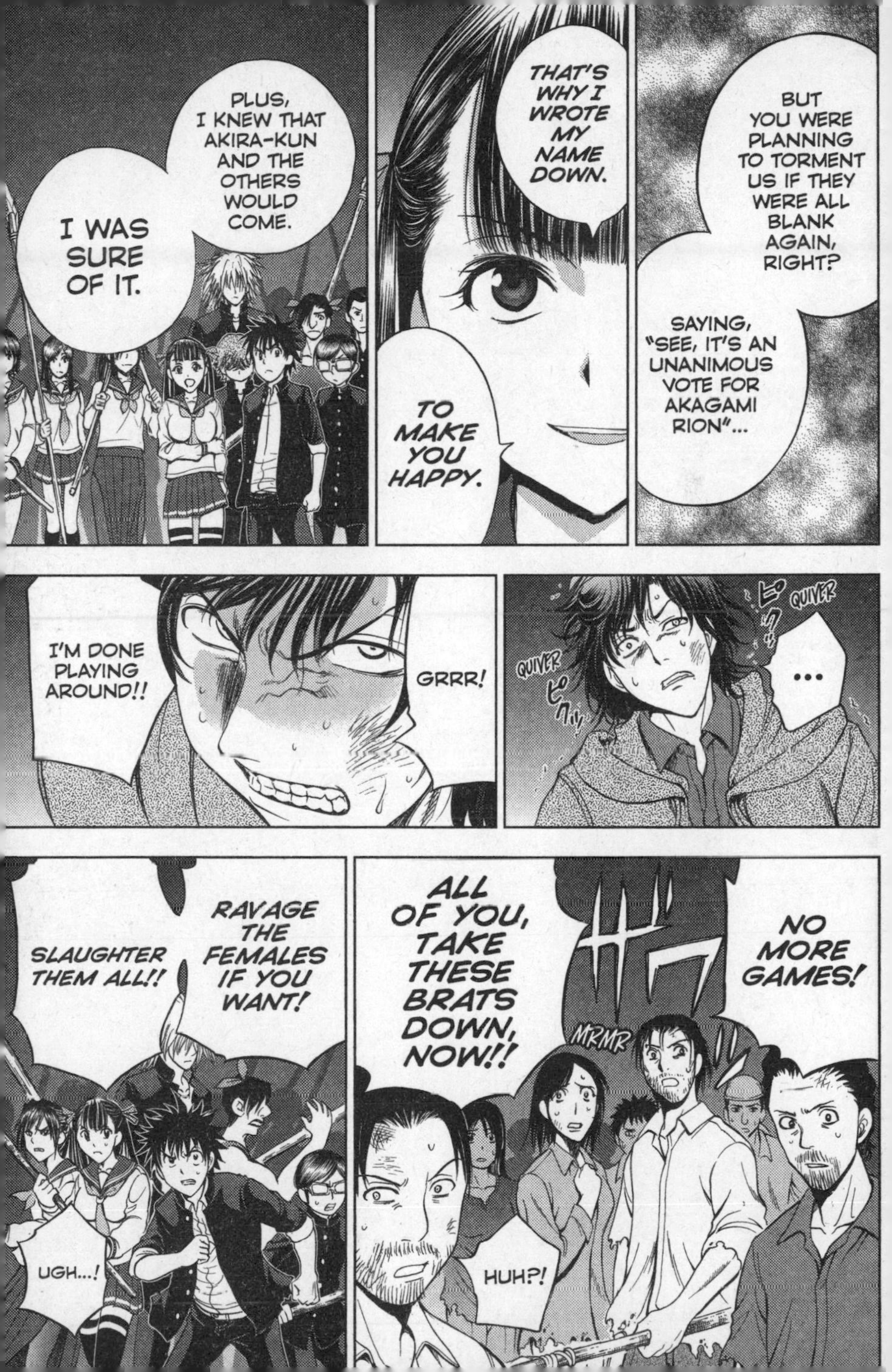
BUT YOU WERE PLANNING TO TORMENT US IF THEY WERE ALL BLANK AGAIN, RIGHT?
SAYING, "SEE, IT'S AN UNANIMOUS VOTE FOR AKAGAMI RION"...
THAT'S WHY I WROTE MY NAME DOWN.
TO MAKE YOU HAPPY.
PLUS, I KNEW THAT AKIRA-KUN AND THE OTHERS WOULD COME.
I WAS SURE OF IT.
QUIVER
...
QUIVER
GRRR!
I'M DONE PLAYING AROUND!!
NO MORE GAMES!
ALL OF YOU, TAKE THESE BRATS DOWN, NOW!!
MRMR
HUH?!
RAVAGE THE FEMALES IF YOU WANT!
SLAUGHTER THEM ALL!!
UGH...!

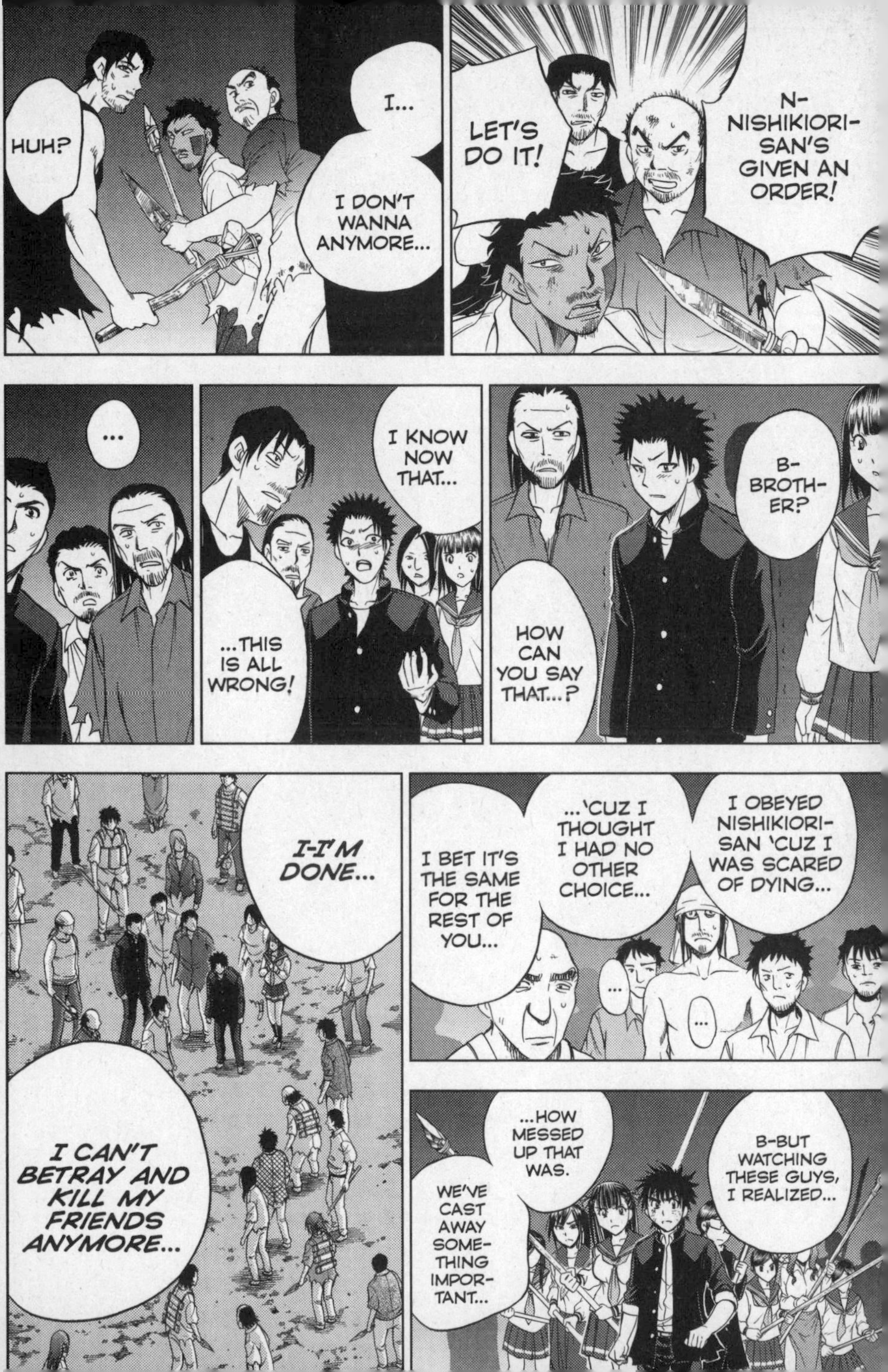

N-NISHIKIORI-SAN'S GIVEN AN ORDER!
LET'S DO IT!
I...
I DON'T WANNA ANYMORE...
HUH?
B-BROTHER?
HOW CAN YOU SAY THAT...?
I KNOW NOW THAT...
...THIS IS ALL WRONG!
...
I OBEYED NISHIKIORI-SAN 'CUZ I WAS SCARED OF DYING...
...'CUZ I THOUGHT I HAD NO OTHER CHOICE...
I BET IT'S THE SAME FOR THE REST OF YOU...
...
...
B-BUT WATCHING THESE GUYS, I REALIZED...
...HOW MESSED UP THAT WAS.
WE'VE CAST AWAY SOME-THING IMPOR-TANT...
I-I'M DONE...
I CAN'T BETRAY AND KILL MY FRIENDS ANYMORE...

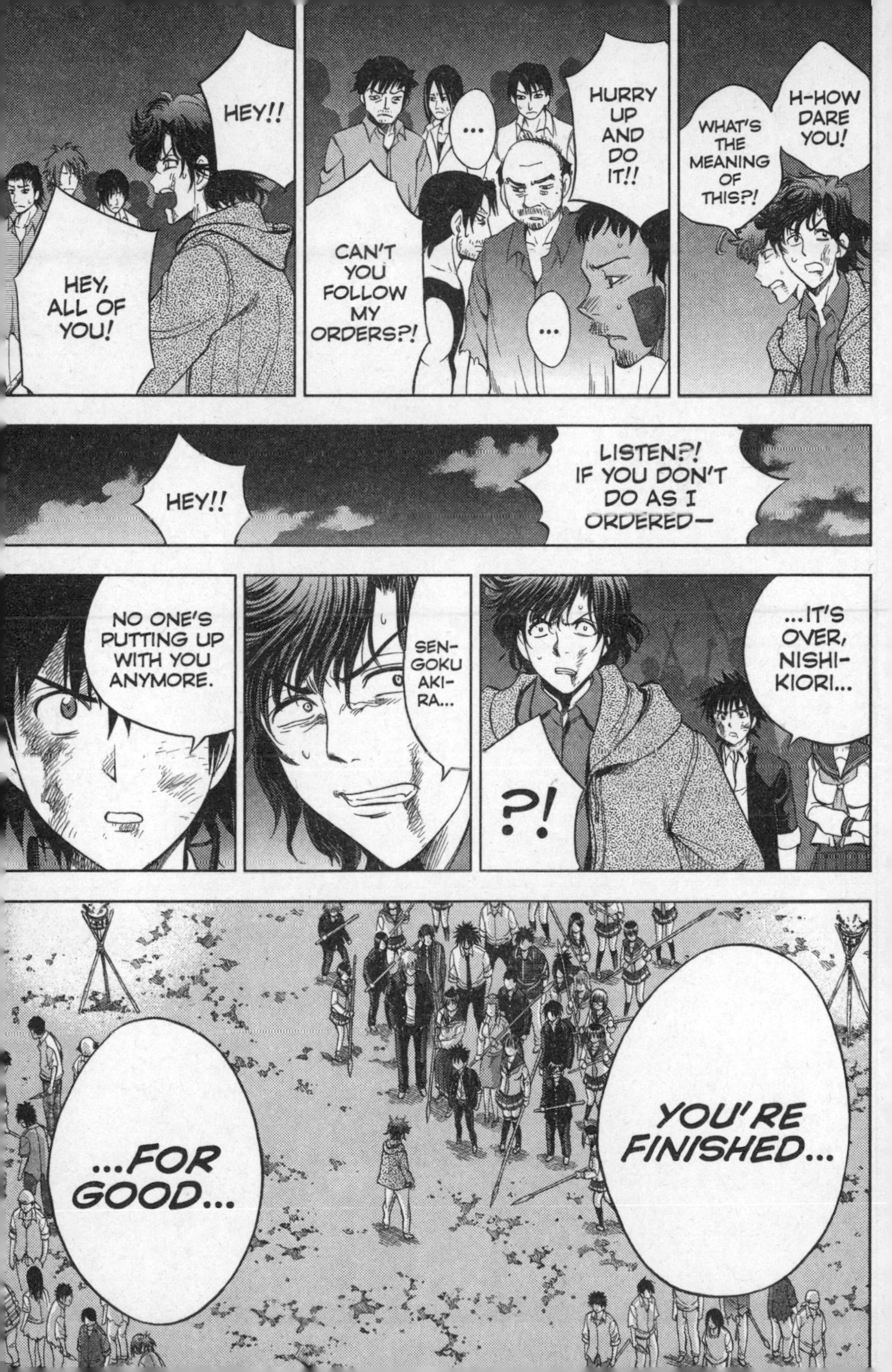
H-HOW DARE YOU!
WHAT'S THE MEANING OF THIS?!
HURRY UP AND DO IT!!
...
CAN'T YOU FOLLOW MY ORDERS?!
...
HEY!!
HEY, ALL OF YOU!
LISTEN?! IF YOU DON'T DO AS I ORDERED—
HEY!!
...IT'S OVER, NISHIKIORI...
?!
SENGOKU AKIRA...
NO ONE'S PUTTING UP WITH YOU ANYMORE.
YOU'RE FINISHED...
...FOR GOOD...

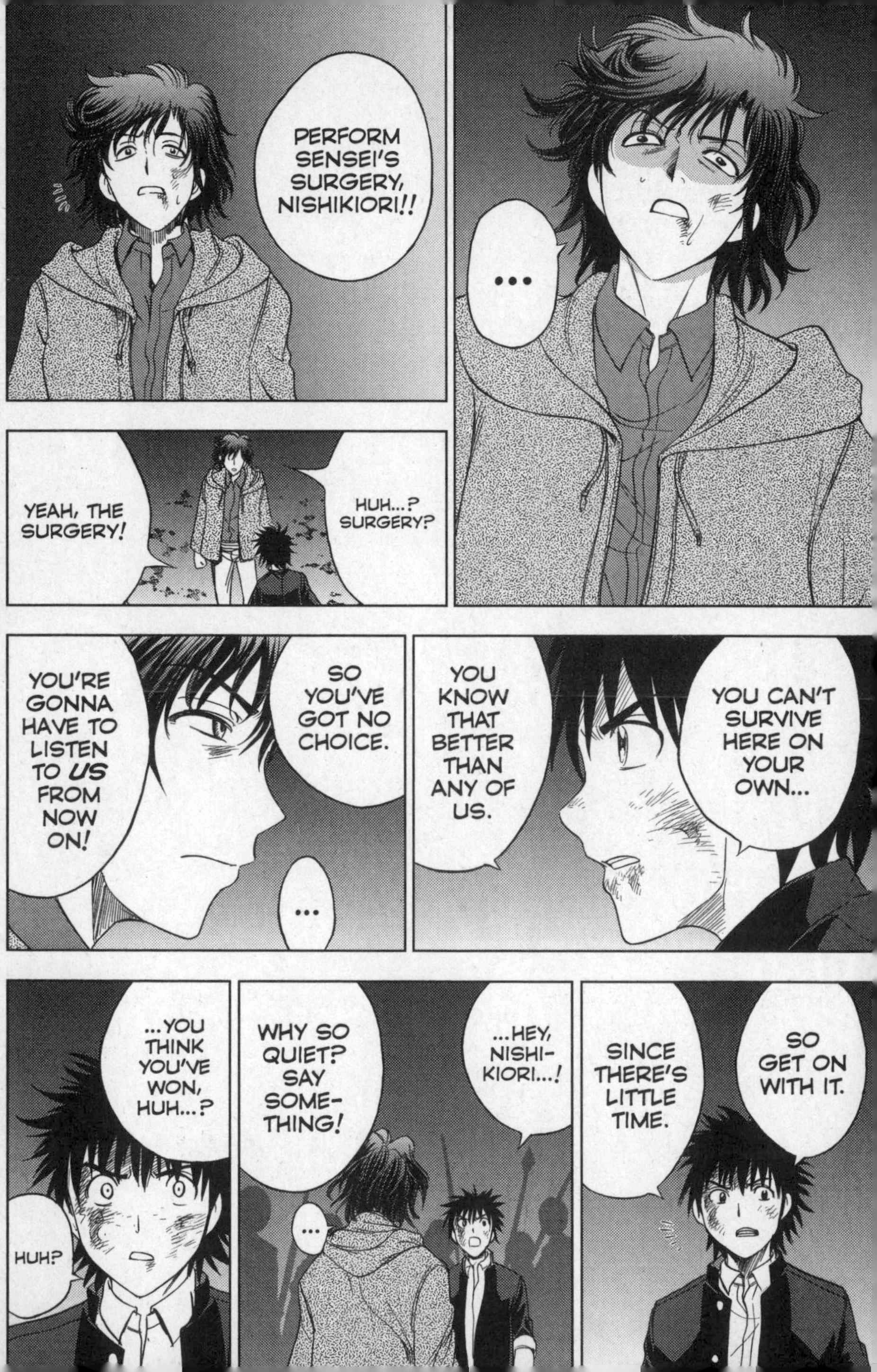
...
PERFORM SENSEI'S SURGERY, NISHIKIORI!!
HUH...? SURGERY?
YEAH, THE SURGERY!
YOU CAN'T SURVIVE HERE ON YOUR OWN...
YOU KNOW THAT BETTER THAN ANY OF US.
SO YOU'VE GOT NO CHOICE.
YOU'RE GONNA HAVE TO LISTEN TO *US* FROM NOW ON!
...
SO GET ON WITH IT.
SINCE THERE'S LITTLE TIME.
...HEY, NISHI-KIORI...!
WHY SO QUIET? SAY SOME-THING!
...
...YOU THINK YOU'VE WON, HUH...?
HUH?

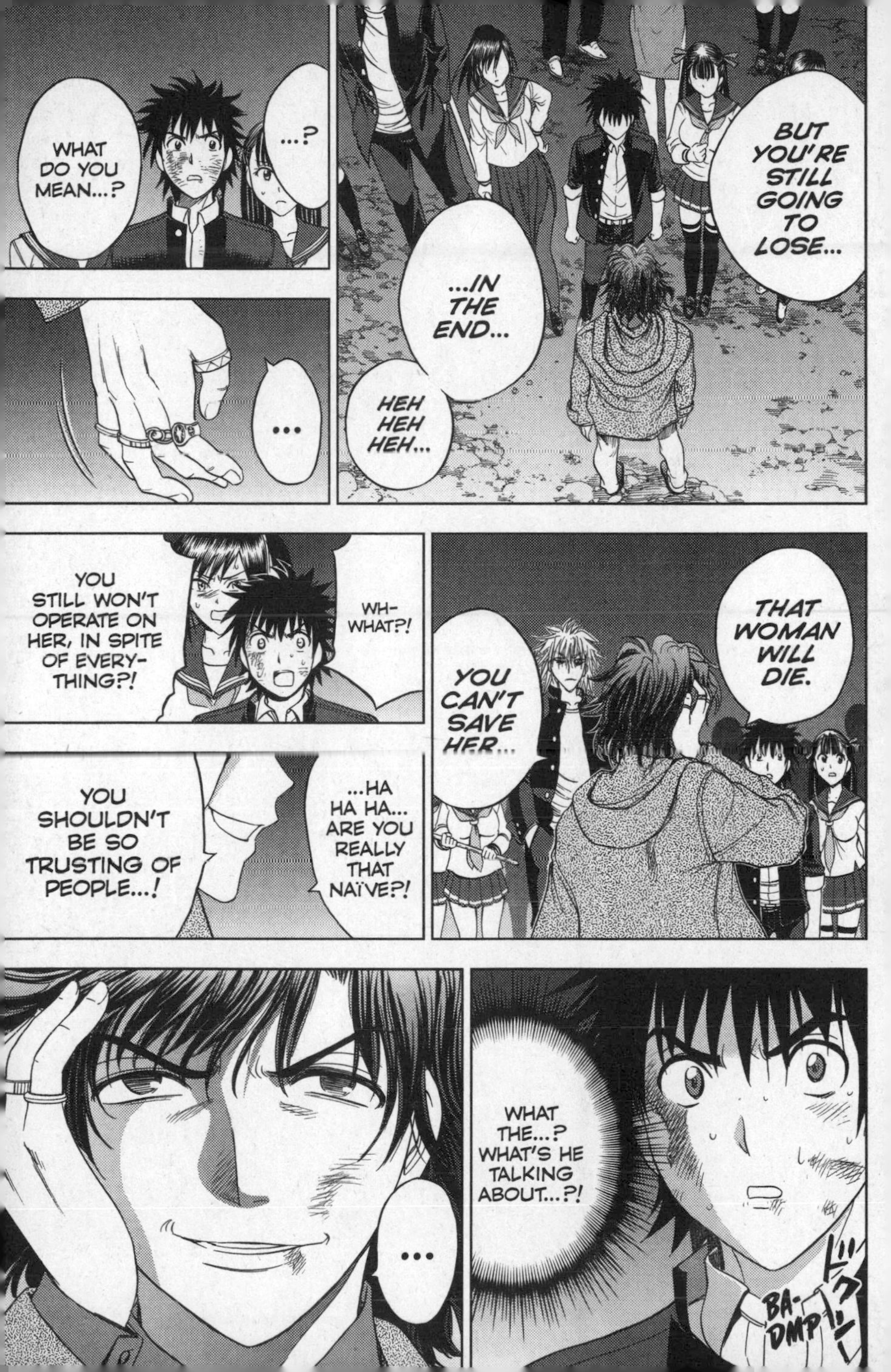
BUT YOU'RE STILL GOING TO LOSE...
...IN THE END...
HEH HEH HEH...
...?
WHAT DO YOU MEAN...?
...
THAT WOMAN WILL DIE.
YOU CAN'T SAVE HER...
WH- WHAT?!
YOU STILL WON'T OPERATE ON HER, IN SPITE OF EVERY-THING?!
...HA HA HA... ARE YOU REALLY THAT NAÏVE?!
YOU SHOULDN'T BE SO TRUSTING OF PEOPLE...!
WHAT THE...? WHAT'S HE TALKING ABOUT...?!
BA-DMP
...

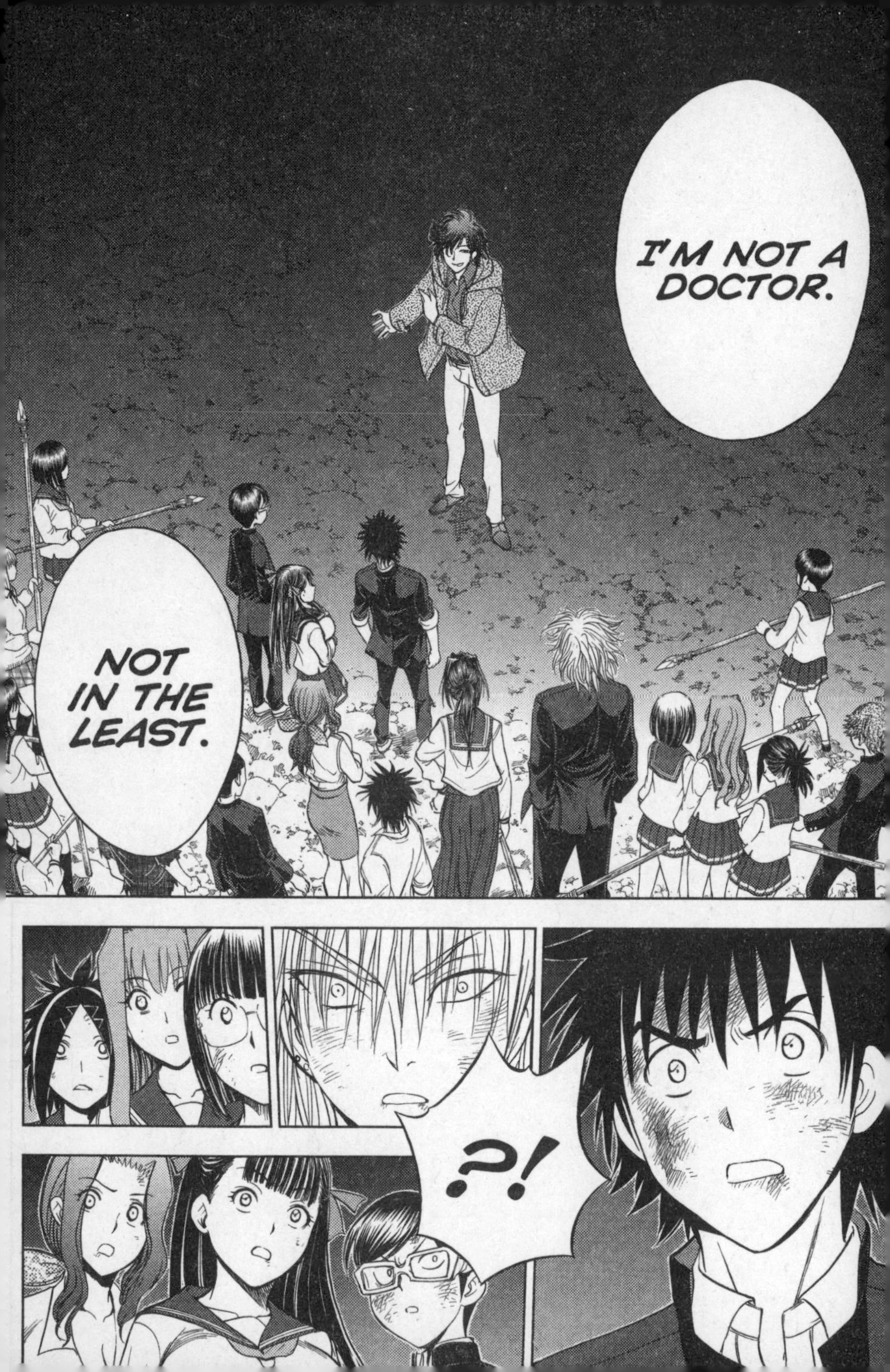
I'M NOT A DOCTOR.
NOT IN THE LEAST.
?!

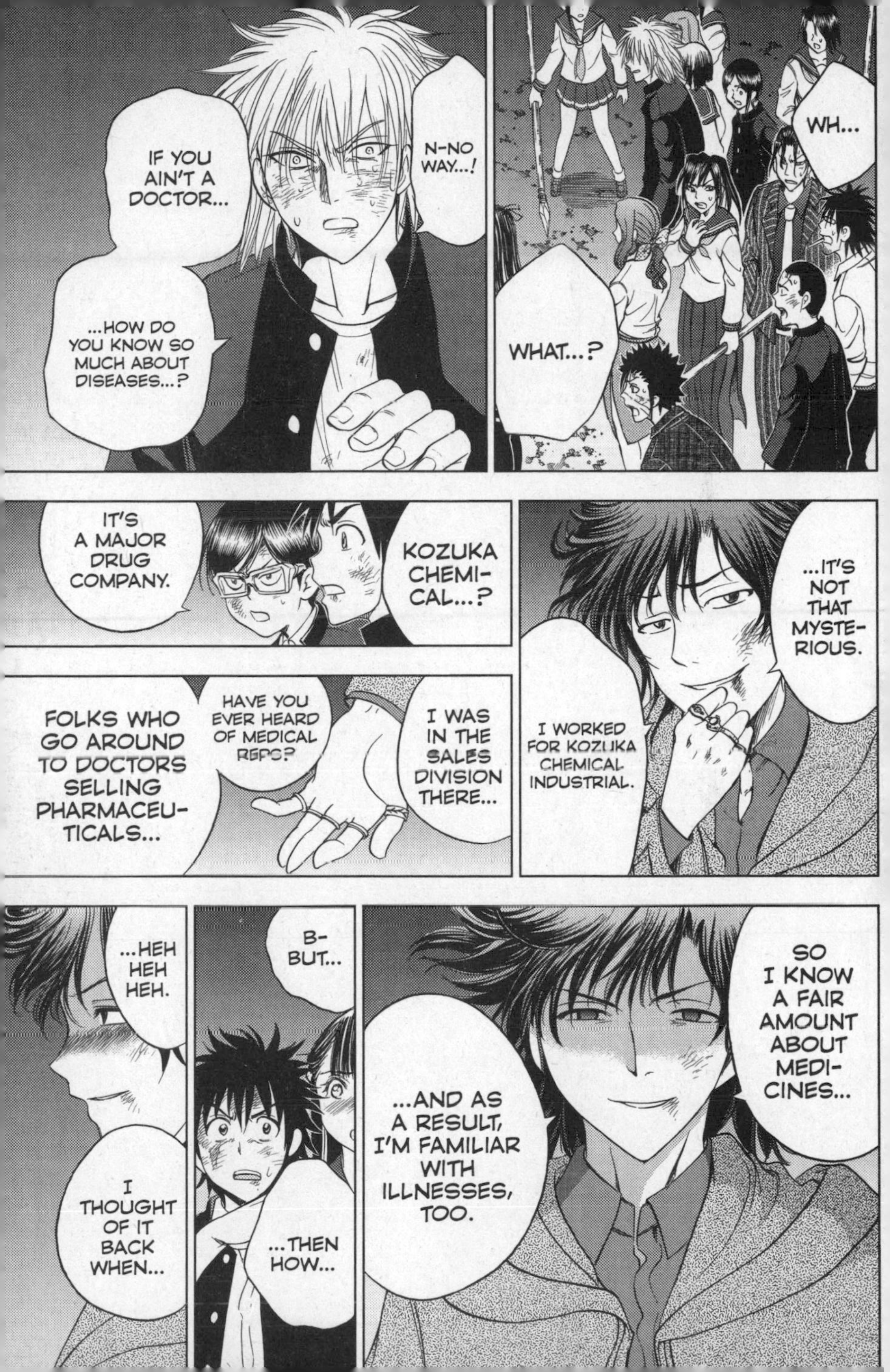
WH...
WHAT...?
N-NO WAY...!
IF YOU AIN'T A DOCTOR...
...HOW DO YOU KNOW SO MUCH ABOUT DISEASES...?
...IT'S NOT THAT MYSTERIOUS.
I WORKED FOR KOZUKA CHEMICAL INDUSTRIAL.
KOZUKA CHEMICAL...?
IT'S A MAJOR DRUG COMPANY.
I WAS IN THE SALES DIVISION THERE...
HAVE YOU EVER HEARD OF MEDICAL REPS?
FOLKS WHO GO AROUND TO DOCTORS SELLING PHARMACEUTICALS...
SO I KNOW A FAIR AMOUNT ABOUT MEDICINES...
...AND AS A RESULT, I'M FAMILIAR WITH ILLNESSES, TOO.
B-BUT...
...THEN HOW...
...HEH HEH HEH.
I THOUGHT OF IT BACK WHEN...

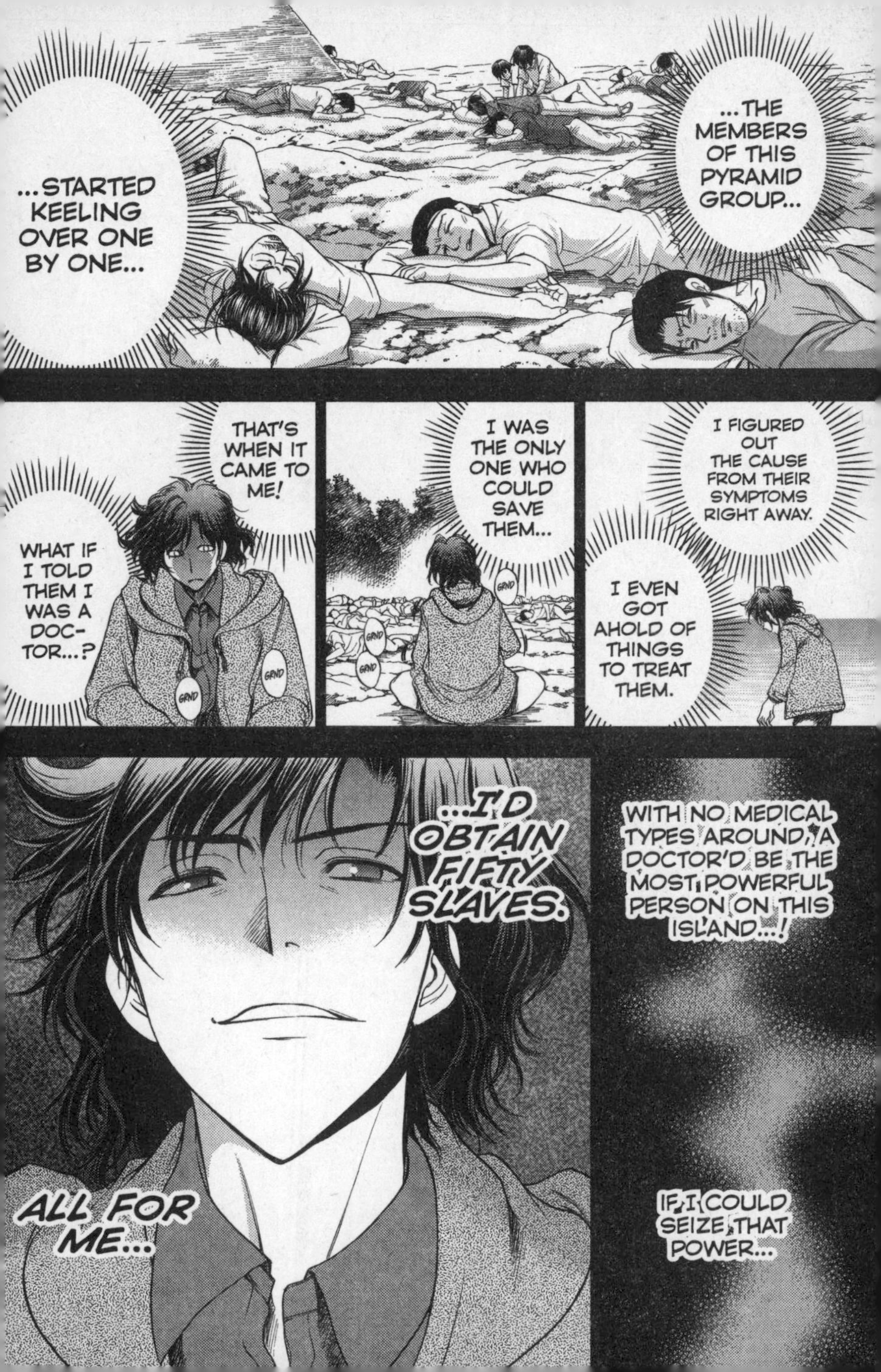
...THE MEMBERS OF THIS PYRAMID GROUP...
...STARTED KEELING OVER ONE BY ONE...
I FIGURED OUT THE CAUSE FROM THEIR SYMPTOMS RIGHT AWAY.
I EVEN GOT AHOLD OF THINGS TO TREAT THEM.
I WAS THE ONLY ONE WHO COULD SAVE THEM...
GRND
GRND
GRND
THAT'S WHEN IT CAME TO ME!
WHAT IF I TOLD THEM I WAS A DOC-TOR...?
GRND
GRND
WITH NO MEDICAL TYPES AROUND, A DOCTOR'D BE THE MOST POWERFUL PERSON ON THIS ISLAND...!
IF I COULD SEIZE THAT POWER...
...I'D OBTAIN FIFTY SLAVES.
ALL FOR ME...

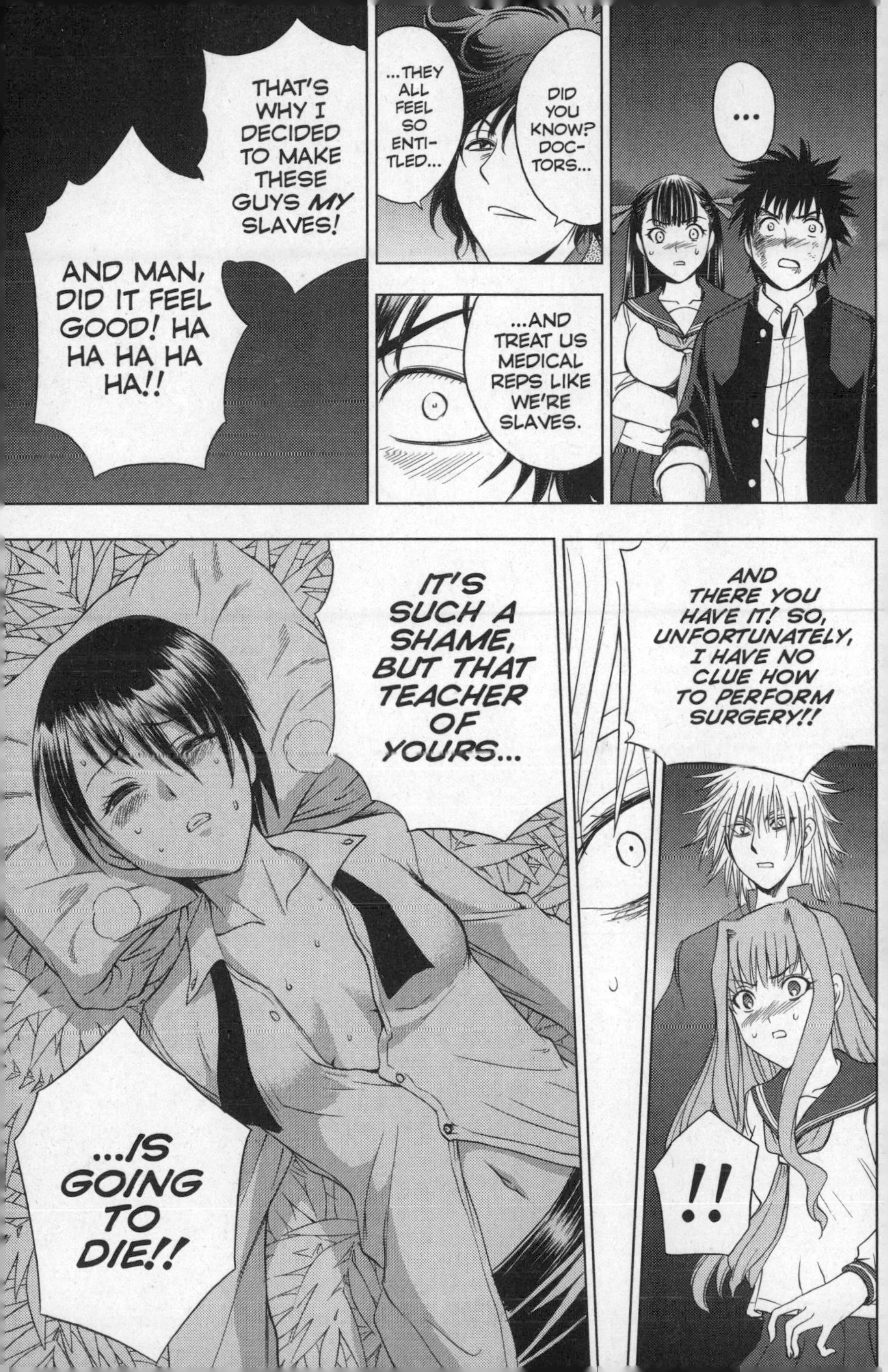
...
DID YOU KNOW? DOCTORS...
...THEY ALL FEEL SO ENTITLED...
...AND TREAT US MEDICAL REPS LIKE WE'RE SLAVES.
THAT'S WHY I DECIDED TO MAKE THESE GUYS MY SLAVES!
AND MAN, DID IT FEEL GOOD! HA HA HA HA HA HA!!
AND THERE YOU HAVE IT! SO, UNFORTUNATELY, I HAVE NO CLUE HOW TO PERFORM SURGERY!!
!!
IT'S SUCH A SHAME, BUT THAT TEACHER OF YOURS...
...IS GOING TO DIE!!

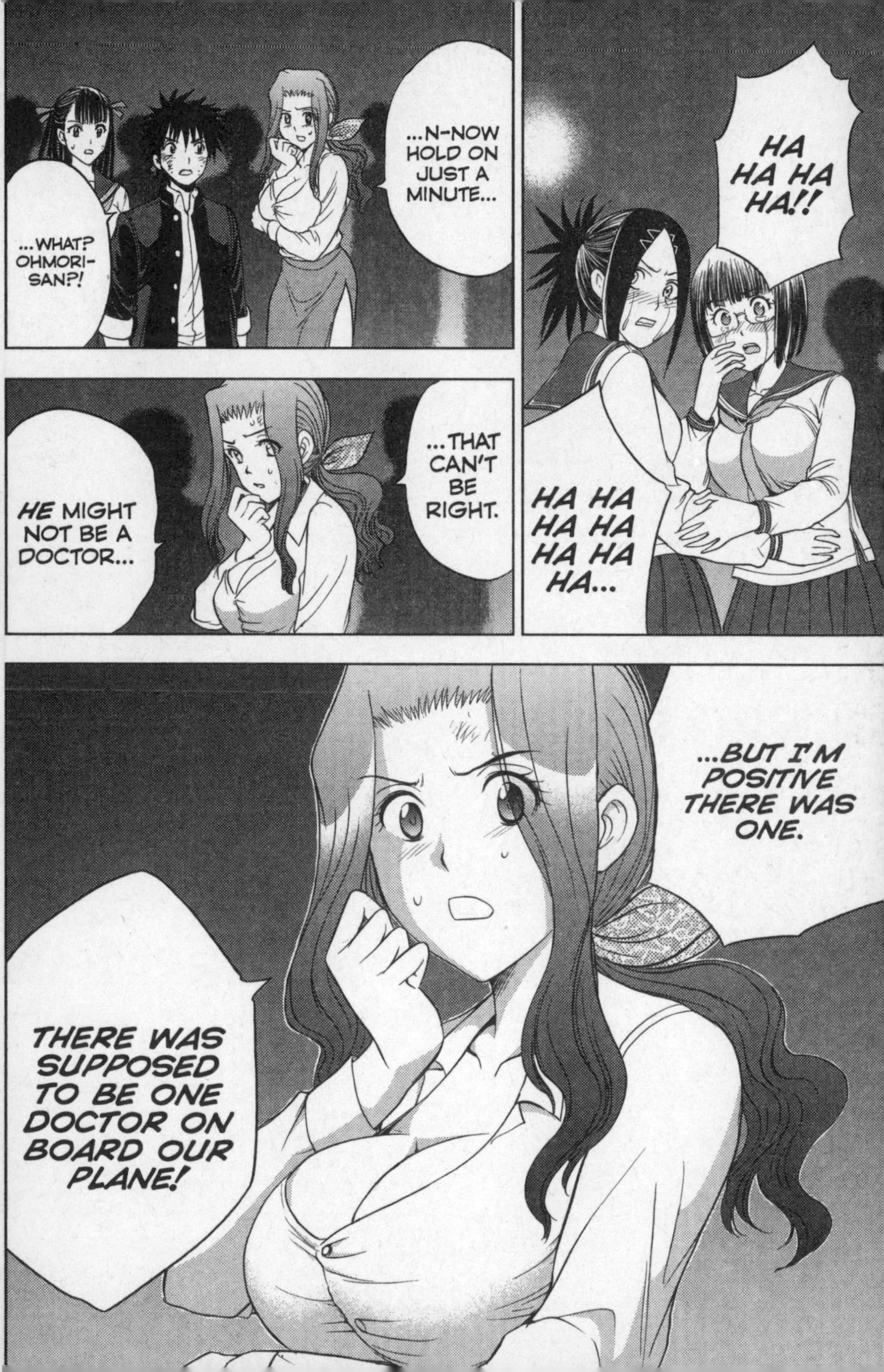
HA HA HA HA!!
HA HA HA HA HA HA HA...
...N-NOW HOLD ON JUST A MINUTE...
...WHAT? OHMORI-SAN?!
...THAT CAN'T BE RIGHT.
HE MIGHT NOT BE A DOCTOR...
...BUT I'M POSITIVE THERE WAS ONE.
THERE WAS SUPPOSED TO BE ONE DOCTOR ON BOARD OUR PLANE!

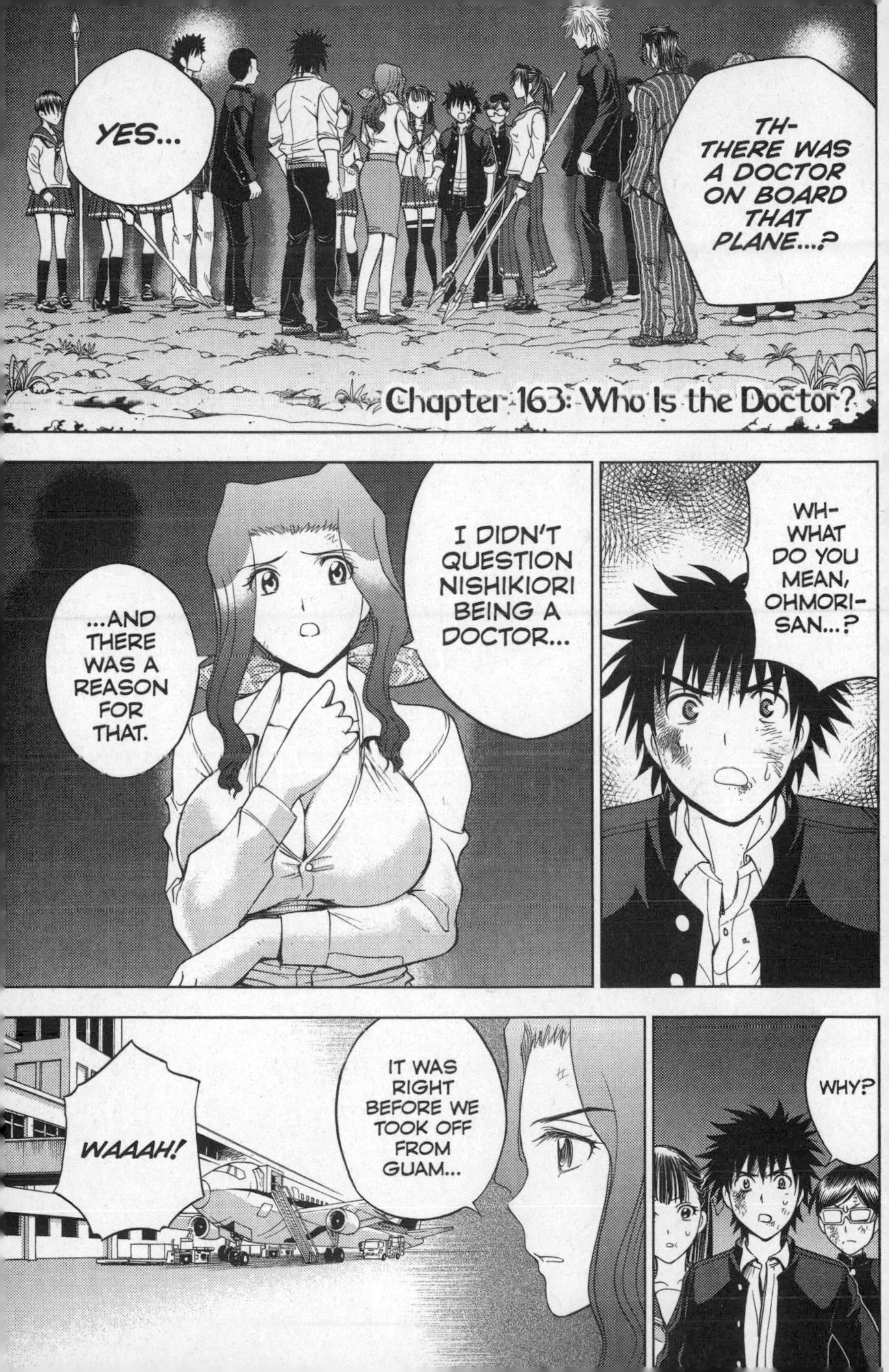
TH- THERE WAS A DOCTOR ON BOARD THAT PLANE...?
YES...
Chapter 163: Who Is the Doctor?
WH- WHAT DO YOU MEAN, OHMORI-SAN...?
I DIDN'T QUESTION NISHIKIORI BEING A DOCTOR...
...AND THERE WAS A REASON FOR THAT.
WHY?
IT WAS RIGHT BEFORE WE TOOK OFF FROM GUAM...
WAAAH!

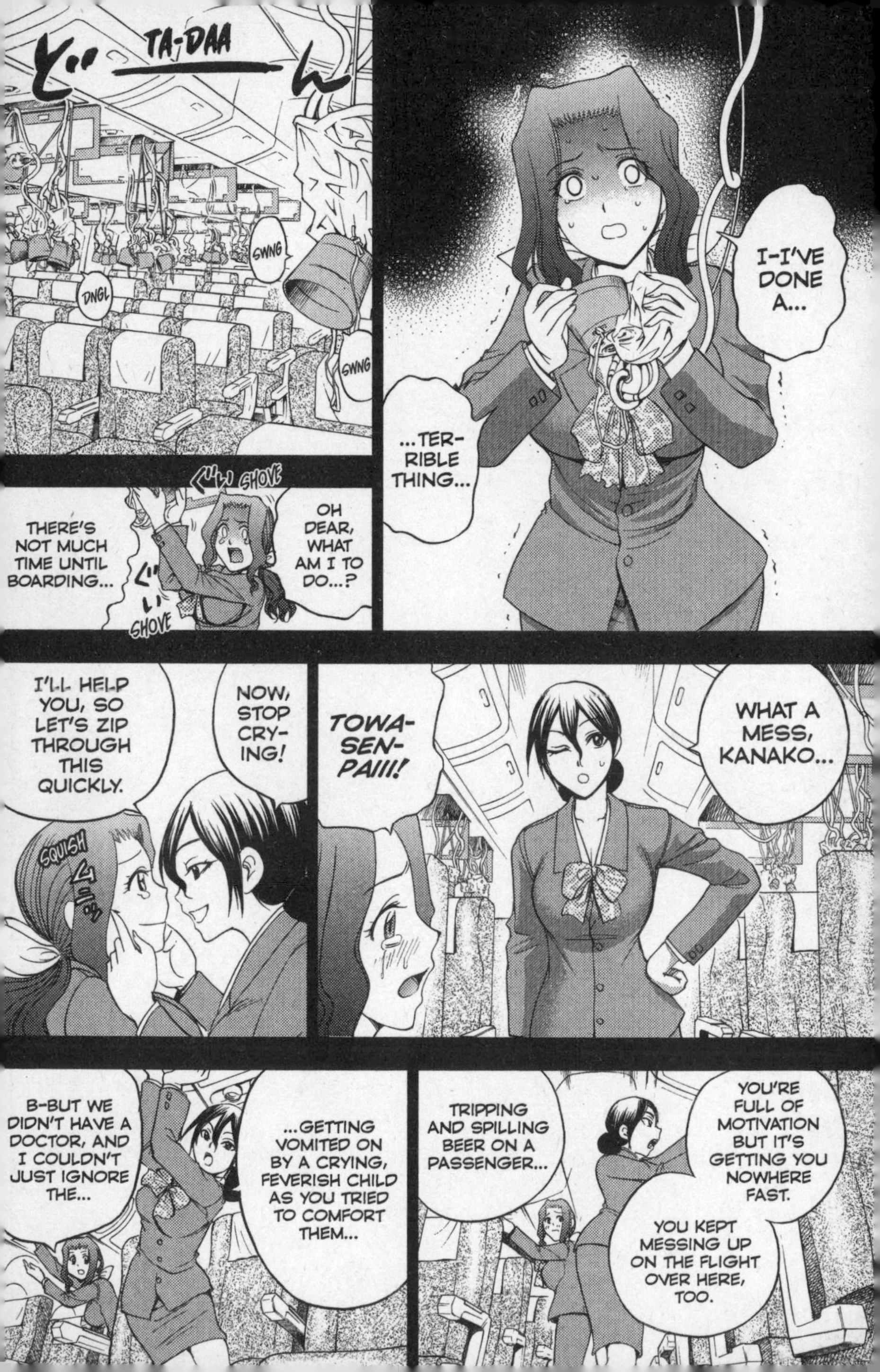
I-I'VE DONE A...
...TER-RIBLE THING...
TA-DAA
SWNG
DNGL
SWNG
OH DEAR, WHAT AM I TO DO...?
SHOVE
THERE'S NOT MUCH TIME UNTIL BOARDING...
SHOVE
WHAT A MESS, KANAKO...
TOWA-SEN-PAIII!
NOW, STOP CRY-ING!
I'LL HELP YOU, SO LET'S ZIP THROUGH THIS QUICKLY.
SQUISH
YOU'RE FULL OF MOTIVATION BUT IT'S GETTING YOU NOWHERE FAST.
TRIPPING AND SPILLING BEER ON A PASSENGER...
YOU KEPT MESSING UP ON THE FLIGHT OVER HERE, TOO.
...GETTING VOMITED ON BY A CRYING, FEVERISH CHILD AS YOU TRIED TO COMFORT THEM...
B-BUT WE DIDN'T HAVE A DOCTOR, AND I COULDN'T JUST IGNORE THE...

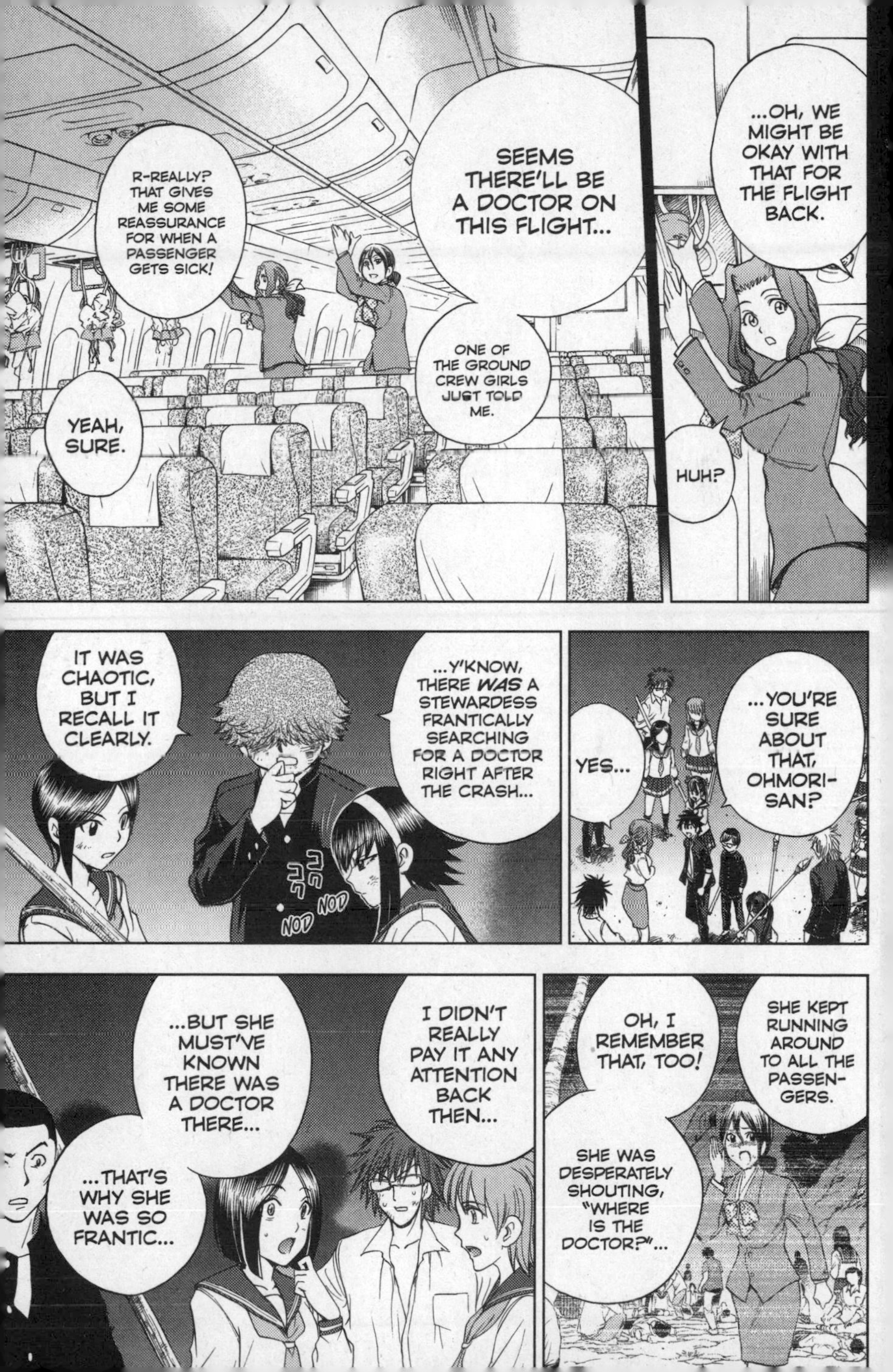
...OH, WE MIGHT BE OKAY WITH THAT FOR THE FLIGHT BACK.
HUH?
SEEMS THERE'LL BE A DOCTOR ON THIS FLIGHT...
ONE OF THE GROUND CREW GIRLS JUST TOLD ME.
R-REALLY? THAT GIVES ME SOME REASSURANCE FOR WHEN A PASSENGER GETS SICK!
YEAH, SURE.
...YOU'RE SURE ABOUT THAT, OHMORI-SAN?
YES...
...Y'KNOW, THERE *WAS* A STEWARDESS FRANTICALLY SEARCHING FOR A DOCTOR RIGHT AFTER THE CRASH...
IT WAS CHAOTIC, BUT I RECALL IT CLEARLY.
コク コク
NOD NOD
SHE KEPT RUNNING AROUND TO ALL THE PASSEN-GERS.
OH, I REMEMBER THAT, TOO!
SHE WAS DESPERATELY SHOUTING, "WHERE IS THE DOCTOR?"...
I DIDN'T REALLY PAY IT ANY ATTENTION BACK THEN...
...BUT SHE MUST'VE KNOWN THERE WAS A DOCTOR THERE...
...THAT'S WHY SHE WAS SO FRANTIC...

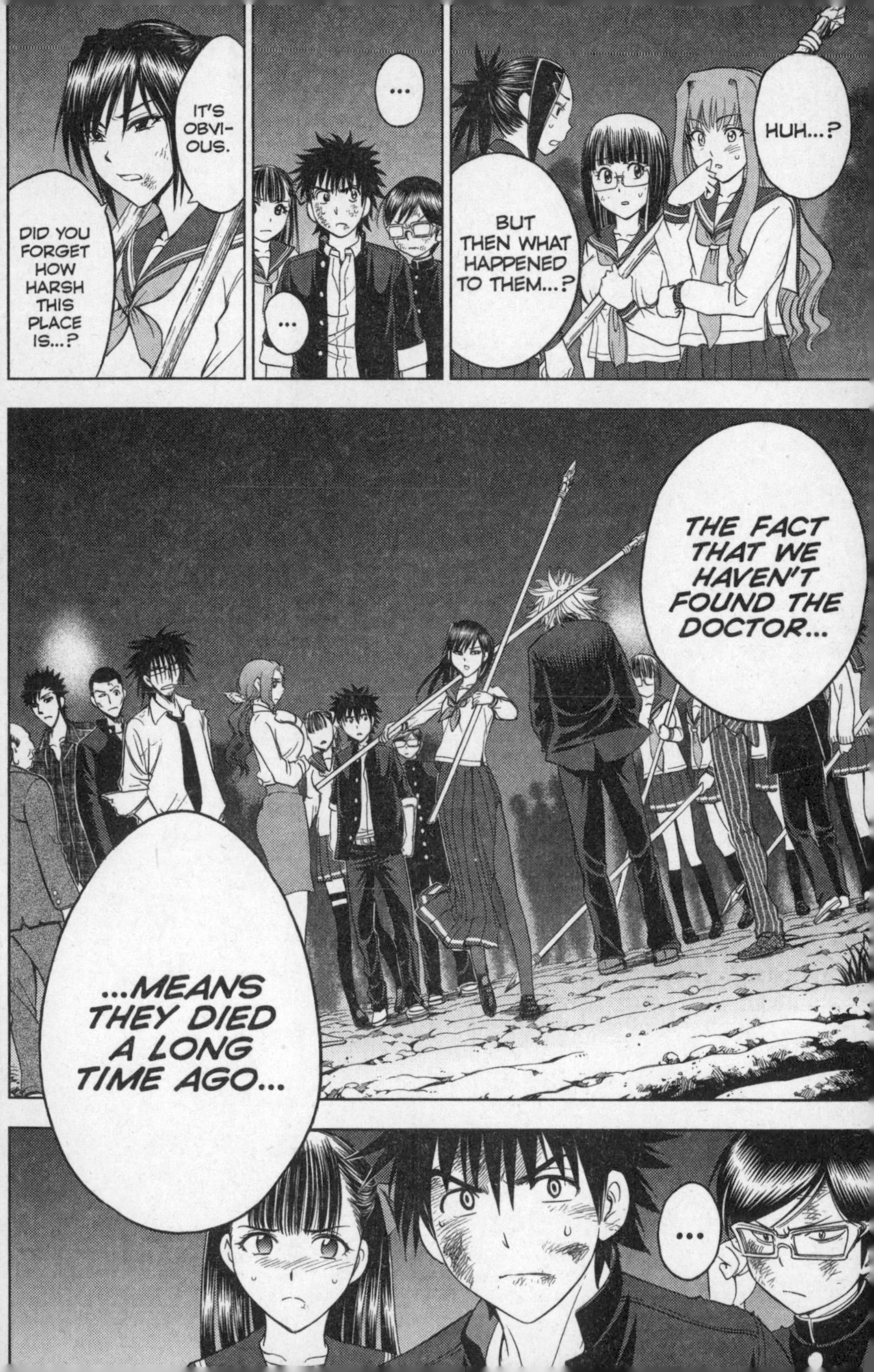
HUH...?
BUT THEN WHAT HAPPENED TO THEM...?
...
...
IT'S OBVI-OUS.
DID YOU FORGET HOW HARSH THIS PLACE IS...?
THE FACT THAT WE HAVEN'T FOUND THE DOCTOR...
...MEANS THEY DIED A LONG TIME AGO...
...

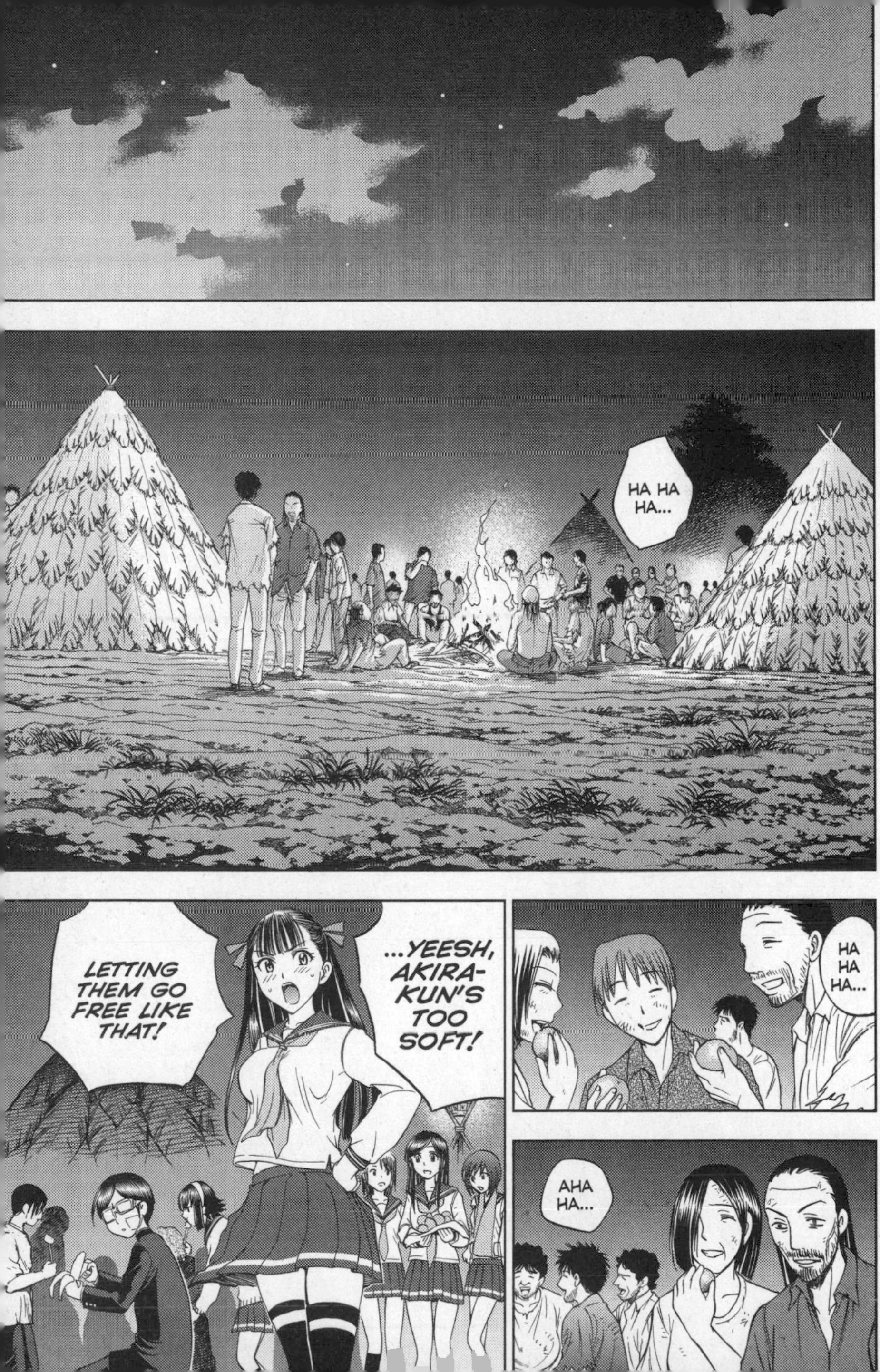
HA HA HA...
HA HA HA...
AHA HA...
...YEESH, AKIRA-KUN'S TOO SOFT!
LETTING THEM GO FREE LIKE THAT!

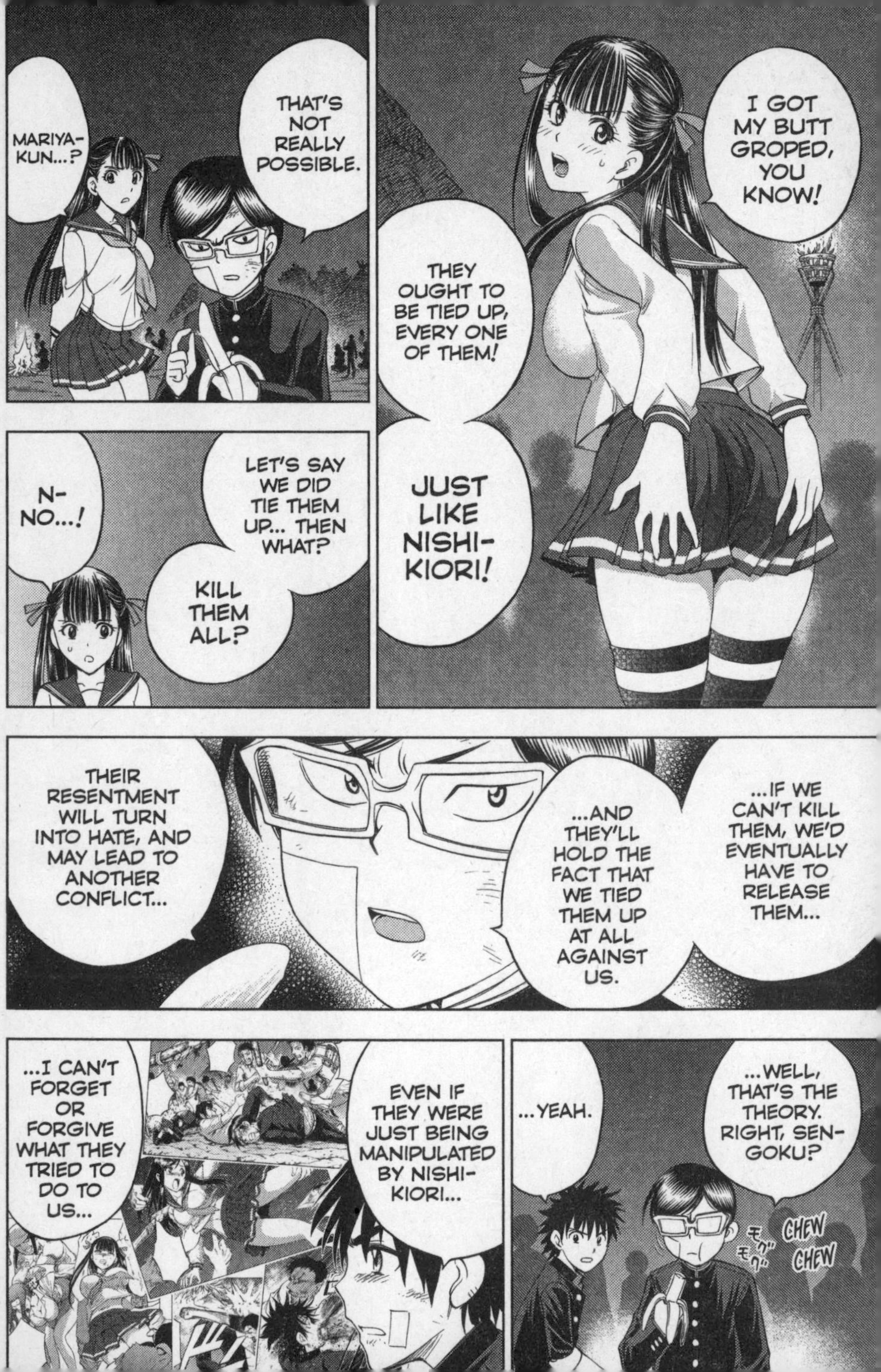
I GOT MY BUTT GROPED, YOU KNOW!
THEY OUGHT TO BE TIED UP, EVERY ONE OF THEM!
JUST LIKE NISHIKIORI!
THAT'S NOT REALLY POSSIBLE.
MARIYA-KUN...?
LET'S SAY WE DID TIE THEM UP... THEN WHAT?
KILL THEM ALL?
N-NO...!
...IF WE CAN'T KILL THEM, WE'D EVENTUALLY HAVE TO RELEASE THEM...
...AND THEY'LL HOLD THE FACT THAT WE TIED THEM UP AT ALL AGAINST US.
THEIR RESENTMENT WILL TURN INTO HATE, AND MAY LEAD TO ANOTHER CONFLICT...
...WELL, THAT'S THE THEORY. RIGHT, SENGOKU?
モグ モグ
CHEW CHEW
...YEAH.
EVEN IF THEY WERE JUST BEING MANIPULATED BY NISHIKIORI...
...I CAN'T FORGET OR FORGIVE WHAT THEY TRIED TO DO TO US...

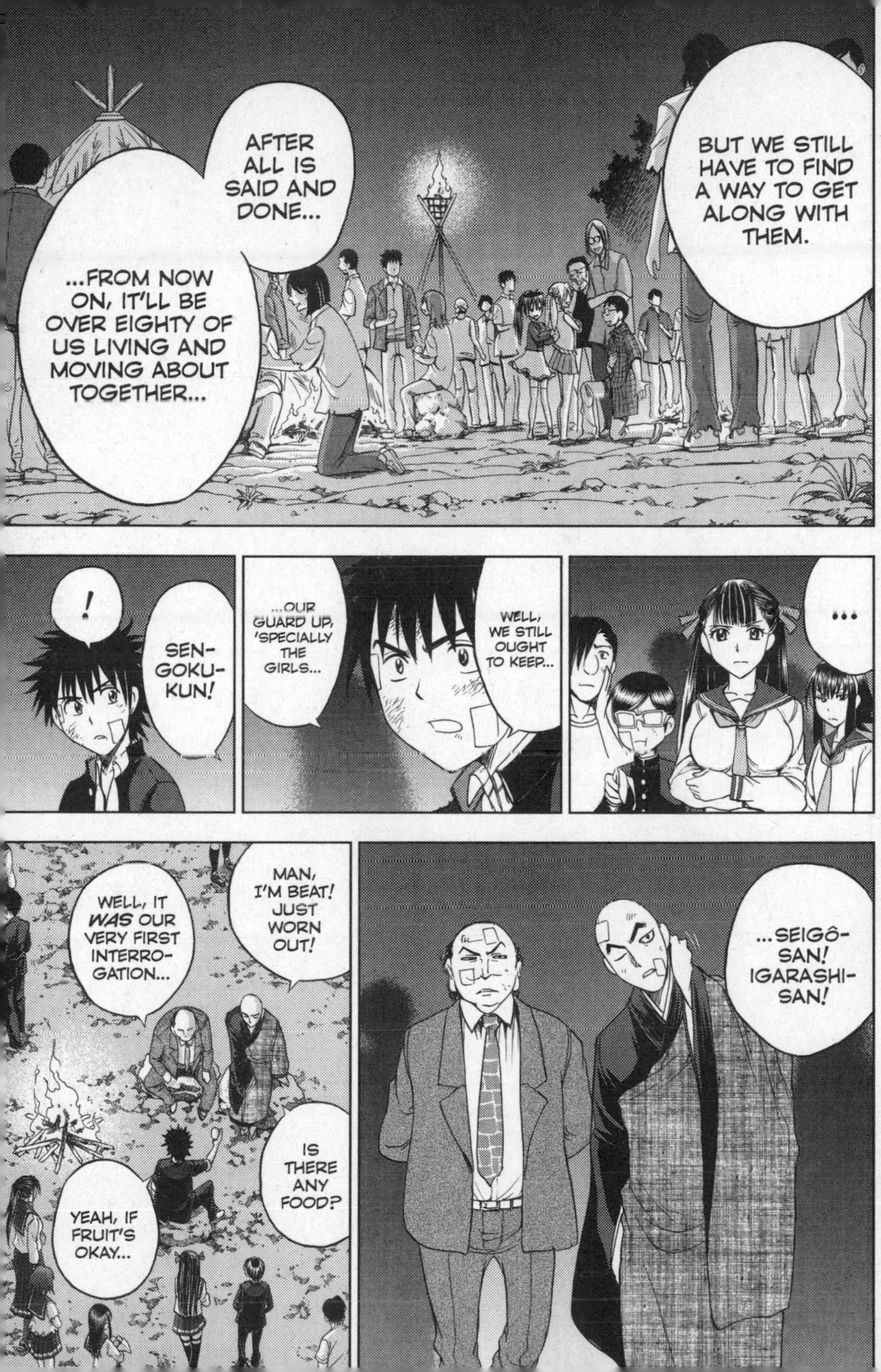
AFTER ALL IS SAID AND DONE...
...FROM NOW ON, IT'LL BE OVER EIGHTY OF US LIVING AND MOVING ABOUT TOGETHER...
BUT WE STILL HAVE TO FIND A WAY TO GET ALONG WITH THEM.
...
WELL, WE STILL OUGHT TO KEEP...
...OUR GUARD UP, 'SPECIALLY THE GIRLS...
!
SEN-GOKU-KUN!
...SEIGÔ-SAN! IGARASHI-SAN!
MAN, I'M BEAT! JUST WORN OUT!
WELL, IT *WAS* OUR VERY FIRST INTERRO-GATION...
IS THERE ANY FOOD?
YEAH, IF FRUIT'S OKAY...

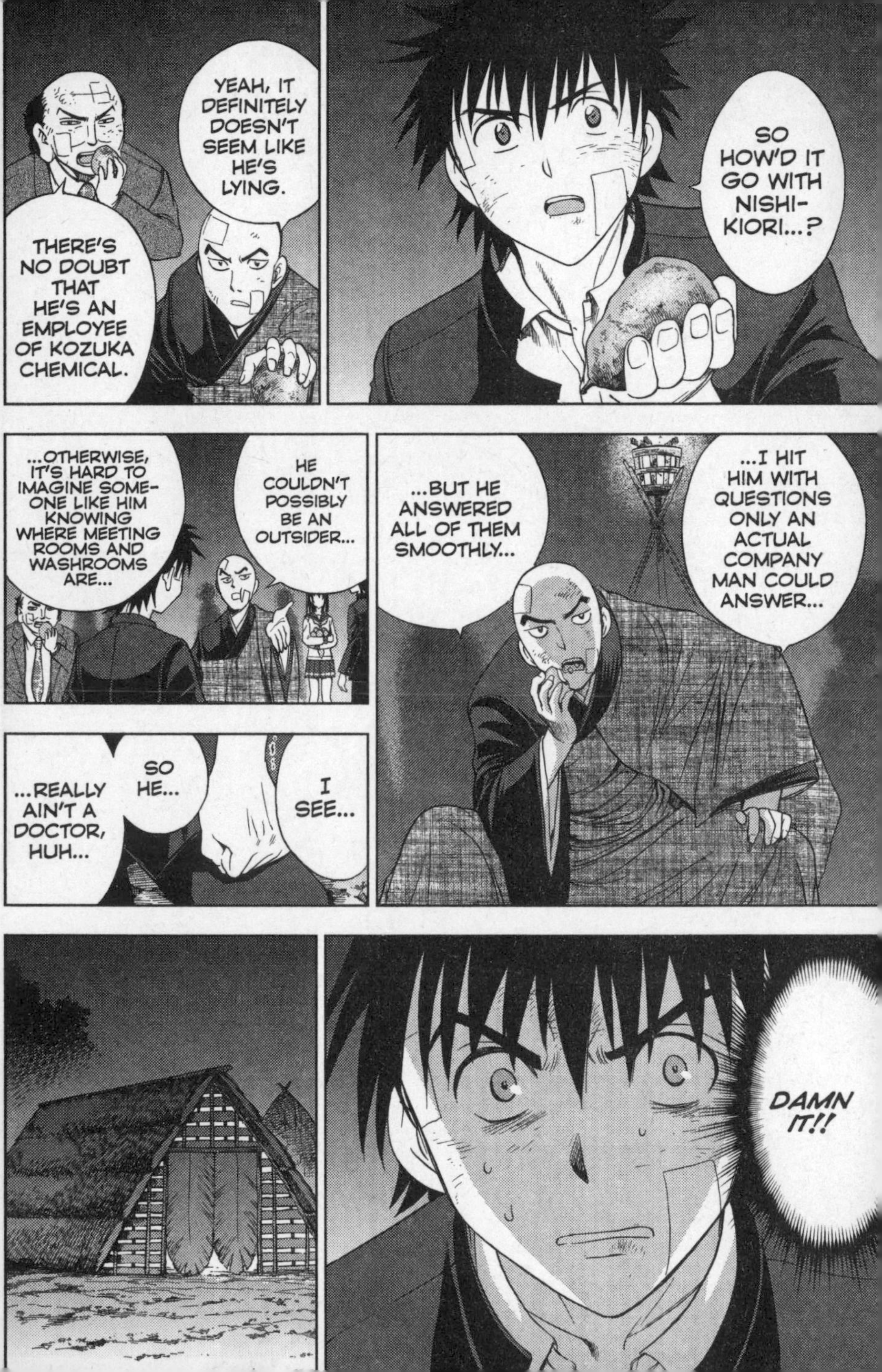
SO HOW'D IT GO WITH NISHI-KIORI...?
YEAH, IT DEFINITELY DOESN'T SEEM LIKE HE'S LYING.
THERE'S NO DOUBT THAT HE'S AN EMPLOYEE OF KOZUKA CHEMICAL.
...I HIT HIM WITH QUESTIONS ONLY AN ACTUAL COMPANY MAN COULD ANSWER...
...BUT HE ANSWERED ALL OF THEM SMOOTHLY...
HE COULDN'T POSSIBLY BE AN OUTSIDER...
...OTHERWISE, IT'S HARD TO IMAGINE SOME-ONE LIKE HIM KNOWING WHERE MEETING ROOMS AND WASHROOMS ARE...
I SEE...
SO HE...
...REALLY AIN'T A DOCTOR, HUH...
DAMN IT!!

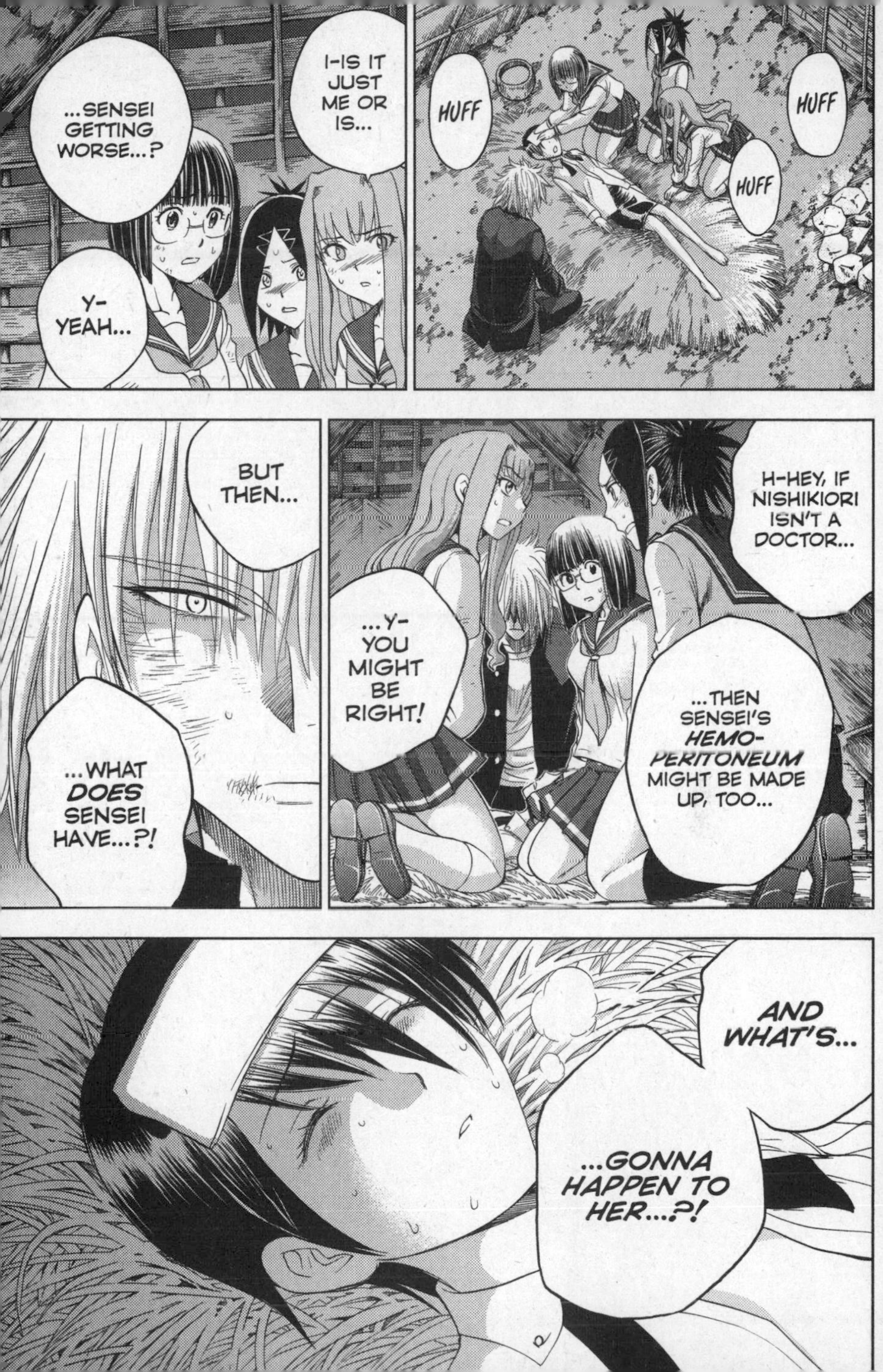
HUFF
HUFF
HUFF
I-IS IT JUST ME OR IS...
...SENSEI GETTING WORSE...?
Y-YEAH...
H-HEY, IF NISHIKIORI ISN'T A DOCTOR...
...THEN SENSEI'S *HEMO-PERITONEUM* MIGHT BE MADE UP, TOO...
...Y-YOU MIGHT BE RIGHT!
BUT THEN...
...WHAT *DOES* SENSEI HAVE...?!
AND WHAT'S...
...GONNA HAPPEN TO HER...?!

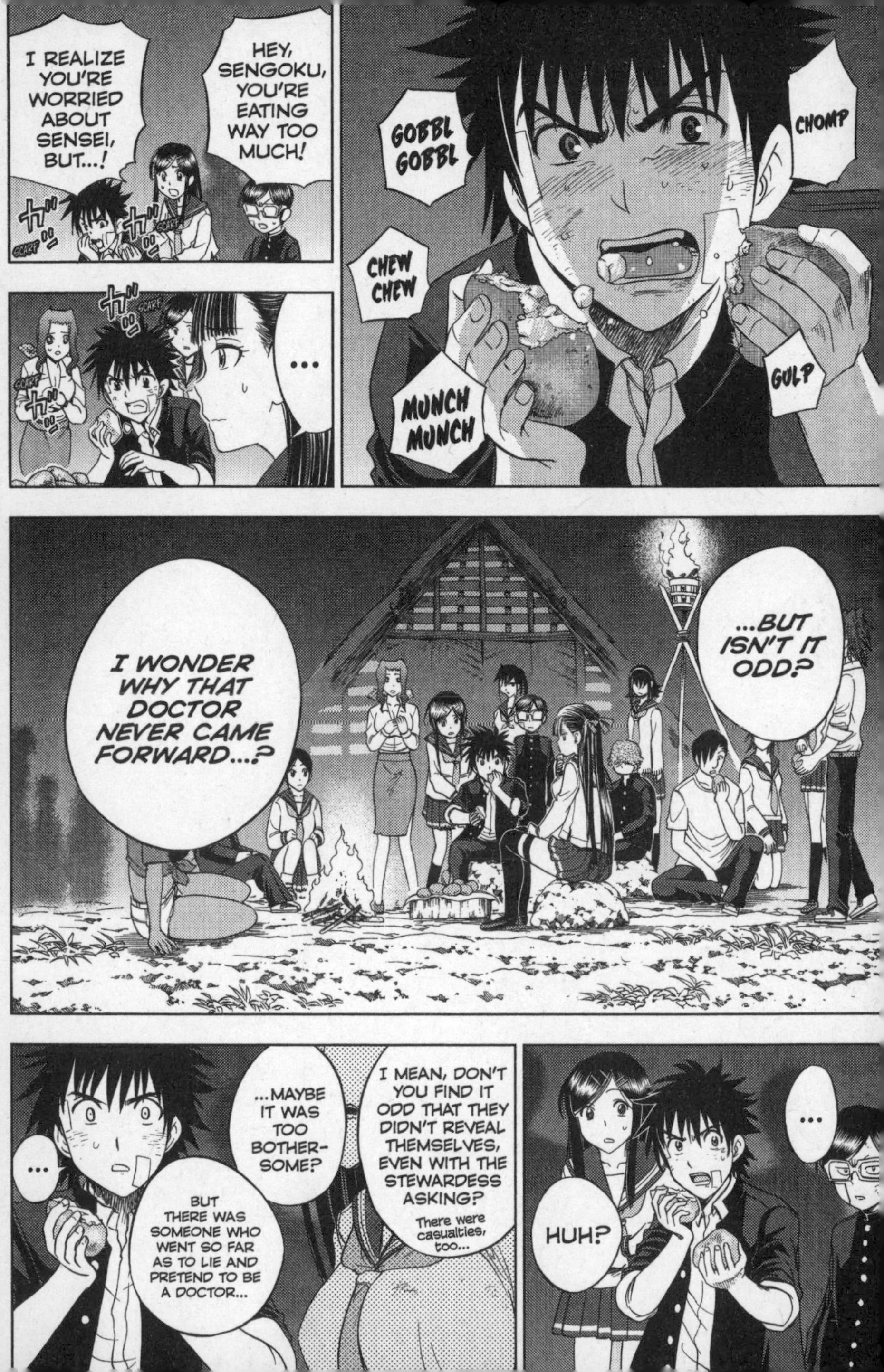
CHOMP
GOBBL GOBBL
CHEW CHEW
GULP
MUNCH MUNCH
HEY, SENGOKU, YOU'RE EATING WAY TOO MUCH!
I REALIZE YOU'RE WORRIED ABOUT SENSEI, BUT...!
SCARF
SCARF
...
SCARF
SCARF
...BUT ISN'T IT ODD?
I WONDER WHY THAT DOCTOR NEVER CAME FORWARD...?
...
HUH?
I MEAN, DON'T YOU FIND IT ODD THAT THEY DIDN'T REVEAL THEMSELVES, EVEN WITH THE STEWARDESS ASKING?
There were casualties, too...
...MAYBE IT WAS TOO BOTHER-SOME?
BUT THERE WAS SOMEONE WHO WENT SO FAR AS TO LIE AND PRETEND TO BE A DOCTOR...
...

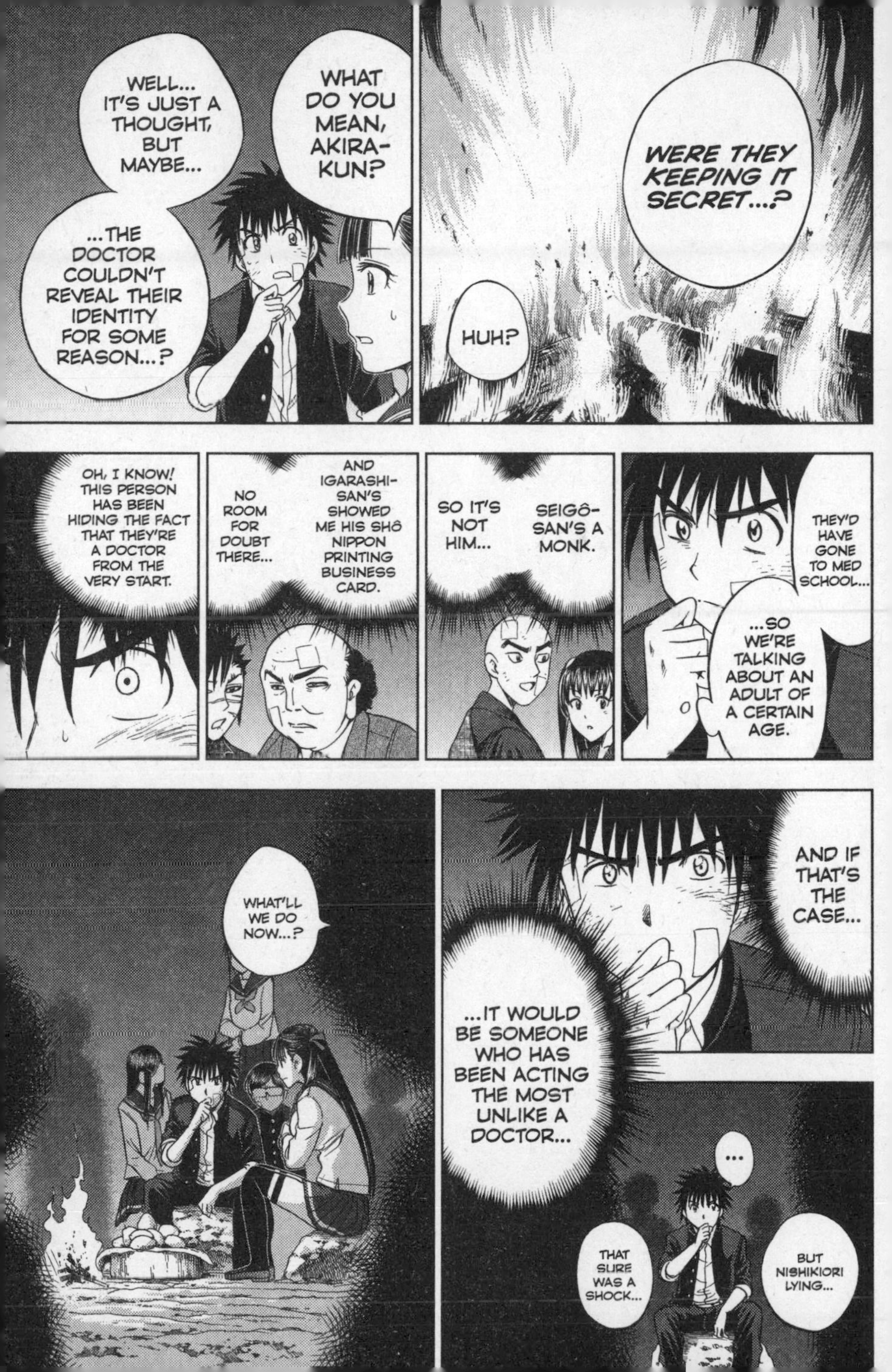
WERE THEY KEEPING IT SECRET...?
HUH?
WHAT DO YOU MEAN, AKIRA-KUN?
WELL... IT'S JUST A THOUGHT, BUT MAYBE...
...THE DOCTOR COULDN'T REVEAL THEIR IDENTITY FOR SOME REASON...?
THEY'D HAVE GONE TO MED SCHOOL...
...SO WE'RE TALKING ABOUT AN ADULT OF A CERTAIN AGE.
SEIGÔ-SAN'S A MONK.
SO IT'S NOT HIM...
AND IGARASHI-SAN'S SHOWED ME HIS SHÔ NIPPON PRINTING BUSINESS CARD.
NO ROOM FOR DOUBT THERE...
OH, I KNOW! THIS PERSON HAS BEEN HIDING THE FACT THAT THEY'RE A DOCTOR FROM THE VERY START.
AND IF THAT'S THE CASE...
...IT WOULD BE SOMEONE WHO HAS BEEN ACTING THE MOST UNLIKE A DOCTOR...
...
BUT NISHIKIORI LYING...
THAT SURE WAS A SHOCK...
WHAT'LL WE DO NOW...?

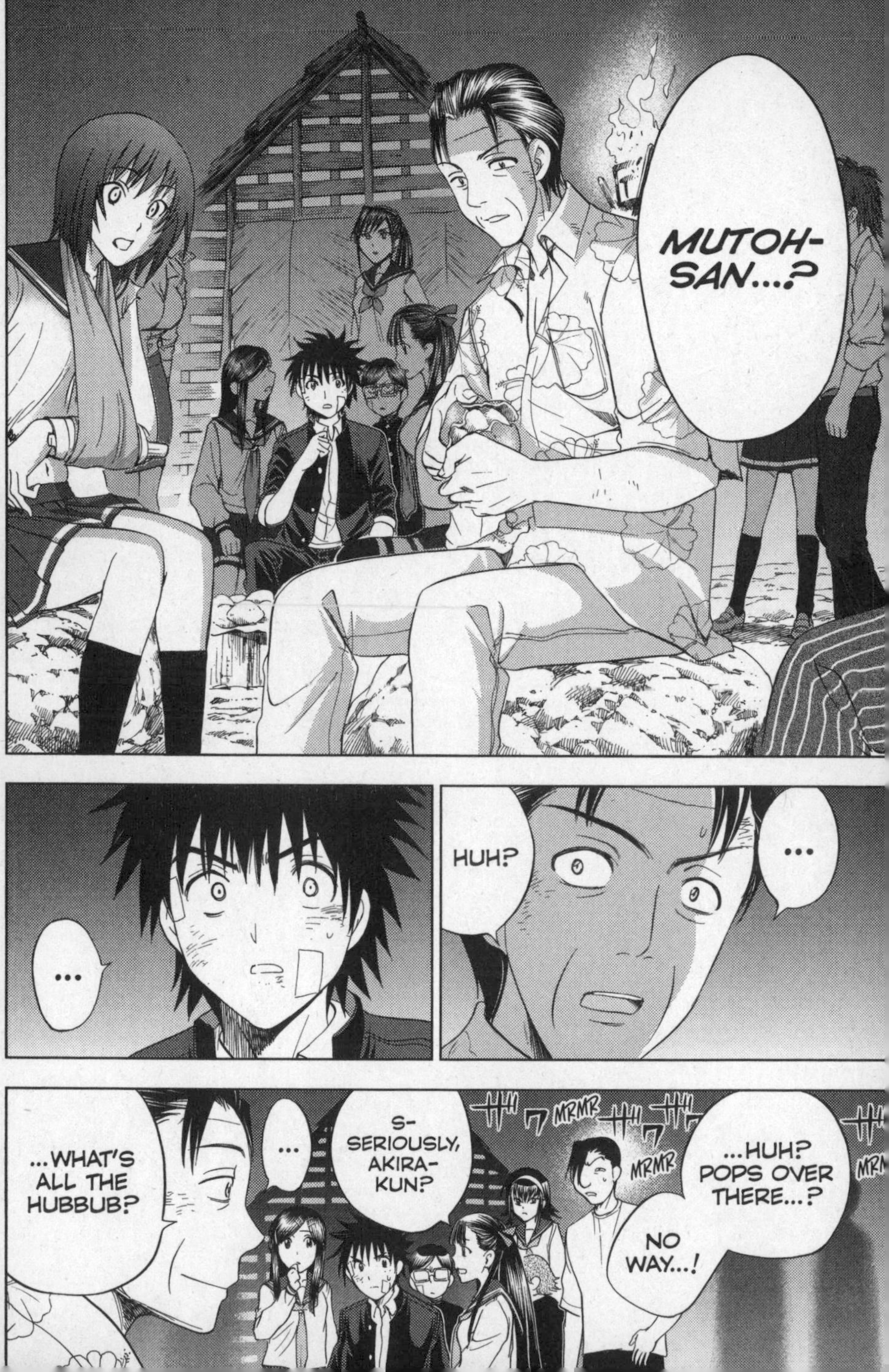
MUTOH-SAN...?
...
HUH?
...
MRMR
...HUH? POPS OVER THERE...?
NO WAY...!
MRMR
S-SERIOUSLY, AKIRA-KUN?
...
...WHAT'S ALL THE HUBBUB?

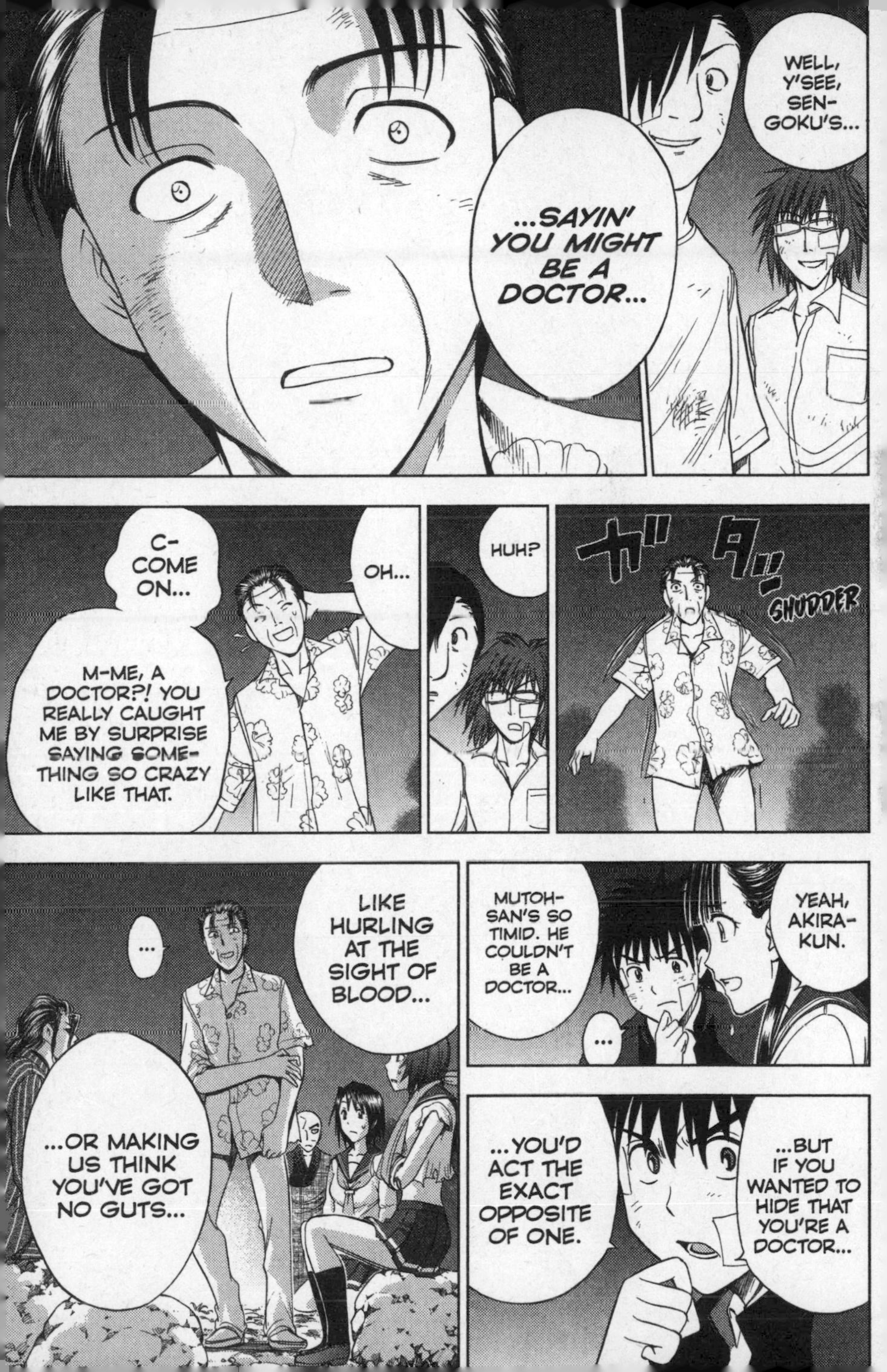
WELL, Y'SEE, SEN-GOKU'S...
...SAYIN' YOU MIGHT BE A DOCTOR...
ガタッ
SHUDDER
HUH?
OH...
C-COME ON...
M-ME, A DOCTOR?! YOU REALLY CAUGHT ME BY SURPRISE SAYING SOME-THING SO CRAZY LIKE THAT.
YEAH, AKIRA-KUN.
MUTOH-SAN'S SO TIMID. HE COULDN'T BE A DOCTOR...
...
...BUT IF YOU WANTED TO HIDE THAT YOU'RE A DOCTOR...
...YOU'D ACT THE EXACT OPPOSITE OF ONE.
LIKE HURLING AT THE SIGHT OF BLOOD...
...
...OR MAKING US THINK YOU'VE GOT NO GUTS...

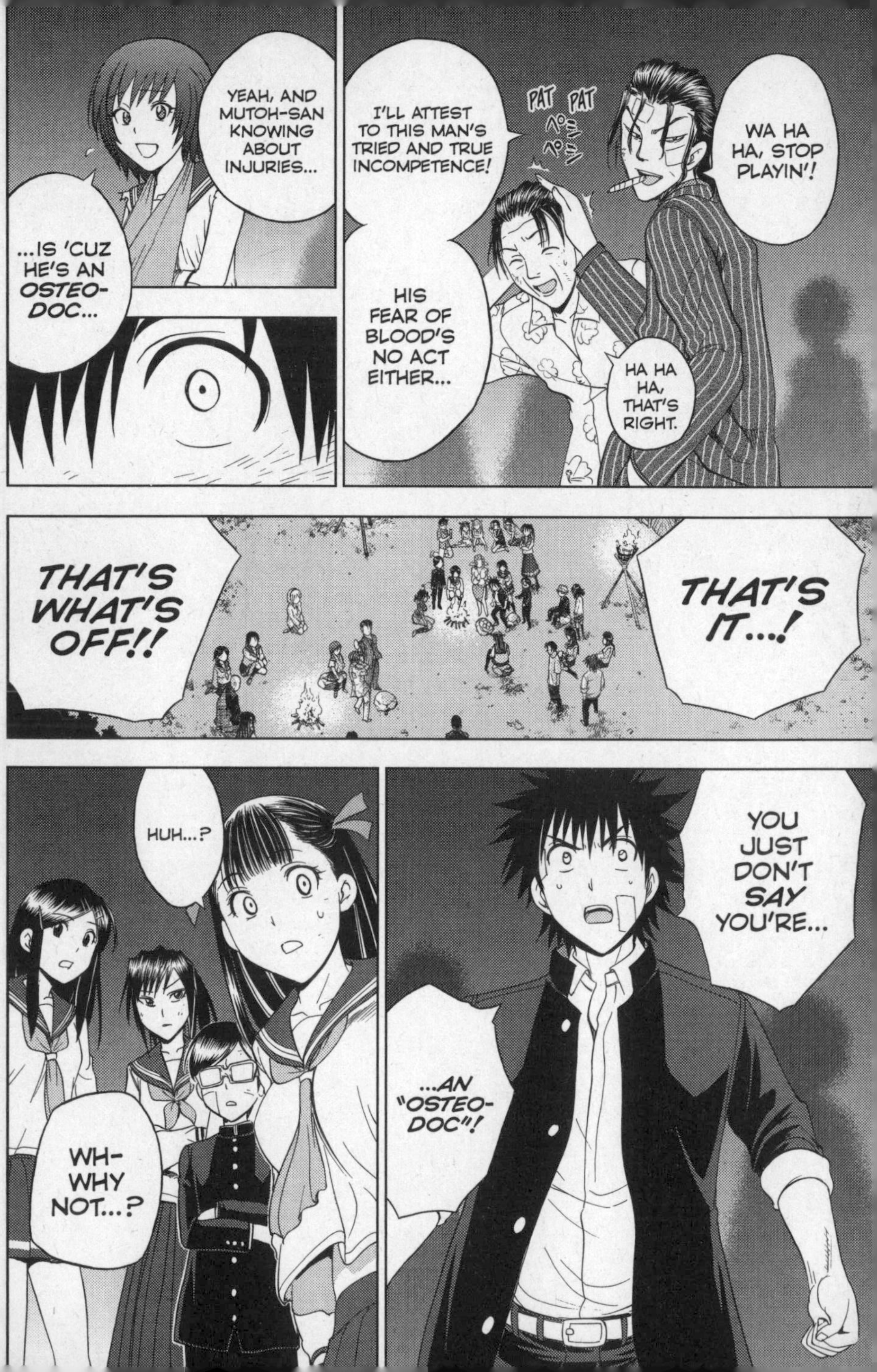
WA HA HA, STOP PLAYIN'!
PAT PAT
I'LL ATTEST TO THIS MAN'S TRIED AND TRUE INCOMPETENCE!
HIS FEAR OF BLOOD'S NO ACT EITHER...
HA HA HA, THAT'S RIGHT.
YEAH, AND MUTOH-SAN KNOWING ABOUT INJURIES...
...IS 'CUZ HE'S AN OSTEO-DOC...
THAT'S IT...!
THAT'S WHAT'S OFF!!
YOU JUST DON'T SAY YOU'RE...
...AN "OSTEO-DOC"!
HUH...?
WH-WHY NOT...?

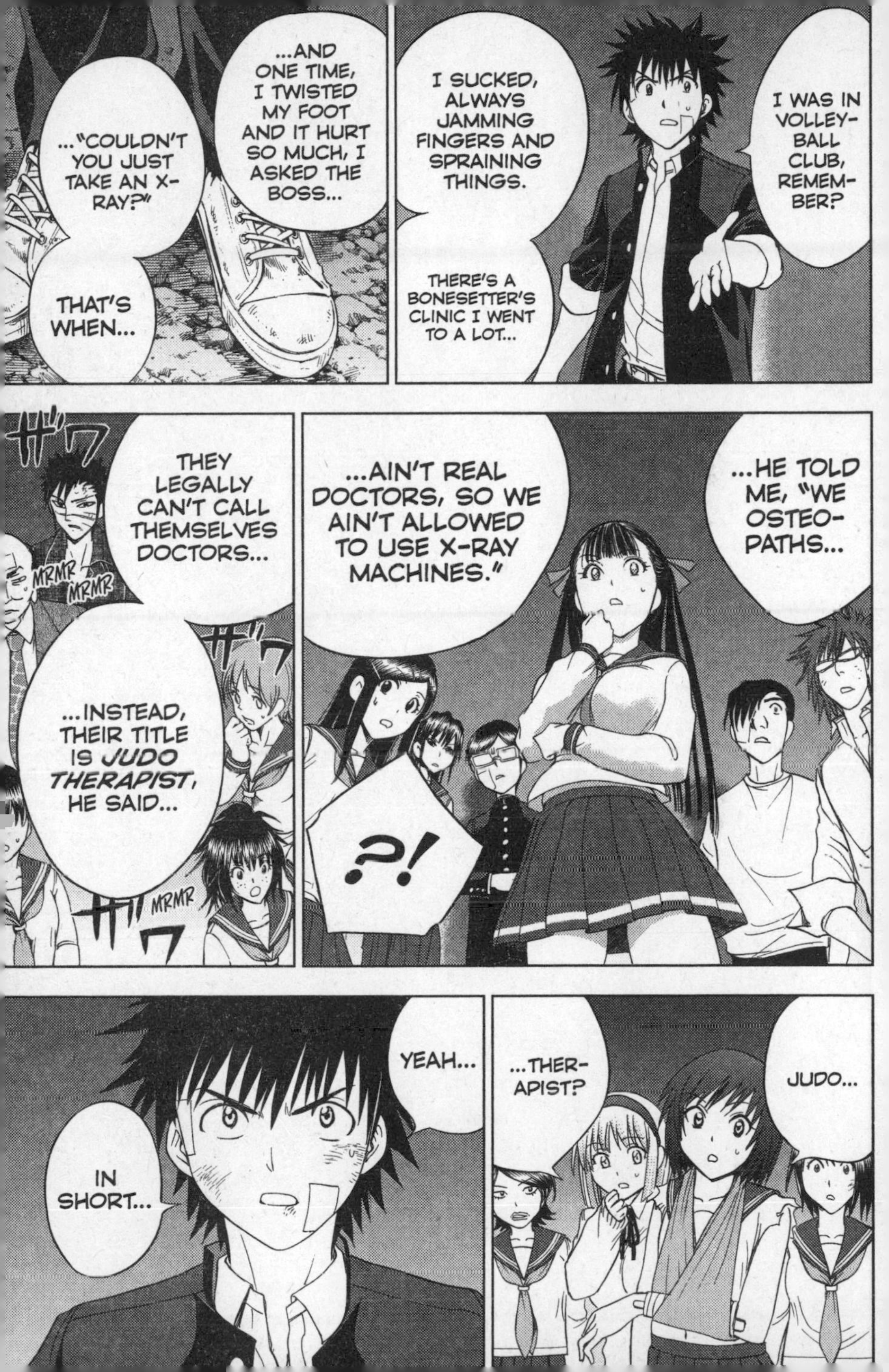
I WAS IN VOLLEY-BALL CLUB, REMEMBER?
I SUCKED, ALWAYS JAMMING FINGERS AND SPRAINING THINGS.
THERE'S A BONESETTER'S CLINIC I WENT TO A LOT...
...AND ONE TIME, I TWISTED MY FOOT AND IT HURT SO MUCH, I ASKED THE BOSS...
..."COULDN'T YOU JUST TAKE AN X-RAY?"
THAT'S WHEN...
...HE TOLD ME, "WE OSTEO-PATHS...
...AIN'T REAL DOCTORS, SO WE AIN'T ALLOWED TO USE X-RAY MACHINES."
?!
ザワ
ザワ
THEY LEGALLY CAN'T CALL THEMSELVES DOCTORS...
MRMR MRMR
...INSTEAD, THEIR TITLE IS *JUDO THERAPIST*, HE SAID...
MRMR
ザワ
JUDO...
...THER-APIST?
YEAH...
IN SHORT...

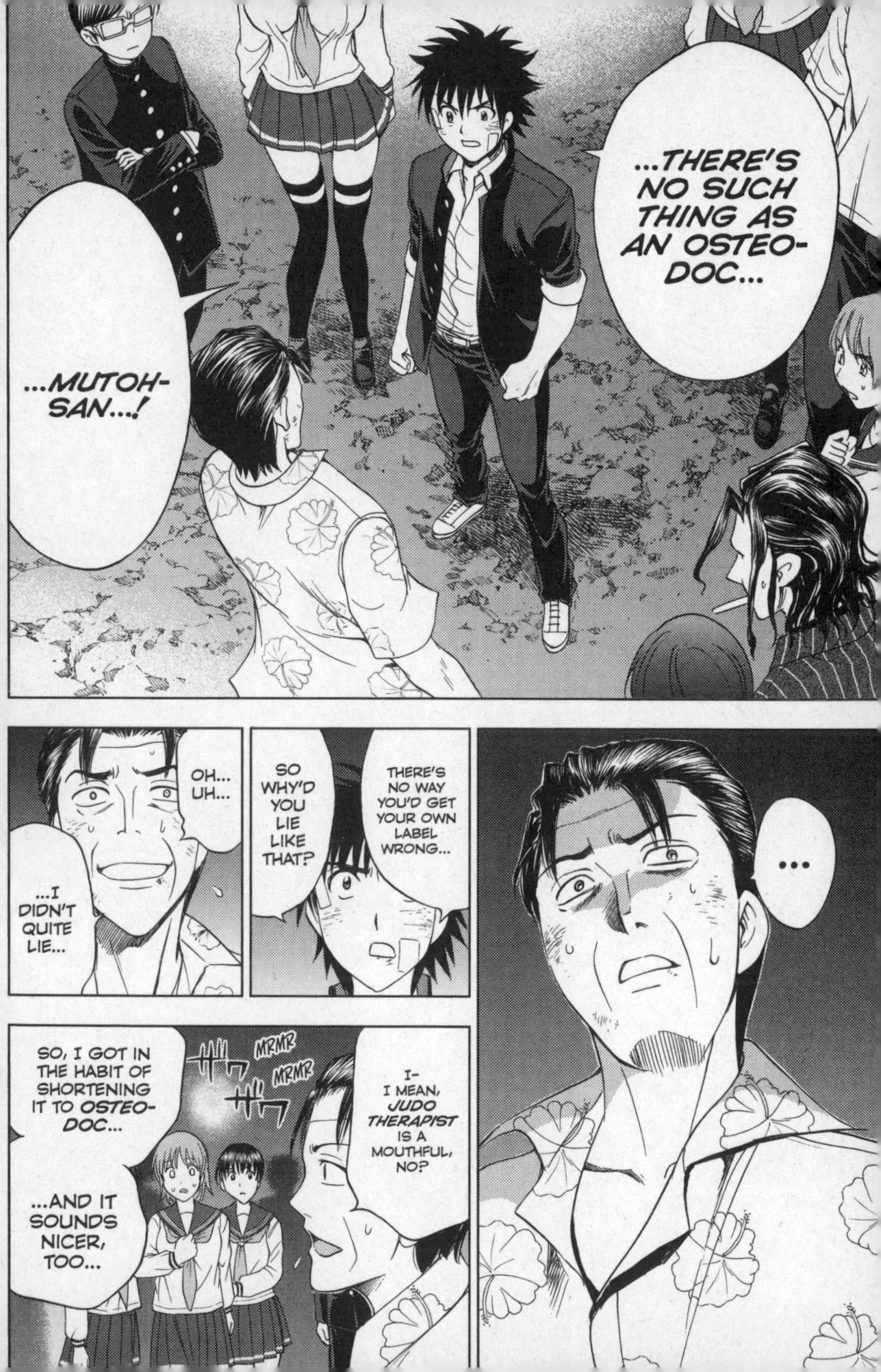
...THERE'S NO SUCH THING AS AN OSTEO-DOC...
...MUTOH-SAN...!
...
THERE'S NO WAY YOU'D GET YOUR OWN LABEL WRONG...
SO WHY'D YOU LIE LIKE THAT?
OH... UH...
...I DIDN'T QUITE LIE...
I- I MEAN, JUDO THERAPIST IS A MOUTHFUL, NO?
SO, I GOT IN THE HABIT OF SHORTENING IT TO OSTEO-DOC...
MRMR
MRMR
...AND IT SOUNDS NICER, TOO...

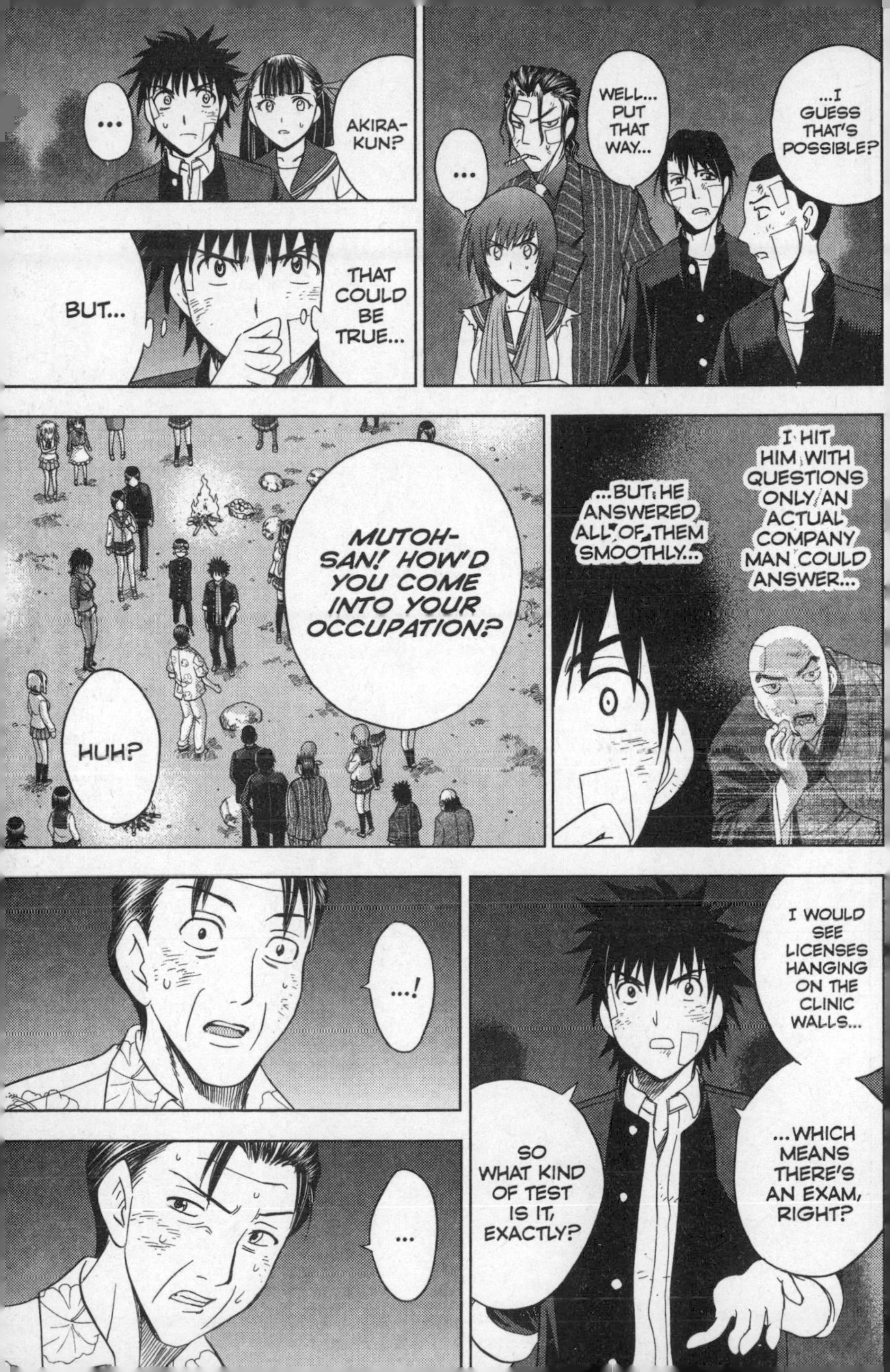
...I GUESS THAT'S POSSIBLE?
WELL... PUT THAT WAY...
...
AKIRA-KUN?
...
THAT COULD BE TRUE...
BUT...
I HIT HIM WITH QUESTIONS ONLY AN ACTUAL COMPANY MAN COULD ANSWER...
...BUT HE ANSWERED ALL OF THEM SMOOTHLY...
MUTOH-SAN! HOW'D YOU COME INTO YOUR OCCUPATION?
HUH?
I WOULD SEE LICENSES HANGING ON THE CLINIC WALLS...
...WHICH MEANS THERE'S AN EXAM, RIGHT?
SO WHAT KIND OF TEST IS IT, EXACTLY?
...!
...

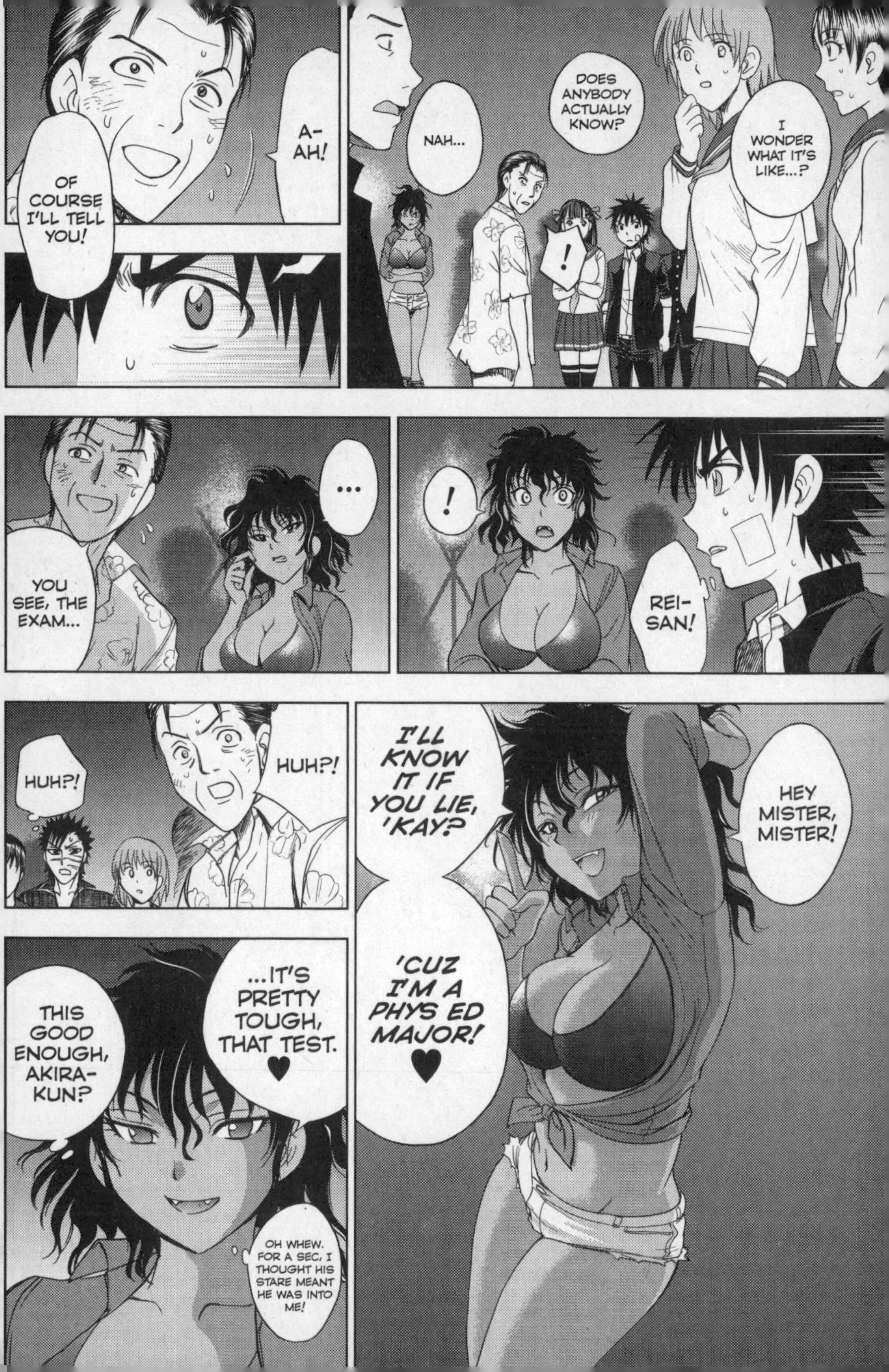
I WONDER WHAT IT'S LIKE...?
DOES ANYBODY ACTUALLY KNOW?
NAH...
!
A-AH!
OF COURSE I'LL TELL YOU!
REI-SAN!
!
...
YOU SEE, THE EXAM...
HEY MISTER, MISTER!
I'LL KNOW IT IF YOU LIE, 'KAY?
'CUZ I'M A PHYS ED MAJOR! ♥
HUH?!
HUH?!
...IT'S PRETTY TOUGH, THAT TEST. ♥
THIS GOOD ENOUGH, AKIRA-KUN?
OH WHEW. FOR A SEC, I THOUGHT HIS STARE MEANT HE WAS INTO ME!

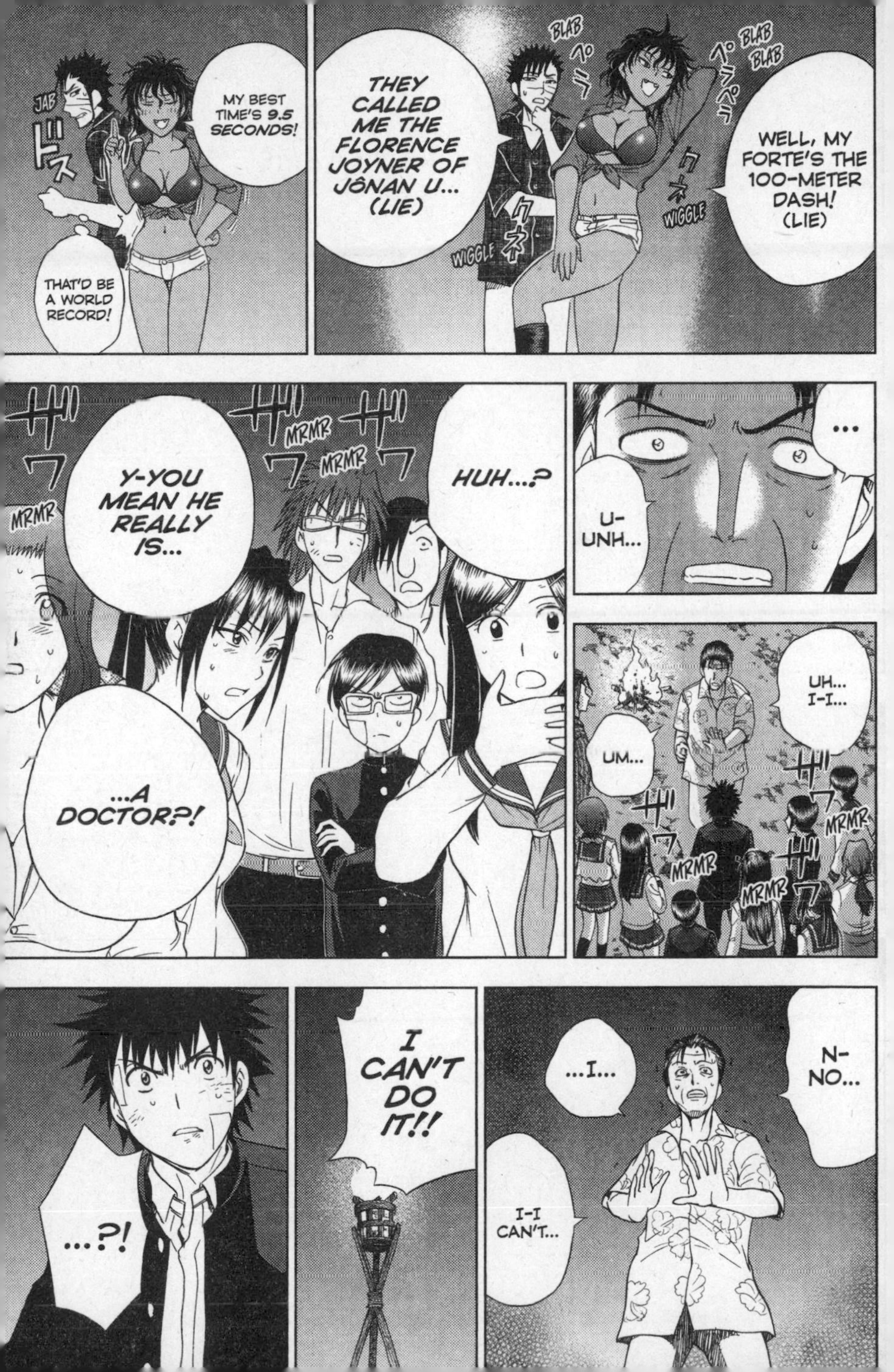
BLAB BLAB
BLAB
WELL, MY FORTE'S THE 100-METER DASH! (LIE)
WIGGLE
THEY CALLED ME THE FLORENCE JOYNER OF JÔNAN U... (LIE)
WIGGLE
MY BEST TIME'S 9.5 SECONDS!
JAB
THAT'D BE A WORLD RECORD!
...
U- UNH...
UH... I-I...
UM...
MRMR
MRMR
HUH...?
MRMR
MRMR
Y-YOU MEAN HE REALLY IS...
MRMR
...A DOCTOR?!
N- NO...
...I...
I-I CAN'T...
I CAN'T DO IT!!
...?!

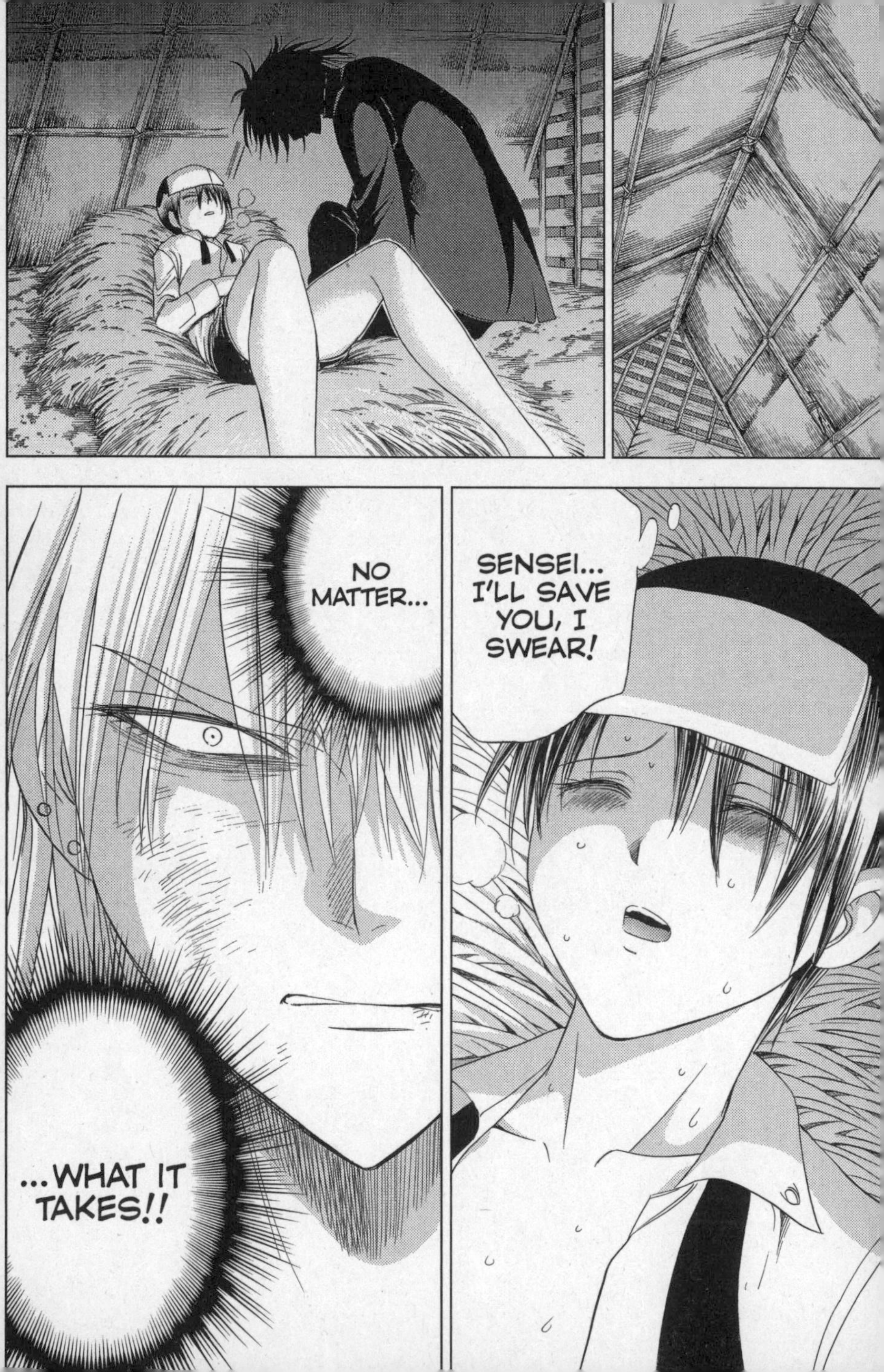
SENSEI... I'LL SAVE YOU, I SWEAR!
NO MATTER...
...WHAT IT TAKES!!

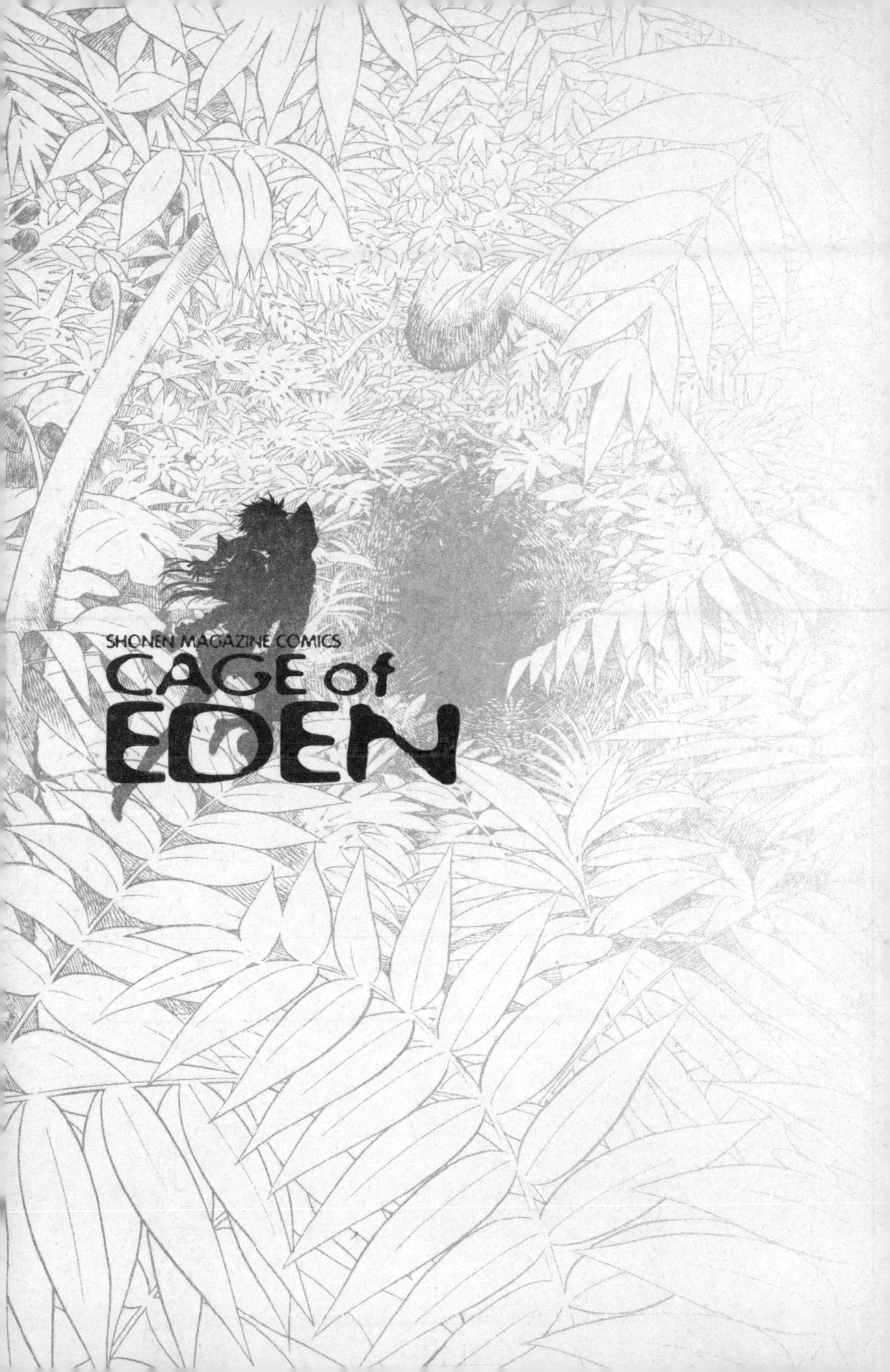
SHONEN MAGAZINE COMICS
CAGE of EDEN

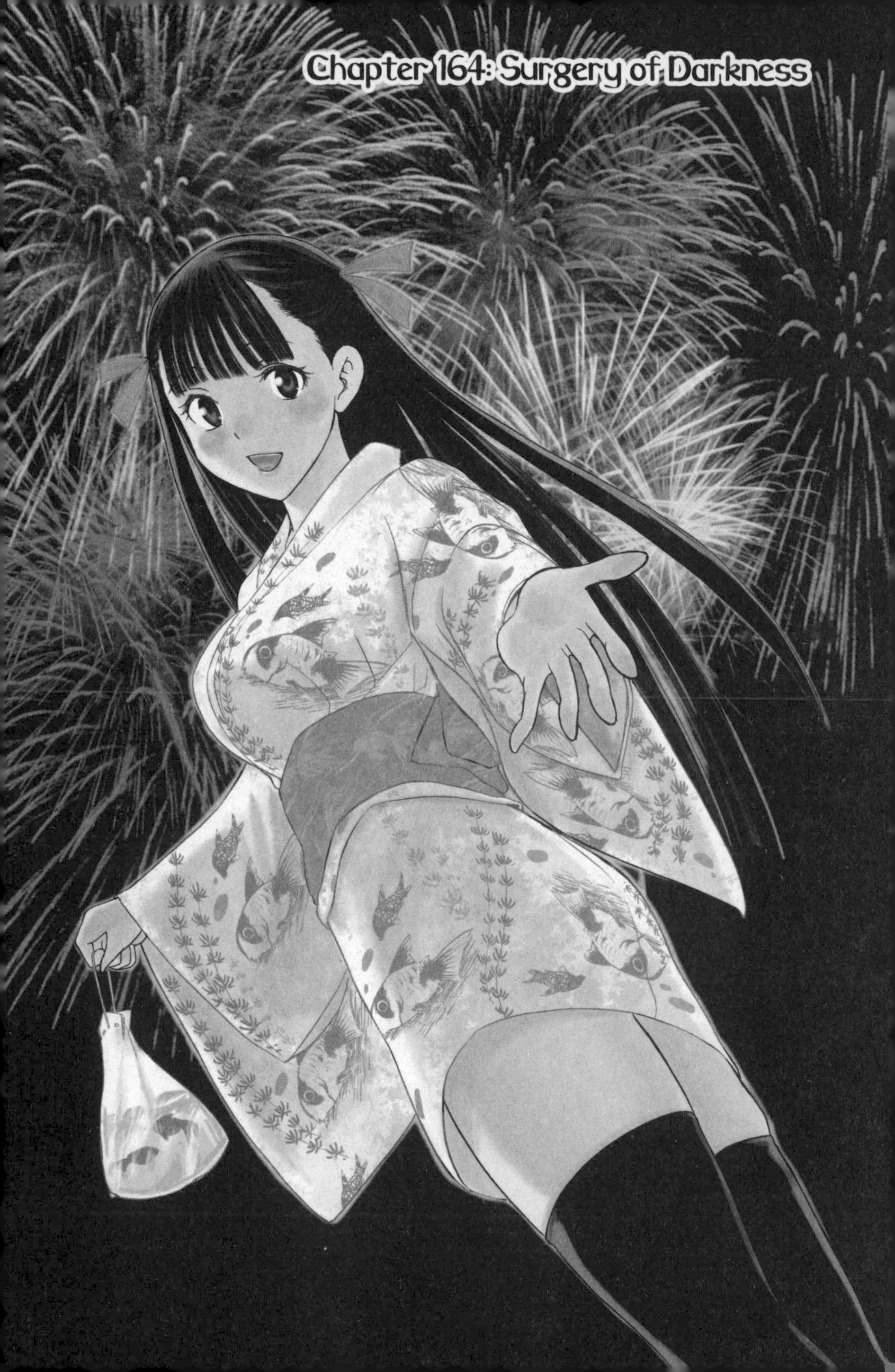
Chapter 164: Surgery of Darkness

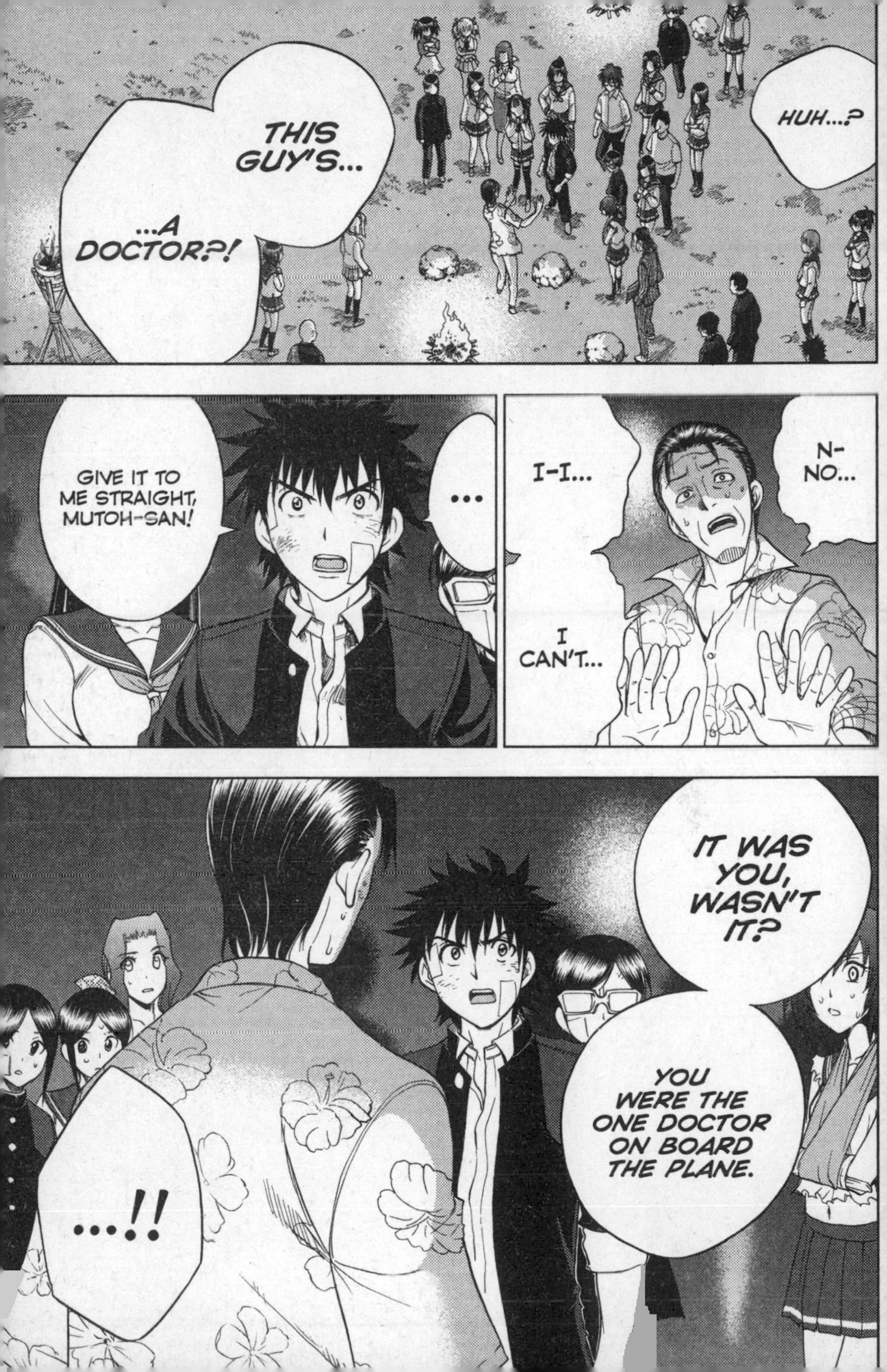
HUH...?
THIS GUY'S... ...A DOCTOR?!
N-NO...
I-I...
I CAN'T...
...
GIVE IT TO ME STRAIGHT, MUTOH-SAN!
IT WAS YOU, WASN'T IT?
YOU WERE THE ONE DOCTOR ON BOARD THE PLANE.
...!!

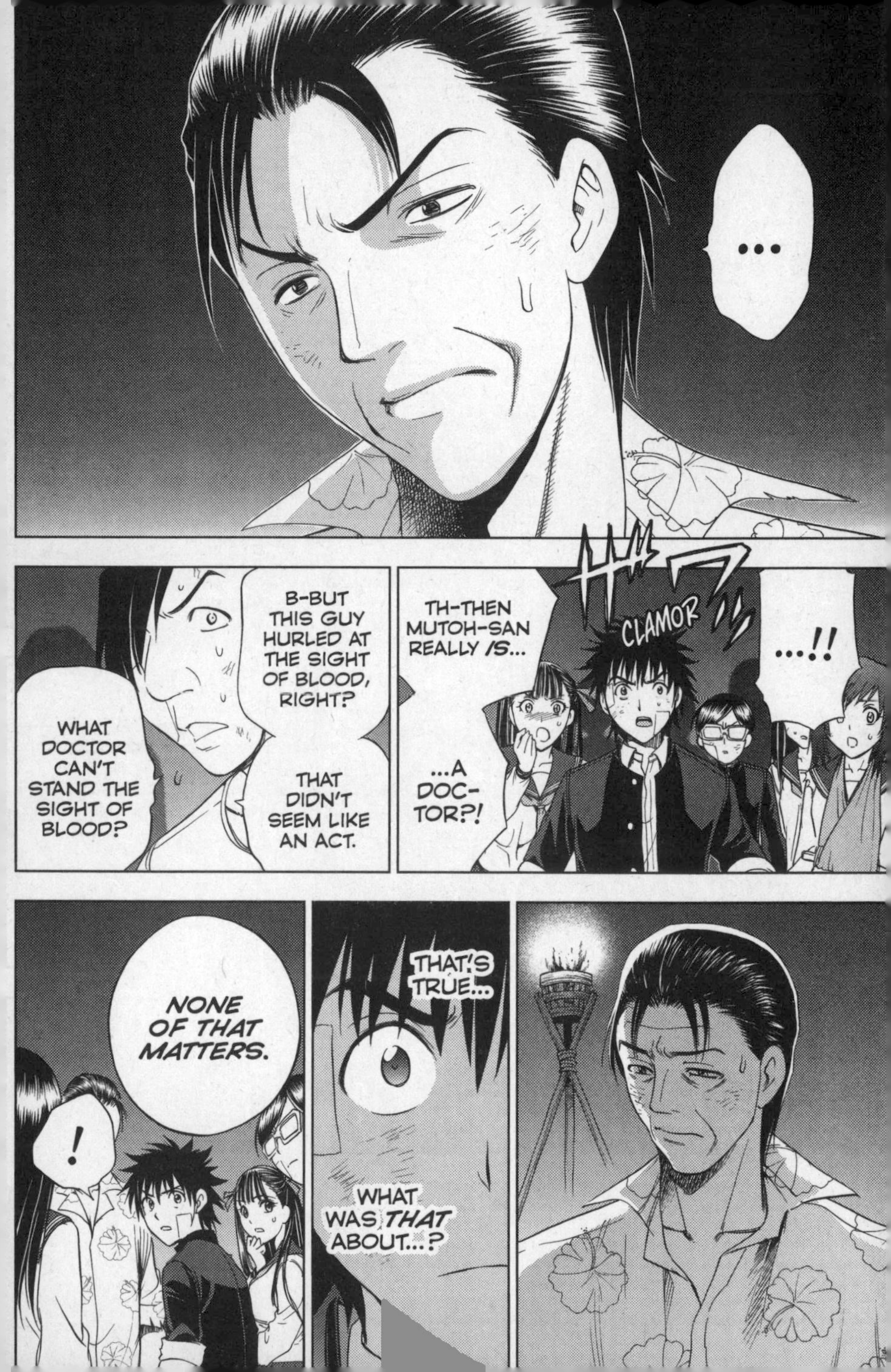
...
TH-THEN MUTOH-SAN REALLY *IS*...
CLAMOR
...!!
...A DOC-TOR?!
B-BUT THIS GUY HURLED AT THE SIGHT OF BLOOD, RIGHT?
THAT DIDN'T SEEM LIKE AN ACT.
WHAT DOCTOR CAN'T STAND THE SIGHT OF BLOOD?
THAT'S TRUE...
WHAT WAS *THAT* ABOUT...?
NONE OF THAT MATTERS.
!

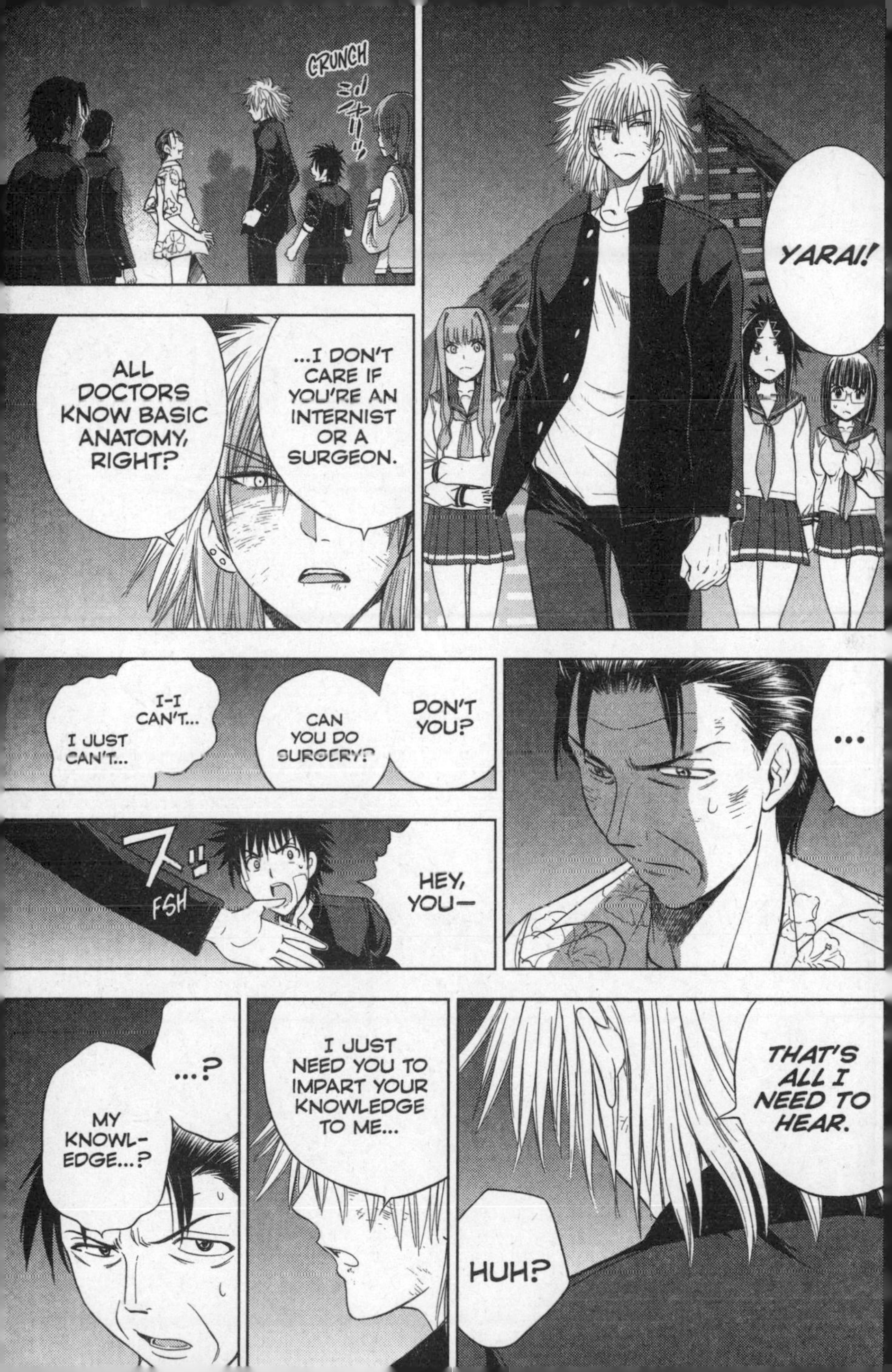
YARAI!
CRUNCH
...I DON'T CARE IF YOU'RE AN INTERNIST OR A SURGEON.
ALL DOCTORS KNOW BASIC ANATOMY, RIGHT?
...
DON'T YOU?
CAN YOU DO SURGERY?
I-I CAN'T...
I JUST CAN'T...
HEY, YOU—
FSH
THAT'S ALL I NEED TO HEAR.
HUH?
I JUST NEED YOU TO IMPART YOUR KNOWLEDGE TO ME...
...?
MY KNOWL-EDGE...?

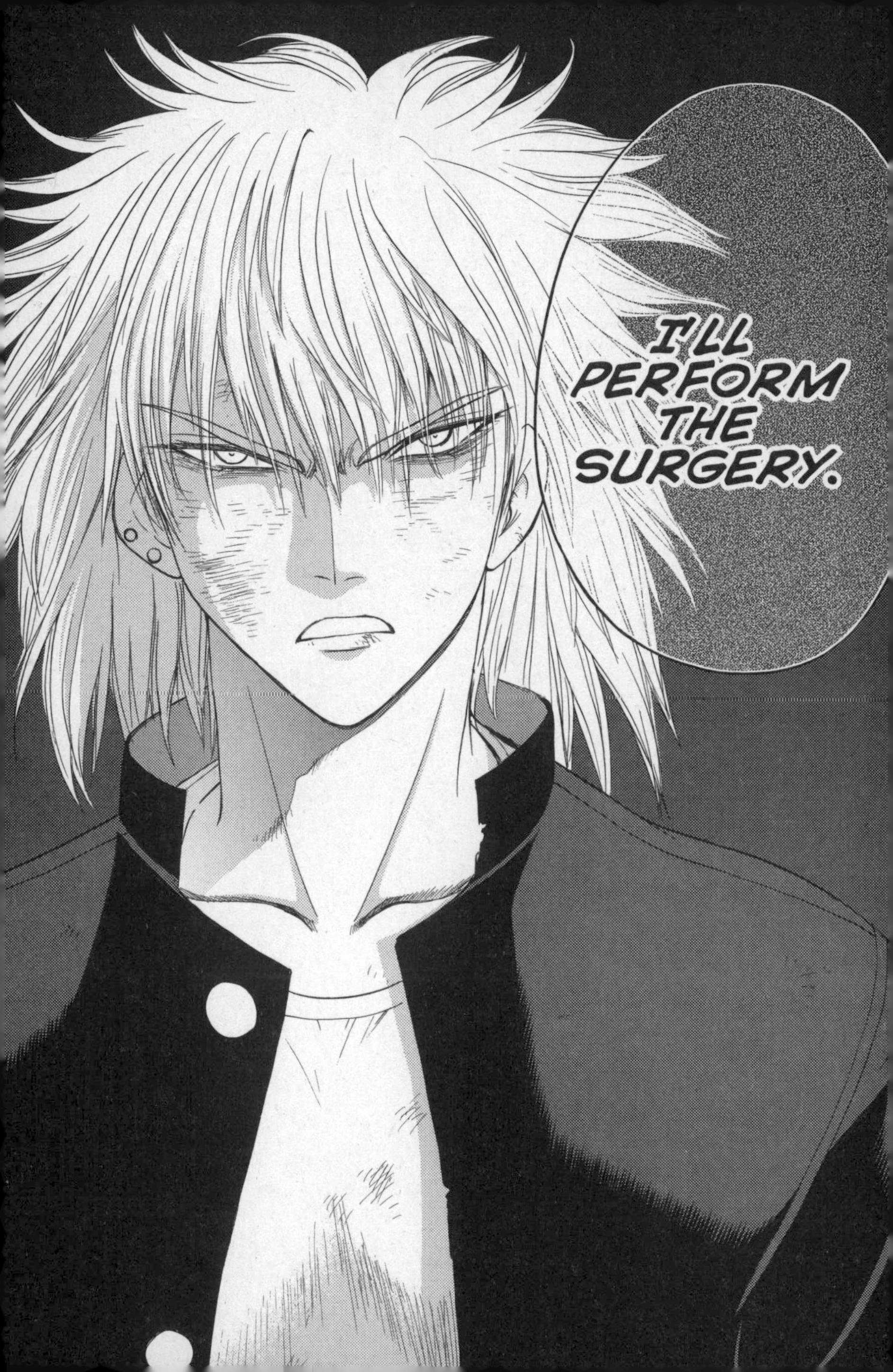
I'LL PERFORM THE SURGERY.

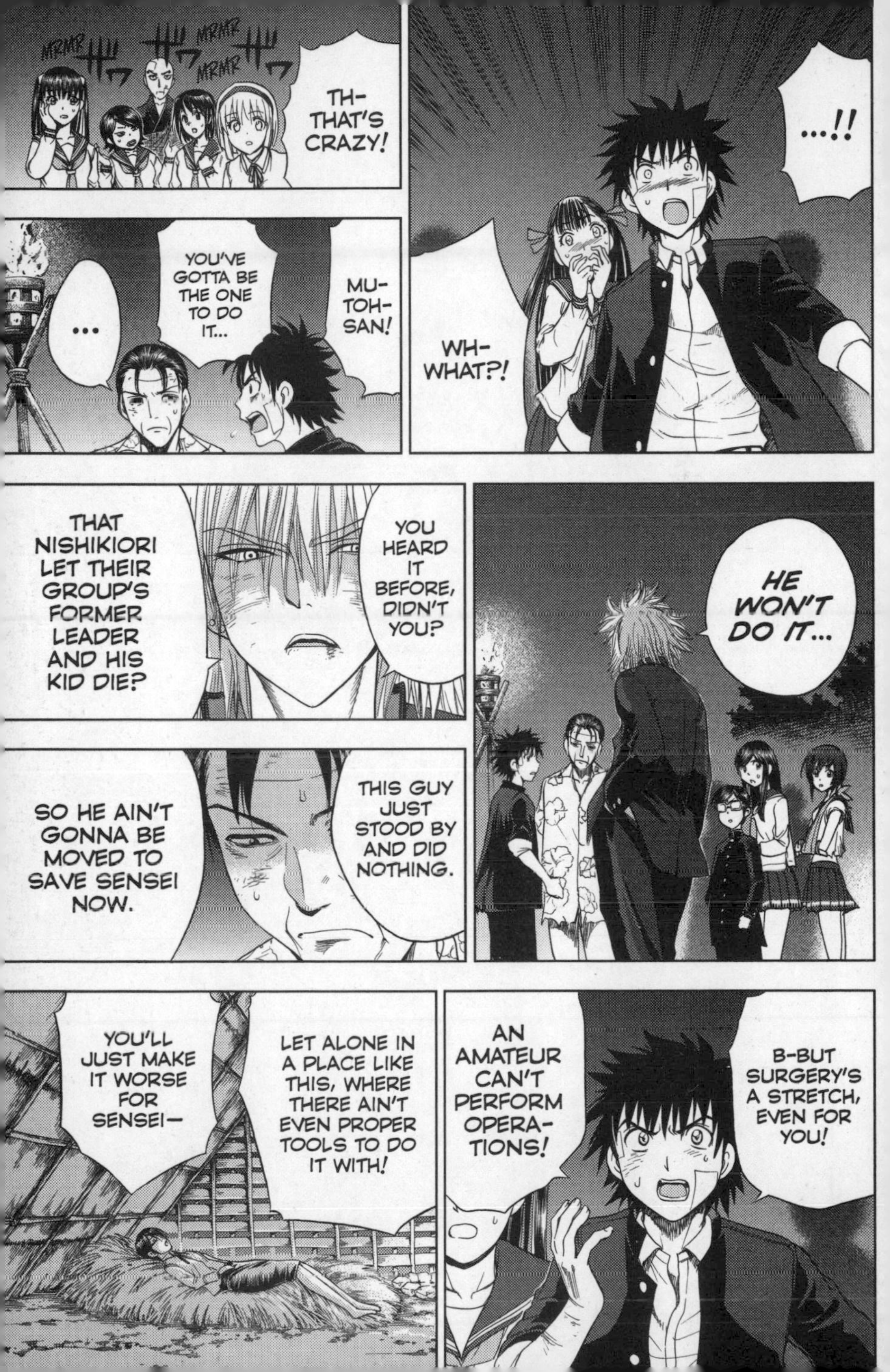
...!!
WH-WHAT?!
MRMR
MRMR
MRMR
TH-THAT'S CRAZY!
MU-TOH-SAN!
YOU'VE GOTTA BE THE ONE TO DO IT...
...
HE WON'T DO IT...
YOU HEARD IT BEFORE, DIDN'T YOU?
THAT NISHIKIORI LET THEIR GROUP'S FORMER LEADER AND HIS KID DIE?
THIS GUY JUST STOOD BY AND DID NOTHING.
SO HE AIN'T GONNA BE MOVED TO SAVE SENSEI NOW.
B-BUT SURGERY'S A STRETCH, EVEN FOR YOU!
AN AMATEUR CAN'T PERFORM OPERA-TIONS!
LET ALONE IN A PLACE LIKE THIS, WHERE THERE AIN'T EVEN PROPER TOOLS TO DO IT WITH!
YOU'LL JUST MAKE IT WORSE FOR SENSEI—

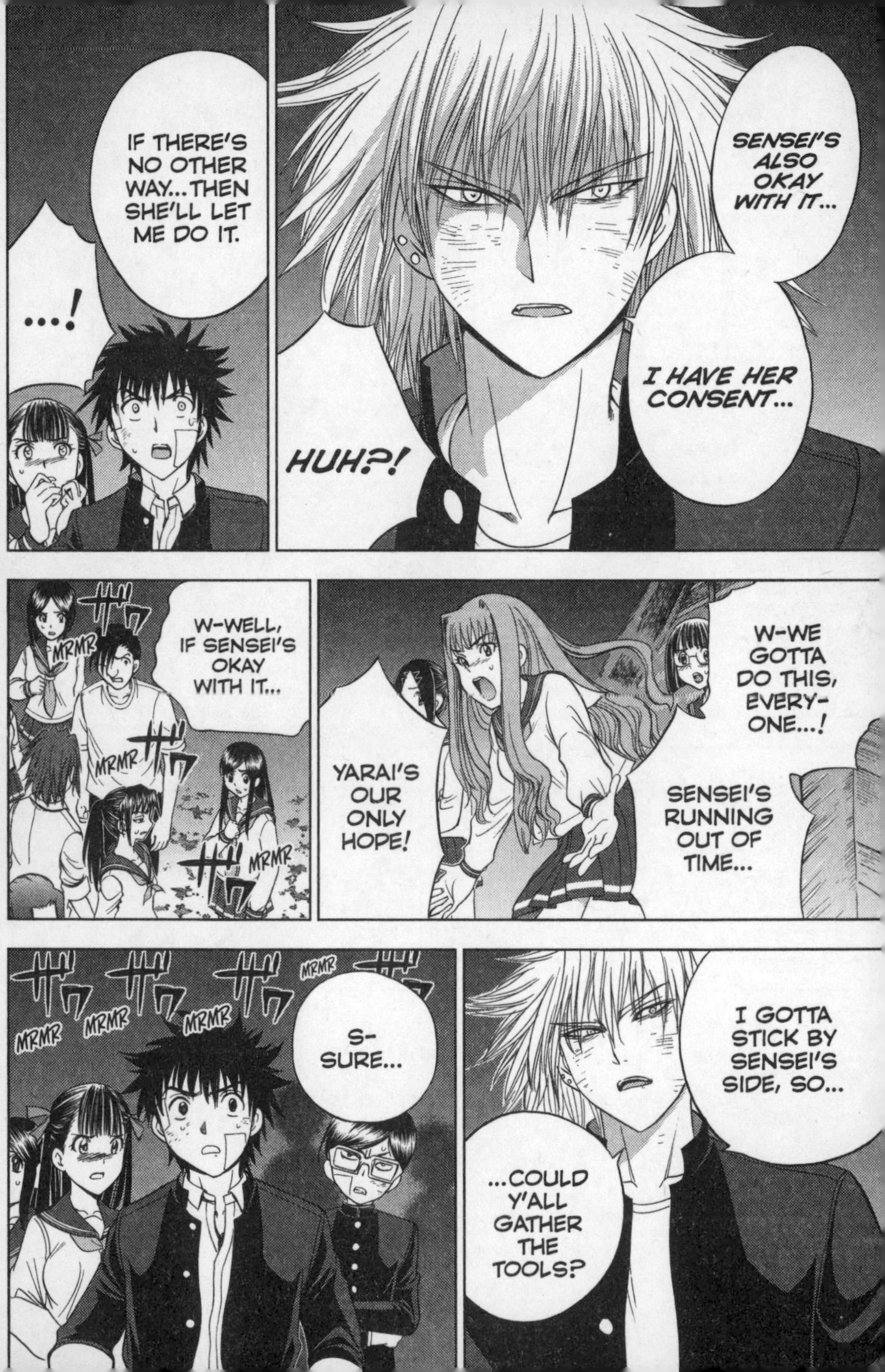

SENSEI'S ALSO OKAY WITH IT...
I HAVE HER CONSENT...
HUH?!
IF THERE'S NO OTHER WAY...THEN SHE'LL LET ME DO IT.
...!
W-WE GOTTA DO THIS, EVERY-ONE...!
SENSEI'S RUNNING OUT OF TIME...
YARAI'S OUR ONLY HOPE!
W-WELL, IF SENSEI'S OKAY WITH IT...
MRMR
MRMR
MRMR
I GOTTA STICK BY SENSEI'S SIDE, SO...
...COULD Y'ALL GATHER THE TOOLS?
S-SURE...
MRMR
MRMR
MRMR
MRMR

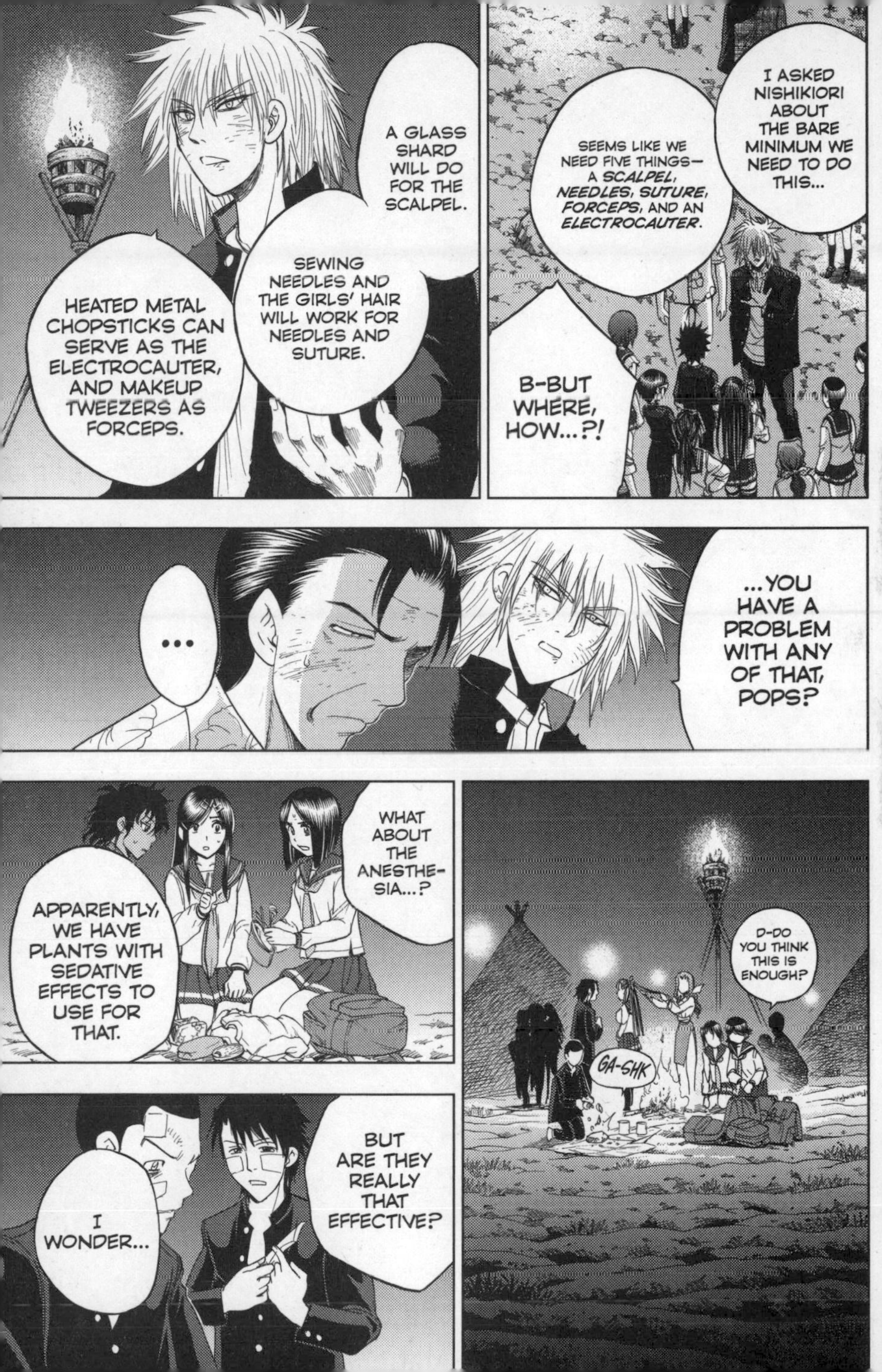
I ASKED NISHIKIORI ABOUT THE BARE MINIMUM WE NEED TO DO THIS...
SEEMS LIKE WE NEED FIVE THINGS— A SCALPEL, NEEDLES, SUTURE, FORCEPS, AND AN ELECTROCAUTER.
B-BUT WHERE, HOW...?!
A GLASS SHARD WILL DO FOR THE SCALPEL.
SEWING NEEDLES AND THE GIRLS' HAIR WILL WORK FOR NEEDLES AND SUTURE.
HEATED METAL CHOPSTICKS CAN SERVE AS THE ELECTROCAUTER, AND MAKEUP TWEEZERS AS FORCEPS.
...YOU HAVE A PROBLEM WITH ANY OF THAT, POPS?
...
D-DO YOU THINK THIS IS ENOUGH?
GA-SHK
WHAT ABOUT THE ANESTHE-SIA...?
APPARENTLY, WE HAVE PLANTS WITH SEDATIVE EFFECTS TO USE FOR THAT.
BUT ARE THEY REALLY THAT EFFECTIVE?
I WONDER...

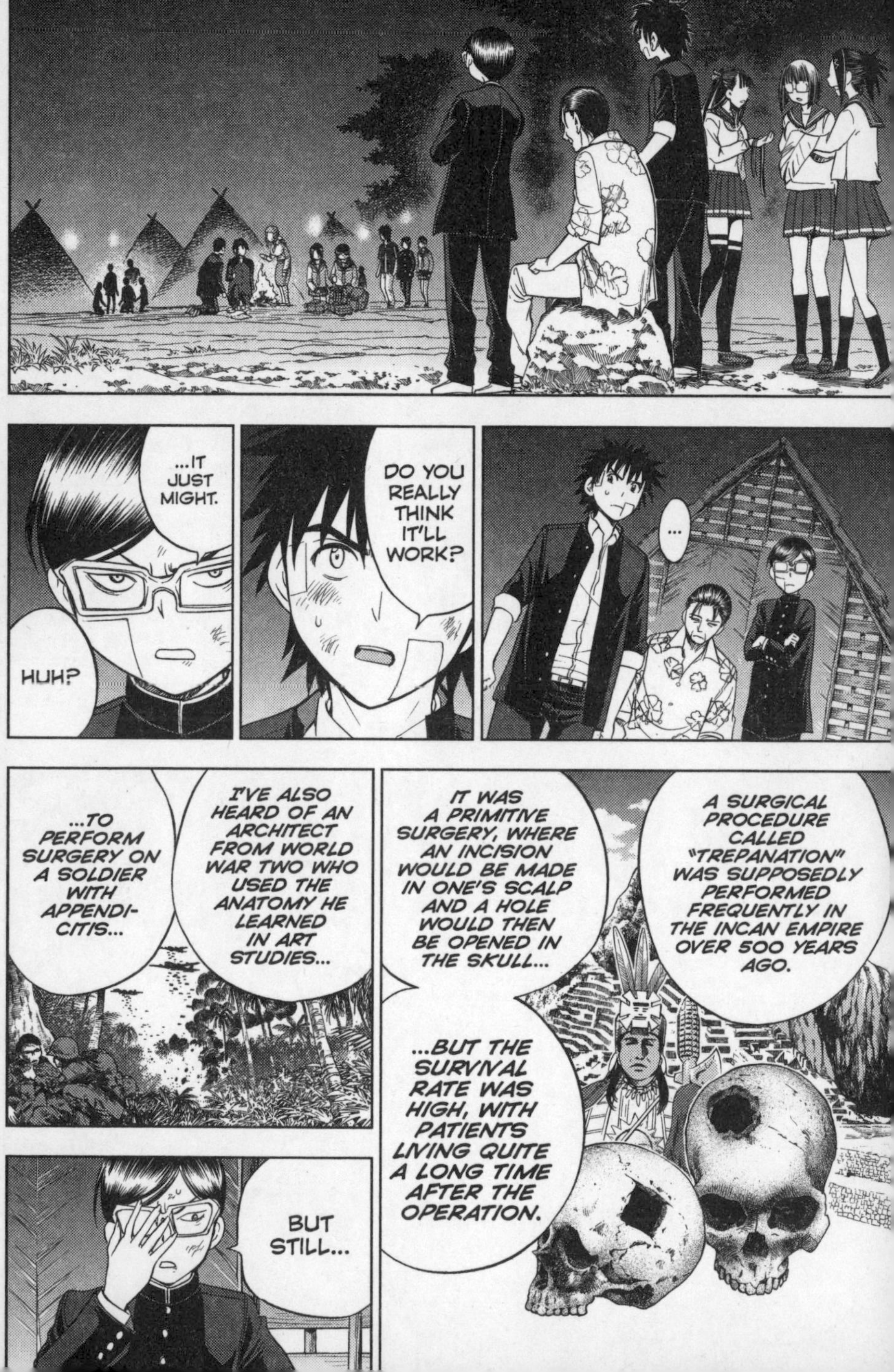
...
DO YOU REALLY THINK IT'LL WORK?
...IT JUST MIGHT.
HUH?
A SURGICAL PROCEDURE CALLED "TREPANATION" WAS SUPPOSEDLY PERFORMED FREQUENTLY IN THE INCAN EMPIRE OVER 500 YEARS AGO.
IT WAS A PRIMITIVE SURGERY, WHERE AN INCISION WOULD BE MADE IN ONE'S SCALP AND A HOLE WOULD THEN BE OPENED IN THE SKULL...
...BUT THE SURVIVAL RATE WAS HIGH, WITH PATIENTS LIVING QUITE A LONG TIME AFTER THE OPERATION.
I'VE ALSO HEARD OF AN ARCHITECT FROM WORLD WAR TWO WHO USED THE ANATOMY HE LEARNED IN ART STUDIES...
...TO PERFORM SURGERY ON A SOLDIER WITH APPENDICITIS...
BUT STILL...

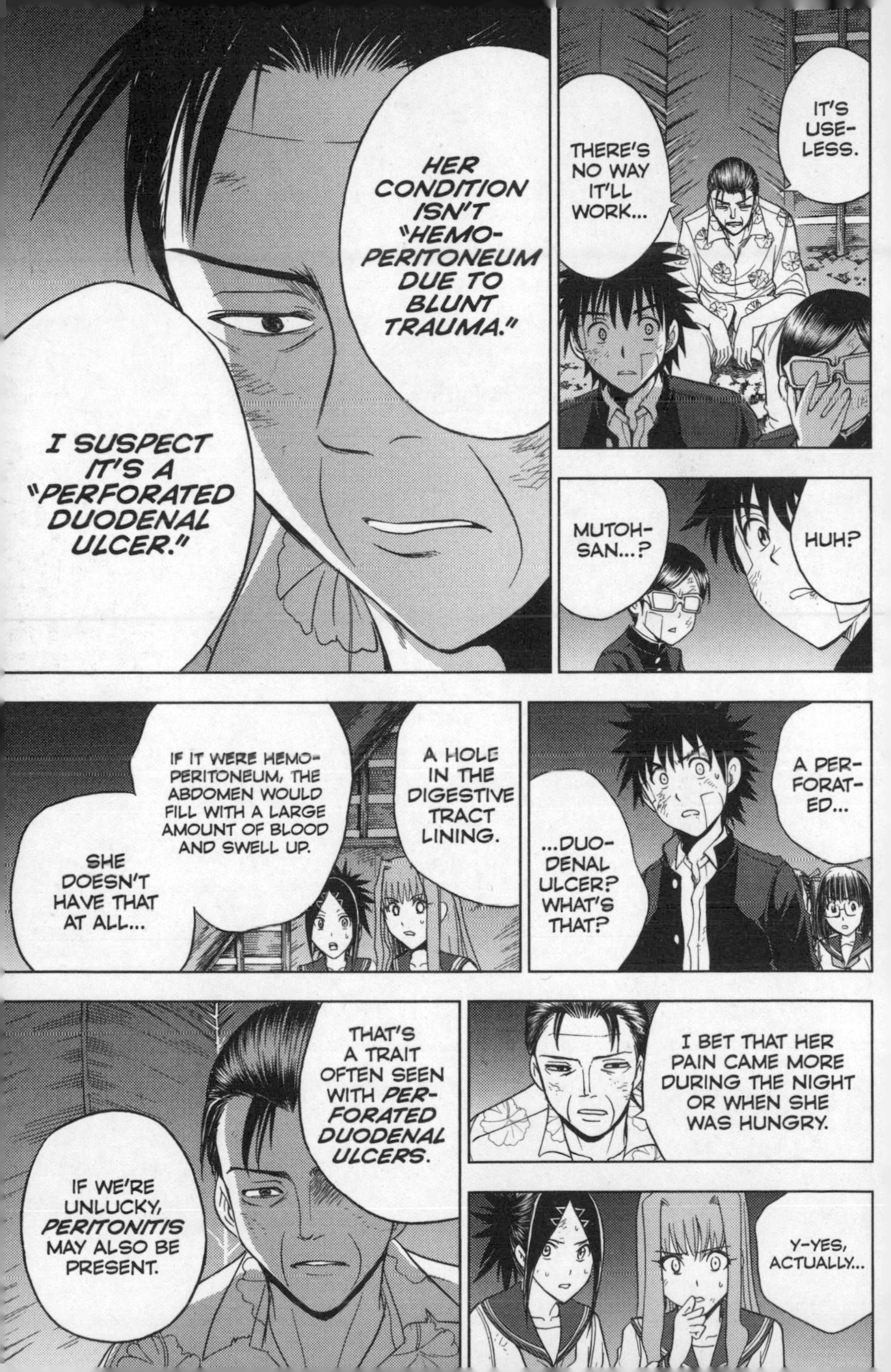
IT'S USELESS.
THERE'S NO WAY IT'LL WORK...
HUH?
MUTOH-SAN...?
HER CONDITION ISN'T "HEMO-PERITONEUM DUE TO BLUNT TRAUMA."
I SUSPECT IT'S A "PERFORATED DUODENAL ULCER."
A PER-FORAT-ED...
...DUODENAL ULCER? WHAT'S THAT?
A HOLE IN THE DIGESTIVE TRACT LINING.
IF IT WERE HEMO-PERITONEUM, THE ABDOMEN WOULD FILL WITH A LARGE AMOUNT OF BLOOD AND SWELL UP.
SHE DOESN'T HAVE THAT AT ALL...
I BET THAT HER PAIN CAME MORE DURING THE NIGHT OR WHEN SHE WAS HUNGRY.
Y-YES, ACTUALLY...
THAT'S A TRAIT OFTEN SEEN WITH PERFORATED DUODENAL ULCERS.
IF WE'RE UNLUCKY, PERITONITIS MAY ALSO BE PRESENT.

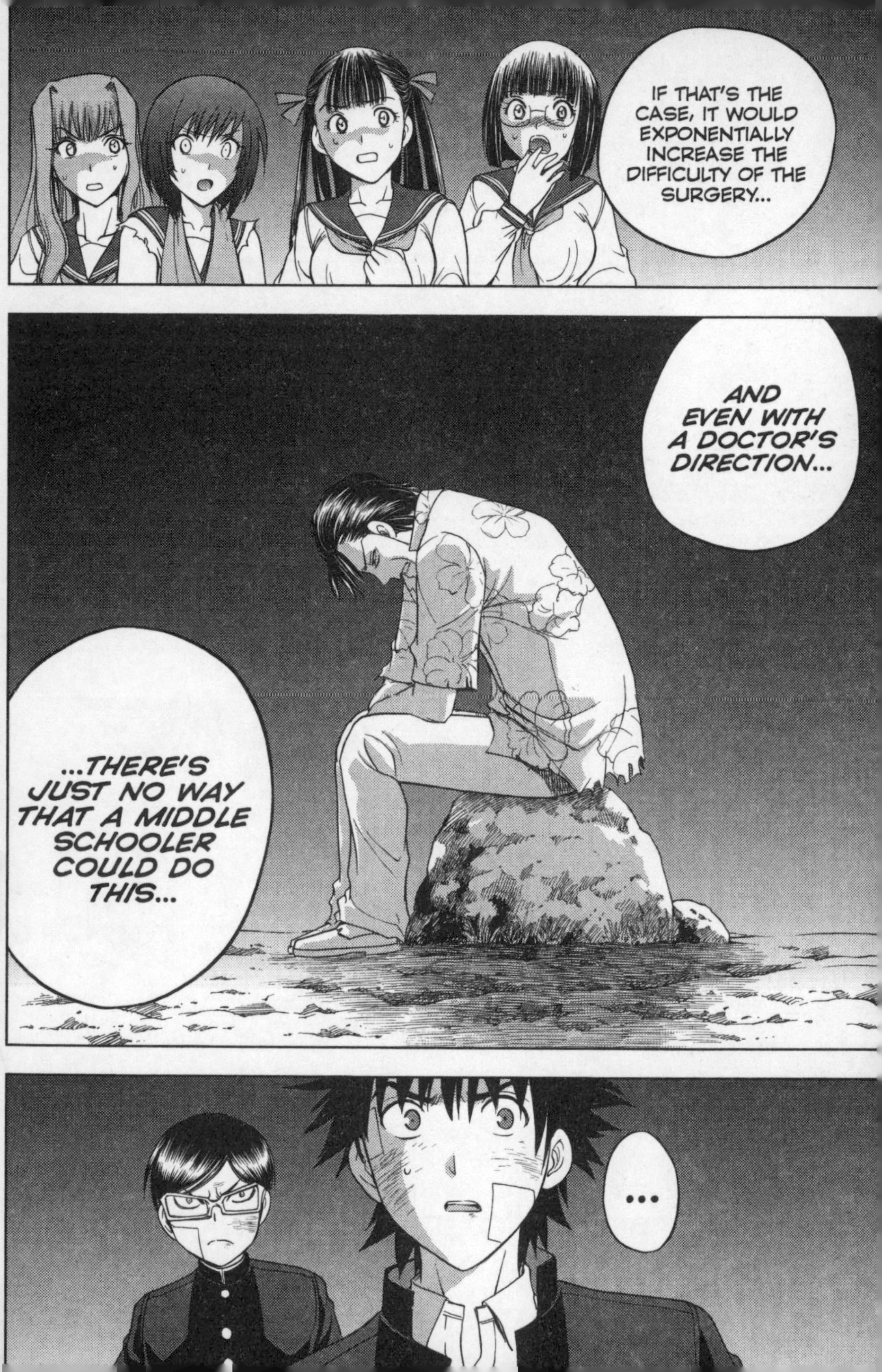
IF THAT'S THE CASE, IT WOULD EXPONENTIALLY INCREASE THE DIFFICULTY OF THE SURGERY...
AND EVEN WITH A DOCTOR'S DIRECTION...
...THERE'S JUST NO WAY THAT A MIDDLE SCHOOLER COULD DO THIS...
...

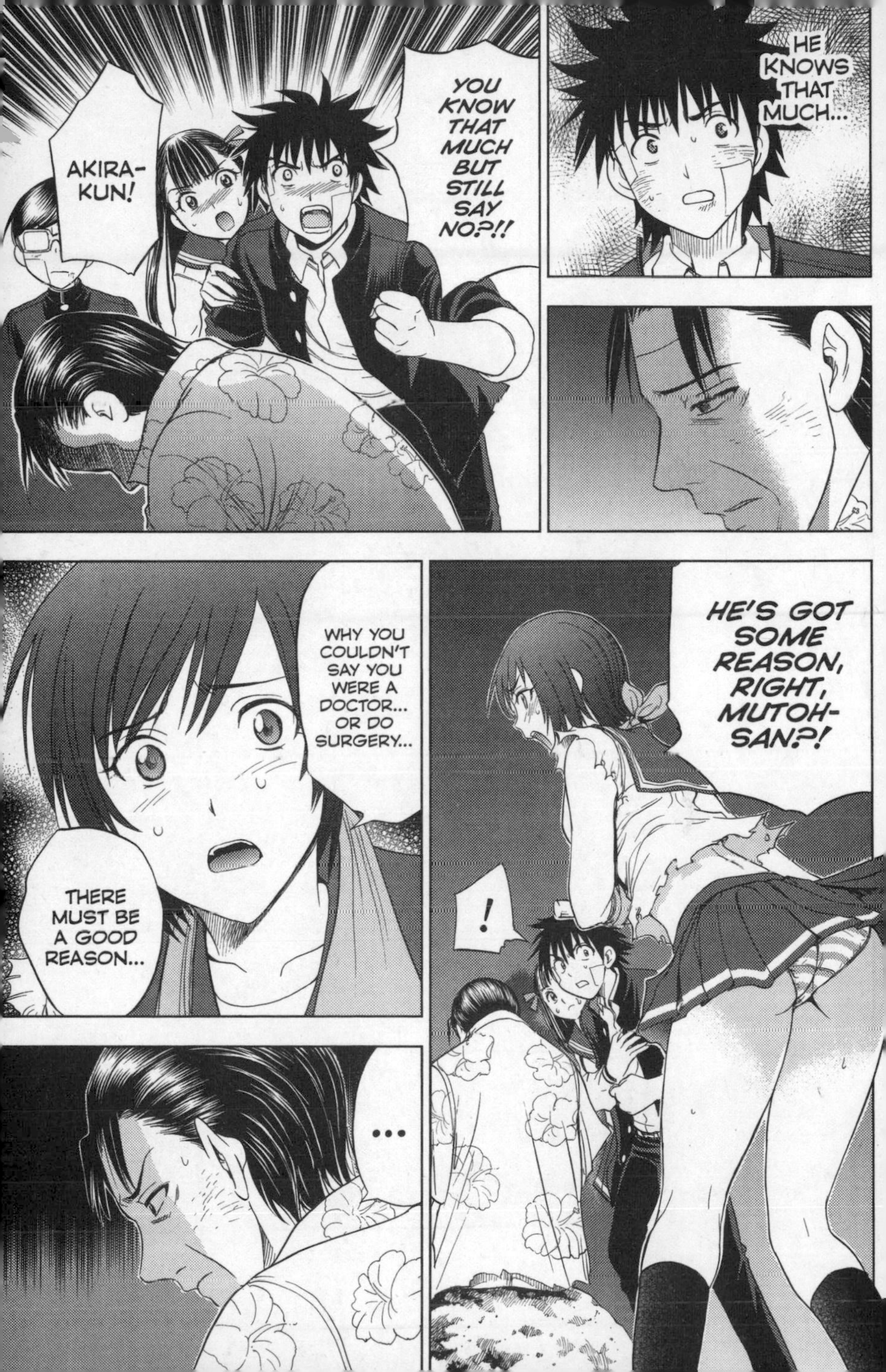

HE KNOWS THAT MUCH...
YOU KNOW THAT MUCH BUT STILL SAY NO?!!
AKIRA-KUN!
HE'S GOT SOME REASON, RIGHT, MUTOH-SAN?!
!
WHY YOU COULDN'T SAY YOU WERE A DOCTOR... OR DO SURGERY...
THERE MUST BE A GOOD REASON...
...

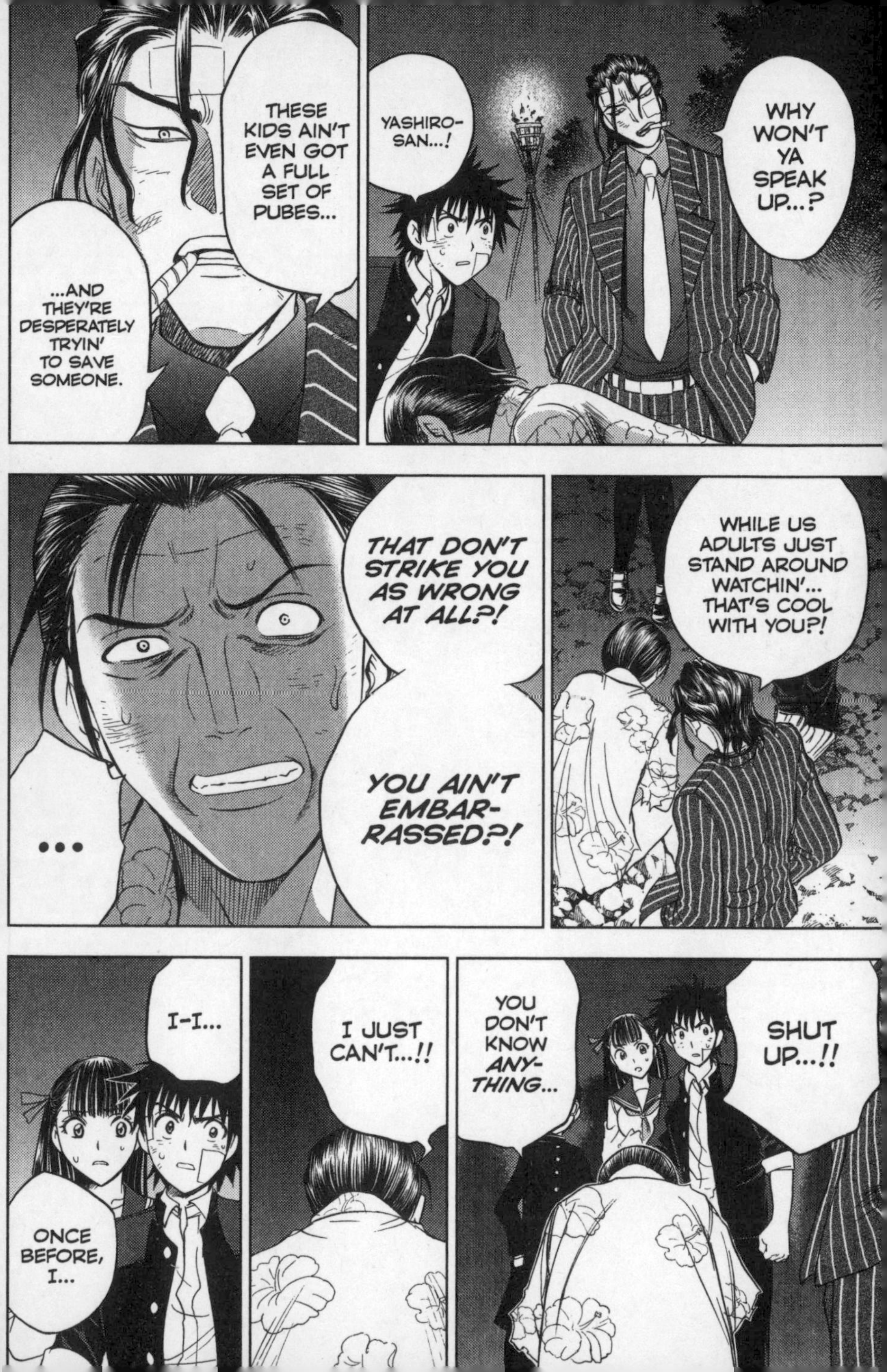
WHY WON'T YA SPEAK UP...?
YASHIRO-SAN...!
THESE KIDS AIN'T EVEN GOT A FULL SET OF PUBES...
...AND THEY'RE DESPERATELY TRYIN' TO SAVE SOMEONE.
WHILE US ADULTS JUST STAND AROUND WATCHIN'... THAT'S COOL WITH YOU?!
THAT DON'T STRIKE YOU AS WRONG AT ALL?!
YOU AIN'T EMBAR-RASSED?!
...
SHUT UP...!!
YOU DON'T KNOW ANY-THING...
I JUST CAN'T...!!
I-I...
ONCE BEFORE, I...

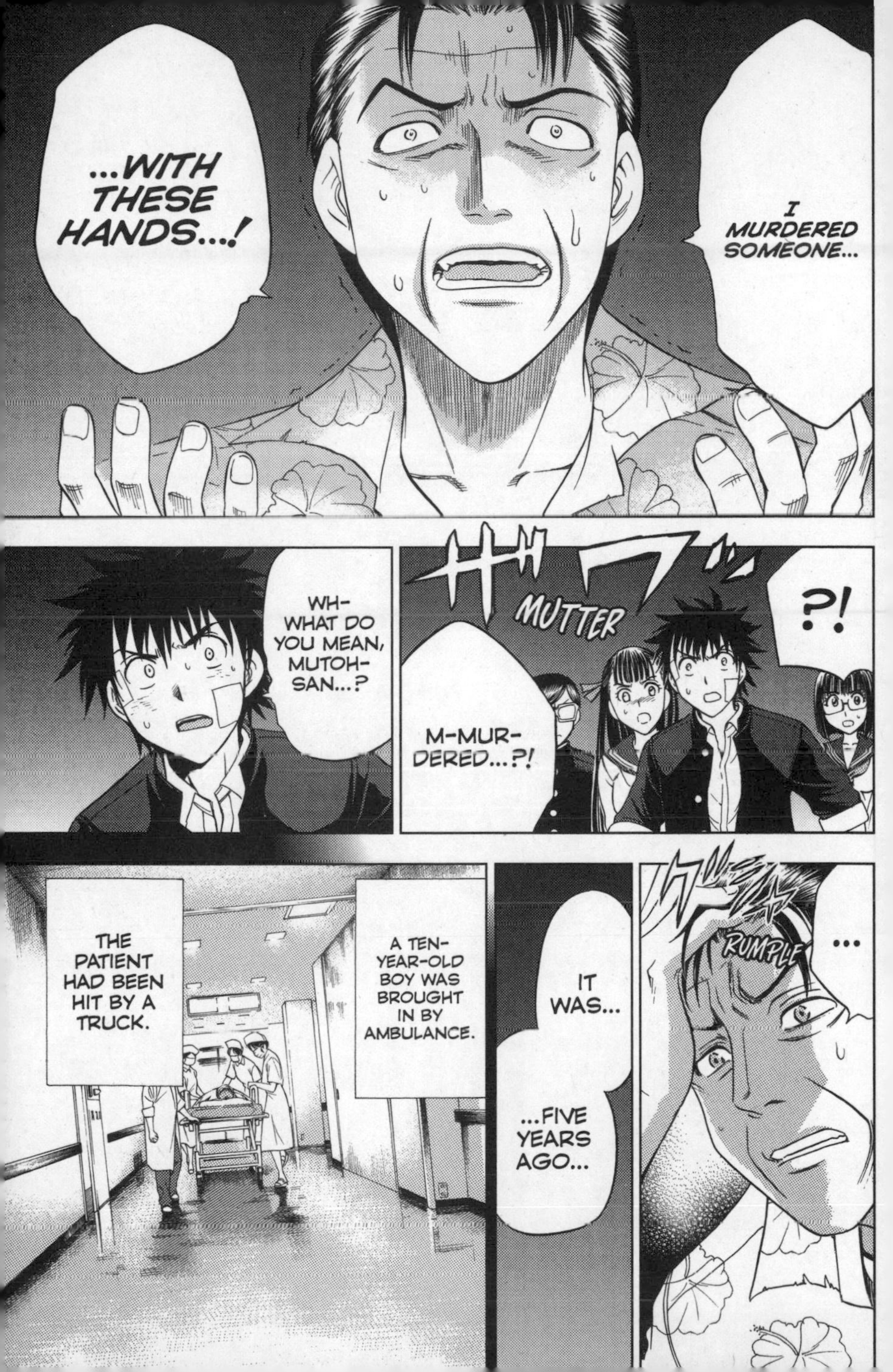
I MURDERED SOMEONE...
...WITH THESE HANDS...!
ザワッ
MUTTER
?!
M-MURDERED...?!
WH- WHAT DO YOU MEAN, MUTOH-SAN...?
...
RUMPLE
IT WAS...
...FIVE YEARS AGO...
A TEN-YEAR-OLD BOY WAS BROUGHT IN BY AMBULANCE.
THE PATIENT HAD BEEN HIT BY A TRUCK.

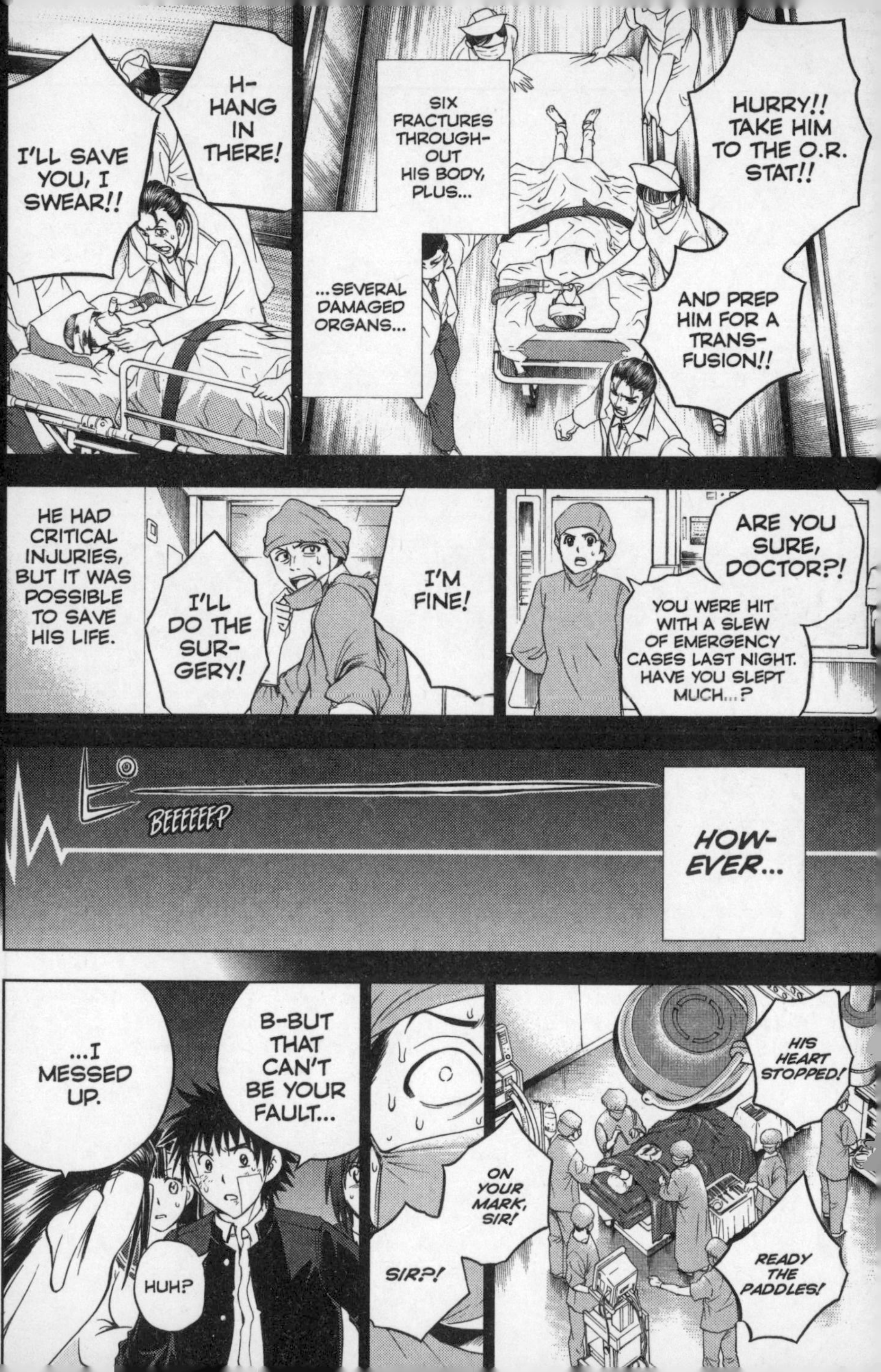
HURRY!! TAKE HIM TO THE O.R. STAT!!
SIX FRACTURES THROUGH-OUT HIS BODY, PLUS...
...SEVERAL DAMAGED ORGANS...
AND PREP HIM FOR A TRANS-FUSION!!
H-HANG IN THERE!
I'LL SAVE YOU, I SWEAR!!
ARE YOU SURE, DOCTOR?!
YOU WERE HIT WITH A SLEW OF EMERGENCY CASES LAST NIGHT. HAVE YOU SLEPT MUCH...?
I'M FINE!
I'LL DO THE SUR-GERY!
HE HAD CRITICAL INJURIES, BUT IT WAS POSSIBLE TO SAVE HIS LIFE.
HOW-EVER...
BEEEEEEP
HIS HEART STOPPED!
READY THE PADDLES!
ON YOUR MARK, SIR!
SIR?!
B-BUT THAT CAN'T BE YOUR FAULT...
...I MESSED UP.
HUH?

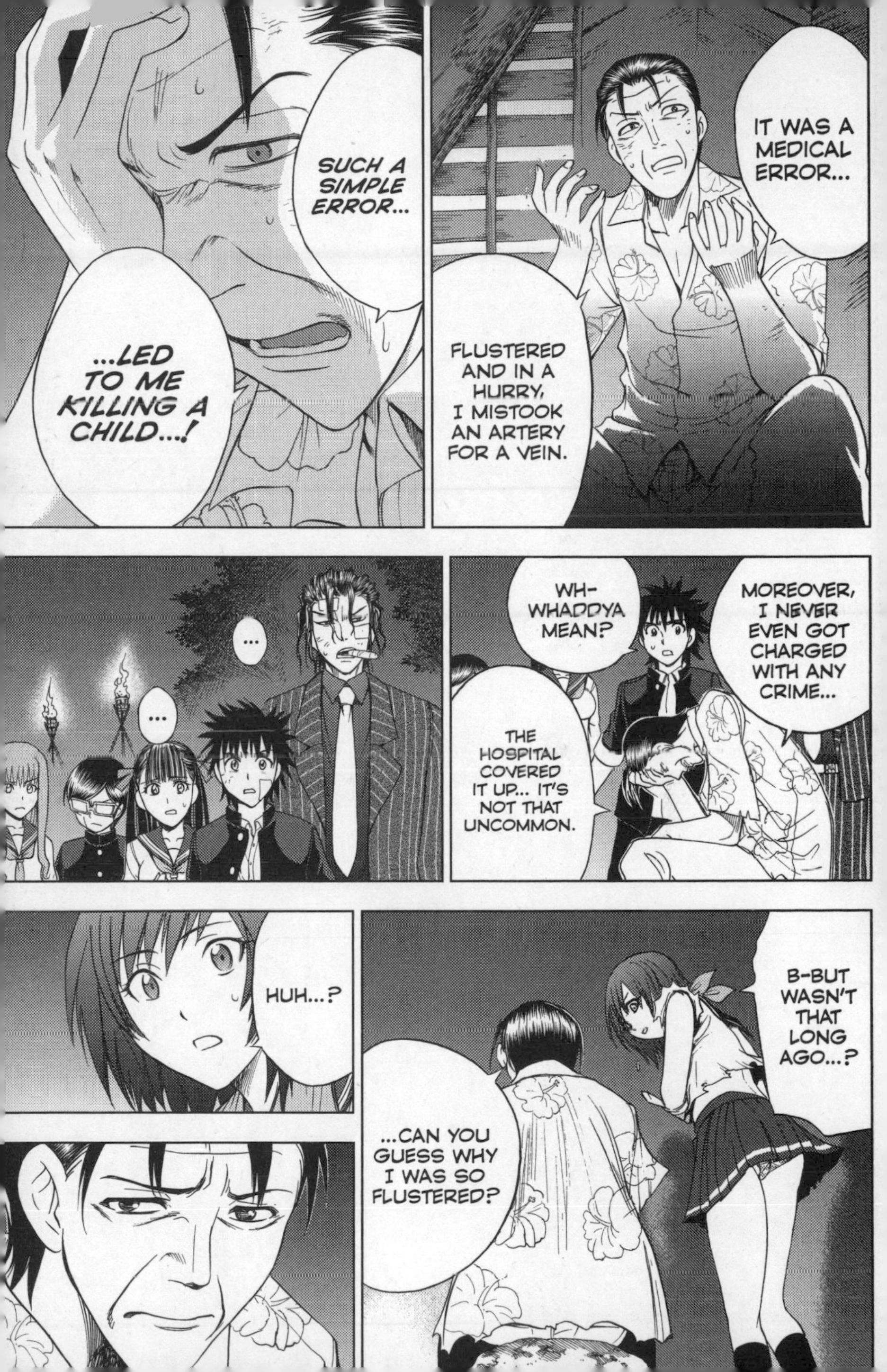
IT WAS A MEDICAL ERROR...
FLUSTERED AND IN A HURRY, I MISTOOK AN ARTERY FOR A VEIN.
SUCH A SIMPLE ERROR...
...LED TO ME KILLING A CHILD...!
MOREOVER, I NEVER EVEN GOT CHARGED WITH ANY CRIME...
WH- WHADDYA MEAN?
THE HOSPITAL COVERED IT UP... IT'S NOT THAT UNCOMMON.
...
...
B-BUT WASN'T THAT LONG AGO...?
...CAN YOU GUESS WHY I WAS SO FLUSTERED?
HUH...?

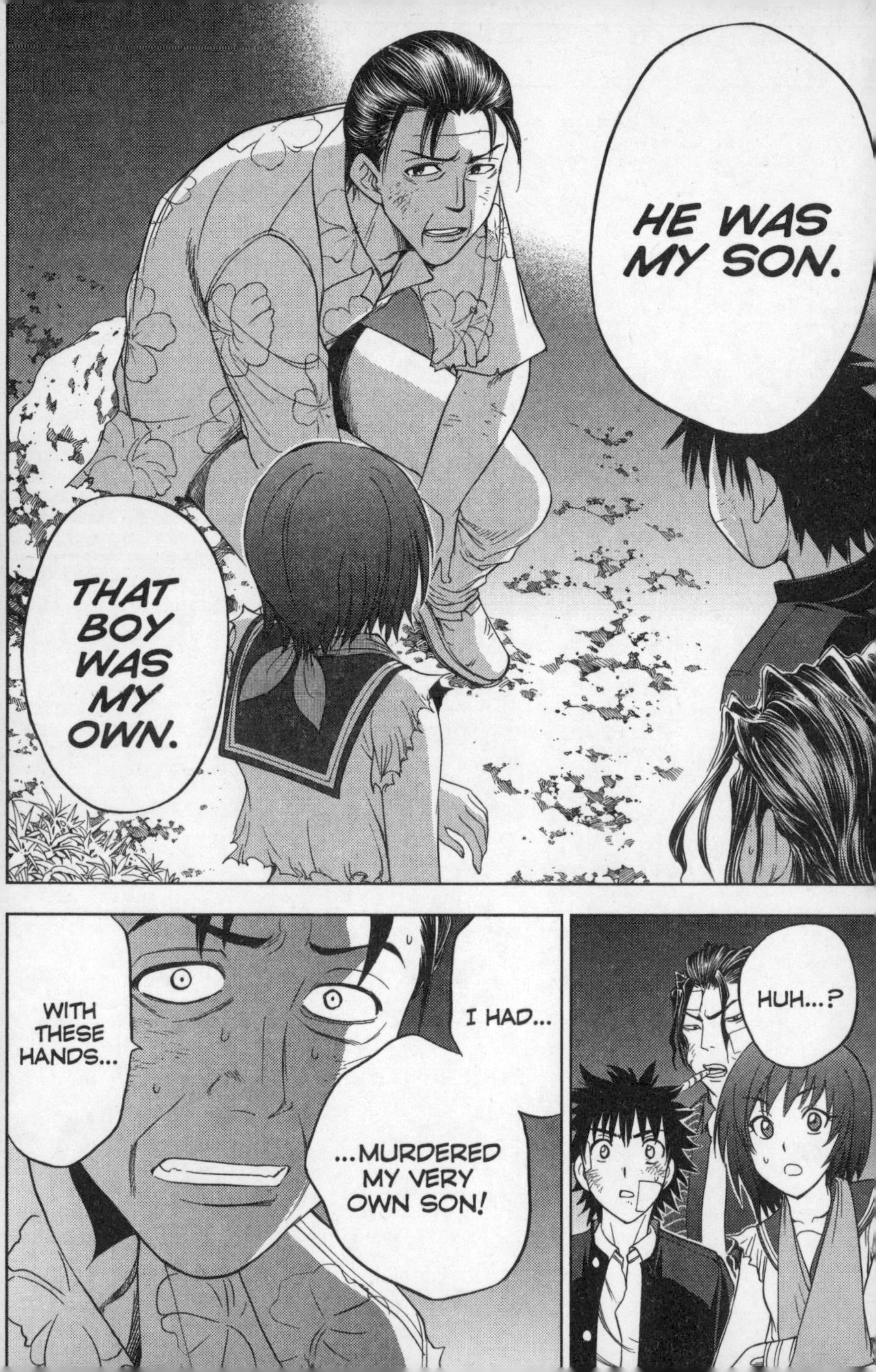
HE WAS MY SON.
THAT BOY WAS MY OWN.
HUH...?
I HAD...
WITH THESE HANDS...
...MURDERED MY VERY OWN SON!

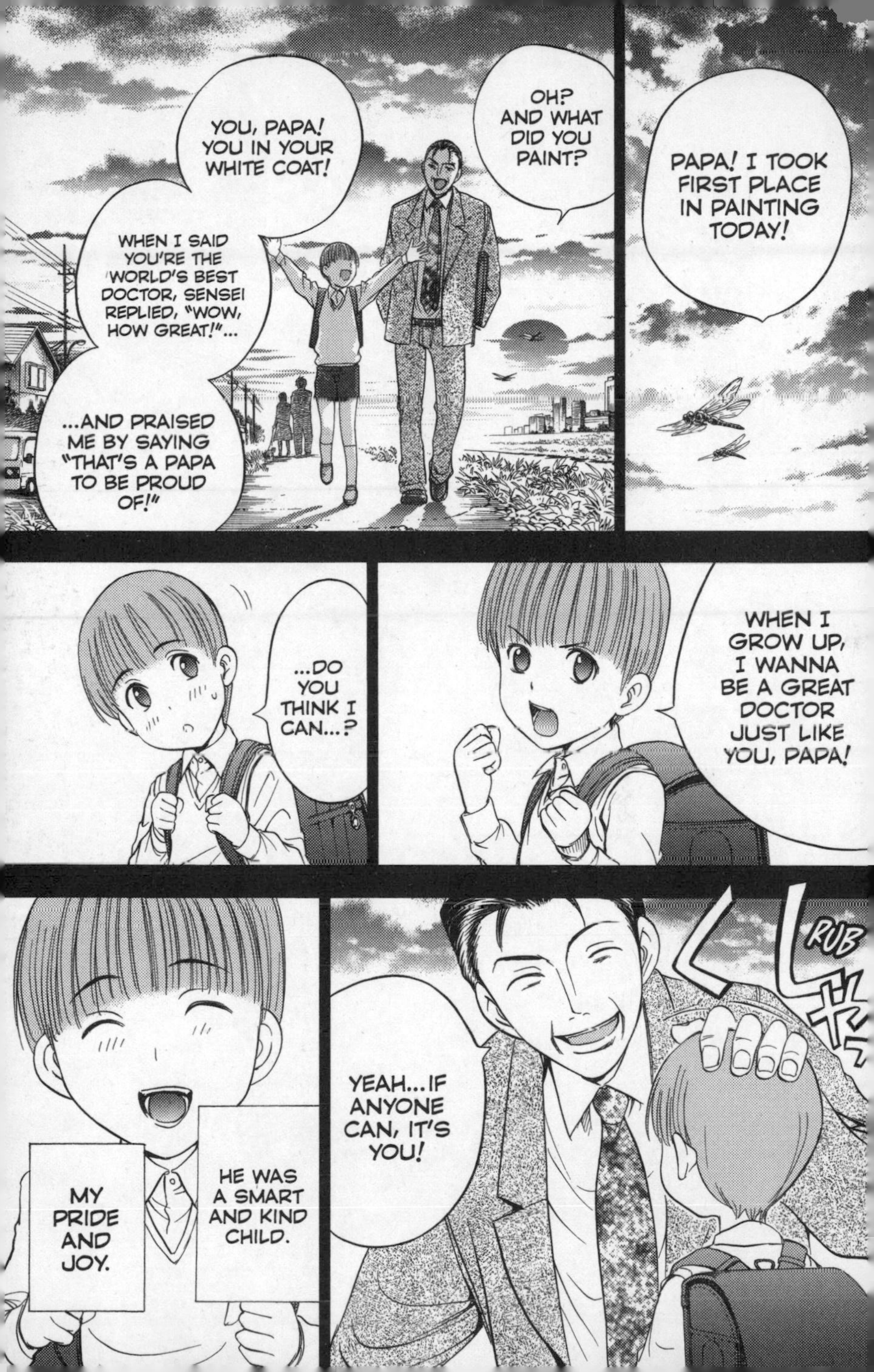
PAPA! I TOOK FIRST PLACE IN PAINTING TODAY!
OH? AND WHAT DID YOU PAINT?
YOU, PAPA! YOU IN YOUR WHITE COAT!
WHEN I SAID YOU'RE THE WORLD'S BEST DOCTOR, SENSEI REPLIED, "WOW, HOW GREAT!"...
...AND PRAISED ME BY SAYING "THAT'S A PAPA TO BE PROUD OF!"
WHEN I GROW UP, I WANNA BE A GREAT DOCTOR JUST LIKE YOU, PAPA!
...DO YOU THINK I CAN...?
RUB
YEAH...IF ANYONE CAN, IT'S YOU!
HE WAS A SMART AND KIND CHILD.
MY PRIDE AND JOY.

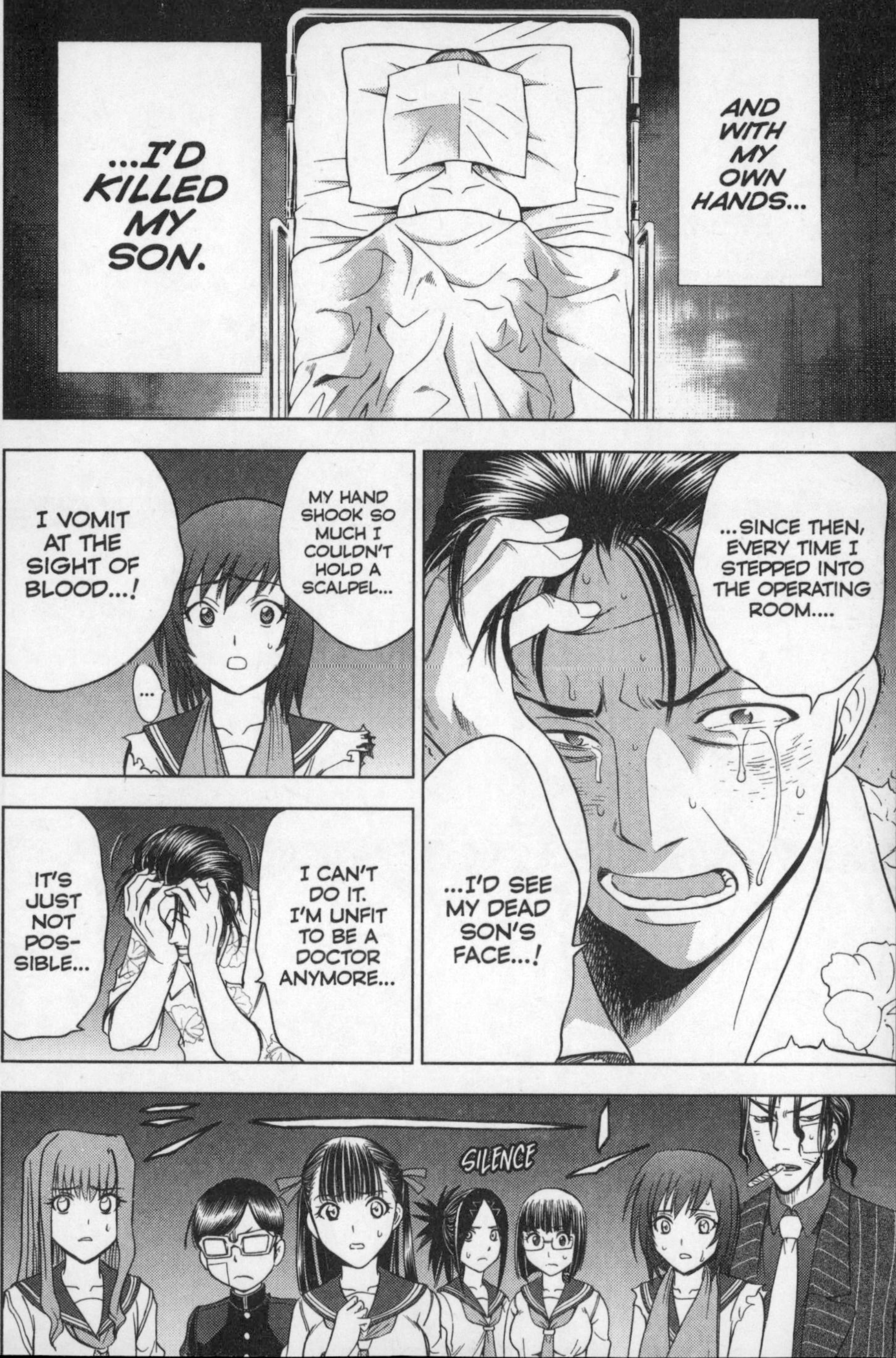
AND WITH MY OWN HANDS...
...I'D KILLED MY SON.
...SINCE THEN, EVERY TIME I STEPPED INTO THE OPERATING ROOM....
...I'D SEE MY DEAD SON'S FACE...!
MY HAND SHOOK SO MUCH I COULDN'T HOLD A SCALPEL...
I VOMIT AT THE SIGHT OF BLOOD...!
...
I CAN'T DO IT. I'M UNFIT TO BE A DOCTOR ANYMORE...
IT'S JUST NOT POS-SIBLE...
SILENCE

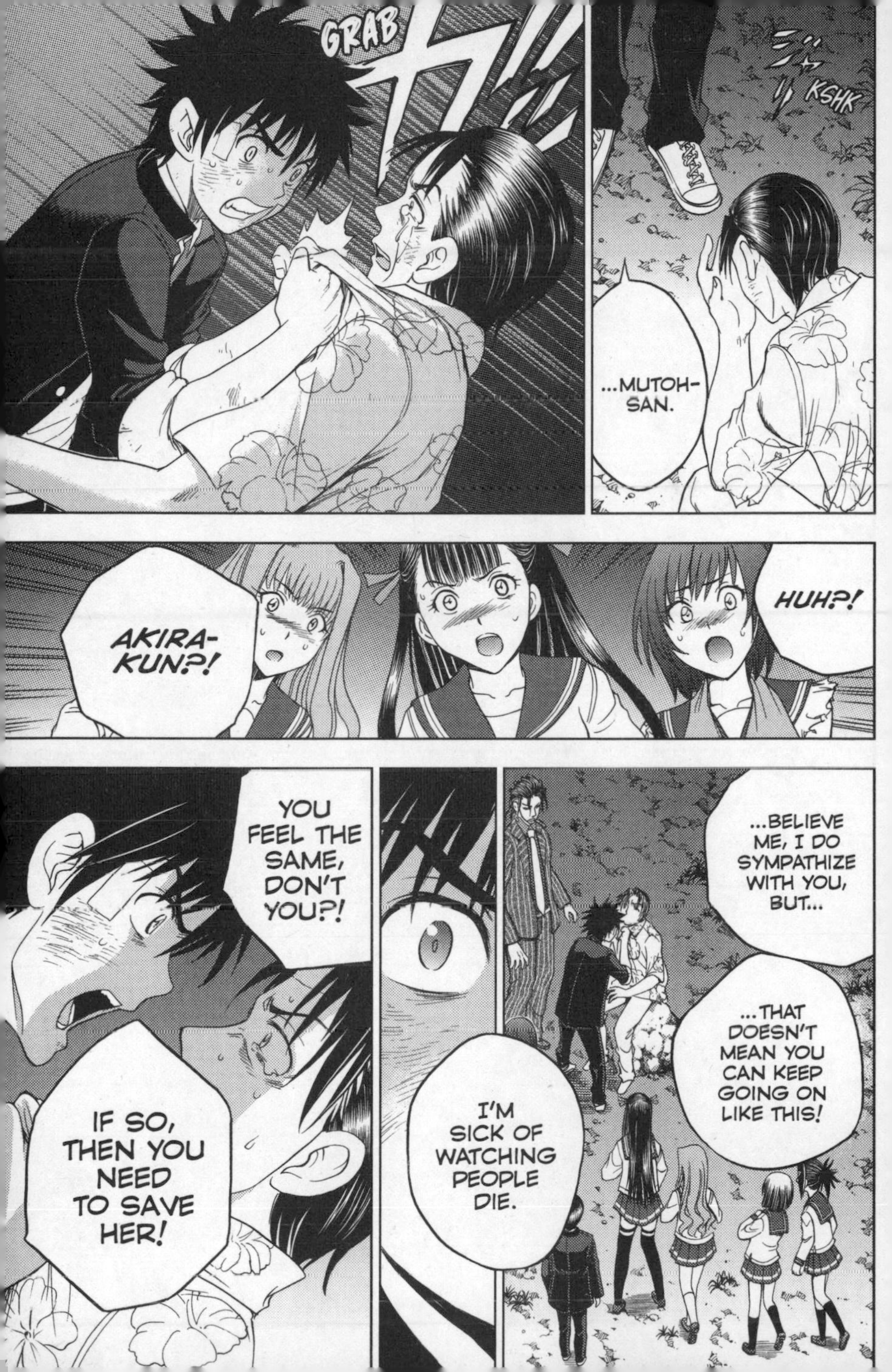
KSHK
...MUTOH-SAN.
GRAB
HUH?!
AKIRA-KUN?!
...BELIEVE ME, I DO SYMPATHIZE WITH YOU, BUT...
...THAT DOESN'T MEAN YOU CAN KEEP GOING ON LIKE THIS!
I'M SICK OF WATCHING PEOPLE DIE.
YOU FEEL THE SAME, DON'T YOU?!
IF SO, THEN YOU NEED TO SAVE HER!

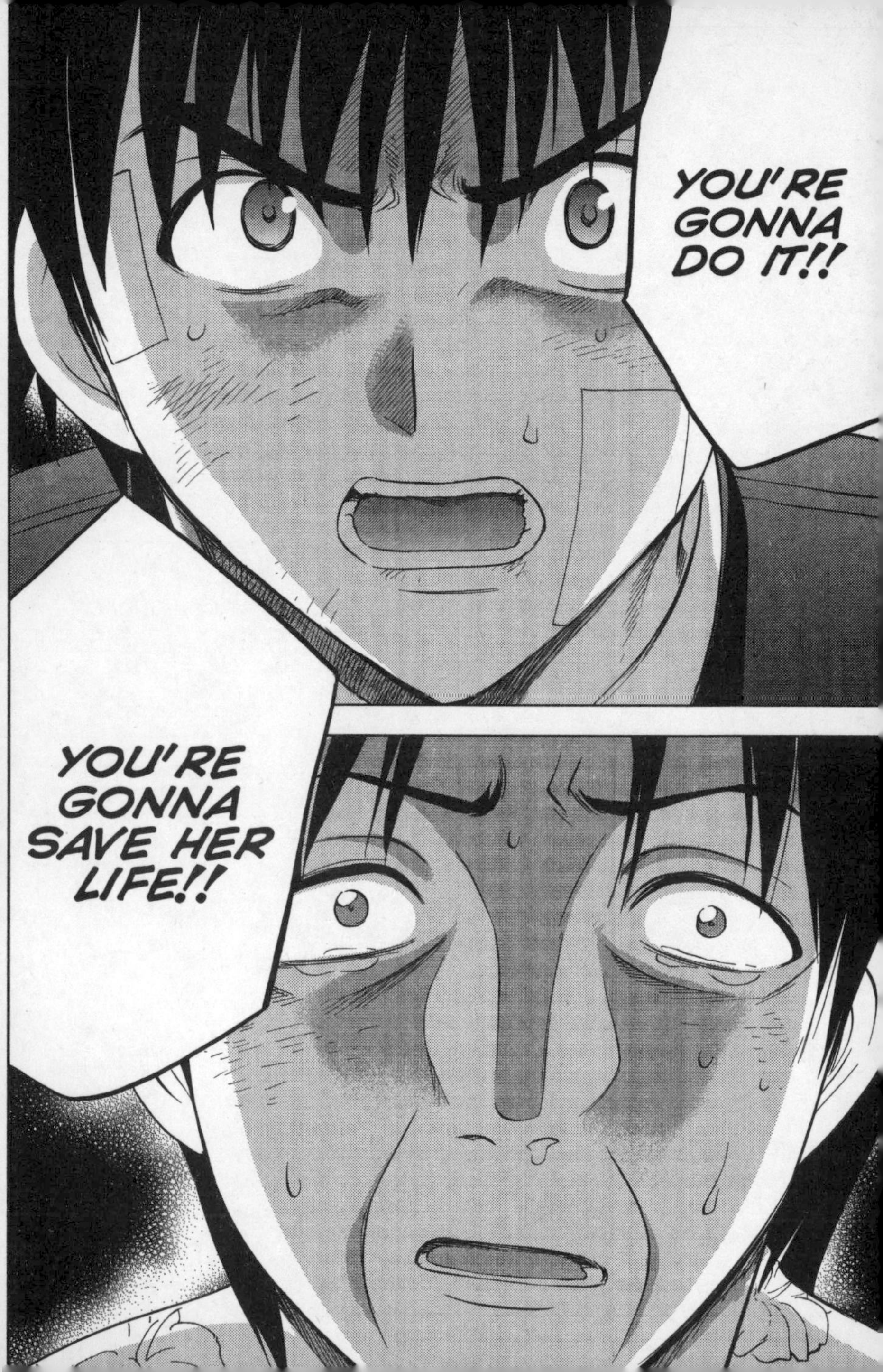
YOU'RE GONNA DO IT!!
YOU'RE GONNA SAVE HER LIFE!!

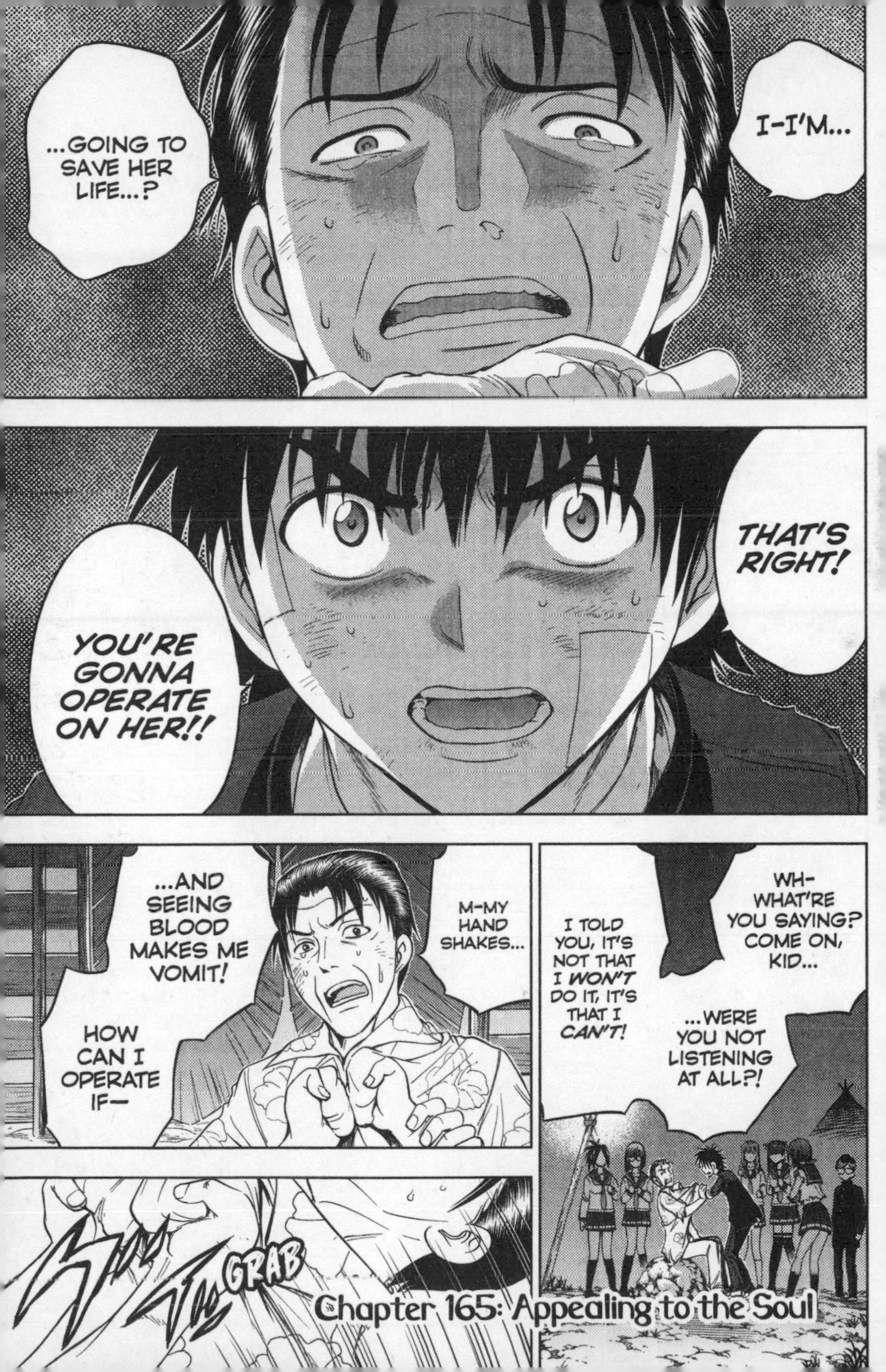
I-I'M...
...GOING TO SAVE HER LIFE...?
THAT'S RIGHT!
YOU'RE GONNA OPERATE ON HER!!
WH- WHAT'RE YOU SAYING? COME ON, KID...
...WERE YOU NOT LISTENING AT ALL?!
I TOLD YOU, IT'S NOT THAT I WON'T DO IT, IT'S THAT I CAN'T!
M-MY HAND SHAKES...
...AND SEEING BLOOD MAKES ME VOMIT!
HOW CAN I OPERATE IF—
GRAB
Chapter 165: Appealing to the Soul

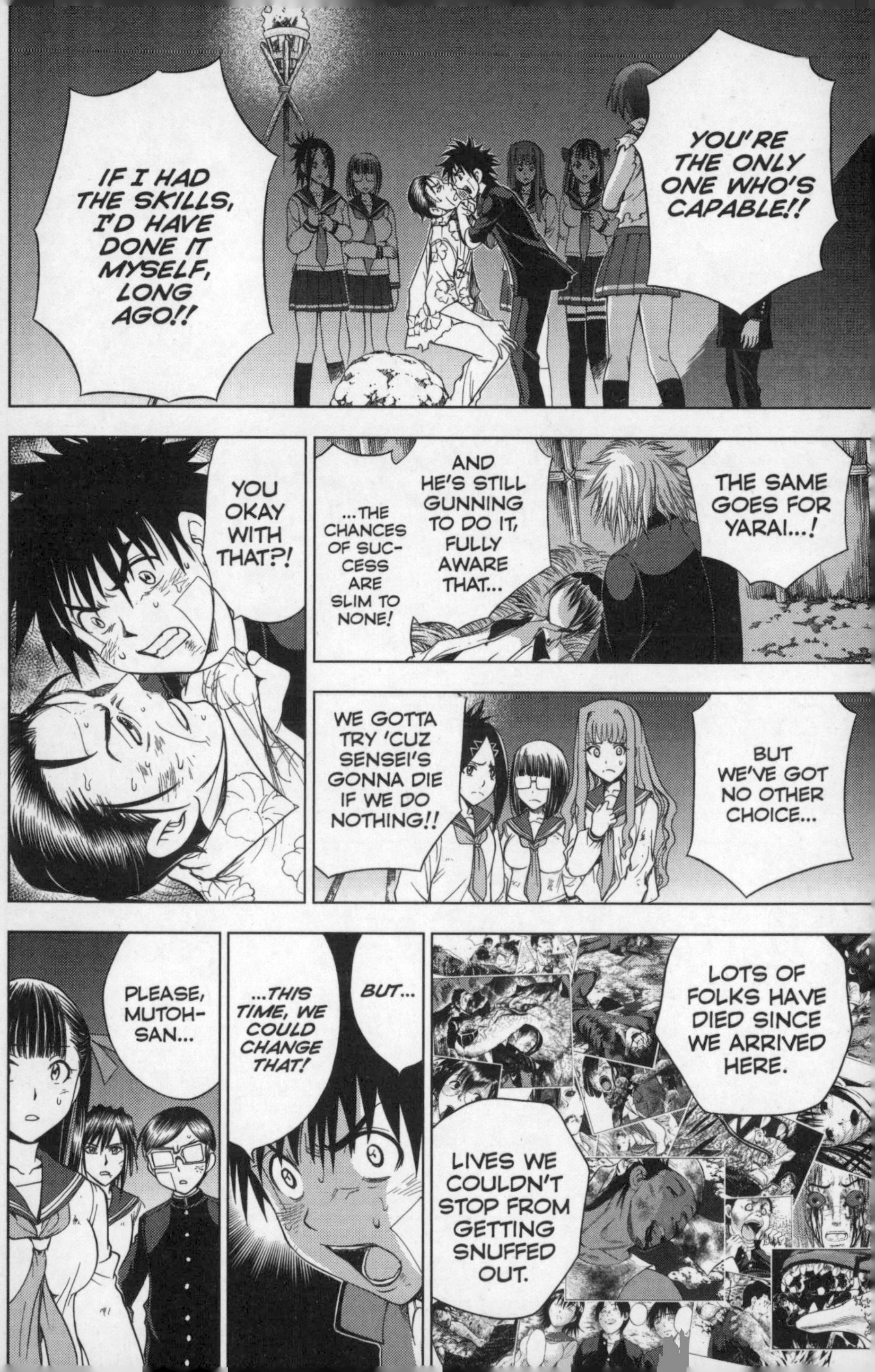
YOU'RE THE ONLY ONE WHO'S CAPABLE!!
IF I HAD THE SKILLS, I'D HAVE DONE IT MYSELF, LONG AGO!!
THE SAME GOES FOR YARAI...!
AND HE'S STILL GUNNING TO DO IT, FULLY AWARE THAT...
...THE CHANCES OF SUC-CESS ARE SLIM TO NONE!
BUT WE'VE GOT NO OTHER CHOICE...
WE GOTTA TRY 'CUZ SENSEI'S GONNA DIE IF WE DO NOTHING!!
YOU OKAY WITH THAT?!
LOTS OF FOLKS HAVE DIED SINCE WE ARRIVED HERE.
LIVES WE COULDN'T STOP FROM GETTING SNUFFED OUT.
BUT...
...THIS TIME, WE COULD CHANGE THAT!
PLEASE, MUTOH-SAN...

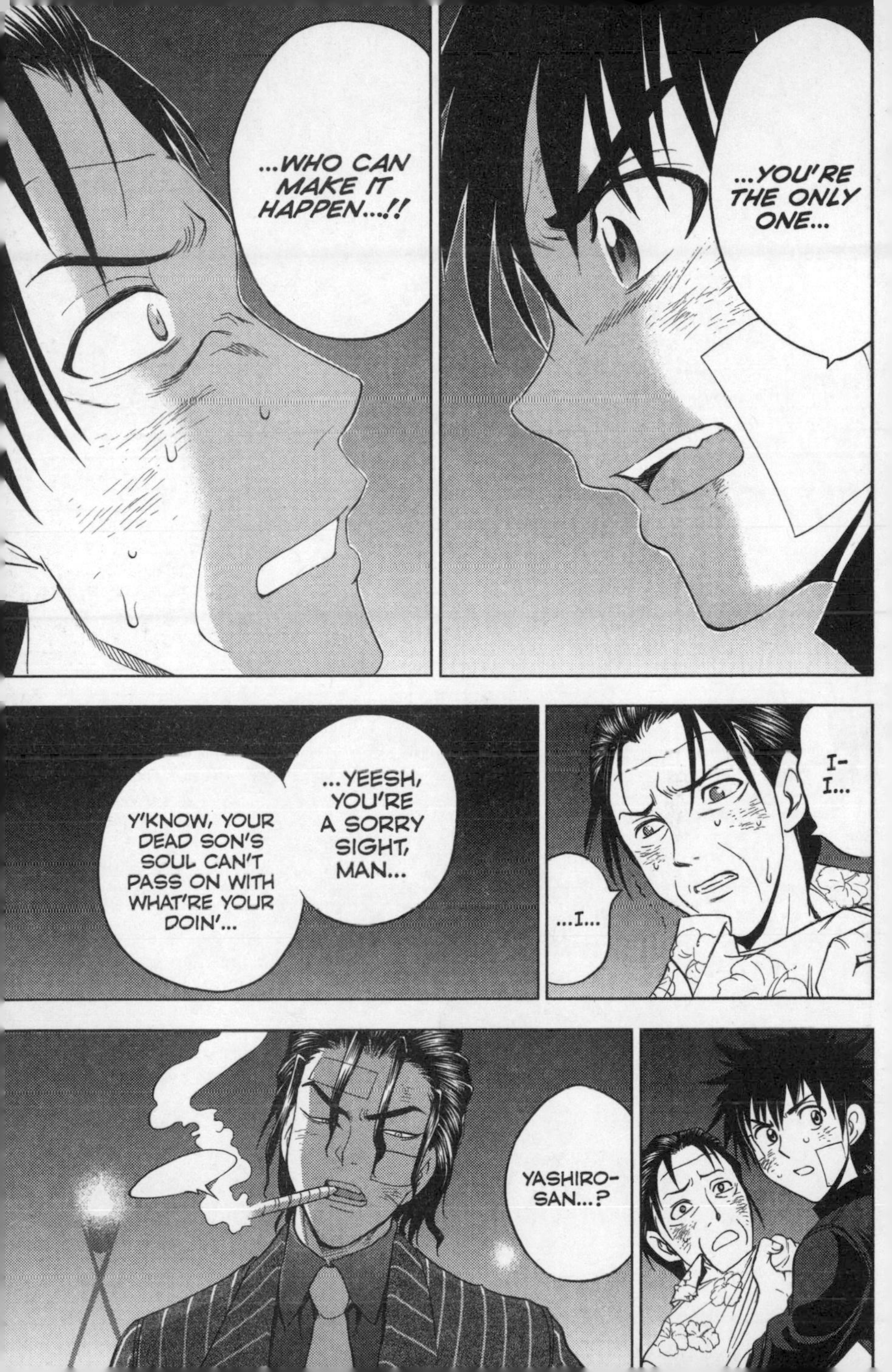
...YOU'RE THE ONLY ONE...
...WHO CAN MAKE IT HAPPEN...!!
I- I...
...I...
...YEESH, YOU'RE A SORRY SIGHT, MAN...
Y'KNOW, YOUR DEAD SON'S SOUL CAN'T PASS ON WITH WHAT'RE YOUR DOIN'...
YASHIRO-SAN...?

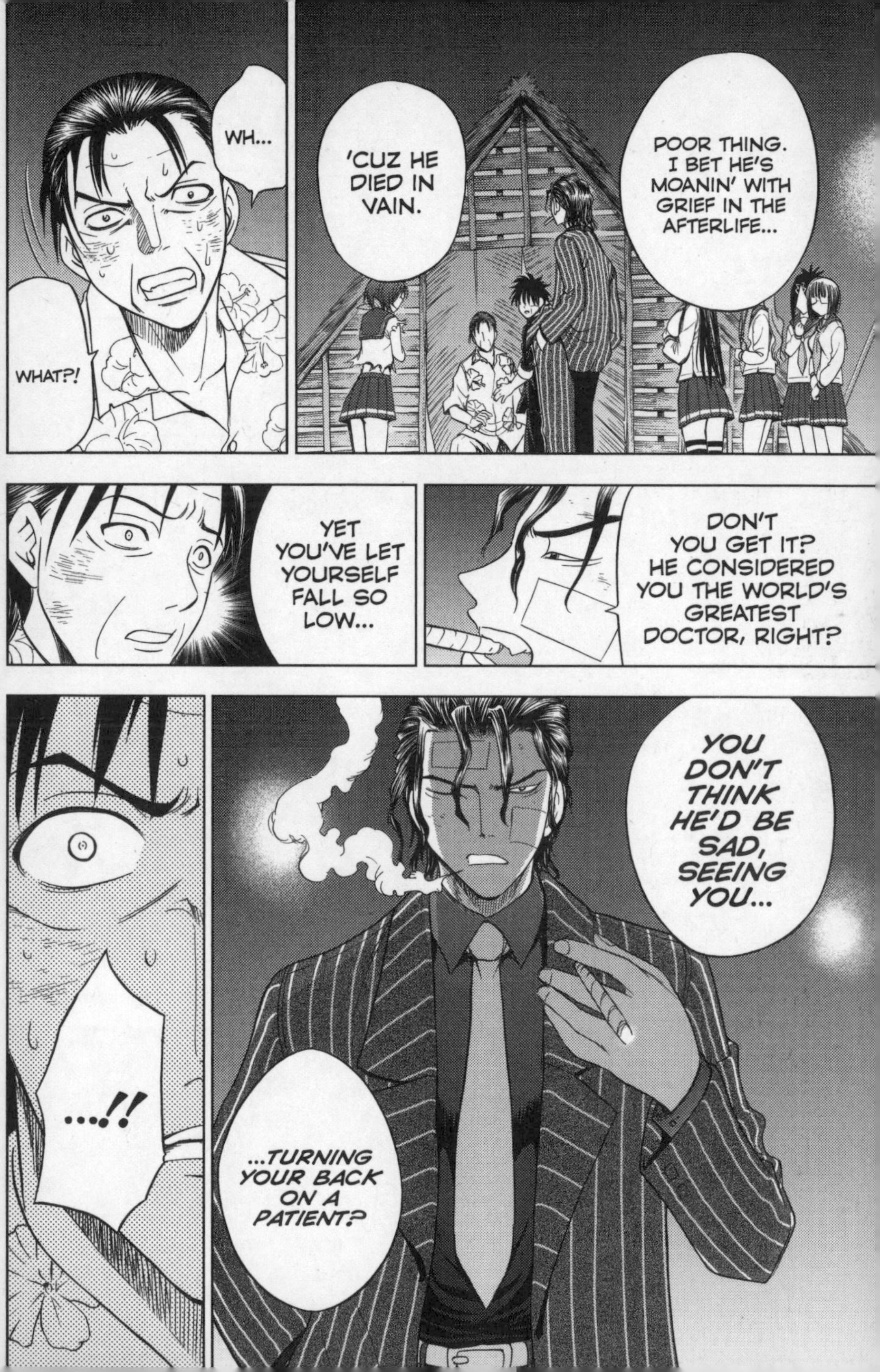
POOR THING. I BET HE'S MOANIN' WITH GRIEF IN THE AFTERLIFE...
'CUZ HE DIED IN VAIN.
WH...
WHAT?!
DON'T YOU GET IT? HE CONSIDERED YOU THE WORLD'S GREATEST DOCTOR, RIGHT?
YET YOU'VE LET YOURSELF FALL SO LOW...
YOU DON'T THINK HE'D BE SAD, SEEING YOU...
...TURNING YOUR BACK ON A PATIENT?
...!!

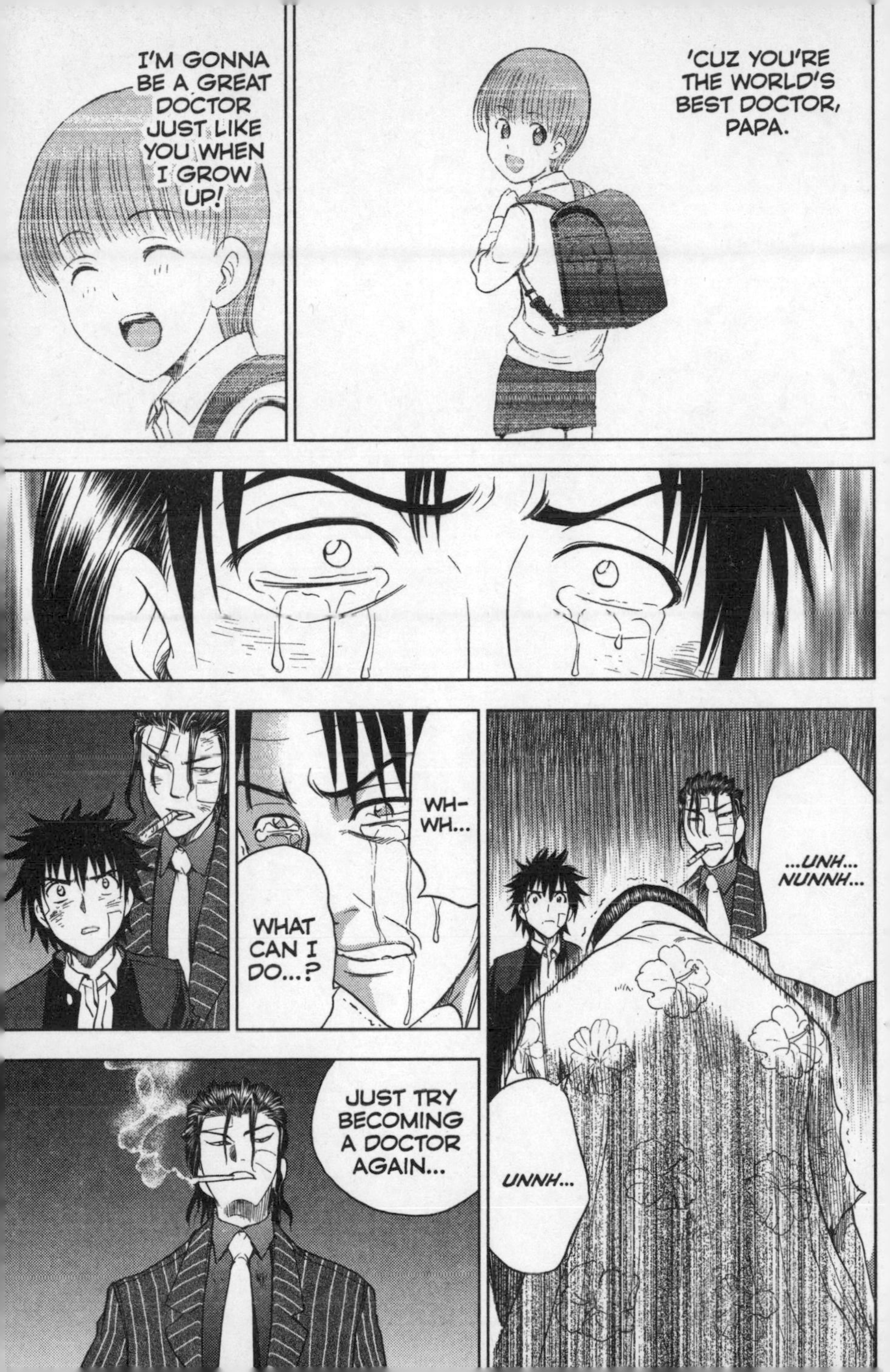
'CUZ YOU'RE THE WORLD'S BEST DOCTOR, PAPA.
I'M GONNA BE A GREAT DOCTOR JUST LIKE YOU WHEN I GROW UP!
...UNH... NUNNH...
UNNH...
WH- WH...
WHAT CAN I DO...?
JUST TRY BECOMING A DOCTOR AGAIN...

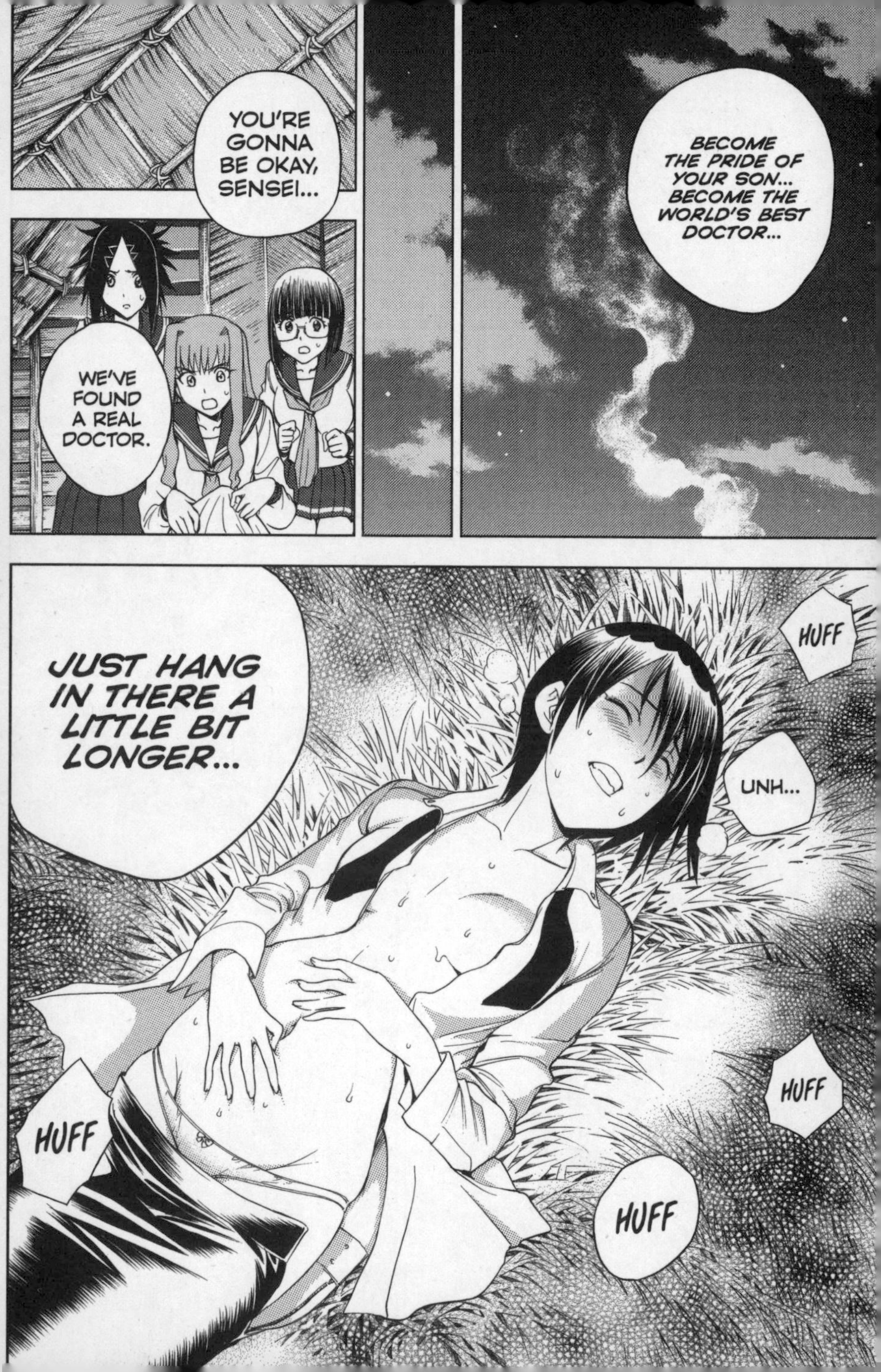
BECOME THE PRIDE OF YOUR SON... BECOME THE WORLD'S BEST DOCTOR...
YOU'RE GONNA BE OKAY, SENSEI...
WE'VE FOUND A REAL DOCTOR.
HUFF
JUST HANG IN THERE A LITTLE BIT LONGER...
UNH...
HUFF
HUFF
HUFF

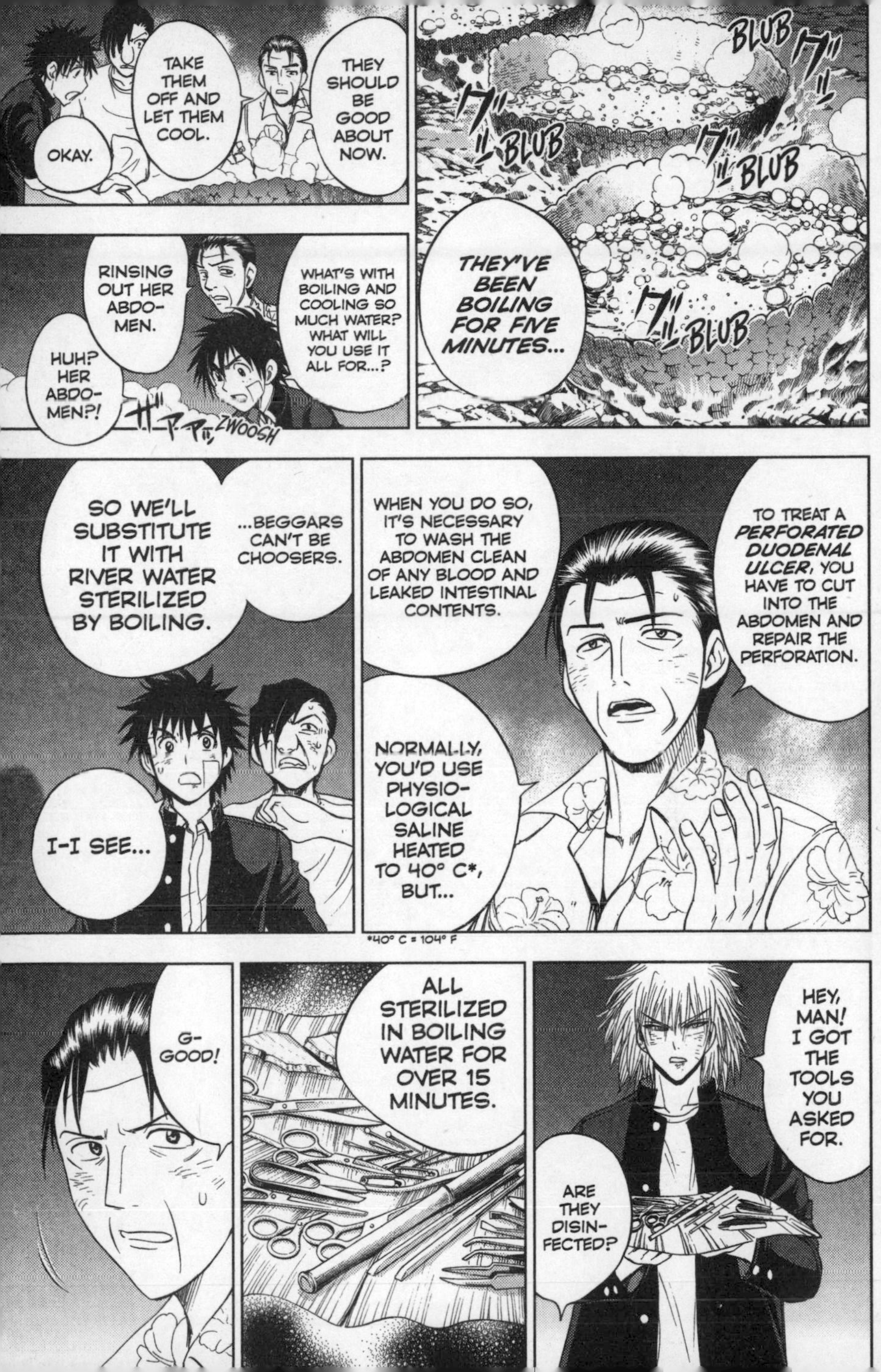
BLUB
BLUB
BLUB
BLUB
THEY'VE BEEN BOILING FOR FIVE MINUTES...
THEY SHOULD BE GOOD ABOUT NOW.
TAKE THEM OFF AND LET THEM COOL.
OKAY.
WHAT'S WITH BOILING AND COOLING SO MUCH WATER? WHAT WILL YOU USE IT ALL FOR...?
RINSING OUT HER ABDOMEN.
HUH? HER ABDOMEN?!
ZWOOSH
TO TREAT A PERFORATED DUODENAL ULCER, YOU HAVE TO CUT INTO THE ABDOMEN AND REPAIR THE PERFORATION.
WHEN YOU DO SO, IT'S NECESSARY TO WASH THE ABDOMEN CLEAN OF ANY BLOOD AND LEAKED INTESTINAL CONTENTS.
NORMALLY, YOU'D USE PHYSIOLOGICAL SALINE HEATED TO 40° C*, BUT...
...BEGGARS CAN'T BE CHOOSERS.
SO WE'LL SUBSTITUTE IT WITH RIVER WATER STERILIZED BY BOILING.
I-I SEE...
HEY, MAN! I GOT THE TOOLS YOU ASKED FOR.
ARE THEY DISINFECTED?
ALL STERILIZED IN BOILING WATER FOR OVER 15 MINUTES.
G-GOOD!

*40° C = 104° F

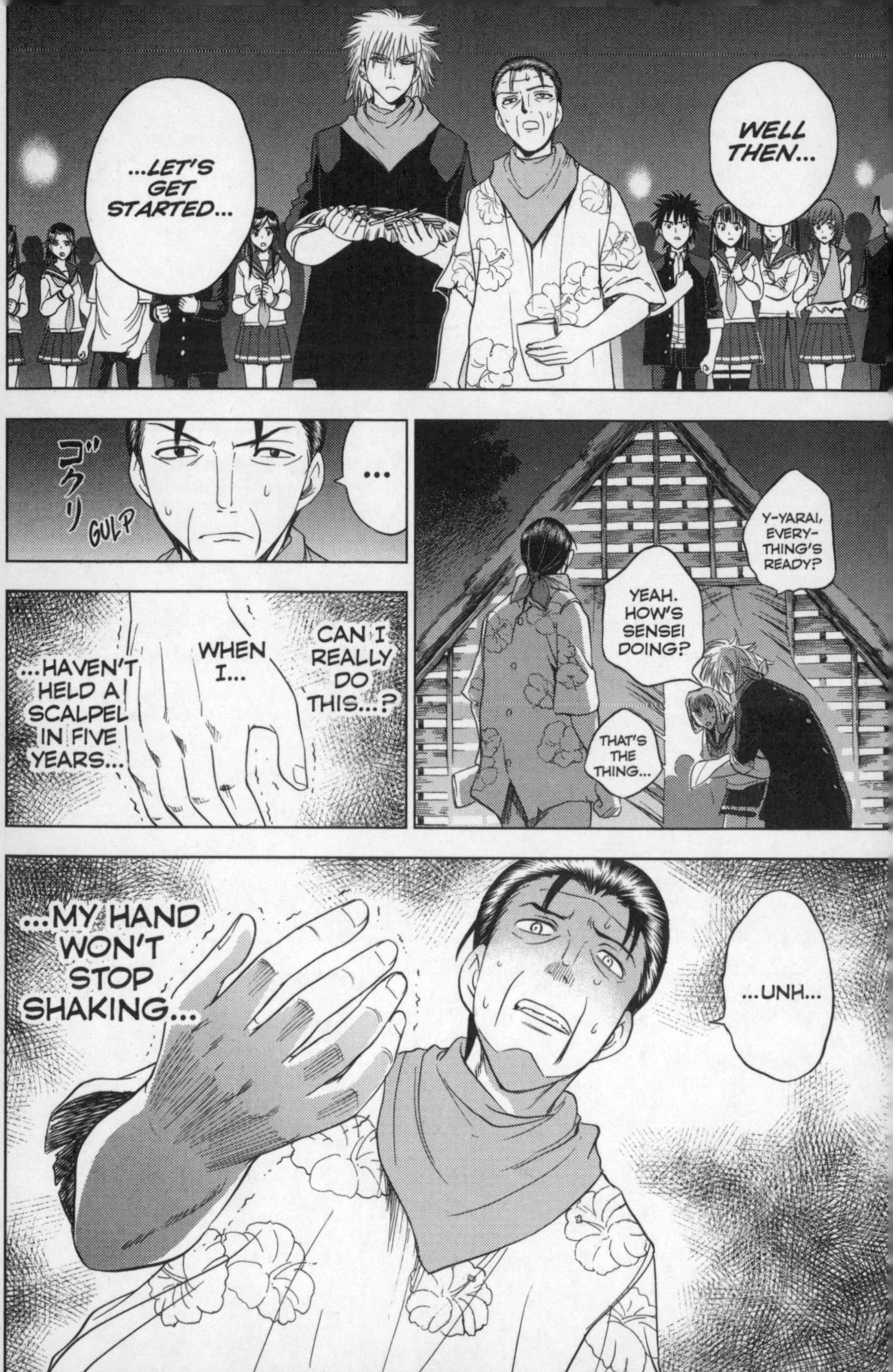
WELL THEN...
...LET'S GET STARTED...
Y-YARAI, EVERYTHING'S READY?
YEAH. HOW'S SENSEI DOING?
THAT'S THE THING...
ゴクリ
GULP
...
CAN I REALLY DO THIS...?
WHEN I...
...HAVEN'T HELD A SCALPEL IN FIVE YEARS...
...UNH...
...MY HAND WON'T STOP SHAKING...

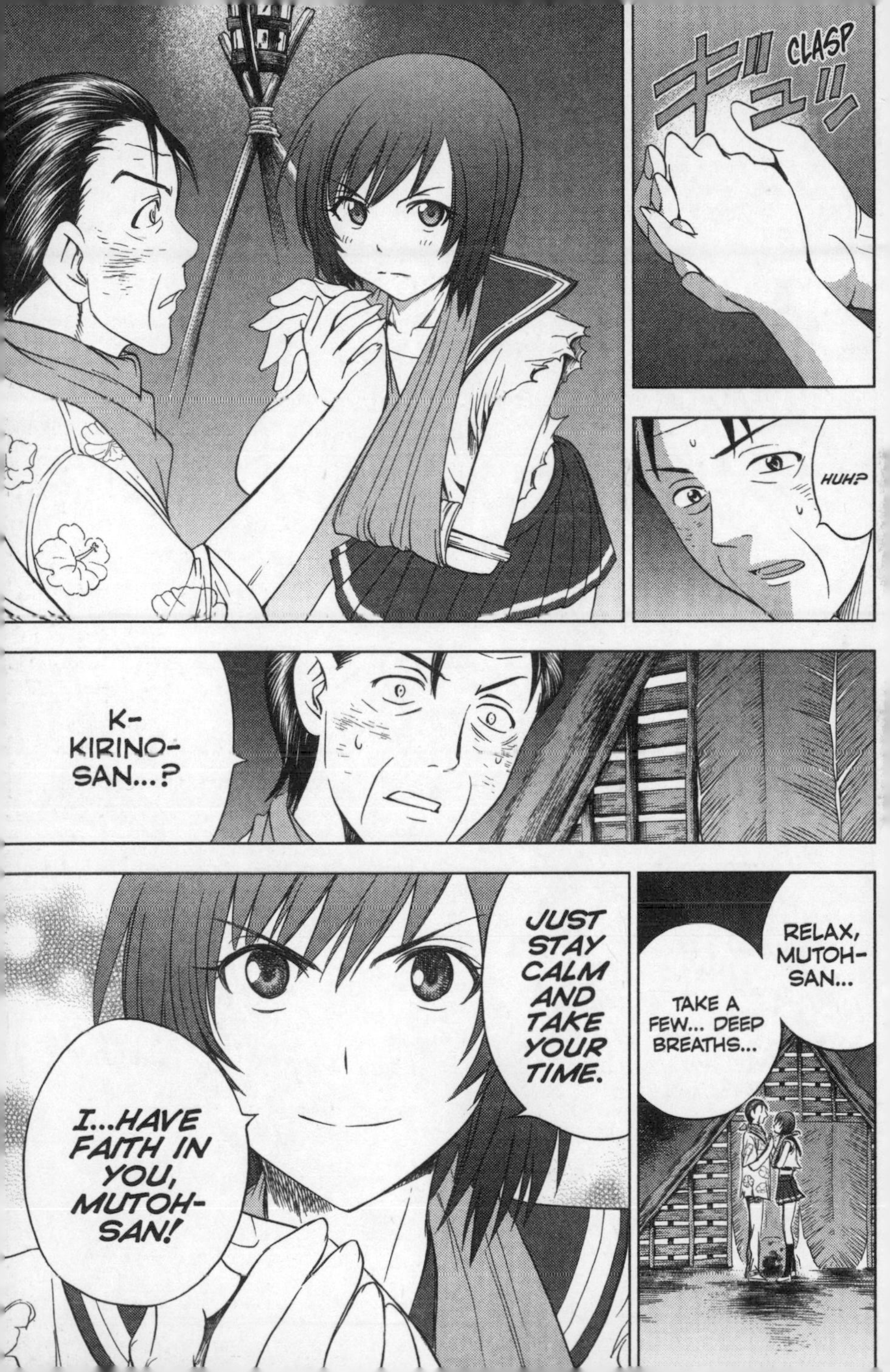
ギュッ
CLASP
HUH?
K-KIRINO-SAN...?
RELAX, MUTOH-SAN...
TAKE A FEW... DEEP BREATHS...
JUST STAY CALM AND TAKE YOUR TIME.
I...HAVE FAITH IN YOU, MUTOH-SAN!

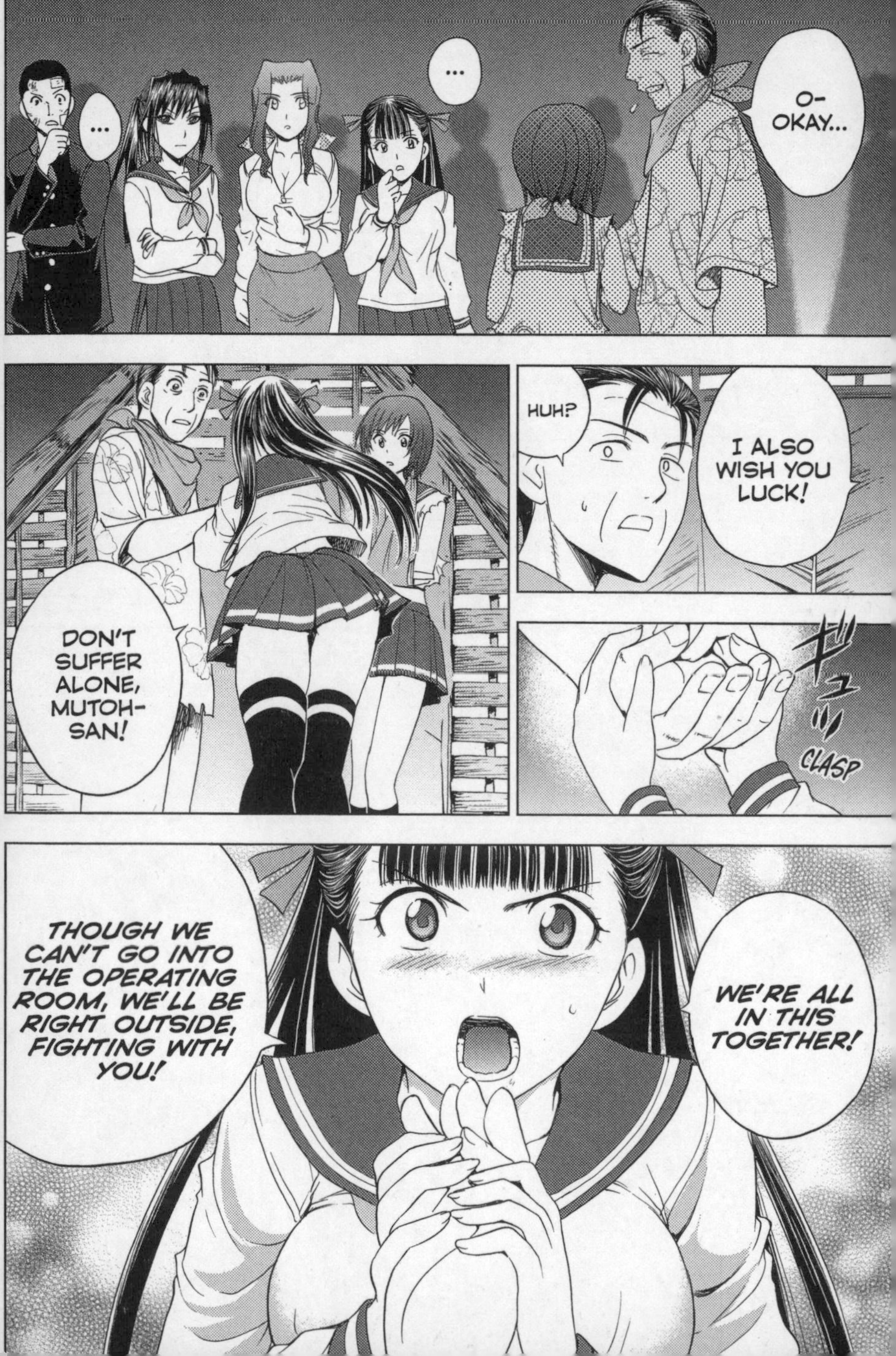
O-OKAY...
...
...
I ALSO WISH YOU LUCK!
HUH?
ギュッ
CLASP
DON'T SUFFER ALONE, MUTOH-SAN!
WE'RE ALL IN THIS TOGETHER!
THOUGH WE CAN'T GO INTO THE OPERATING ROOM, WE'LL BE RIGHT OUTSIDE, FIGHTING WITH YOU!

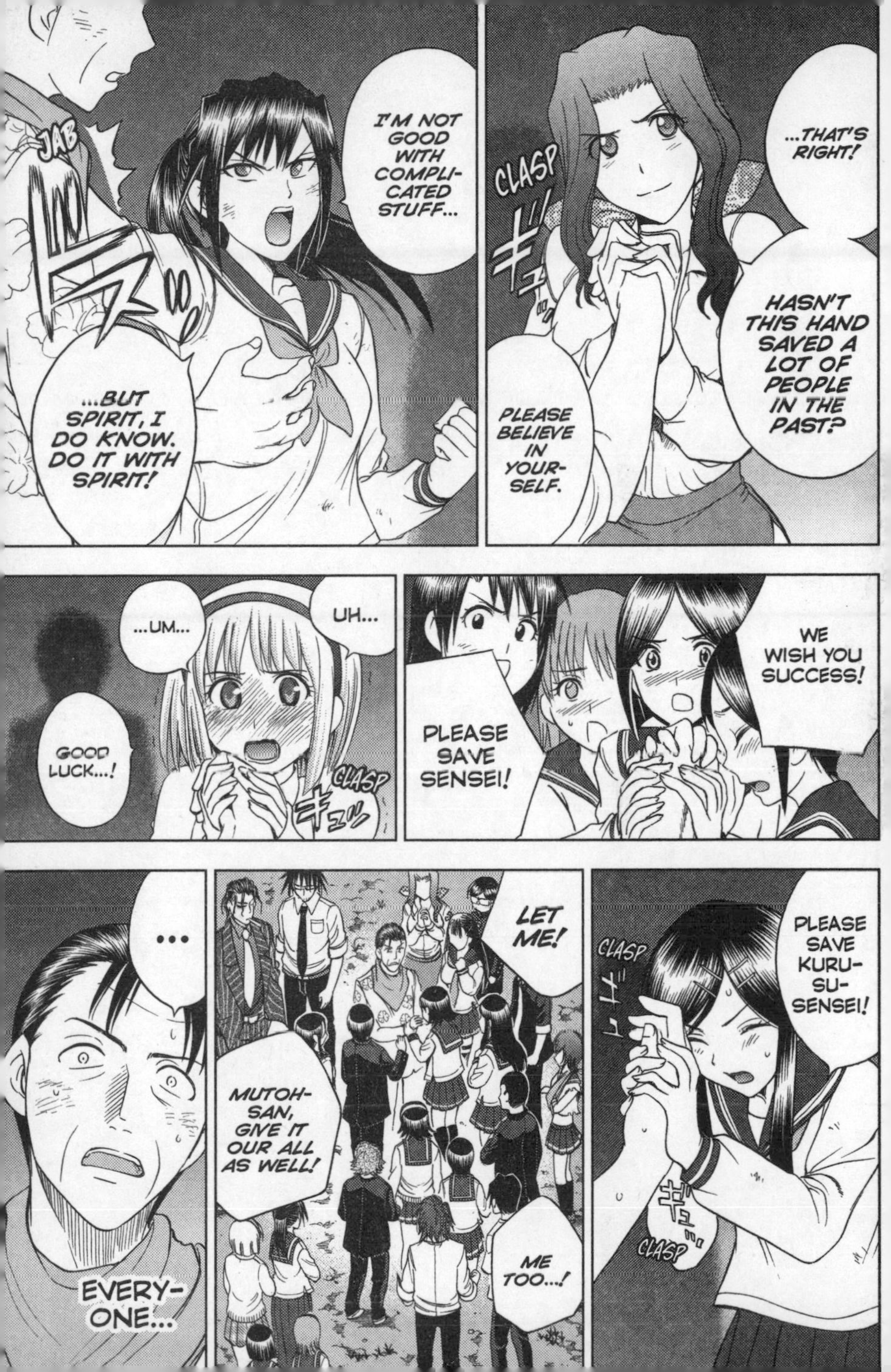
...THAT'S RIGHT!
CLASP
HASN'T THIS HAND SAVED A LOT OF PEOPLE IN THE PAST?
PLEASE BELIEVE IN YOURSELF.
JAB
I'M NOT GOOD WITH COMPLICATED STUFF...
...BUT SPIRIT, I DO KNOW. DO IT WITH SPIRIT!
WE WISH YOU SUCCESS!
PLEASE SAVE SENSEI!
UH...
...UM...
GOOD LUCK...!
CLASP
PLEASE SAVE KURUSU-SENSEI!
CLASP
CLASP
LET ME!
MUTOH-SAN, GIVE IT OUR ALL AS WELL!
ME TOO...!
...
EVERYONE...

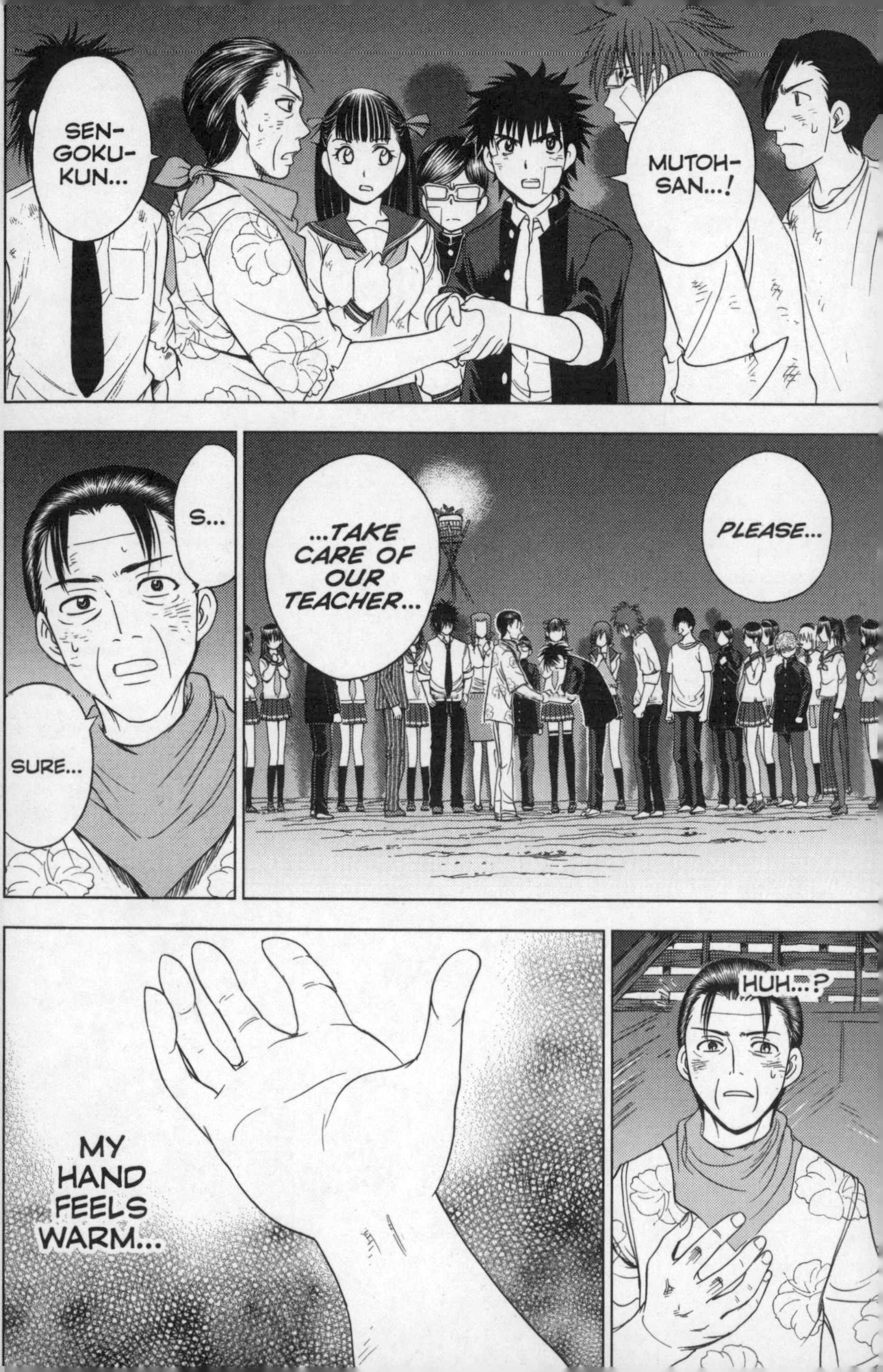
MUTOH-SAN...!
SEN-GOKU-KUN...
PLEASE...
...TAKE CARE OF OUR TEACHER...
S...
SURE...
HUH...?
MY HAND FEELS WARM...

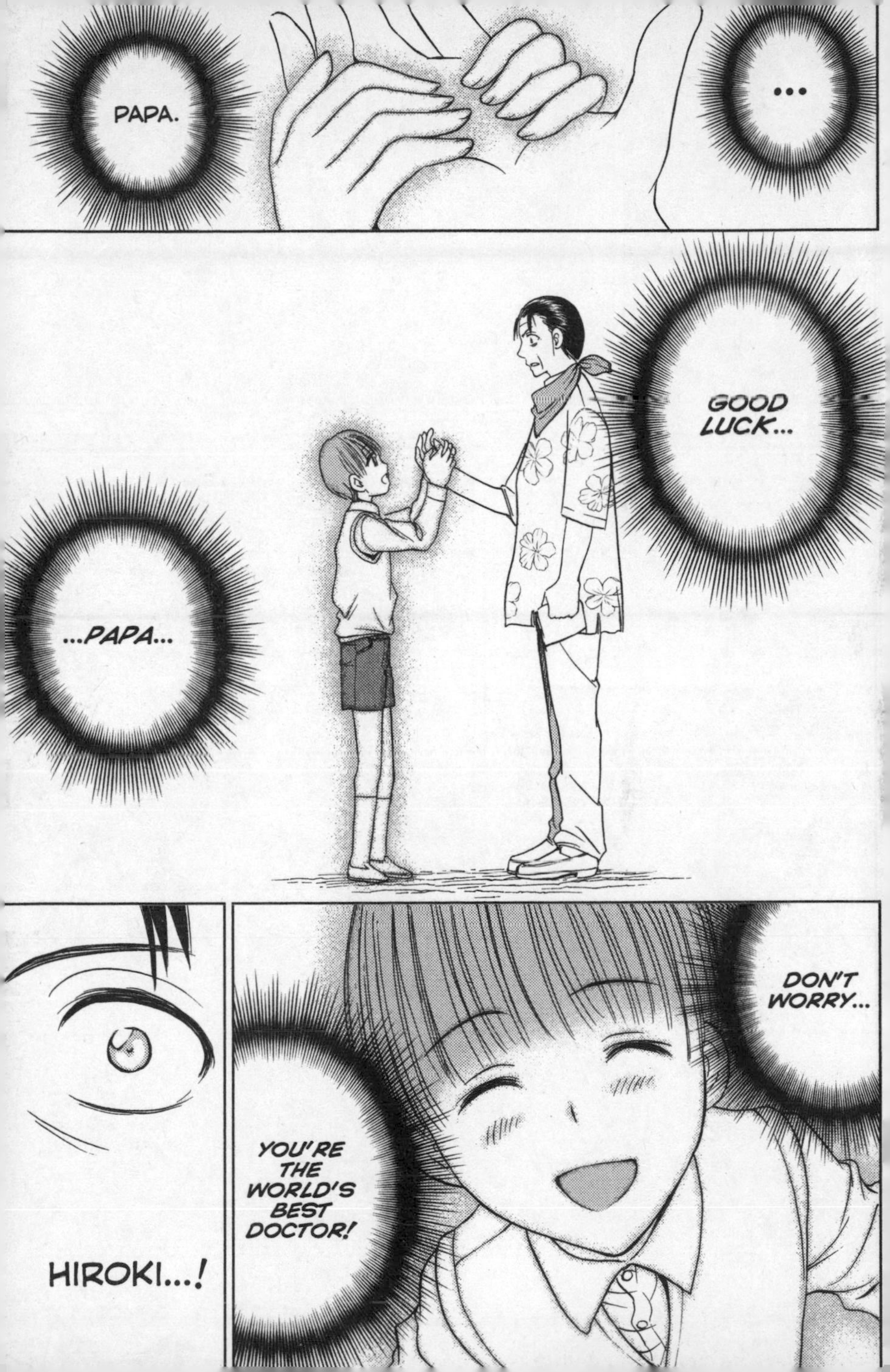
...
PAPA.
GOOD LUCK...
...PAPA...
DON'T WORRY...
YOU'RE THE WORLD'S BEST DOCTOR!
HIROKI...!

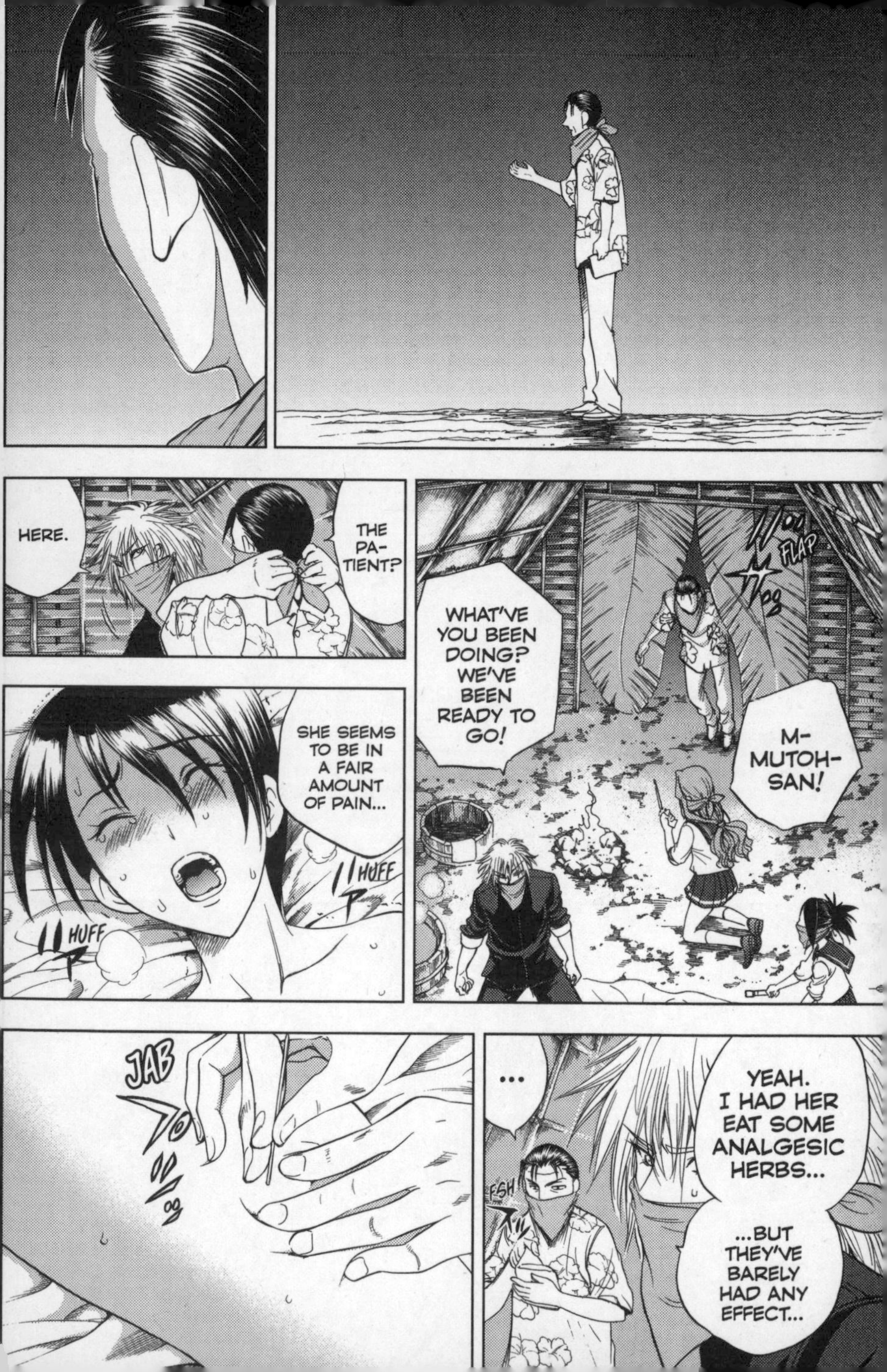
FLAP
WHAT'VE YOU BEEN DOING? WE'VE BEEN READY TO GO!
M-MUTOH-SAN!
THE PATIENT?
HERE.
SHE SEEMS TO BE IN A FAIR AMOUNT OF PAIN...
HUFF
HUFF
YEAH. I HAD HER EAT SOME ANALGESIC HERBS...
...BUT THEY'VE BARELY HAD ANY EFFECT...
FSH
...
JAB

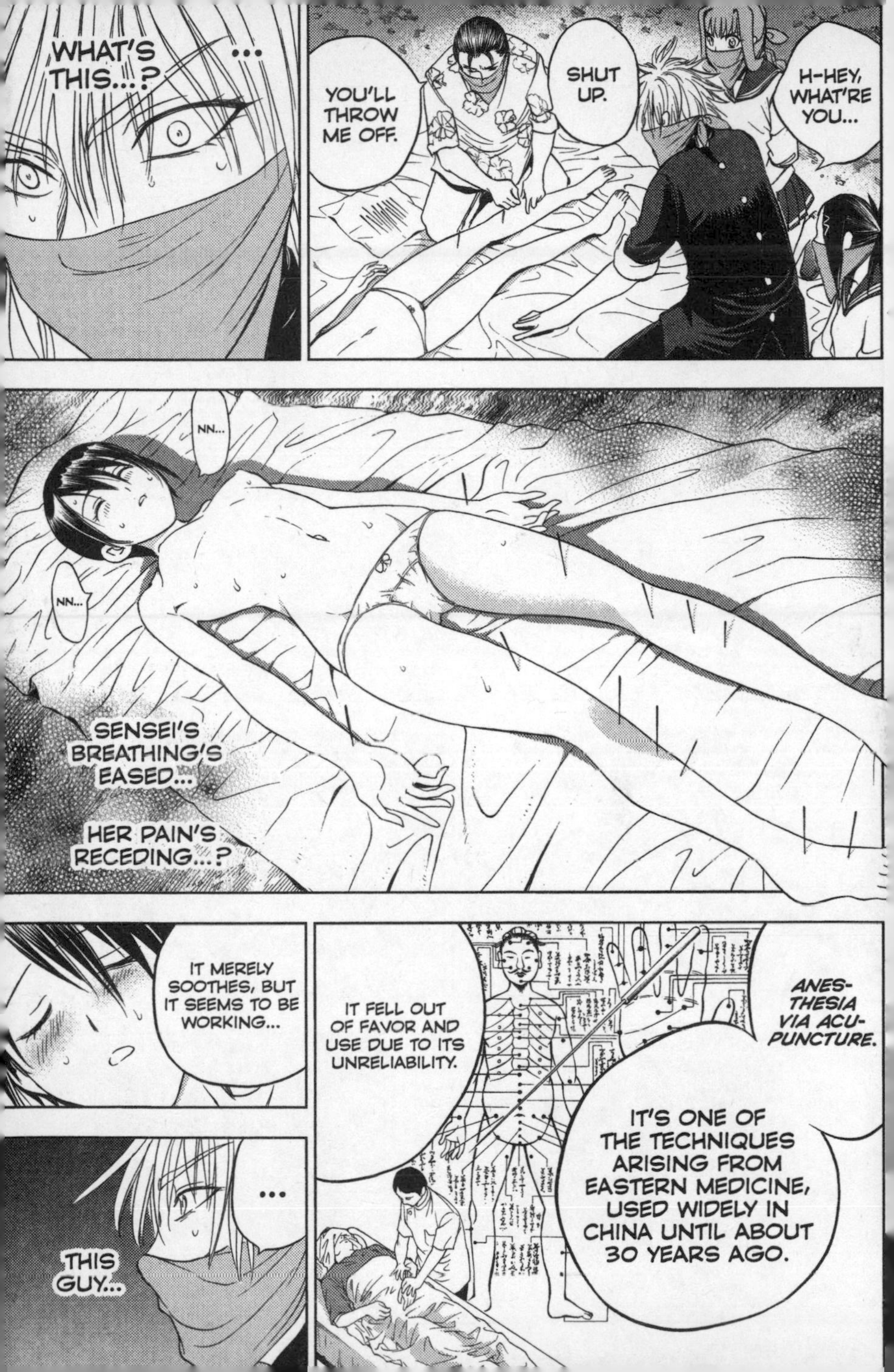
H-HEY, WHAT'RE YOU...
SHUT UP.
YOU'LL THROW ME OFF.
...
WHAT'S THIS...?
NN...
NN...
SENSEI'S BREATHING'S EASED...
HER PAIN'S RECEDING...?
ANES-THESIA VIA ACU-PUNCTURE.
IT'S ONE OF THE TECHNIQUES ARISING FROM EASTERN MEDICINE, USED WIDELY IN CHINA UNTIL ABOUT 30 YEARS AGO.
IT FELL OUT OF FAVOR AND USE DUE TO ITS UNRELIABILITY.
IT MERELY SOOTHES, BUT IT SEEMS TO BE WORKING...
...
THIS GUY...

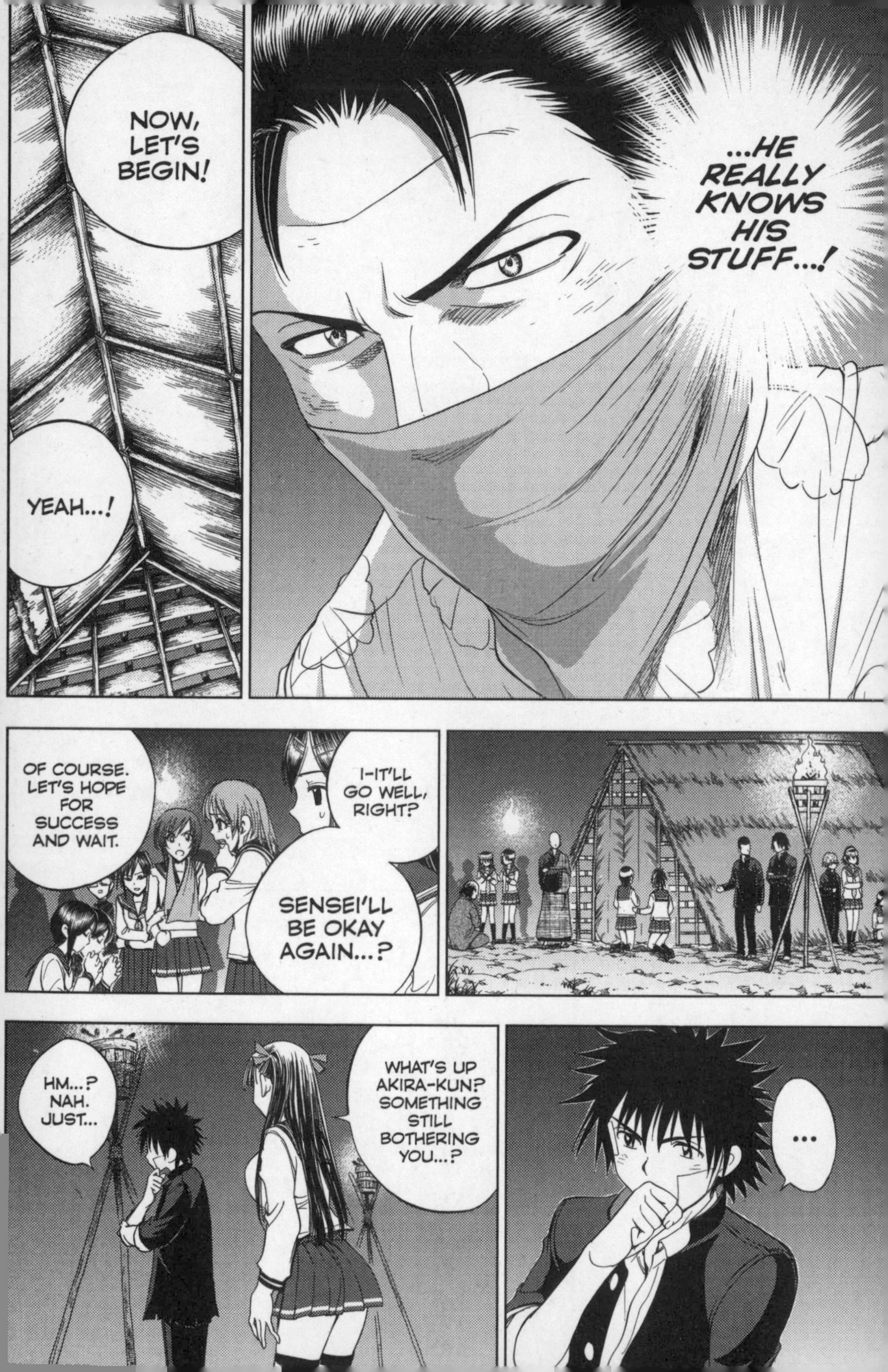
...HE REALLY KNOWS HIS STUFF...!
NOW, LET'S BEGIN!
YEAH...!
I-IT'LL GO WELL, RIGHT?
SENSEI'LL BE OKAY AGAIN...?
OF COURSE. LET'S HOPE FOR SUCCESS AND WAIT.
...
WHAT'S UP AKIRA-KUN? SOMETHING STILL BOTHERING YOU...?
HM...? NAH. JUST...

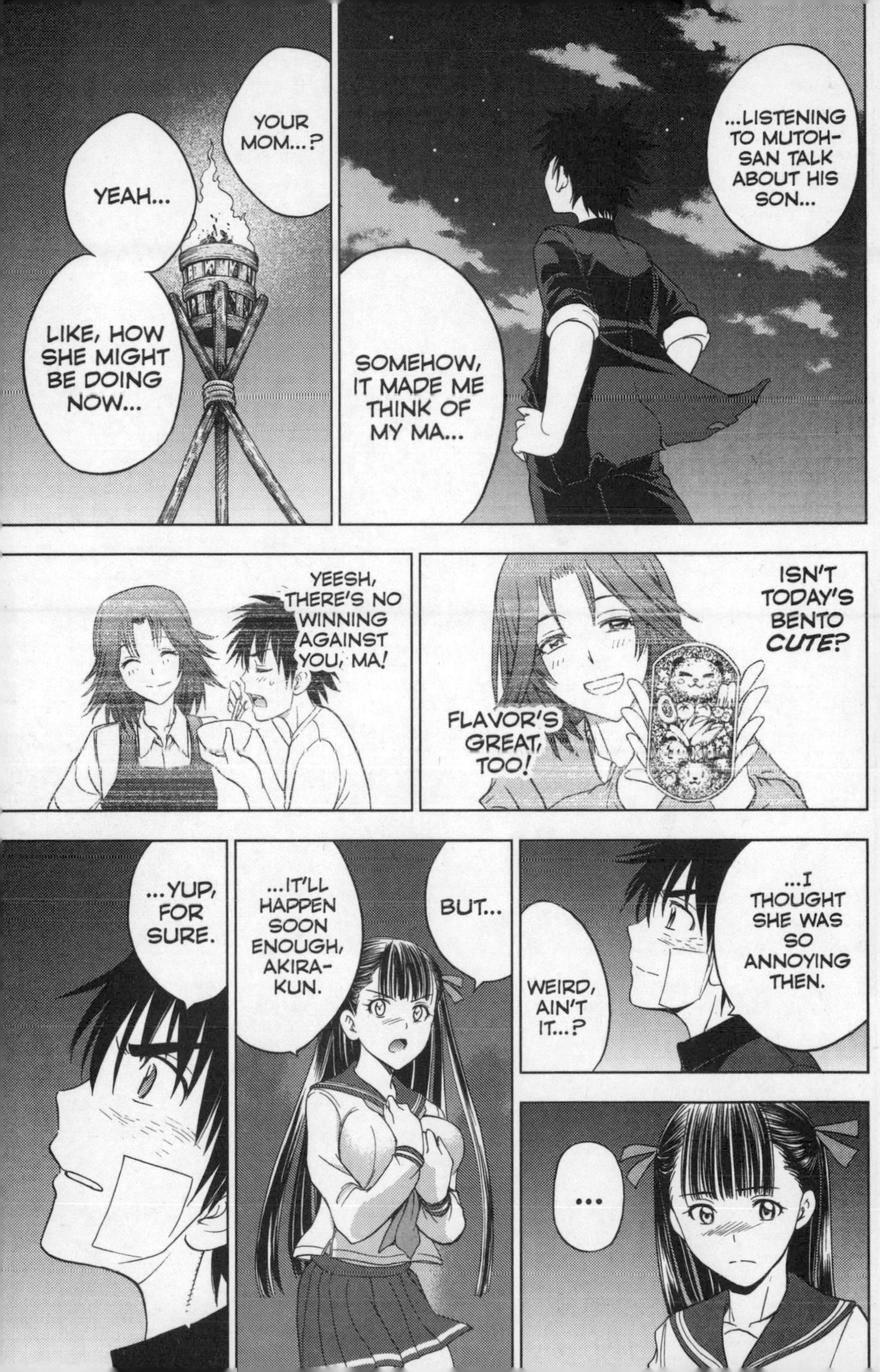
...LISTENING TO MUTOH-SAN TALK ABOUT HIS SON...
SOMEHOW, IT MADE ME THINK OF MY MA...
YOUR MOM...?
YEAH...
LIKE, HOW SHE MIGHT BE DOING NOW...
ISN'T TODAY'S BENTO *CUTE*?
FLAVOR'S GREAT, TOO!
YEESH, THERE'S NO WINNING AGAINST YOU, MA!
...I THOUGHT SHE WAS SO ANNOYING THEN.
WEIRD, AIN'T IT...?
...
BUT...
...IT'LL HAPPEN SOON ENOUGH, AKIRA-KUN.
...YUP, FOR SURE.

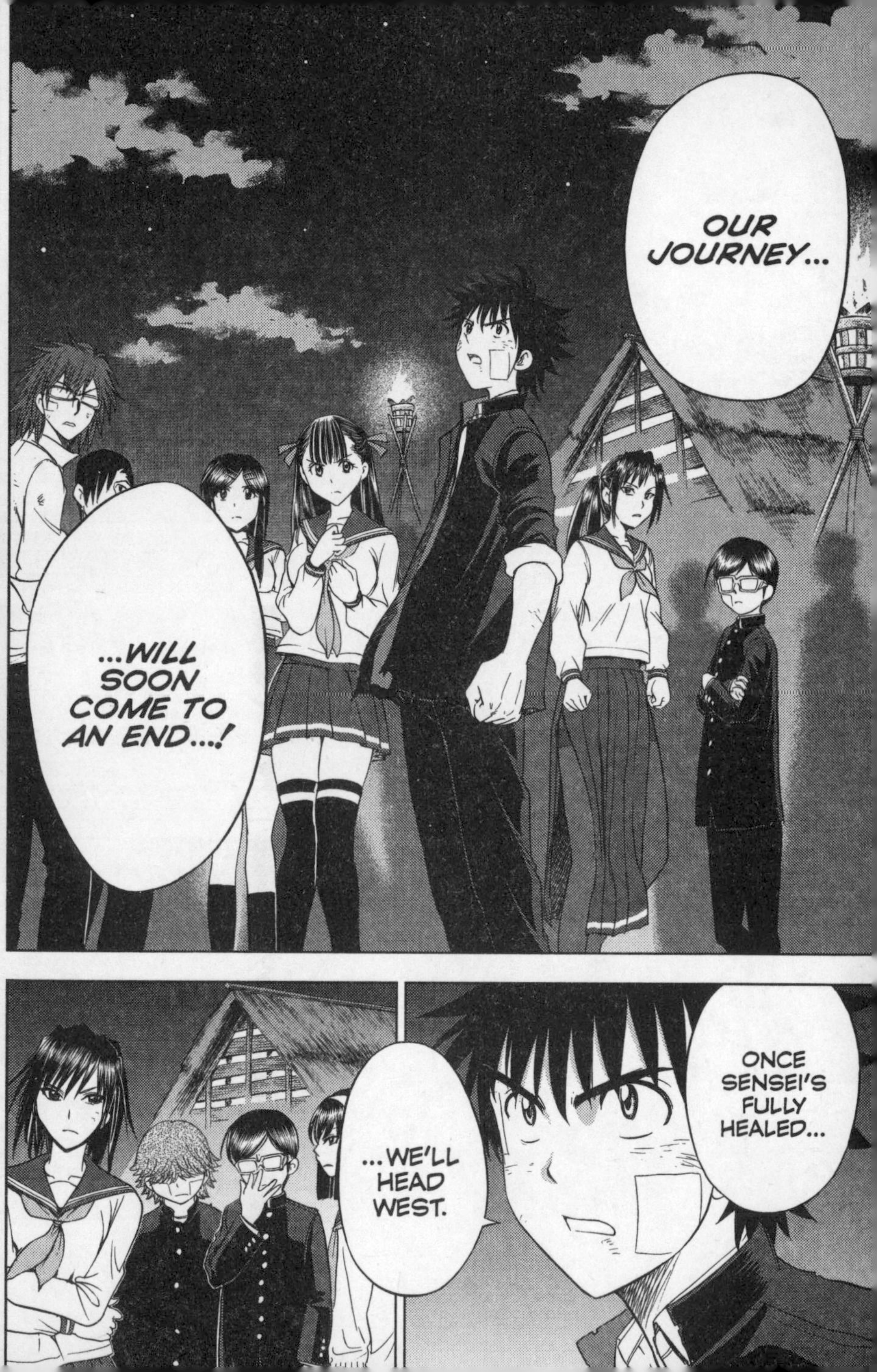
OUR JOURNEY...
...WILL SOON COME TO AN END...!
ONCE SENSEI'S FULLY HEALED...
...WE'LL HEAD WEST.

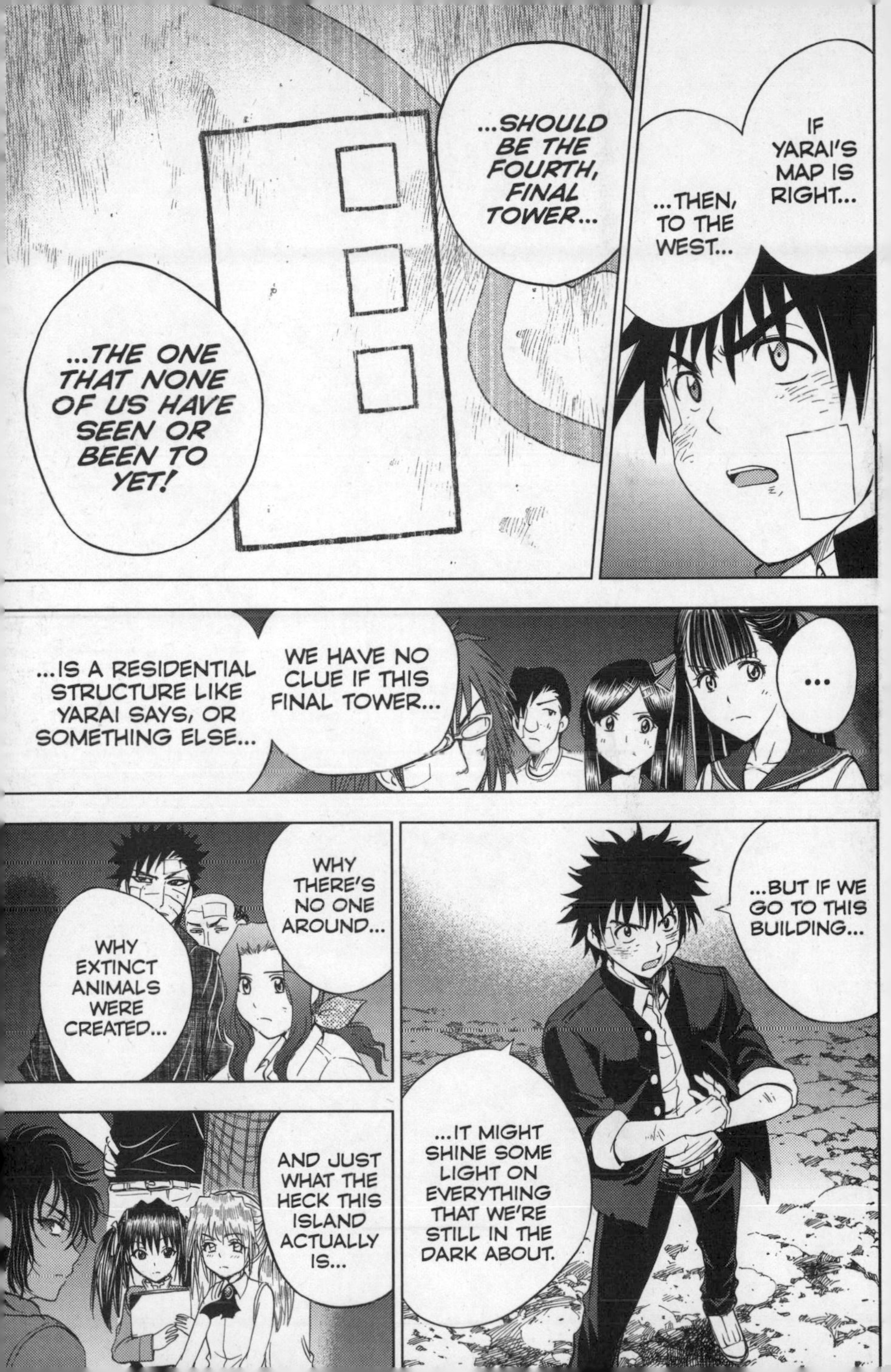
IF YARAI'S MAP IS RIGHT...
...THEN, TO THE WEST...
...SHOULD BE THE FOURTH, FINAL TOWER...
...THE ONE THAT NONE OF US HAVE SEEN OR BEEN TO YET!
...
WE HAVE NO CLUE IF THIS FINAL TOWER...
...IS A RESIDENTIAL STRUCTURE LIKE YARAI SAYS, OR SOMETHING ELSE...
...BUT IF WE GO TO THIS BUILDING...
...IT MIGHT SHINE SOME LIGHT ON EVERYTHING THAT WE'RE STILL IN THE DARK ABOUT.
WHY THERE'S NO ONE AROUND...
WHY EXTINCT ANIMALS WERE CREATED...
AND JUST WHAT THE HECK THIS ISLAND ACTUALLY IS...

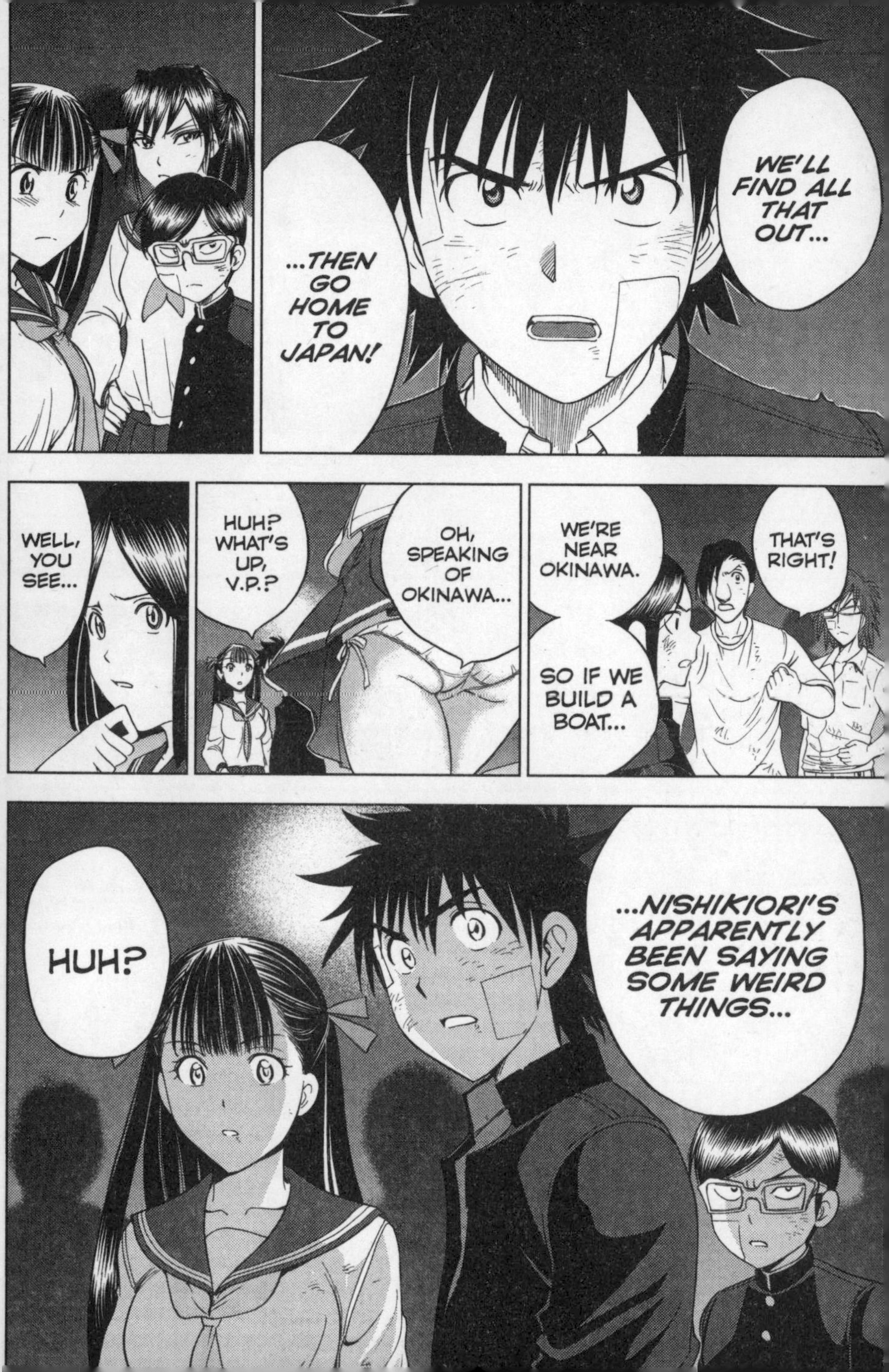
WE'LL FIND ALL THAT OUT...
...THEN GO HOME TO JAPAN!
THAT'S RIGHT!
WE'RE NEAR OKINAWA.
SO IF WE BUILD A BOAT...
OH, SPEAKING OF OKINAWA...
HUH? WHAT'S UP, V.P.?
WELL, YOU SEE...
...NISHIKIORI'S APPARENTLY BEEN SAYING SOME WEIRD THINGS...
HUH?

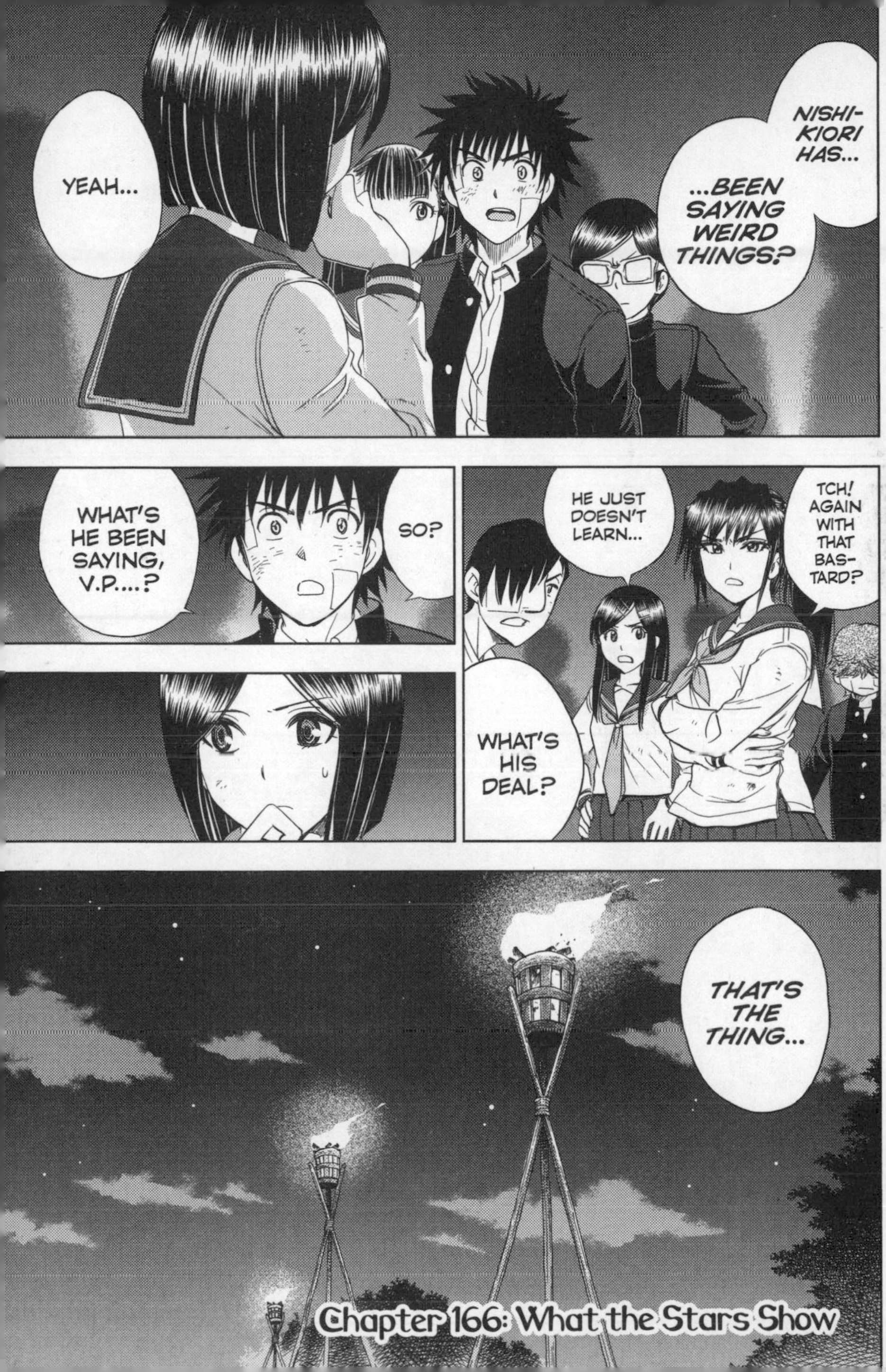
NISHI-KIORI HAS...
...BEEN SAYING WEIRD THINGS?
YEAH...
TCH! AGAIN WITH THAT BAS-TARD?
HE JUST DOESN'T LEARN...
WHAT'S HIS DEAL?
SO?
WHAT'S HE BEEN SAYING, V.P....?
THAT'S THE THING...
Chapter 166: What the Stars Show

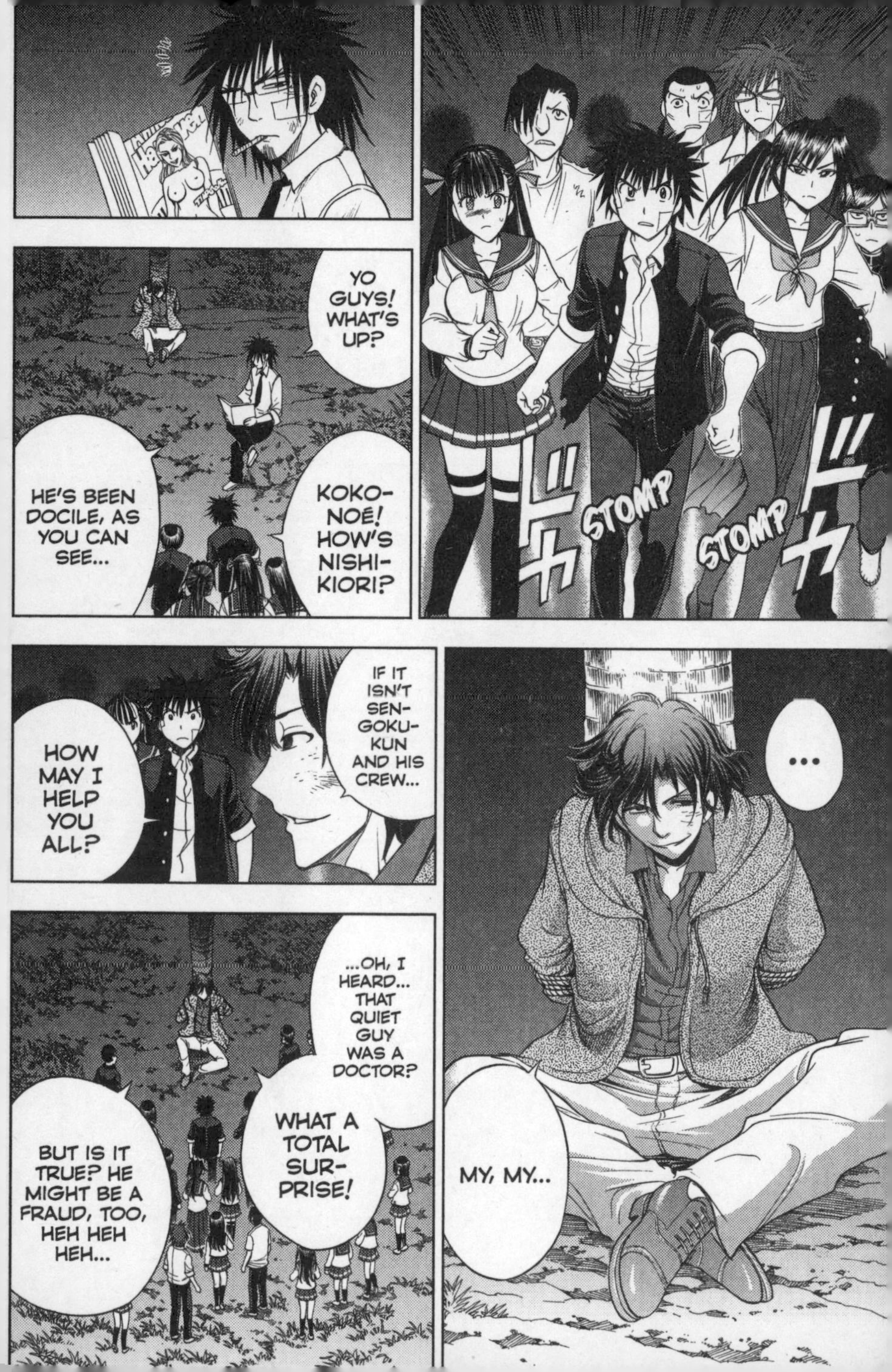
STOMP
STOMP
YO GUYS! WHAT'S UP?
KOKO-NOÉ! HOW'S NISHI-KIORI?
HE'S BEEN DOCILE, AS YOU CAN SEE...
...
MY, MY...
IF IT ISN'T SEN-GOKU-KUN AND HIS CREW...
HOW MAY I HELP YOU ALL?
...OH, I HEARD... THAT QUIET GUY WAS A DOCTOR?
WHAT A TOTAL SUR-PRISE!
BUT IS IT TRUE? HE MIGHT BE A FRAUD, TOO, HEH HEH HEH...

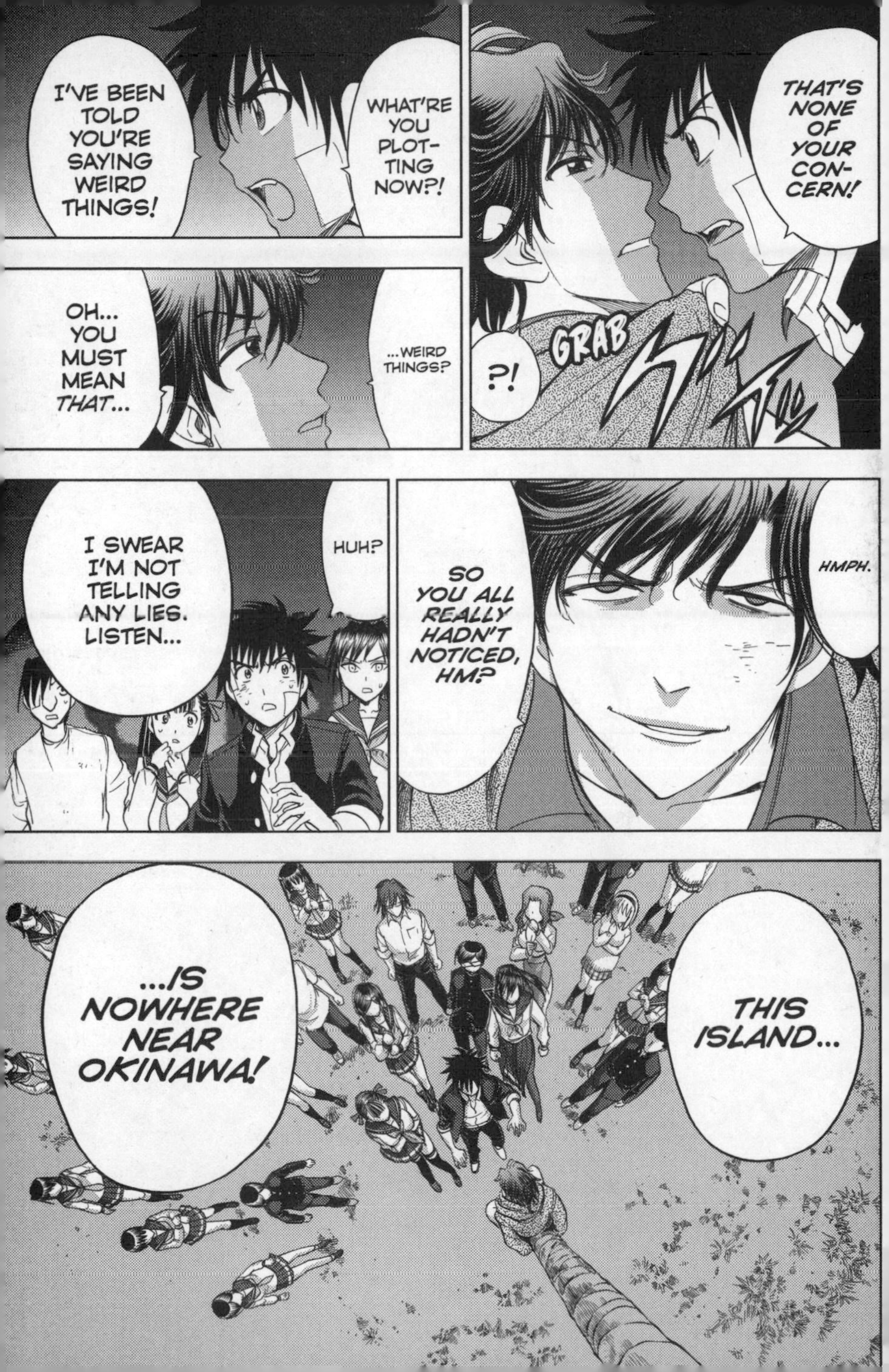
THAT'S NONE OF YOUR CONCERN!
GRAB
?!
WHAT'RE YOU PLOTTING NOW?!
I'VE BEEN TOLD YOU'RE SAYING WEIRD THINGS!
...WEIRD THINGS?
OH... YOU MUST MEAN *THAT*...
HMPH.
SO *YOU ALL REALLY* HADN'T NOTICED, HM?
HUH?
I SWEAR I'M NOT TELLING ANY LIES. LISTEN...
THIS ISLAND...
...IS NOWHERE NEAR OKINAWA!

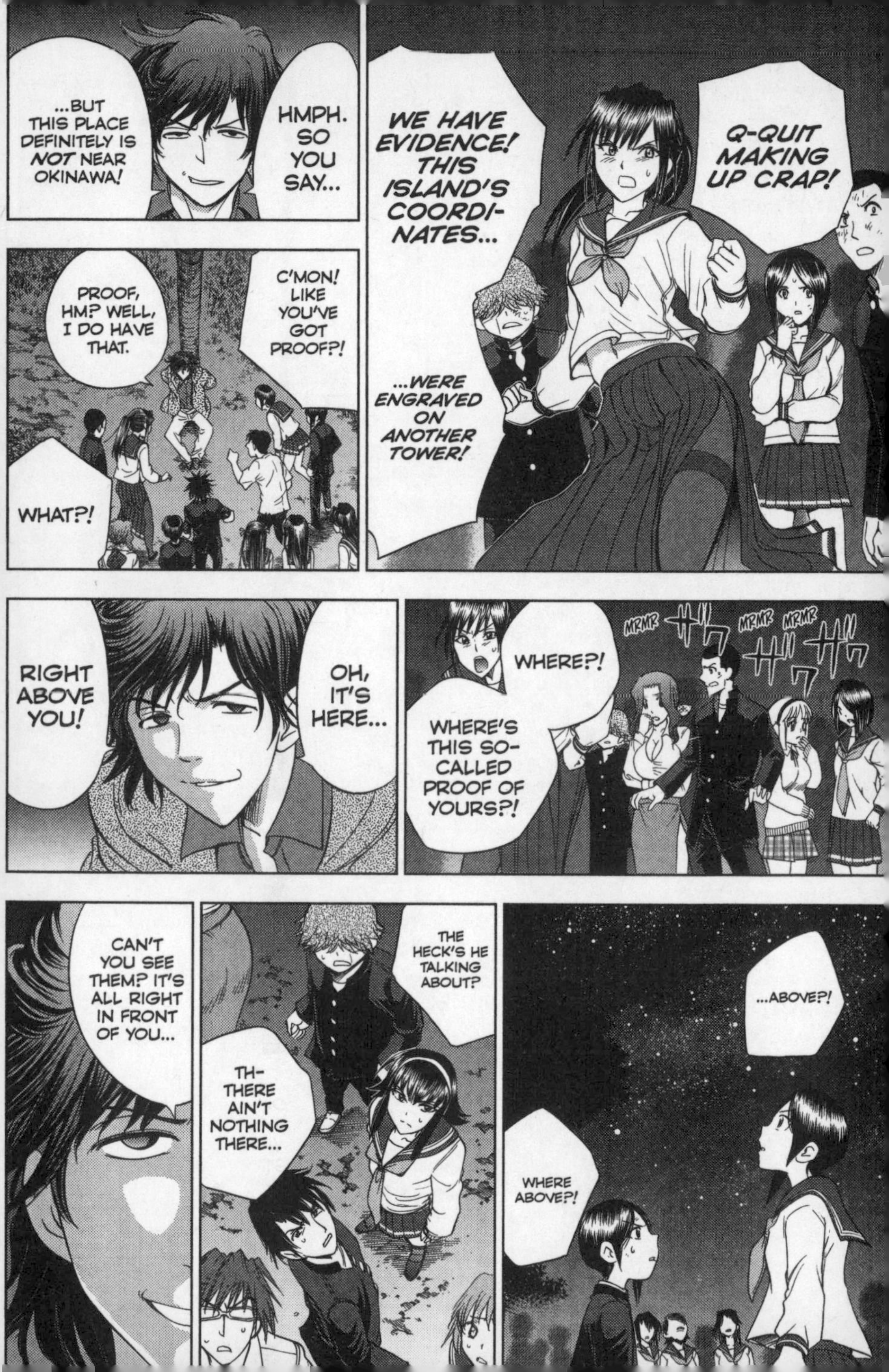
Q-QUIT MAKING UP CRAP!
WE HAVE EVIDENCE! THIS ISLAND'S COORDINATES...
...WERE ENGRAVED ON ANOTHER TOWER!
HMPH. SO YOU SAY...
...BUT THIS PLACE DEFINITELY IS *NOT* NEAR OKINAWA!
C'MON! LIKE YOU'VE GOT PROOF?!
PROOF, HM? WELL, I DO HAVE THAT.
WHAT?!
MRMR ザワ
MRMR MRMR ザワ ザワ
WHERE?!
WHERE'S THIS SO-CALLED PROOF OF YOURS?!
OH, IT'S HERE...
RIGHT ABOVE YOU!
...ABOVE?!
WHERE ABOVE?!
THE HECK'S HE TALKING ABOUT?
TH-THERE AIN'T NOTHING THERE...
CAN'T YOU SEE THEM? IT'S ALL RIGHT IN FRONT OF YOU...

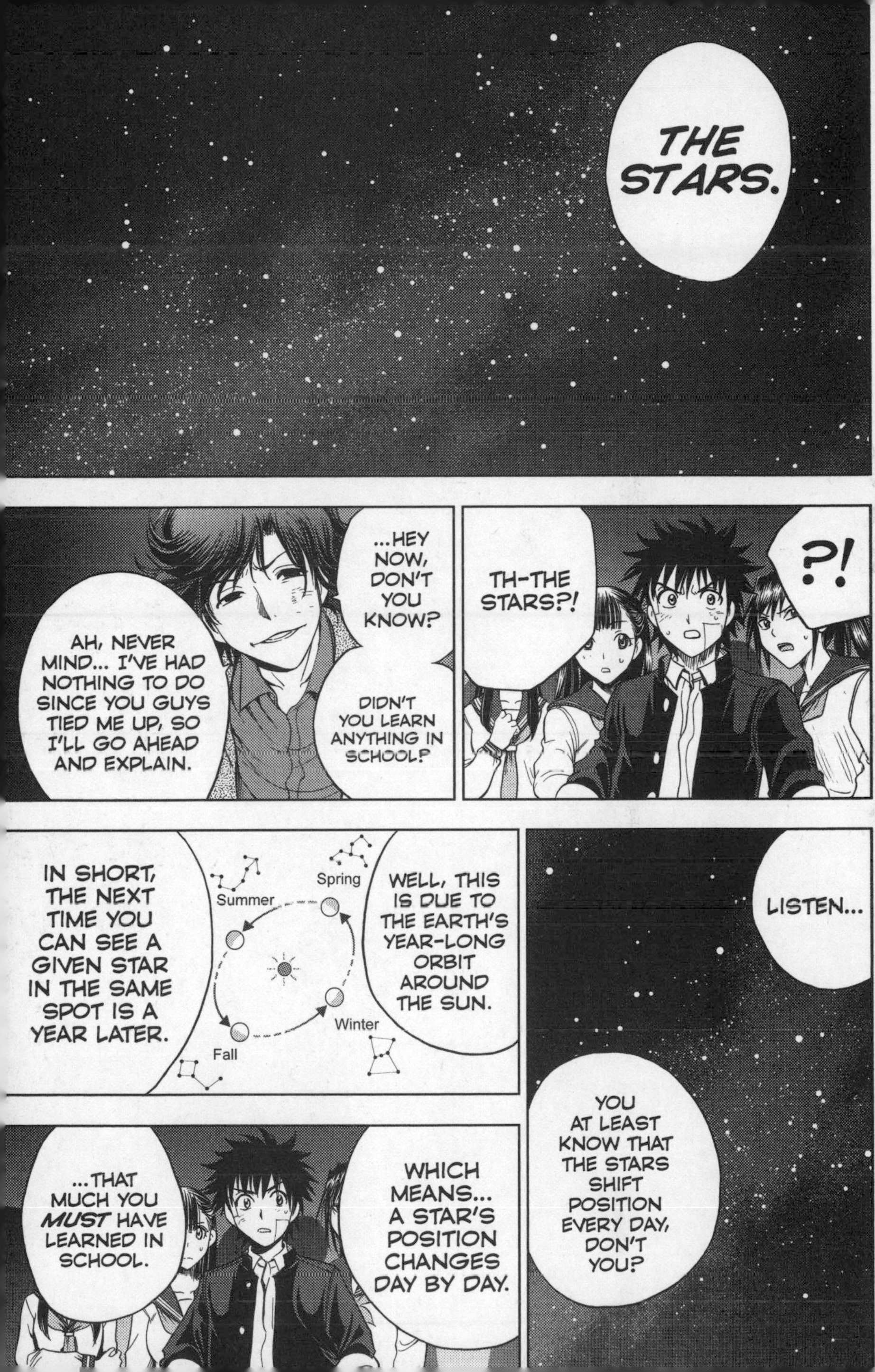
THE STARS.
?!
TH-THE STARS?!
...HEY NOW, DON'T YOU KNOW?
DIDN'T YOU LEARN ANYTHING IN SCHOOL?
AH, NEVER MIND... I'VE HAD NOTHING TO DO SINCE YOU GUYS TIED ME UP, SO I'LL GO AHEAD AND EXPLAIN.
LISTEN...
YOU AT LEAST KNOW THAT THE STARS SHIFT POSITION EVERY DAY, DON'T YOU?
WELL, THIS IS DUE TO THE EARTH'S YEAR-LONG ORBIT AROUND THE SUN.
Spring
Summer
Winter
Fall
IN SHORT, THE NEXT TIME YOU CAN SEE A GIVEN STAR IN THE SAME SPOT IS A YEAR LATER.
WHICH MEANS... A STAR'S POSITION CHANGES DAY BY DAY.
...THAT MUCH YOU *MUST* HAVE LEARNED IN SCHOOL.

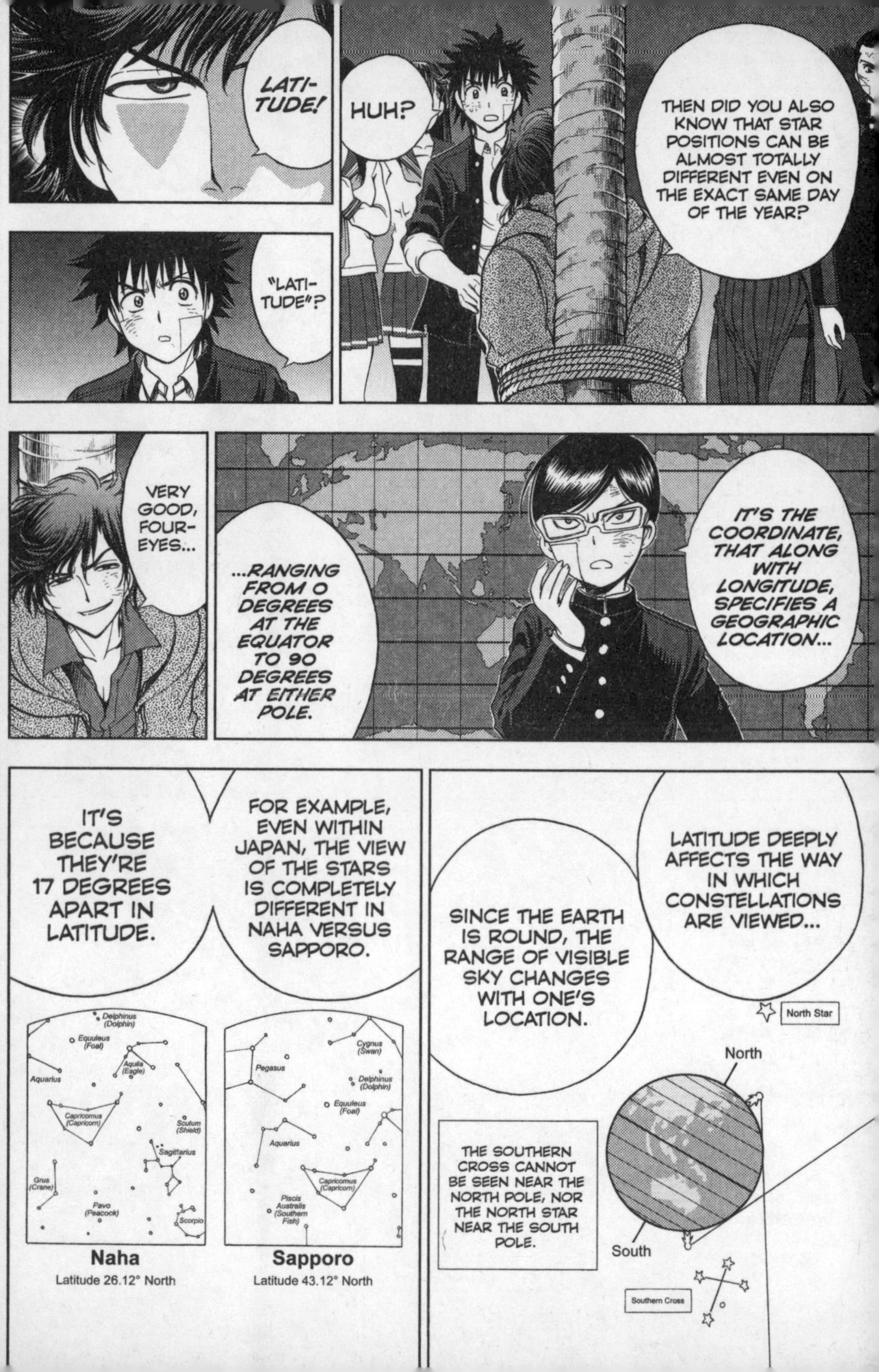

THEN DID YOU ALSO KNOW THAT STAR POSITIONS CAN BE ALMOST TOTALLY DIFFERENT EVEN ON THE EXACT SAME DAY OF THE YEAR?
HUH?
LATI-TUDE!
"LATI-TUDE"?
IT'S THE COORDINATE, THAT ALONG WITH LONGITUDE, SPECIFIES A GEOGRAPHIC LOCATION...
...RANGING FROM 0 DEGREES AT THE EQUATOR TO 90 DEGREES AT EITHER POLE.
VERY GOOD, FOUR-EYES...
LATITUDE DEEPLY AFFECTS THE WAY IN WHICH CONSTELLATIONS ARE VIEWED...
SINCE THE EARTH IS ROUND, THE RANGE OF VISIBLE SKY CHANGES WITH ONE'S LOCATION.
North Star
North
South
THE SOUTHERN CROSS CANNOT BE SEEN NEAR THE NORTH POLE, NOR THE NORTH STAR NEAR THE SOUTH POLE.
Southern Cross
FOR EXAMPLE, EVEN WITHIN JAPAN, THE VIEW OF THE STARS IS COMPLETELY DIFFERENT IN NAHA VERSUS SAPPORO.
IT'S BECAUSE THEY'RE 17 DEGREES APART IN LATITUDE.
Cygnus (Swan)
Pegasus
Delphinus (Dolphin)
Equuleus (Foal)
Aquarius
Capricornus (Capricorn)
Piscis Australis (Southern Fish)
Sapporo
Latitude 43.12° North
Delphinus (Dolphin)
Equuleus (Foal)
Aquila (Eagle)
Aquarius
Capricornus (Capricorn)
Scutum (Shield)
Sagittarius
Grus (Crane)
Pavo (Peacock)
Scorpio
Naha
Latitude 26.12° North

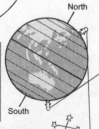

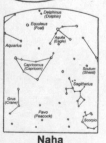

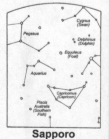

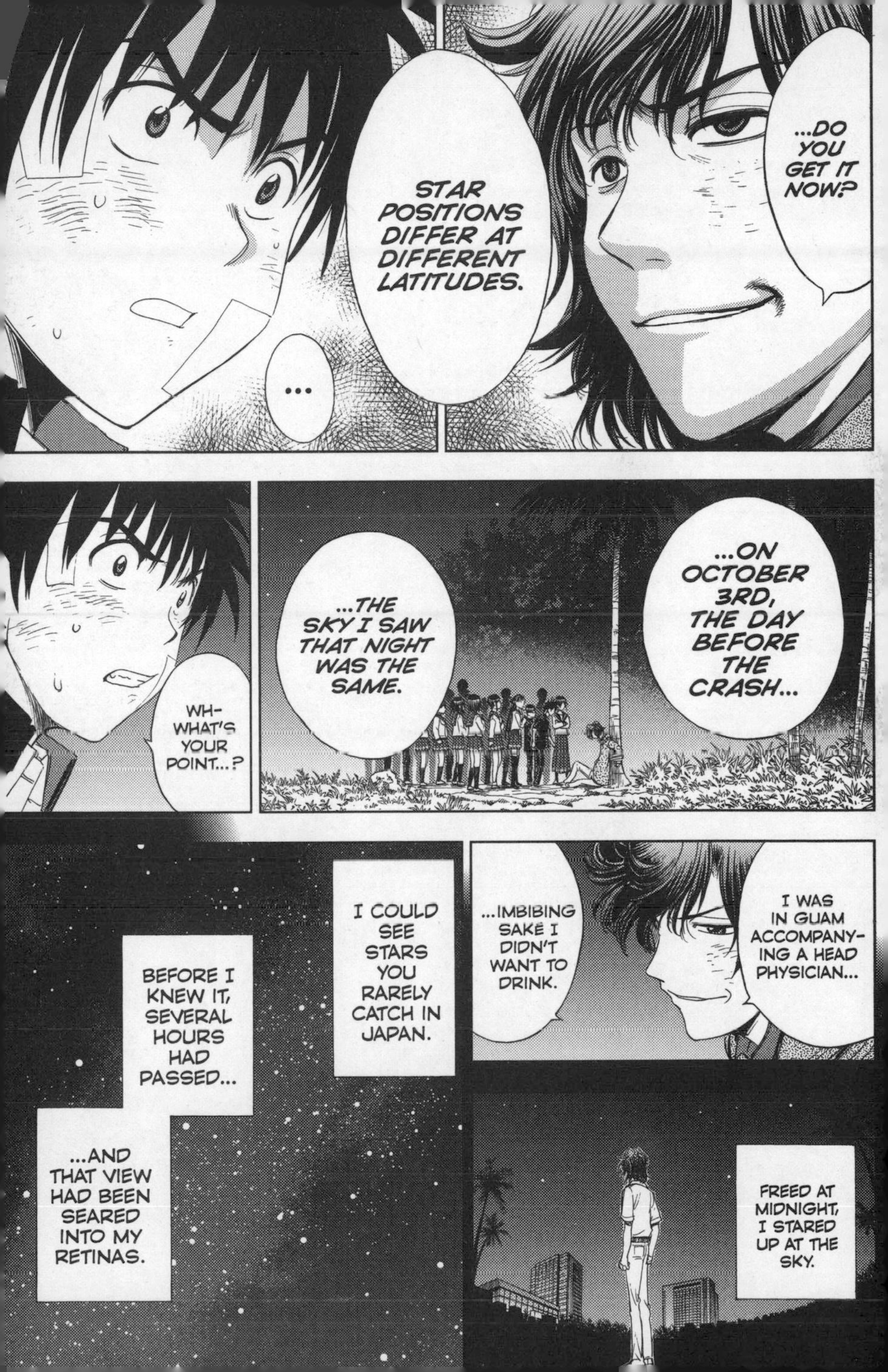
...DO YOU GET IT NOW?
STAR POSITIONS DIFFER AT DIFFERENT LATITUDES.
...
...ON OCTOBER 3RD, THE DAY BEFORE THE CRASH...
...THE SKY I SAW THAT NIGHT WAS THE SAME.
WH-WHAT'S YOUR POINT...?
I WAS IN GUAM ACCOMPANYING A HEAD PHYSICIAN...
...IMBIBING SAKE I DIDN'T WANT TO DRINK.
FREED AT MIDNIGHT, I STARED UP AT THE SKY.
I COULD SEE STARS YOU RARELY CATCH IN JAPAN.
BEFORE I KNEW IT, SEVERAL HOURS HAD PASSED...
...AND THAT VIEW HAD BEEN SEARED INTO MY RETINAS.

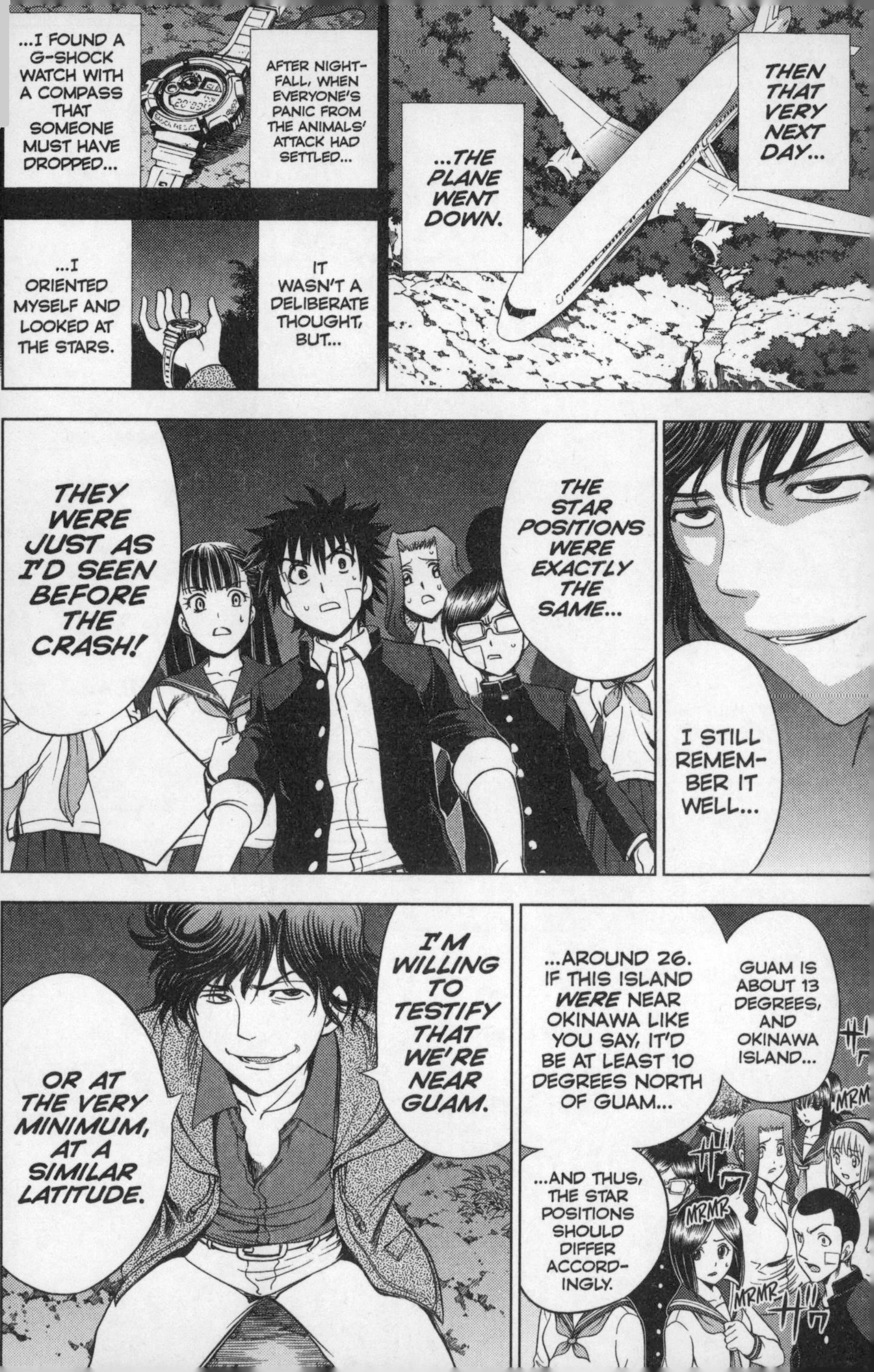
THEN THAT VERY NEXT DAY...
...THE PLANE WENT DOWN.
AFTER NIGHTFALL, WHEN EVERYONE'S PANIC FROM THE ANIMALS' ATTACK HAD SETTLED...
...I FOUND A G-SHOCK WATCH WITH A COMPASS THAT SOMEONE MUST HAVE DROPPED...
IT WASN'T A DELIBERATE THOUGHT, BUT...
...I ORIENTED MYSELF AND LOOKED AT THE STARS.
I STILL REMEMBER IT WELL...
THE STAR POSITIONS WERE EXACTLY THE SAME...
THEY WERE JUST AS I'D SEEN BEFORE THE CRASH!
GUAM IS ABOUT 13 DEGREES, AND OKINAWA ISLAND...
...AROUND 26. IF THIS ISLAND WERE NEAR OKINAWA LIKE YOU SAY, IT'D BE AT LEAST 10 DEGREES NORTH OF GUAM...
...AND THUS, THE STAR POSITIONS SHOULD DIFFER ACCORDINGLY.
MRMR
MRMR
MRMR
I'M WILLING TO TESTIFY THAT WE'RE NEAR GUAM.
OR AT THE VERY MINIMUM, AT A SIMILAR LATITUDE.

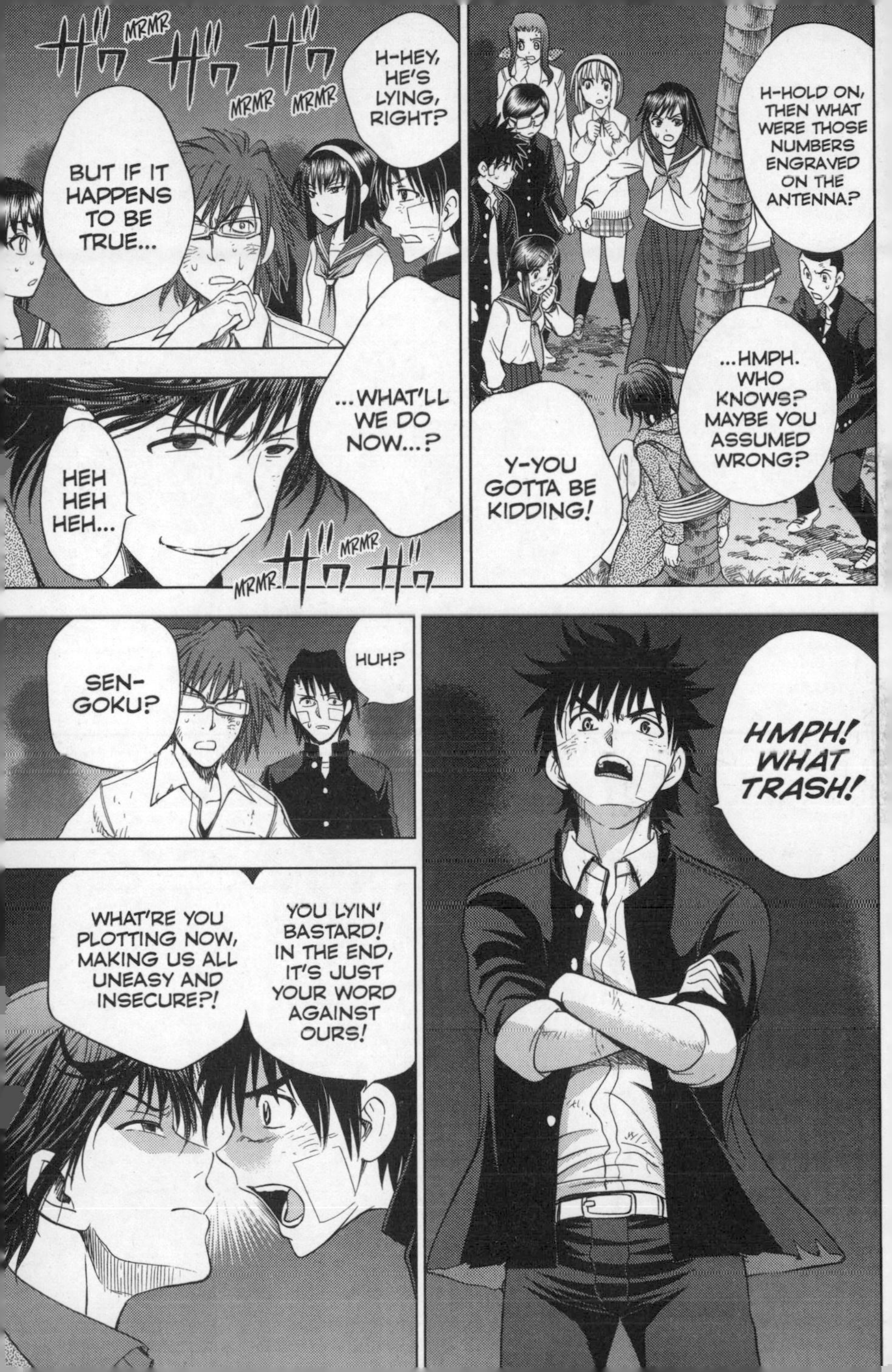
H-HOLD ON, THEN WHAT WERE THOSE NUMBERS ENGRAVED ON THE ANTENNA?
...HMPH. WHO KNOWS? MAYBE YOU ASSUMED WRONG?
Y-YOU GOTTA BE KIDDING!
MRMR
MRMR MRMR
H-HEY, HE'S LYING, RIGHT?
BUT IF IT HAPPENS TO BE TRUE...
...WHAT'LL WE DO NOW...?
HEH HEH HEH...
MRMR MRMR
HMPH! WHAT TRASH!
HUH?
SEN-GOKU?
YOU LYIN' BASTARD! IN THE END, IT'S JUST YOUR WORD AGAINST OURS!
WHAT'RE YOU PLOTTING NOW, MAKING US ALL UNEASY AND INSECURE?!

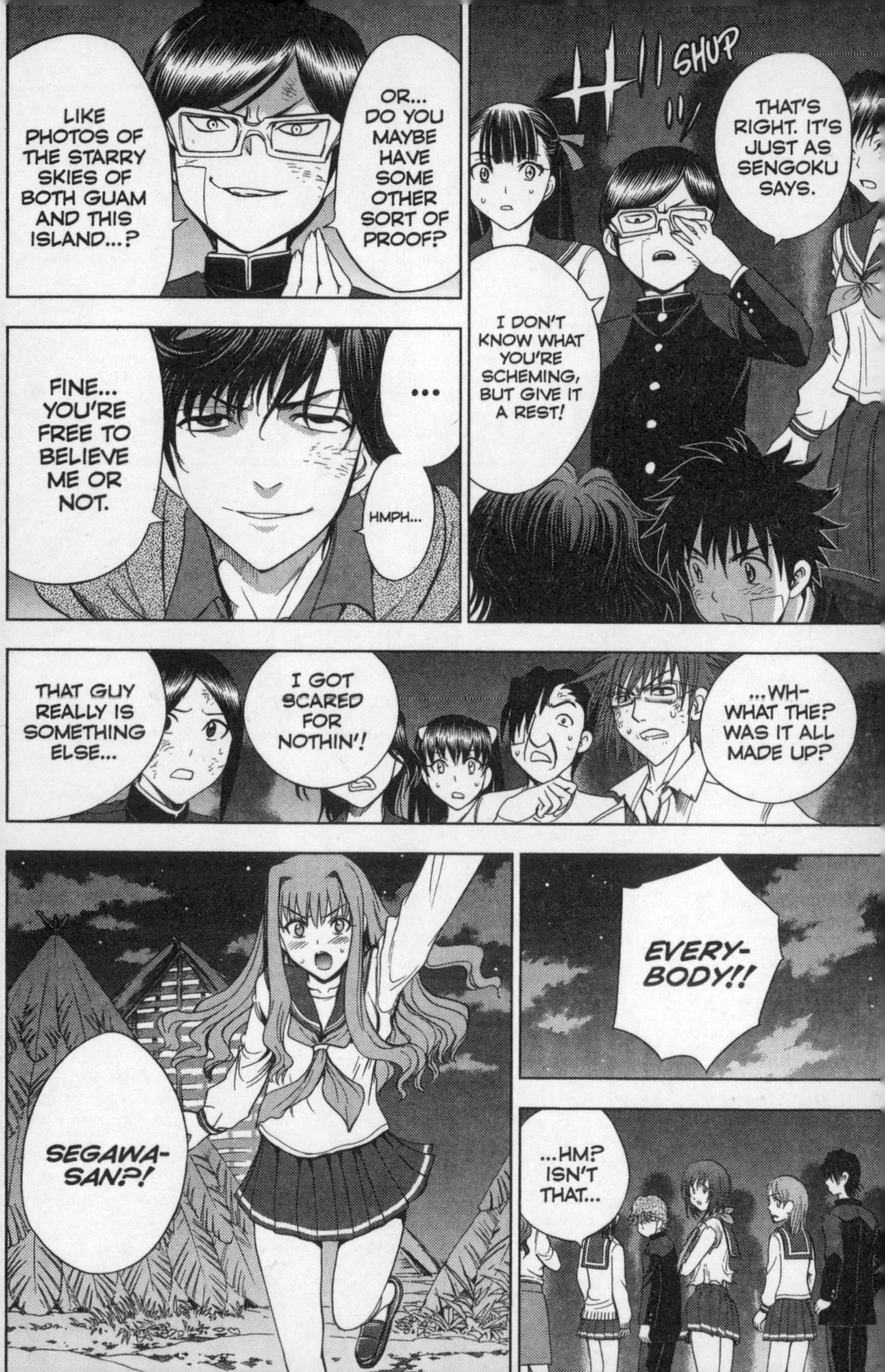
SHUP
THAT'S RIGHT. IT'S JUST AS SENGOKU SAYS.
I DON'T KNOW WHAT YOU'RE SCHEMING, BUT GIVE IT A REST!
OR... DO YOU MAYBE HAVE SOME OTHER SORT OF PROOF?
LIKE PHOTOS OF THE STARRY SKIES OF BOTH GUAM AND THIS ISLAND...?
...
HMPH...
FINE... YOU'RE FREE TO BELIEVE ME OR NOT.
...WH- WHAT THE? WAS IT ALL MADE UP?
I GOT SCARED FOR NOTHIN'!
THAT GUY REALLY IS SOMETHING ELSE...
EVERY-BODY!!
...HM? ISN'T THAT...
SEGAWA-SAN?!

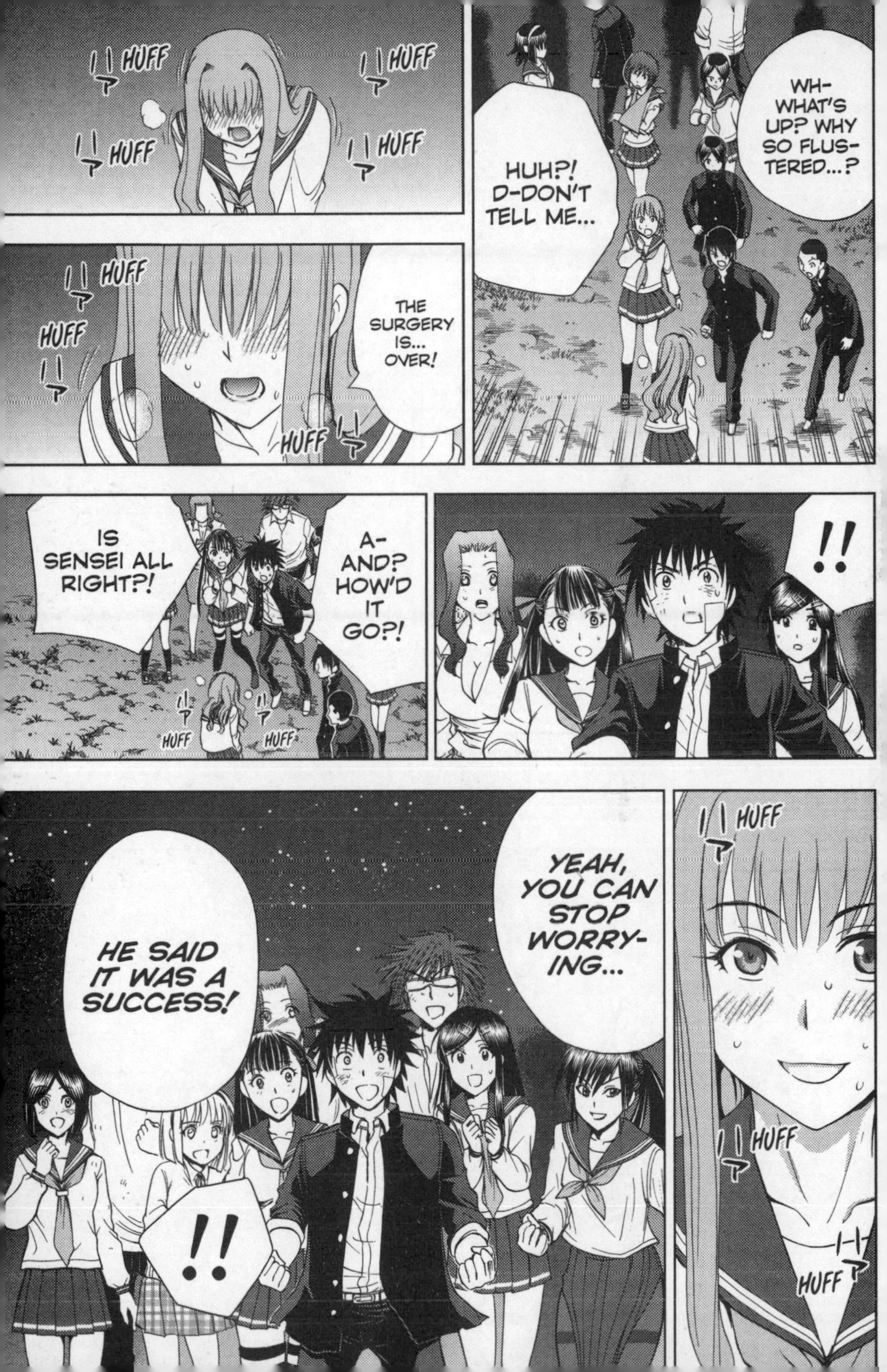
WH- WHAT'S UP? WHY SO FLUSTERED...?
HUH?! D-DON'T TELL ME...
HUFF
HUFF
HUFF
HUFF
HUFF
HUFF
THE SURGERY IS... OVER!
HUFF
!!
A- AND? HOW'D IT GO?!
IS SENSEI ALL RIGHT?!
HUFF
HUFF
HUFF
HUFF
HUFF
YEAH, YOU CAN STOP WORRYING...
HE SAID IT WAS A SUCCESS!
!!

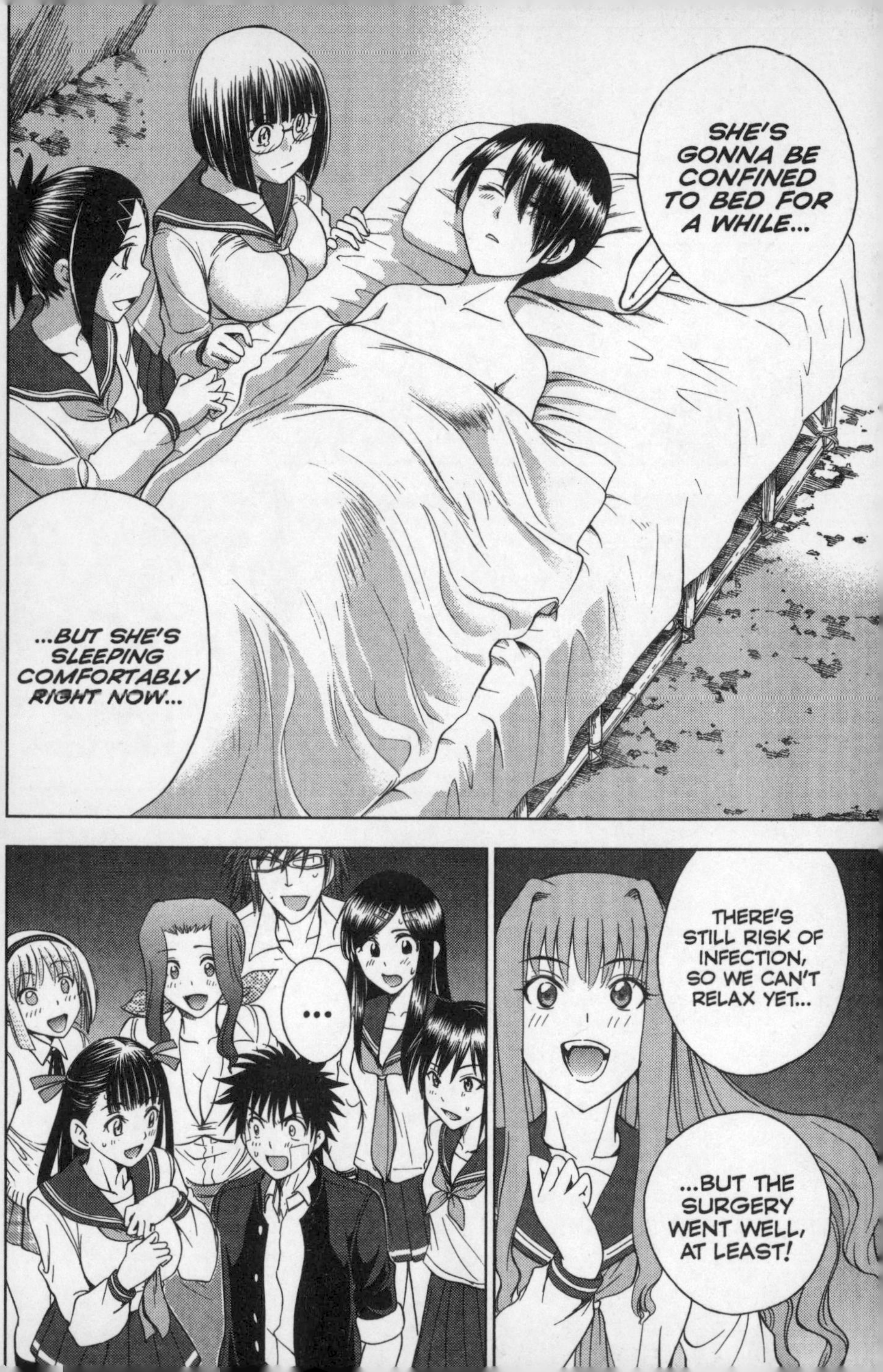
SHE'S GONNA BE CONFINED TO BED FOR A WHILE...
...BUT SHE'S SLEEPING COMFORTABLY RIGHT NOW...
THERE'S STILL RISK OF INFECTION, SO WE CAN'T RELAX YET...
...BUT THE SURGERY WENT WELL, AT LEAST!
...

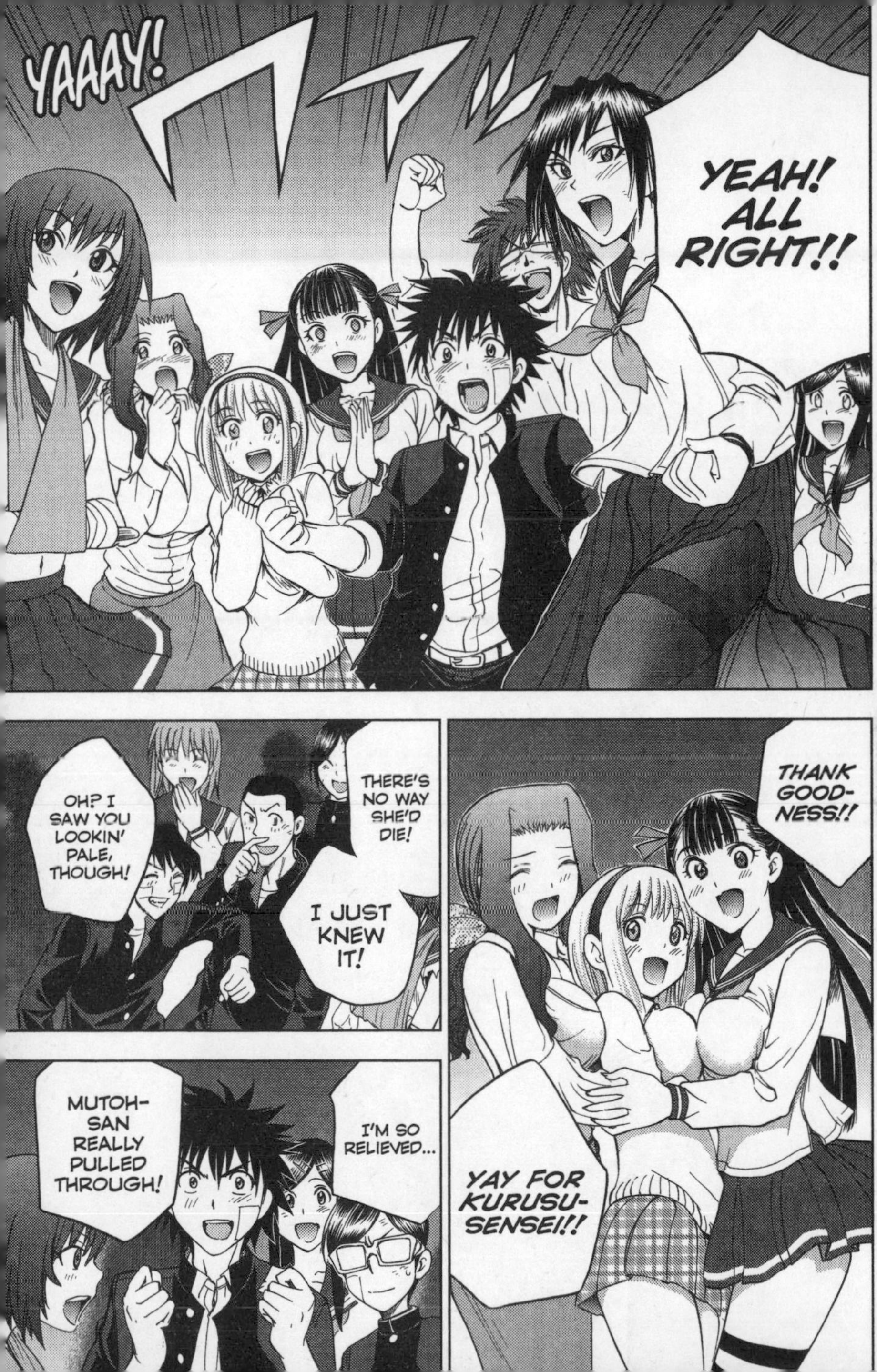
YEAH! ALL RIGHT!!
YAAAY!
THANK GOODNESS!!
YAY FOR KURUSU-SENSEI!!
THERE'S NO WAY SHE'D DIE!
I JUST KNEW IT!
OH? I SAW YOU LOOKIN' PALE, THOUGH!
I'M SO RELIEVED...
MUTOH-SAN REALLY PULLED THROUGH!

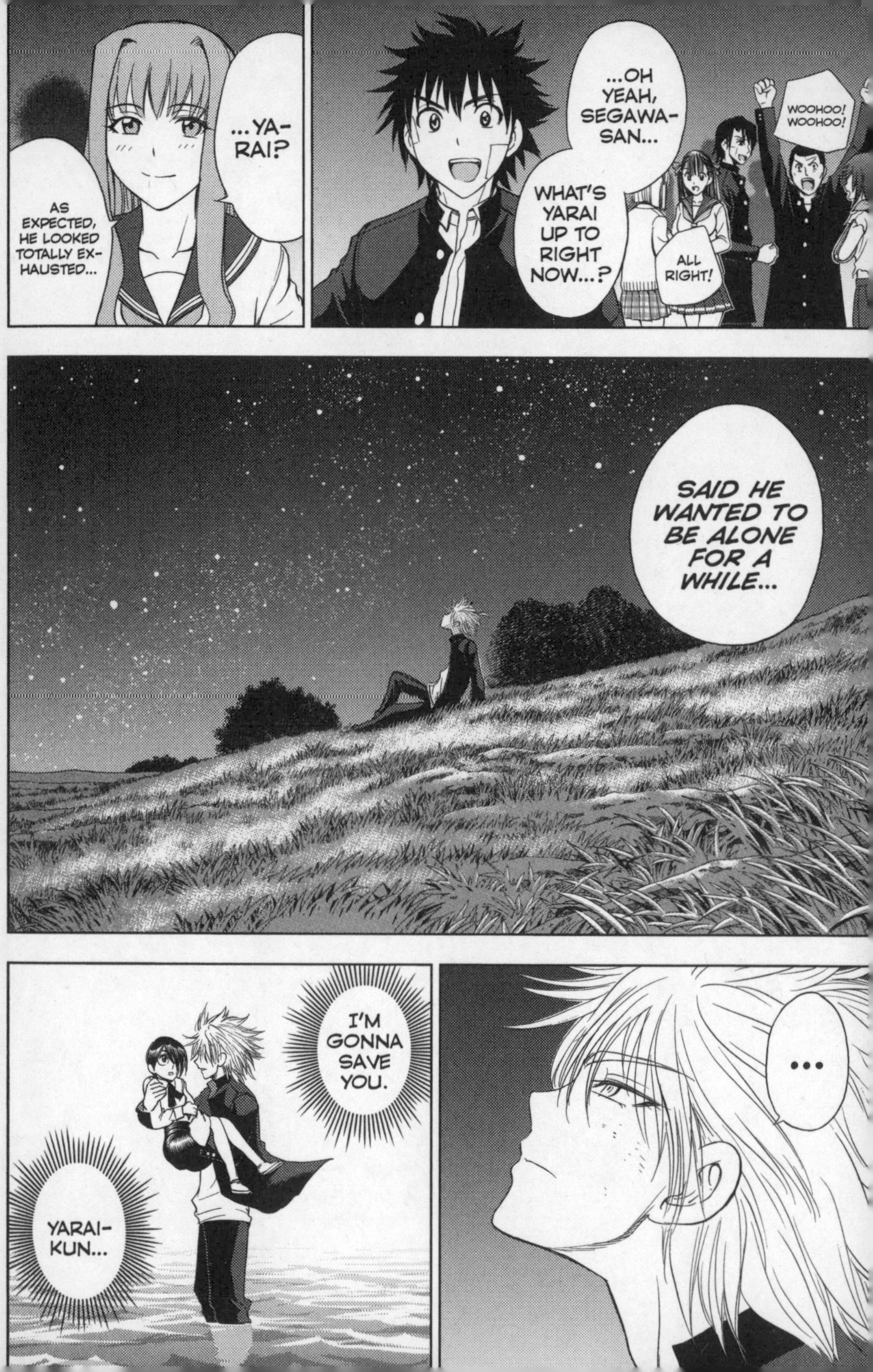
WOOHOO! WOOHOO!
...OH YEAH, SEGAWA-SAN...
WHAT'S YARAI UP TO RIGHT NOW...?
ALL RIGHT!
...YA-RAI?
AS EXPECTED, HE LOOKED TOTALLY EX-HAUSTED...
SAID HE WANTED TO BE ALONE FOR A WHILE...
...
I'M GONNA SAVE YOU.
YARAI-KUN...

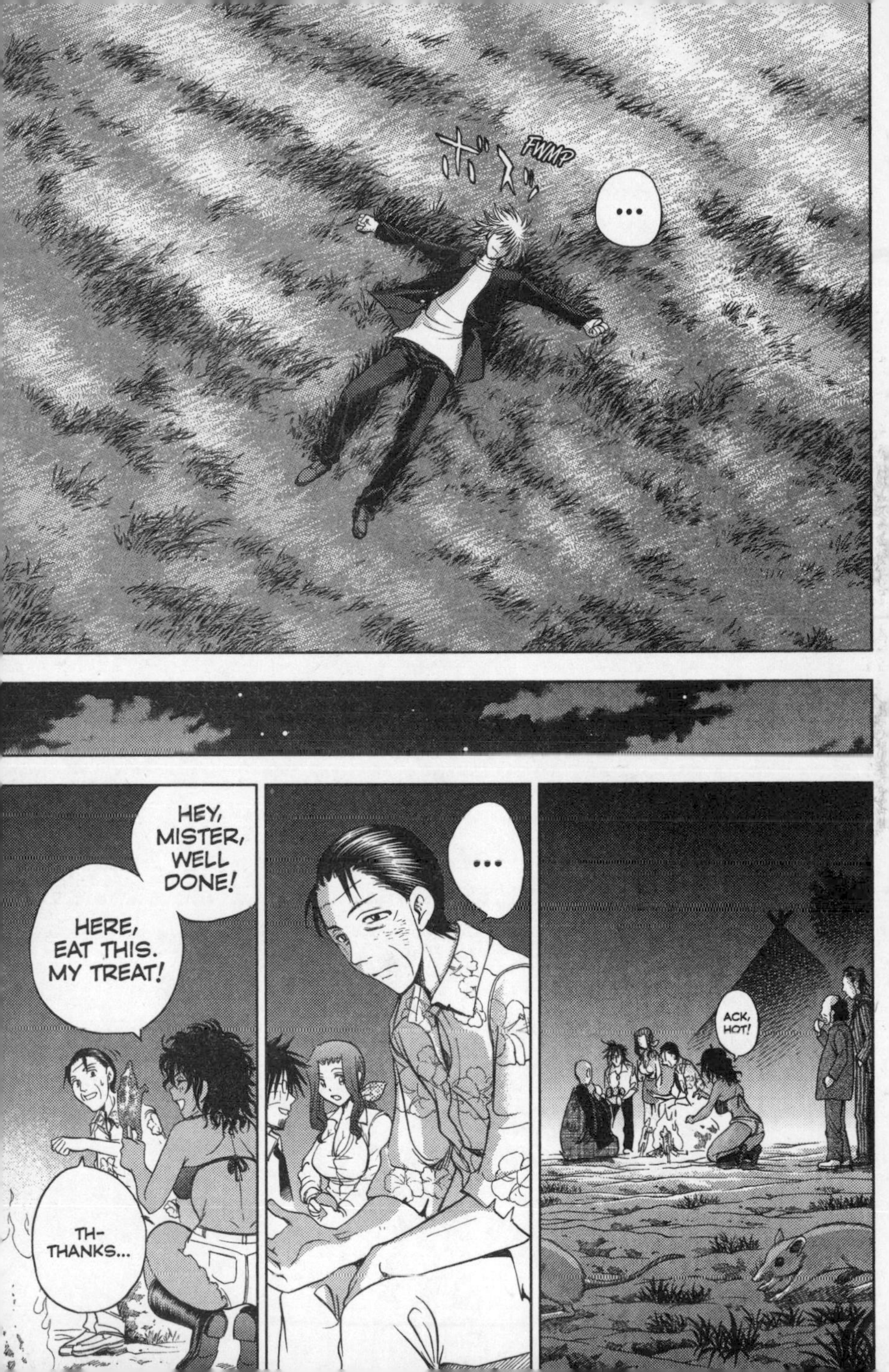
FWMP
...
ACK, HOT!
...
HEY, MISTER, WELL DONE!
HERE, EAT THIS. MY TREAT!
TH-THANKS...

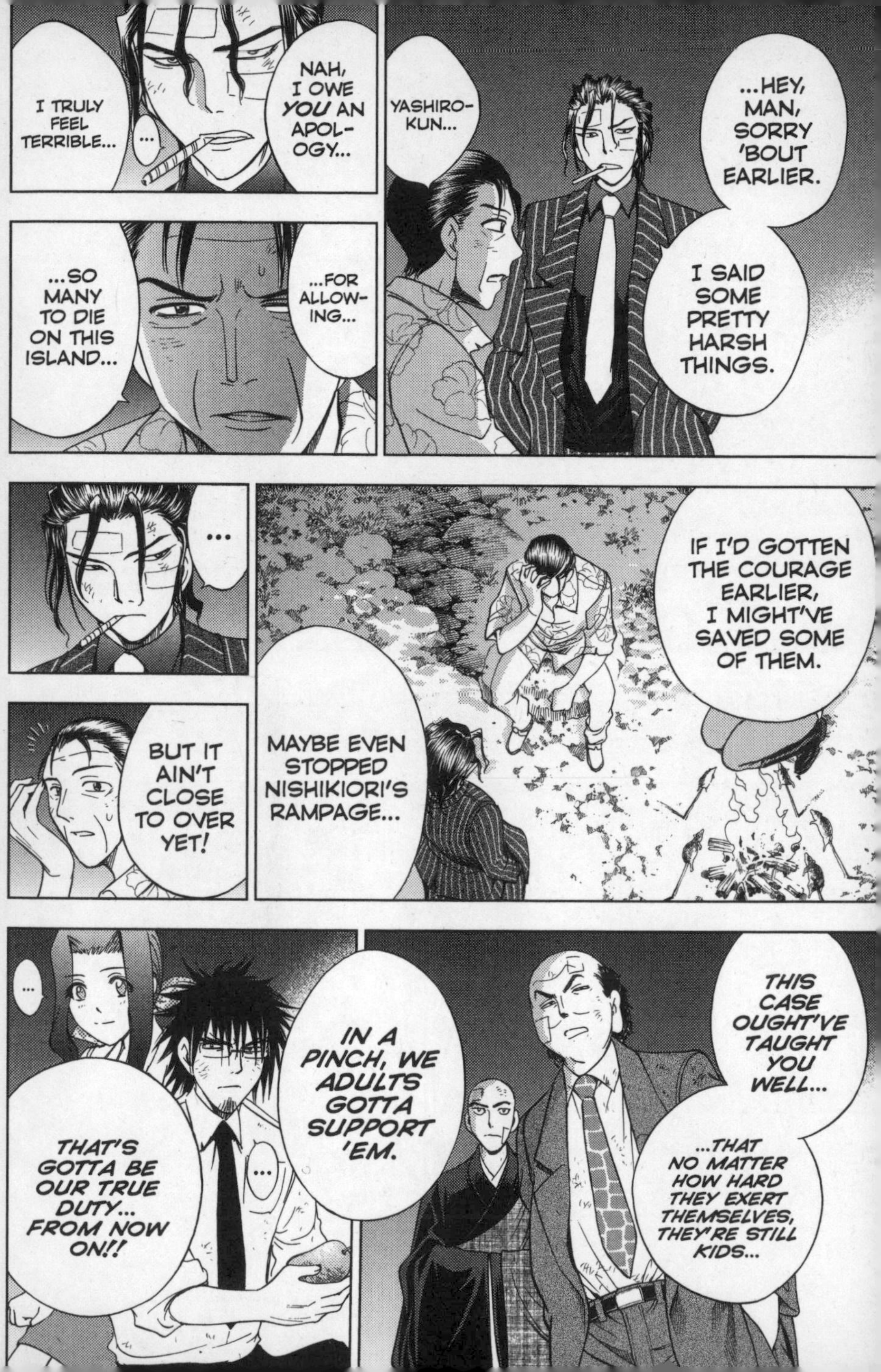
...HEY, MAN, SORRY 'BOUT EARLIER.
I SAID SOME PRETTY HARSH THINGS.
YASHIRO-KUN...
NAH, I OWE YOU AN APOLOGY...
...
I TRULY FEEL TERRIBLE...
...FOR ALLOWING...
...SO MANY TO DIE ON THIS ISLAND...
IF I'D GOTTEN THE COURAGE EARLIER, I MIGHT'VE SAVED SOME OF THEM.
MAYBE EVEN STOPPED NISHIKIORI'S RAMPAGE...
...
BUT IT AIN'T CLOSE TO OVER YET!
THIS CASE OUGHT'VE TAUGHT YOU WELL...
...THAT NO MATTER HOW HARD THEY EXERT THEMSELVES, THEY'RE STILL KIDS...
IN A PINCH, WE ADULTS GOTTA SUPPORT 'EM.
...
...
THAT'S GOTTA BE OUR TRUE DUTY... FROM NOW ON!!

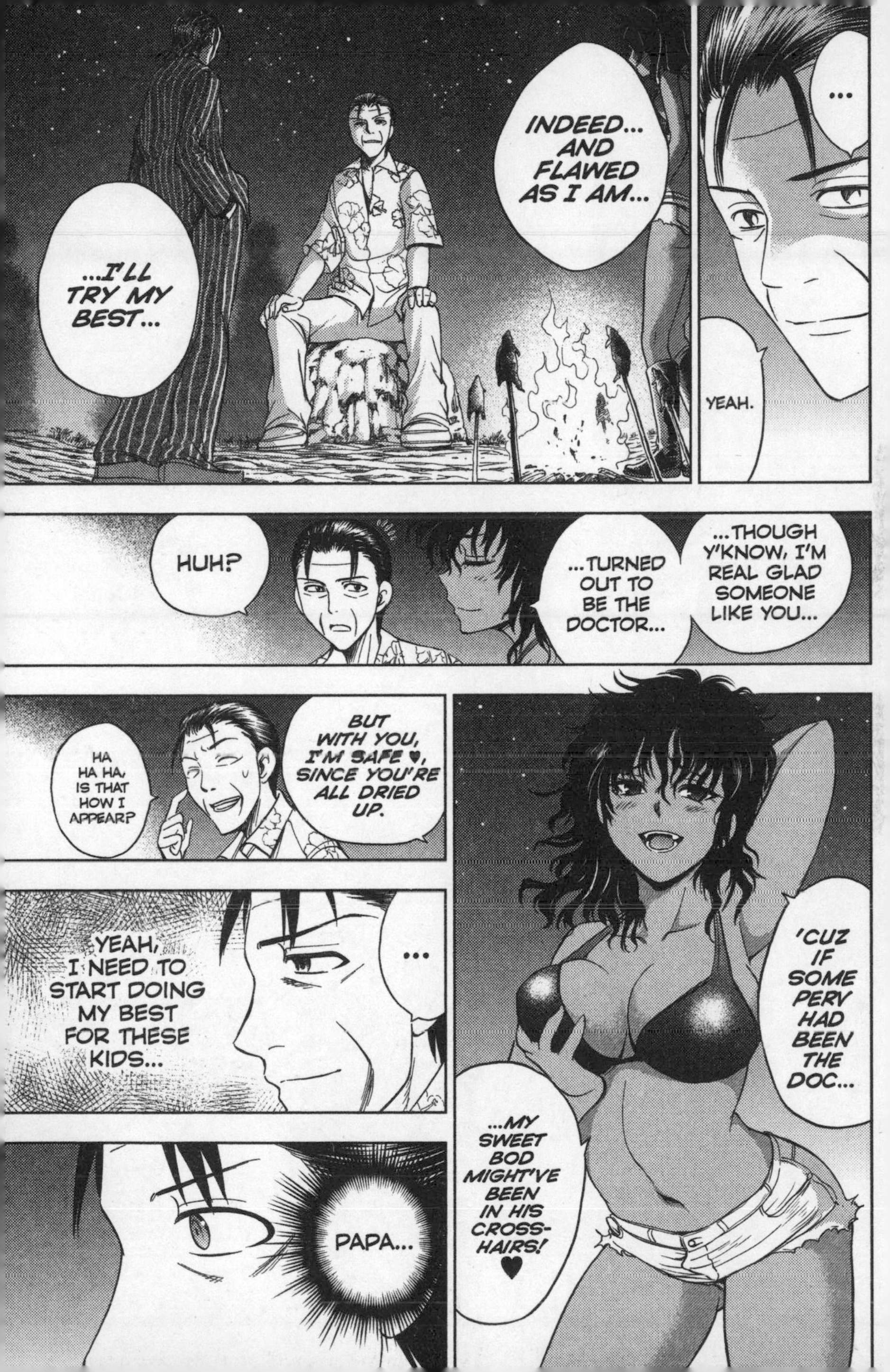
...
YEAH.
INDEED... AND FLAWED AS I AM...
...I'LL TRY MY BEST...
...THOUGH Y'KNOW, I'M REAL GLAD SOMEONE LIKE YOU...
...TURNED OUT TO BE THE DOCTOR...
HUH?
'CUZ IF SOME PERV HAD BEEN THE DOC...
...MY SWEET BOD MIGHT'VE BEEN IN HIS CROSS-HAIRS! ♥
BUT WITH YOU, I'M SAFE ♥, SINCE YOU'RE ALL DRIED UP.
HA HA HA, IS THAT HOW I APPEAR?
...
YEAH, I NEED TO START DOING MY BEST FOR THESE KIDS...
PAPA...

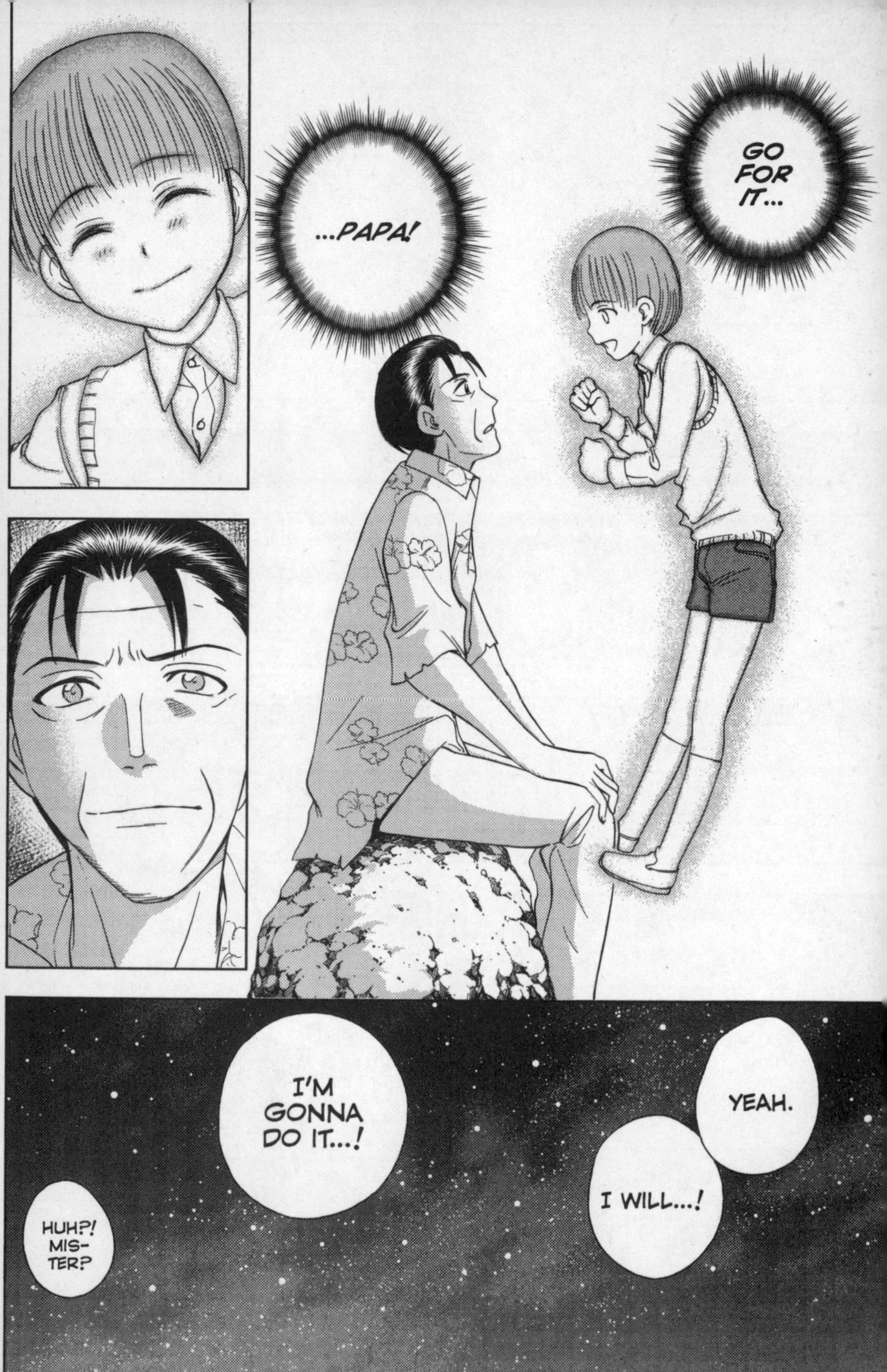
GO FOR IT...
...PAPA!
YEAH.
I WILL...!
I'M GONNA DO IT...!
HUH?! MISTER?

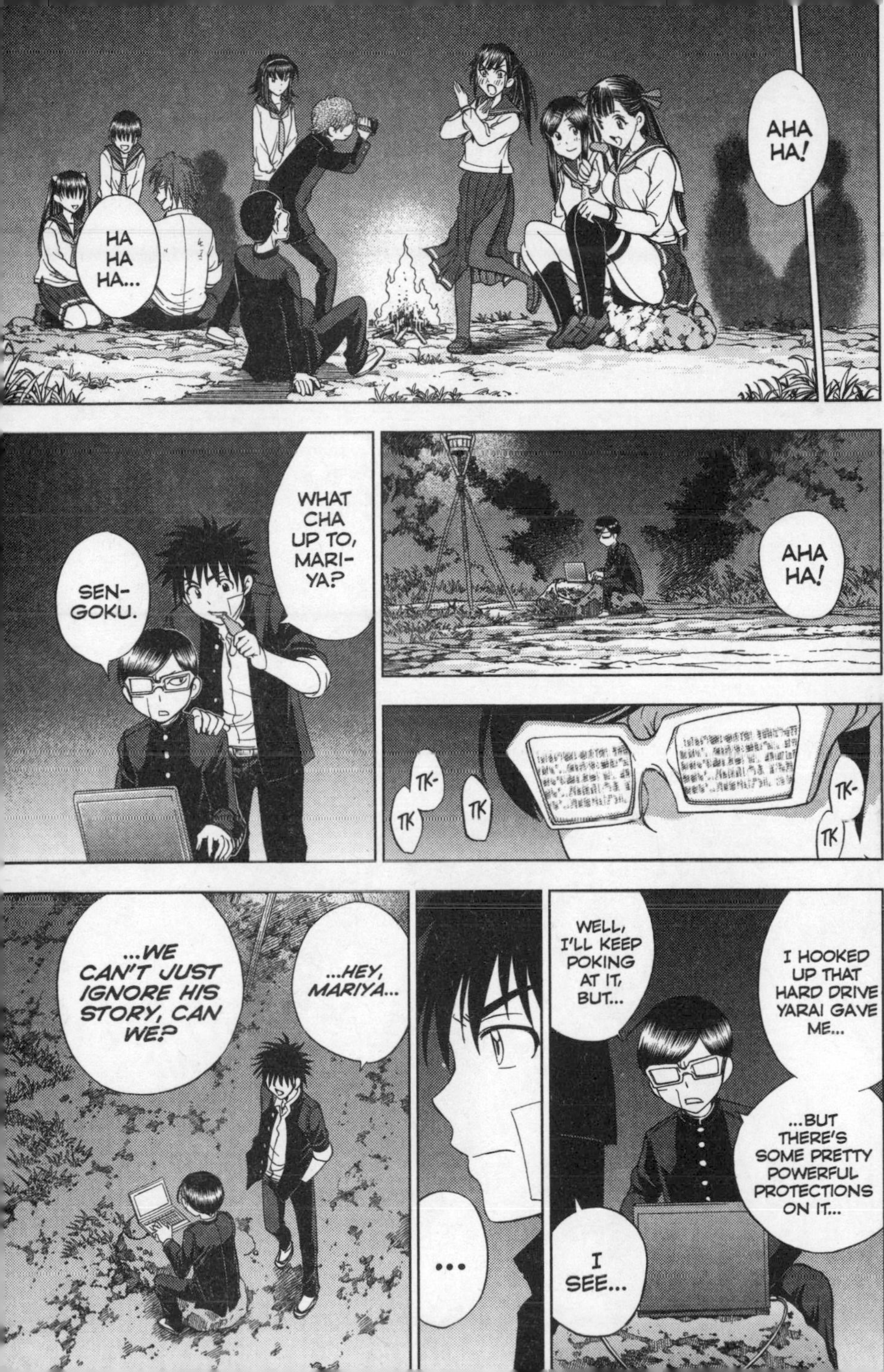
AHA HA!
HA HA HA...
AHA HA!
TK-TK
TK
TK-TK
WHAT CHA UP TO, MARIYA?
SEN-GOKU.
I HOOKED UP THAT HARD DRIVE YARAI GAVE ME...
...BUT THERE'S SOME PRETTY POWERFUL PROTECTIONS ON IT...
WELL, I'LL KEEP POKING AT IT, BUT...
I SEE...
...
...HEY, MARIYA...
...WE CAN'T JUST IGNORE HIS STORY, CAN WE?

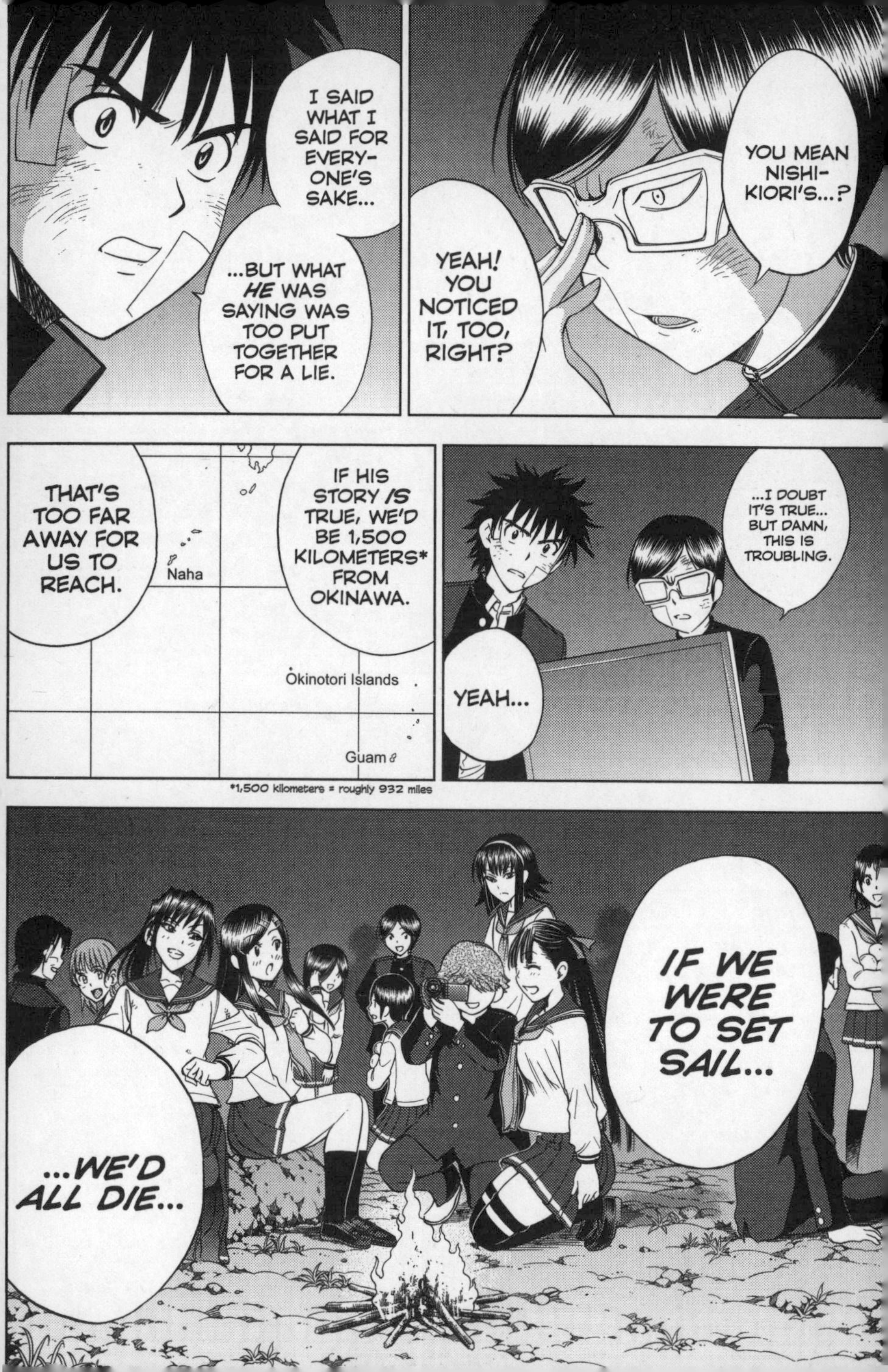
YOU MEAN NISHI-KIORI'S...?
YEAH! YOU NOTICED IT, TOO, RIGHT?
I SAID WHAT I SAID FOR EVERY-ONE'S SAKE...
...BUT WHAT *HE* WAS SAYING WAS TOO PUT TOGETHER FOR A LIE.
...I DOUBT IT'S TRUE... BUT DAMN, THIS IS TROUBLING.
YEAH...
IF HIS STORY *IS* TRUE, WE'D BE 1,500 KILOMETERS* FROM OKINAWA.
THAT'S TOO FAR AWAY FOR US TO REACH.
Naha
Okinotori Islands
Guam
*1,500 kilometers = roughly 932 miles
IF WE WERE TO SET SAIL...
...WE'D ALL DIE...

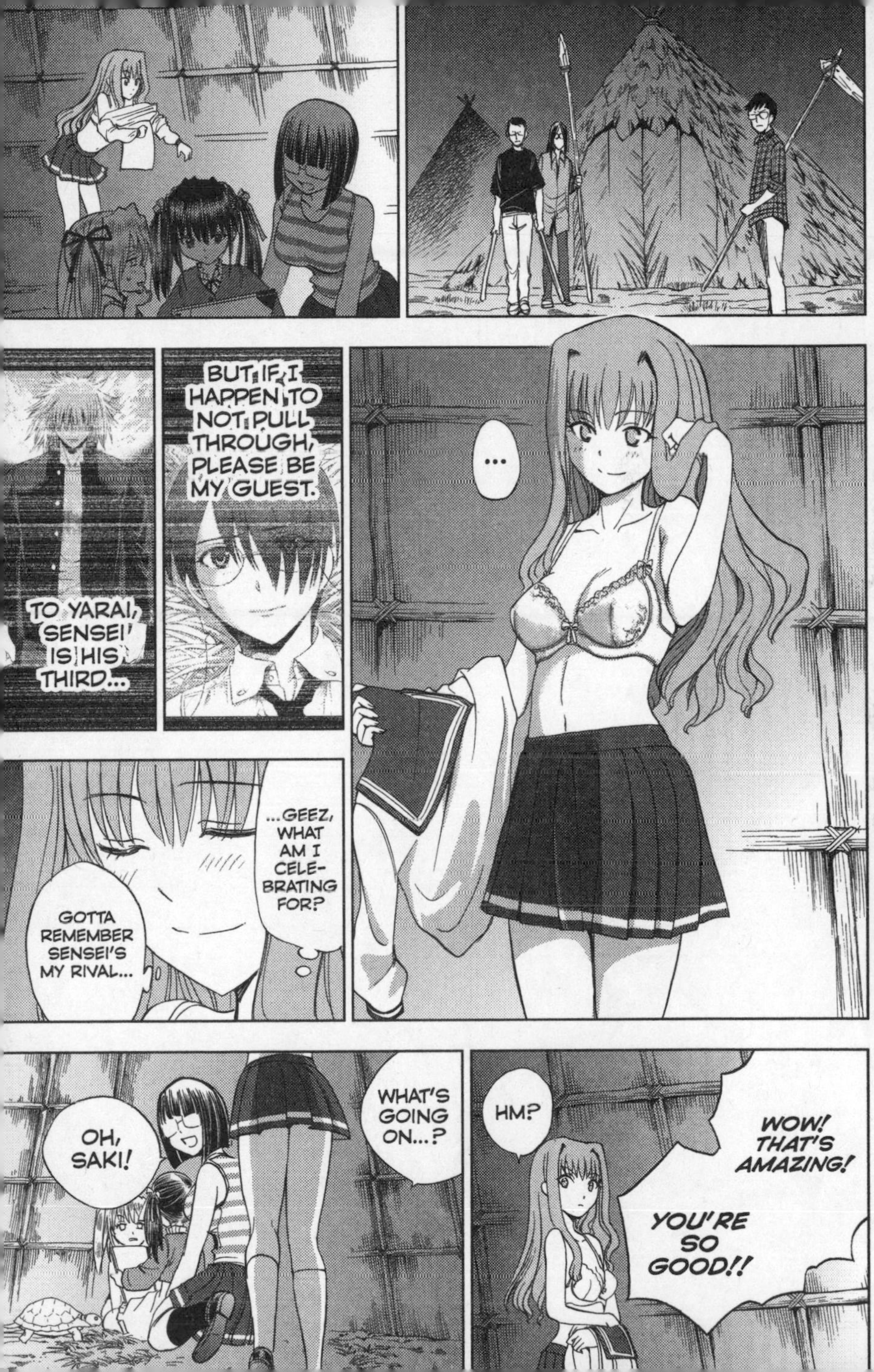
...
BUT IF I HAPPEN TO NOT PULL THROUGH, PLEASE BE MY GUEST.
TO YARAI, SENSEI IS HIS THIRD...
...GEEZ, WHAT AM I CELE-BRATING FOR?
GOTTA REMEMBER SENSEI'S MY RIVAL...
WOW! THAT'S AMAZING!
YOU'RE SO GOOD!!
HM?
WHAT'S GOING ON...?
OH, SAKI!

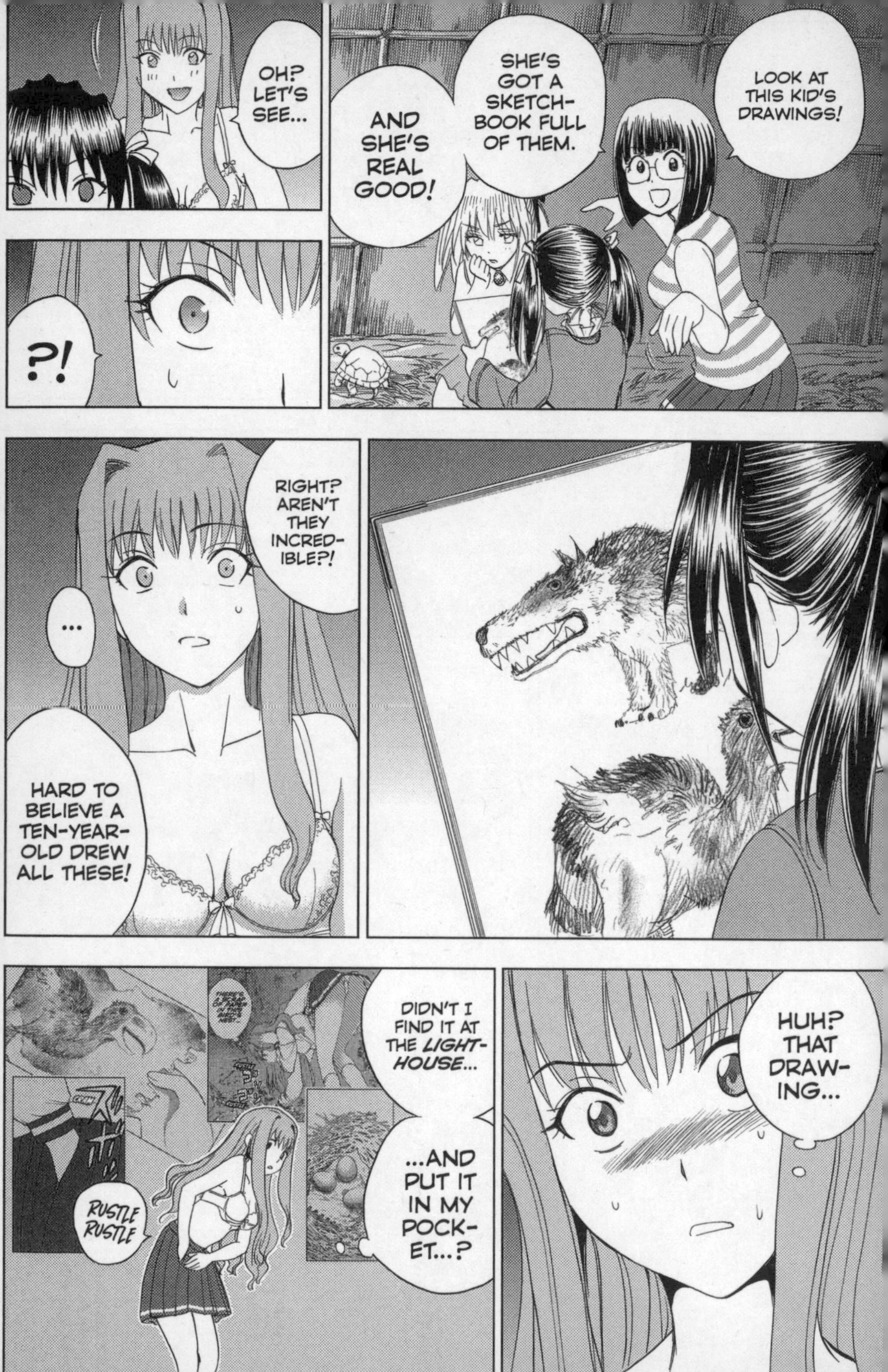
LOOK AT THIS KID'S DRAWINGS!
SHE'S GOT A SKETCH-BOOK FULL OF THEM.
AND SHE'S REAL GOOD!
OH? LET'S SEE...
?!
RIGHT? AREN'T THEY INCRED-IBLE?!
...
HARD TO BELIEVE A TEN-YEAR-OLD DREW ALL THESE!
HUH? THAT DRAW-ING...
DIDN'T I FIND IT AT THE *LIGHT-HOUSE*...
...AND PUT IT IN MY POCK-ET...?
THERE'S A SCRAP OF PAPER IN THIS BIRD'S NEST...
RUSTLE RUSTLE

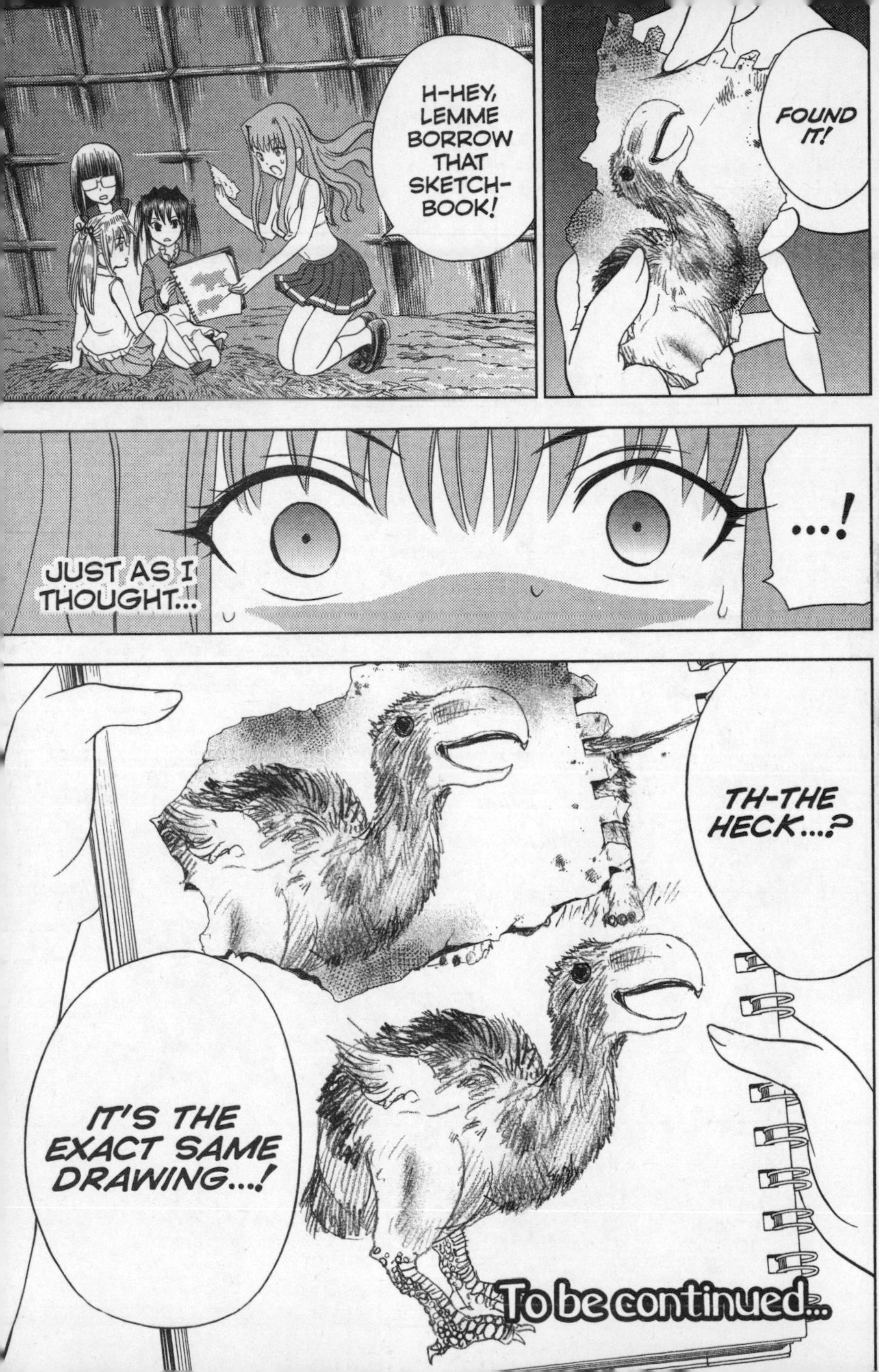
FOUND IT!
H-HEY, LEMME BORROW THAT SKETCH-BOOK!
...!
JUST AS I THOUGHT...
TH-THE HECK...?
IT'S THE EXACT SAME DRAWING...!
To be continued...

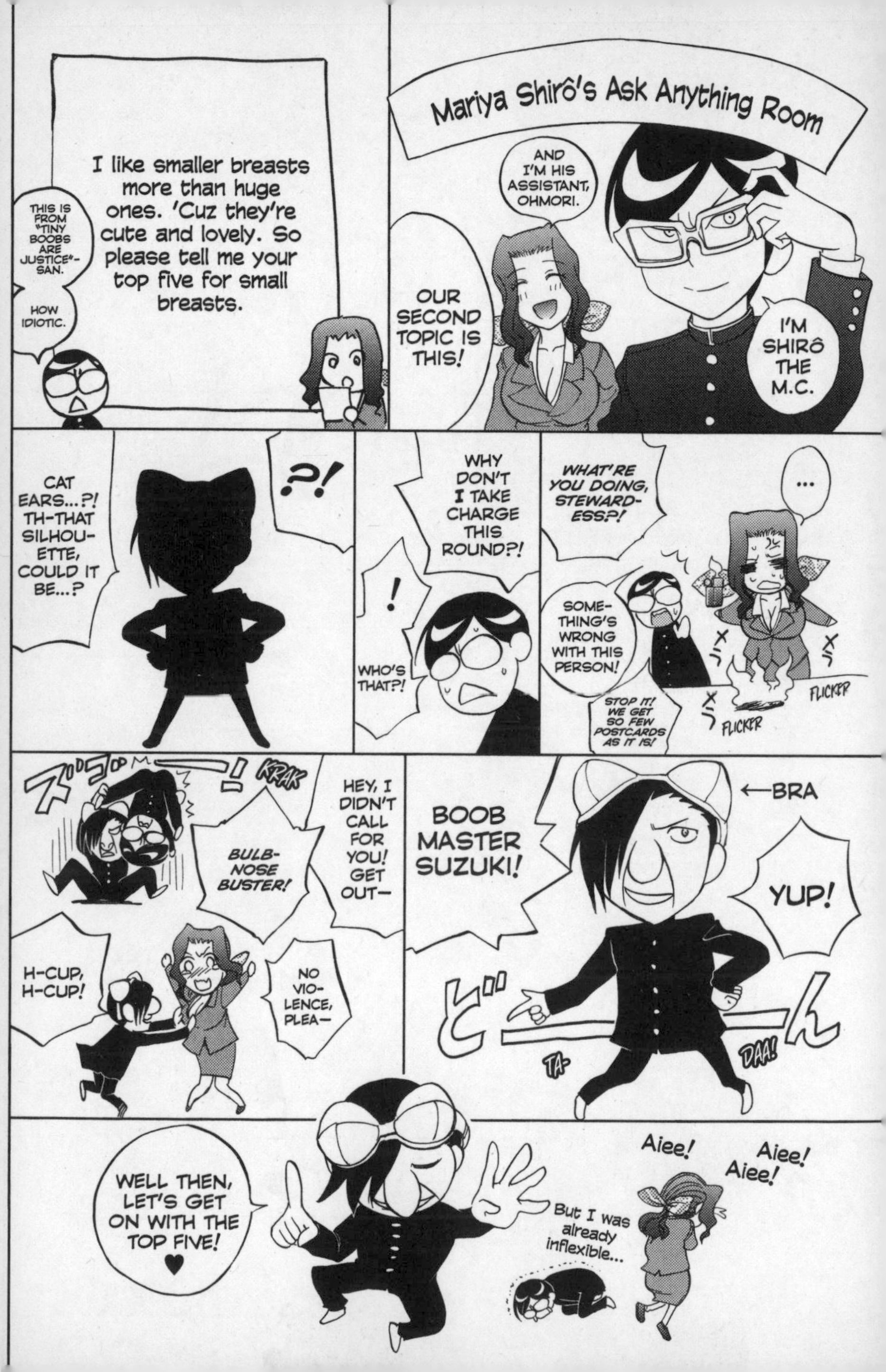

Mariya Shirô's Ask Anything Room
I'M SHIRÔ THE M.C.
AND I'M HIS ASSISTANT, OHMORI.
OUR SECOND TOPIC IS THIS!
I like smaller breasts more than huge ones. 'Cuz they're cute and lovely. So please tell me your top five for small breasts.
THIS IS FROM "TINY BOOBS ARE JUSTICE"-SAN.
HOW IDIOTIC.
...
WHAT'RE YOU DOING, STEWARDESS?!
SOMETHING'S WRONG WITH THIS PERSON!
STOP IT! WE GET SO FEW POSTCARDS AS IT IS!
FLICKER
FLICKER
WHY DON'T I TAKE CHARGE THIS ROUND?!
!
WHO'S THAT?!
?!
CAT EARS...?! TH-THAT SILHOUETTE, COULD IT BE...?
←BRA
BOOB MASTER SUZUKI!
YUP!
TA-
DAA!
HEY, I DIDN'T CALL FOR YOU! GET OUT—
KRAK
BULB-NOSE BUSTER!
NO VIOLENCE, PLEA—
H-CUP, H-CUP!
Aiee!
Aiee!
Aiee!
But I was already inflexible...
WELL THEN, LET'S GET ON WITH THE TOP FIVE! ♥

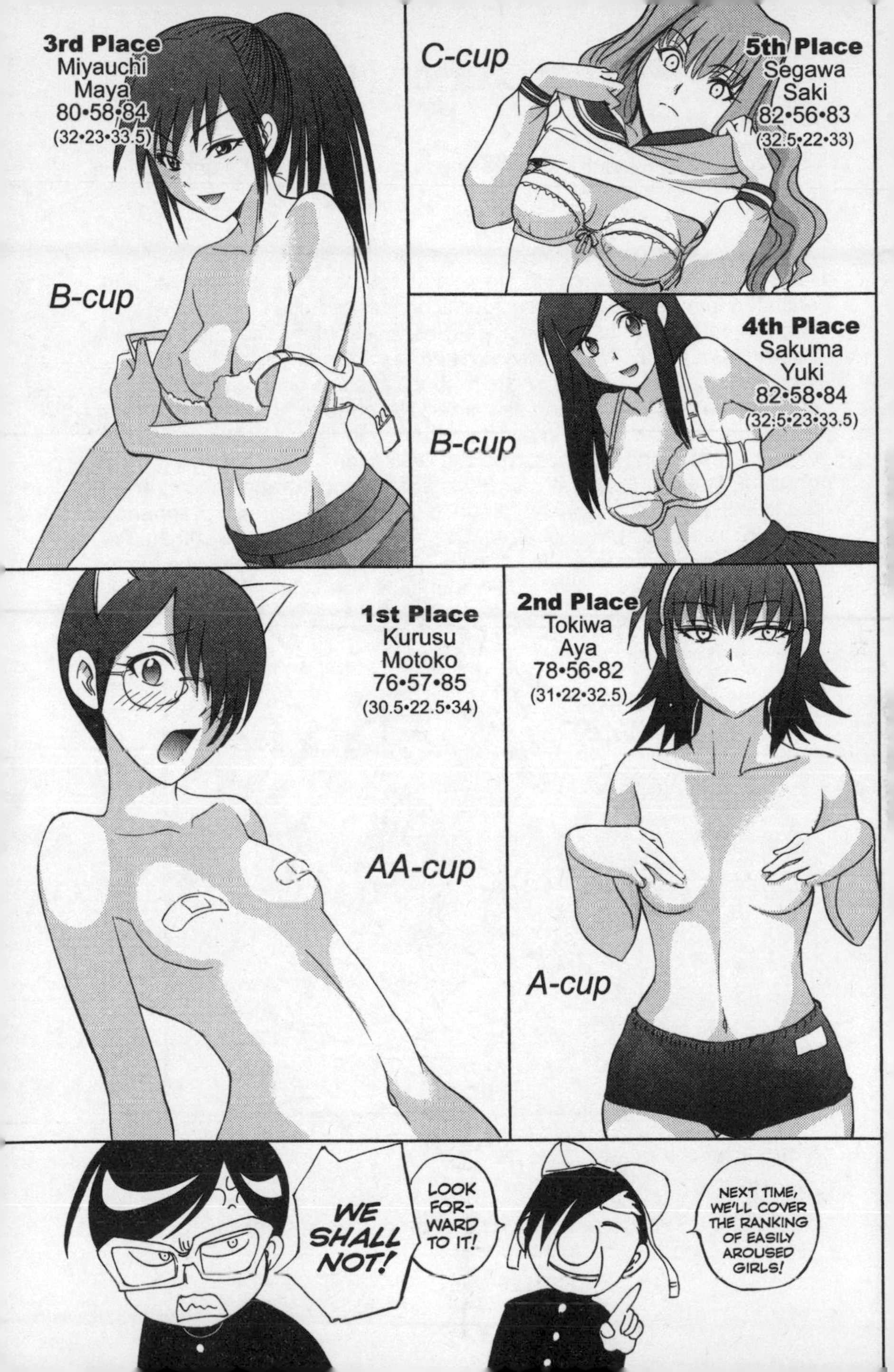
5th Place
Segawa
Saki
82•56•83
(32.5•22•33)
C-cup
4th Place
Sakuma
Yuki
82•58•84
(32.5•23•33.5)
B-cup
3rd Place
Miyauchi
Maya
80•58•84
(32•23•33.5)
B-cup
2nd Place
Tokiwa
Aya
78•56•82
(31•22•32.5)
A-cup
1st Place
Kurusu
Motoko
76•57•85
(30.5•22.5•34)
AA-cup
NEXT TIME, WE'LL COVER THE RANKING OF EASILY AROUSED GIRLS!
LOOK FOR-WARD TO IT!
WE SHALL NOT!

Translation Notes

***Daimyôjin*, page 9**

A Shinto deity title. I.e., Fake Miina is audaciously calling herself a Shinto goddess.

Amulets, page 9

Traditionally in Japan, amulets are sold at both temples and shrines and dedicated to particular Buddhist figures or Shinto deities, respectively. They are considered talismans or charms that confer either luck, protection, or both, upon the individual carrying it on their person or the object it is placed within (such as a car or apartment), and are often given as gifts or souvenirs. Though often seen as a small rectangular brocade bag with a string loop, they can come in various other shapes and forms, including bumper stickers and figurines. Specific protections include warding off evil, improving financial luck, traffic or travel safety, good grades and exam results, commercial prosperity, romantic or marital bliss, safe pregnancy and birth, as well as physical protection of a household against theft, fire, etc. In this particular case, the pouch is labeled “traffic safety” and Miina passing herself off as a Shinto deity identifies it as a fake Shinto amulet.

...WHAT IS THIS...?
IT'S AN AMULET.
交通安全
ミイナ大明神
MIINA GAVE IT TO ME.

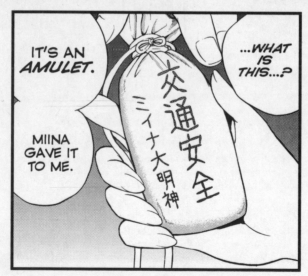

“A monk for the dead,” page 37

In Japan, death rites are associated with Buddhism. This association is similar to how Priests are linked with funerary rites in Christianity.

Quatre, Heero, Duo, and "Mission, accepted," page 42

Quatre, Heero, and Duo are three of the five pilots appearing in the anime series *Mobile Suit Gundam Wing*, and "Mission, accepted" is an oft-uttered line of dialogue by said characters.

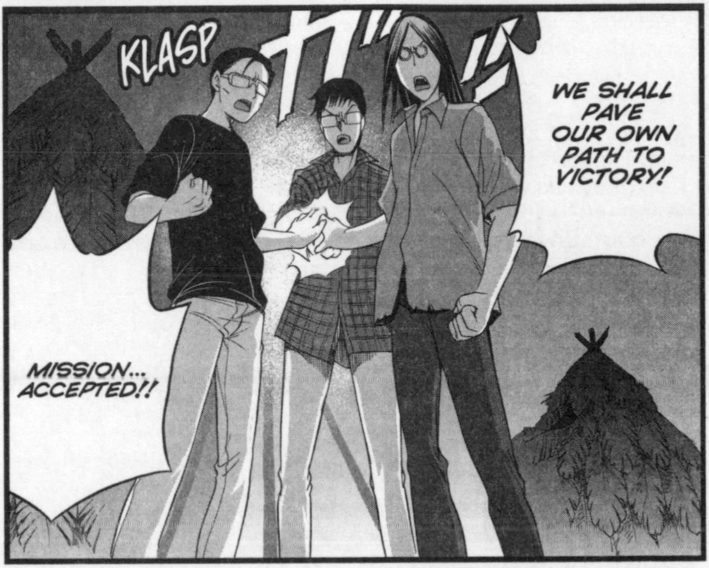
WE SHALL PAVE OUR OWN PATH TO VICTORY!
KLASP
MISSION... ACCEPTED!!

Operation Meteo(r), "Mission, accomplished," page 80

Operation Meteor is an infamous military retaliation plot within the storyline of *Mobile Suit Gundam Wing* and its spinoffs, though it apparently never succeeded in the original story. "Mission, accomplished" is another oft-uttered line of dialogue by the Gundam Wing pilots.

Kozuka Chemical Industrial, page 99

The company Nishikiori works for (whose name translates into "Little Mound Chemical Industrial") is probably an homage to Otsuka Chemical Industrial Company, Ltd. ("Big Mound Chemical Industrial Company, Ltd.").

Bust/Bra measurements, page 189

The three numbers listed refer to the circumference measurements (in centimeters) of the above bust, under bust or band, and bust sizes, respectively. Originally intended for the purpose of finding the correct brassiere, it is also used by women in their personal ads or profiles to describe their proportions to the viewer.

Cage of Eden volume 19 is a work of fiction. Names, characters, places, and incidents are the products of the author's imagination or are used fictitiously. Any resemblance to actual events, locales, or persons, living or dead, is entirely coincidental.

A Kodansha Comics Trade Paperback Original.

Published in the United States by Kodansha Comics, an imprint of Kodansha USA Publishing, LLC, New York.

Publication rights for this English edition arranged through Kodansha Ltd., Tokyo.

First published in Japan in 2012 by Kodansha Ltd., Tokyo, as Eden no Ori 19

ISBN 978-1-61262-984-1

Printed in the United States of America.

www.kodanshacomics.com

9 8 7 6 5 4 3 2 1

Translator: Mari Morimoto
Lettering: Morgan Hart
Kodansha Comics edition cover design: Phil Balsman